"G" Is for Grafton

"G" Is for

Natalie Hevener Kaufman
and
Carol McGinnis Kay

Grafton

THE WORLD OF KINSEY MILLHONE

A Marian Wood Book

HENRY HOLT AND COMPANY
NEW YORK

A Marian Wood Book
Henry Holt and Company, Inc.
Publishers since 1866
115 West 18th Street
New York, New York 10011

Henry Holt® is a registered
trademark of Henry Holt and Company, Inc.

Published in Canada by Fitzhenry & Whiteside Ltd.,
195 Allstate Parkway, Markham, Ontario L3R 4T8.

Library of Congress Cataloging-in-Publication Data
Kaufman, Natalie Hevener.
"G" is for Grafton : the world of Kinsey Millhone /
Natalie Hevener Kaufman and Carol McGinnis Kay.
— 1st ed.
p.   cm.
"A Marian Wood book"—T.p. verso.
Includes bibliographical references (p.   ) and index.
ISBN 0-8050-5446-4 (hb : alk. paper)
1. Grafton, Sue—Characters—Kinsey Millhone.   2. Detective
and mystery stories, American—History and criticism.
3. Millhone, Kinsey (Fictitious character)
4. Women detectives in literature.
I. Kay, Carol McGinnis, 1941–   . II. Title.
PS3557.R13Z75   1997
813′.54—dc21   97-27861

Henry Holt books are available for special promotions and
premiums. For details contact: Director, Special Markets.

First Edition 1997

Designed by Kate Nichols

Printed in the United States of America
All first editions are printed on acid-free paper. ∞

1   2   3   4   5   6   7   8   9   10

For Lee Jane's mother, Helen Carroll Kaufman,
who taught her that good literature includes the best detective fiction,
and in memory of her father, Manny Kaufman,

and

In memory of Carol's parents,
Ruth Owen McGinnis and Gaston Grady McGinnis,
who taught her the value of examining life
through the truths of fiction.

Contents

"Can I ask about the autopsy?": Kinsey's Relationship with
the Police · Kinsey's Case Log
Kinsey Laughs At . . .

Acknowledgments

The authors wish to express their gratitude to the following persons for their invaluable assistance: Judy Thomason, Patricia Gilmartin, Martha Thomas, Judith James, Kate Brown, Cynthia Davis, Allen Marshall and the staff at Architrave, Catherine Fry, Ann Cargill, Kelly Frank, Amy Hausser, Lisa Kerr, Ken Rogerson, the Women of Ms.tery, Julie Anderson, Marilyn McManus (especially for the dust jacket sketch of Kinsey's apartment), Cynthia Colbert, Robyn Newkumet, Anita Floyd, Sarah Fox, Kathlyn Fritz, Carolyn Matalene, Carter Blackmar, Beckay Blanchard, Donald Kay, Robert Newman, Matt Bruccoli, Don Rausch, the English Faculty Colloquium, Grace Owen, Barbara Toohey, colleagues in the Popular Culture Association, Jane Bakerman, the kind staffs at the Richland County Library, the Thomas Cooper Library, and the Happy Bookseller, and the University of South Carolina Venture Fund for support of our travel related to this book.

Special thanks go to Sue Grafton and Steven Humphrey, whose graciousness in responding to "one more question" about Kinsey was boundless and to Marian Wood, whose editorial pen and encouragement were equally boundless.

Finally, we want to express appreciation to our patient families, who gave us both support and specific assistance: David Kay, Gaston and Betty McGinnis, Carrollee Kaufman Hevener, Athey Kaufman, David Whiteman, Susan Kaufman, Helene Kaufman, and Ted Kaufman.

"G" Is for Grafton

Preface

And this is where Renata jumped," Sue Grafton said, gesturing down at the rocks.

The four of us were leaning over the waist-high concrete wall lining the seaward side of the breakwater curving around the marina. We could hear the snap of the flags immediately behind us on the inner side of the walkway. Inside the marina were scores of boats, many wearing bright blue covers, their white masts bobbing up and down. Beyond them the town of Santa Barbara snuggled against the Santa Ynez Mountains.

We all looked down at the dark, pockmarked rocks directly below us, waves churning and foaming around them. So this was the site of Renata Huff's suicide attempt and Kinsey's abortive efforts to save her in the final scene of *"J" Is for Judgment*. Unlike the tourist-brochure perfection of sunlight, blue sky, and blue ocean surrounding us, the rocks looked brutal and forbidding.

Steve Humphrey, Sue's husband, studied the rocks and waves for a moment and said, "I still say that anyone jumping onto those rocks would be killed immediately. There's not enough water here."

"Isn't this low tide?" one of us asked.

"The rocks are close to the surface even at high tide," replied Steve.

"Well, the rocks may be too close to the surface in Santa Barbara, but they're not in *Santa Teresa*," Sue responded.

We all laughed with her and turned to continue our tour of the real world on which Sue Grafton has constructed Kinsey Millhone's fictional world. Having already covered the area of Kinsey's apartment and jogging path, Santa Barbara's Four Seasons Biltmore (which we know as the Edgewater Hotel) and wharf, we were ready to head for the downtown locations of Kinsey's two offices, the police station, the library, and the courthouse, before seeing the more outlying sections of Hope Ranch (Horton Ravine), Montecito (Montebello), and the Bird Refuge.

Kinsey Millhone's world is one many of us have been visiting for fifteen years through the pages of Grafton's popular alphabet detective series. By now, with Grafton halfway through the alphabet (*N* will be available in 1998), many readers have become thoroughly addicted to this appealing private detective who lives and works in Santa Teresa, California. We want to know everything we can about her.

Most readers will cite Kinsey as the major reason they rush to the library or bookstore for the latest Grafton. Kinsey's combination of toughness and vulnerability, bravery and intellectual keenness, compassion and aloofness, engages a wide range of readers of all ages and careers. Her ability to defeat the enemy in a terrifying final confrontation encourages us to think that someone might actually be able to clean up the mess we see all around us in the late twentieth century. At the same time, the personal struggles she goes through in order to do that clean-up reassure us that our own fears and phobias are both normal and manageable. If Kinsey is scared of getting an injection from a nurse yet is also capable of running after a murderer and tackling him to the ground, then maybe we can gather up our nerve to ask the boss for a raise, or hold our teenagers to a curfew, or perform whatever bit of daily living is a challenge for us. Things gone awry can be corrected, at least to some extent, and, equally important, they can be corrected by someone who has foibles much like our own.

Much of the appeal of these novels, then, lies in the dual appeal of *escape from* our daily lives and of reassurance that we can *cope with* our daily lives. While most of us don't chase scam artists into Mexico or become the target of a contract killer, we do know the fears of being the next person to be downsized at the office, or being mugged on downtown streets, or finding drug paraphernalia in our child's room. Grafton's novels allow us to confront those fears by fictionalizing and exaggerating the bogeyman into the worst possible situation—murder—and offering Kinsey Millhone as the knight who slays the dragon for us. We get the thrill of the big scare, but all in the safety of our comfortable chair (or wherever we like to read), plus we have the reassurance that the dragon *can* be slain—and by someone not all that different from us.

The intriguing world of Kinsey Millhone, a dragon-slayer who is frightened by dogs, is our focus throughout this book. We look closely at the details of Kinsey's life, work, and thoughts, the patterns they form, and the insights they may suggest about the reasons for Grafton's place among the most popular and influential writers of detective fiction in the twentieth century. We show those details through several lenses that are unique to this book: maps, floor plans, photographs, a time line of Kinsey's biography, case logs, and charts of the murderers' punishments, as well as description and analysis. Sometimes we speak and sometimes Grafton speaks, but Kinsey's is the voice heard most often.

To make this investigation, our primary resources have been the thirteen novels and Sue Grafton herself. She could not have been more cooperative and gracious in assisting us in our scrutiny of Kinsey and her world. In addition to showing us Kinsey's Santa Barbara/ Santa Teresa, she helped make the maps in Chapter Five as accurate as possible. Likewise, she gave invaluable tips for the accuracy of the floor plans of Kinsey's two apartments in Chapter Three. And most important, she gave us hours of interviews about Kinsey, her own life and work, and herself in relation to Kinsey. We are delighted to be able to quote liberally from these interviews in the book, especially in Chapter Nine, where Grafton talks about Kinsey. Unless we note otherwise, all quotations from Grafton are from our interviews at her Kentucky residence in October 1996 and at her primary residence in Santa Barbara in February 1997.

Sue has also given us access to the journals she keeps as she writes the novels. The journal is, in her words, "a daily log of work in progress," which notes, among other things, when and where she gets stuck with a problem—of plot or character or tone—and how she chooses names and locales. "The journal functions as a play-ground for the mind, a haven where the imagination can cavort at will." These working documents make fascinating reading for anyone interested in Grafton, Kinsey, or the process of writing fiction.

We also drew on the eight Kinsey short stories published in several venues and collected by Steve Humphrey as a gift for Sue in a limited edition, *Kinsey and Me*. Because the edition was limited to only 350 copies, many readers may not know it. We have quoted extensively from it because this particular publication is highly personal: it also contains eight stories about her relationship with her mother written shortly after her mother's death. Sue's introductions to all the stories are candid revelations about her own life and her approach to her work. These introductions were an invaluable resource for us.

We should mention that our final resource was the expected one of reviews, critical articles, interviews, and book chapters on Grafton or Kinsey. The bibliography makes a distinction between works we've cited and related works that we thought might be of general interest for readers. A complete listing of Grafton's publications and awards to date is also included.

Each chapter of the book explores some aspect of Kinsey's life or character, beginning with the specifics of her biography, her daily life, her friends, her favorite places, and her work, and moving toward more abstract topics, such as her awareness of contemporary social issues, her ideas about death, and her sense of morality and justice. Each chapter draws on scenes from all the novels through *"M" Is for Malice*. Each chapter is a self-contained unit and may be read by itself. At the same time, the book forms a totality, moving from Kinsey as a person to Grafton as a person, and concluding with Grafton's own views on Kinsey, an analysis of Grafton's writing style, and commentary on her place of leadership in reshaping the genre of detective fiction.

Though the book is an organic whole, readers may want to use it for specific questions from time to time. In order to make this easier, the table of contents is detailed enough to allow a reader who, for example, wants to know how Kinsey found Henry Pitts and her apart-ment (or when her apartment was bombed and rebuilt, or exactly what the two versions look like) to find answers in Chapter Three: Kinsey's Daily Life, under "Apartments." The reader who wants to know exactly how she met Jonah Robb, how their affair developed and dwindled, and what Kinsey thinks of him by the time of *"M" Is for Malice* will find the answers in Chapter Four: Kinsey's Personal Relationships, under "Lovers and Ex-husbands." Want to know Rosie's last name? Check under "Major Friends" in Chapter Four, where you will find out why you'll never know her full name. Want to know why Kinsey once claimed Lt. Dolan was her boyfriend? Look in the same chapter for the section on Dolan. Would you like to know who taught Kinsey to put her notes on index cards? Look in Chapter Six: Kinsey at Work under "Training and Job History."

Those of us who read detective fiction love the pleasure of details and we love seeing the pattern behind the details. The authors of this book hope this investigation of Kinsey and her world will bring her many friends both the pleasure of recognizing some familiar details and patterns and an occasional frisson of insight into the unfamiliar.

Kinsey always likes to start a case by looking quickly at the overall picture and then going back to fill in gaps and make connections as she learns more and more about the various pieces of the puzzle. Following her lead, let's begin with a look at Kinsey's biography.

Kinsey's Biography

*"I like my history
just as it is."*

Sue Grafton says she lets Kinsey Millhone's personal history unfold from novel to novel at the pace Kinsey chooses. In some novels we learn more about her life than in others. Now that Grafton is halfway through the alphabet, the biography we can assemble is amazingly consistent, psychologically coherent, and detailed. From the thirteen novels, a vivid picture emerges—like a Polaroid taken at a family picnic—of the past Kinsey who shaped the present Kinsey we like so much.

Early Childhood

Looming above everything else in Kinsey's life is the death of her parents when she was a young child. She herself sees the event as pivotal: "In many ways, my whole sense of myself was embedded in the fact of my parents' death in an automobile wreck when I was five" (*J* 32). The trauma of this event and her subsequent eccentric rearing by her Aunt Virginia have affected virtually everything about who she is now and how she lives.*

* Early in elementary school, Kinsey had another firsthand experience with death. At the age of eight she watched a neighborhood playmate die at his own birthday party of

From bits and pieces in the novels from *A* to *M,* we can put together a narrative of the car accident in which Kinsey's parents, Randy and Rita Millhone, were killed. On Memorial Day weekend, 1955, Kinsey was barely five years old (b. May 5, 1950). She was in the back seat of the family car, her father was driving, and her mother was in the front passenger seat. They were en route to Lompoc, California, on a visit to Rita's estranged family, when a boulder crashed down the mountainside and struck the car. Her father lost control of the vehicle and was killed in the crash. Kinsey was "thrust down against the floorboards on impact, wedged in by the crushed frame" (*C* 64). She carefully "reached around the edge of the front seat, where I found my father's hand, unresisting, passive, and soft. I tucked my fingers around his, not understanding he was dead, simply thinking everything would be all right as long as I had him" (*F* 260). Kinsey couldn't reach her mother, who died after several hours of weeping. She remembers, "My mother cried for a while and then she stopped. I still hear it sometimes in my sleep. Not the sobs. The silence after that" (*A* 142). It took six hours for rescuers from the fire department to pry Kinsey from the "wreckage, trapped there with the dead whom I loved who had left me for all time" (*C* 65).

In every novel, Kinsey refers to the deaths of her parents, sometimes only in passing and sometimes for a page or two. The lengthier passages always focus on the same details: the boulder, the immediacy of her father's death, the crying and then the silence of her mother, the lengthy entrapment, and the sense of abandonment. Significantly, in every account, long and short, Kinsey mentions her own age at the time of the accident. Five is a highly vulnerable and impressionable age at which to endure such an overwhelming loss. Such a child is still greatly dependent on adults for meeting the most basic physical and emotional needs. The impact of so big a loss at so young an age must be great, essentially reshaping the adult that the child becomes. It's no wonder that as late as *"M" Is for Malice,* Kinsey will still be struggling with fear of abandonment in all of her personal relationships.

---

anaphylactic shock following a yellow-jacket sting. He "was dead before his mother reached the backyard" (*F* 204). Since she mentions this only once, in order to explain how she understands what is happening to Ori Fowler, we may assume it did not have a major effect, perhaps because her first encounter had been so much more traumatic.

Kinsey doesn't tell us much about the following days except that she "felt cold and little . . . just after the accident" (*G* 76). She refers once to the funeral service (*C* 104), but she never tells us anything about the service nor does she mention shedding any tears. She went to live with her mother's sister, Virginia Kinsey, a secretary at California Fidelity Insurance in Santa Teresa, who was unmarried and unprepared, financially or emotionally, for suddenly acquiring a child. We must assume she was also in deep grief herself, since she and Rita had been so close. There is no description of the aunt and niece adjusting to each other. Instead, totally ignoring her aunt, who, she only later realizes, must have hovered nearby, worried and concerned, Kinsey "established a separate residence in an oversize cardboard box" (*I* 48). Kinsey remembers: "I created a little world for myself in a cardboard box, filled with blankets and pillows, lighted by a table lamp with a sixty-watt bulb. I was very particular about what I ate. I would make sandwiches for myself, cheese and pickle, or Kraft olive pimento cheese, cut in four equal fingers, which I would arrange on a plate. I had to do everything myself, and it all had to be just so [in *"I" Is for Innocent* she explains that she made the sandwiches exactly the way her mother had, 48] . . . I would take my food and crawl into my container, where I would look at picture books and nibble, stare at the cardboard ceiling, hum to myself, and sleep. For four months, maybe five, I withdrew into that ecosphere of artificial warmth, that cocoon of grief" (*J* 133).

Inside "this small corrugated refuge," Kinsey taught herself to read and to tie her own shoes (*J* 133). She amused herself with shadow puppets and "endless picture books" filled with fantasies and stories about exotic places (*I* 48). She ran her own "home cinema" of mental projections of her parents (*J* 133). She looked after herself— preparing food, eating, sleeping, teaching, and entertaining herself— inside an enclosed space that remained under her exclusive control.

Kinsey used her "little closed-circuit system designed to deal with grief" quite effectively (*I* 48). She learned in a few lonely months to parent herself, another way of saying she grew up. Of course, this was not the healthy maturing process of a child who gradually learns to internalize lessons from trusted parent-figures and to develop a sense of independence throughout childhood and teenage years. This was an abrupt and brutal maturation process that forced Kinsey into adult responsibility for her own physical and emotional needs before she had the skills necessary to meet either category of need fully.

With this traumatic childhood experience, there can be little surprise that the adult Kinsey has "a special weakness for small, enclosed spaces, a barely disguised longing to return to the womb" (*I* 48). Just as the five-year-old sought refuge in the cardboard box, the adult likes her *small* one-room apartment, her *small* office without a secretary, her *small* VW bug, and she often sleeps naked, wrapped in a quilt on the sofa. Neither are we surprised that the only food we see Kinsey prepare is a variety of egg, cheese, or peanut-butter sandwiches. Above all, we are not surprised that this self-contained child becomes a self-contained adult who values independence, autonomy, and privacy more than almost everything else.

Out of pain has come enormous adult strength. The young Kinsey established an important lifelong pattern of behavior, one that characterizes much of her later success both as a human being and as a detective. She learned to find the solution within the problem itself. Plus, she learned to find that solution *herself,* without turning to others for solace or assistance.

These strengths, though, have come at a high price. The outside world that the child finally emerged into was the cold of her aunt's trailer and the terrors of kindergarten (*J* 133–34). (Kinsey often says they lived in trailers all the time, but in *Evidence* [66], she says she grew up in a tiny stucco bungalow, one of the rare inconsistencies in the series—but even that reference stresses the small size.) She and her aunt had a relationship that "entailed more theory than affection" (*H* 16). There was clearly mutual respect, trust, and commitment, but not much of the cuddling or playfulness that most small children need. Kinsey says, "I was raised by a no-nonsense aunt who had done her best, who had loved me deeply, but with a matter-of-factness that had failed to nourish some part of me" (*C* 65).

Two of the more painful stories of life with her aunt occur in a conversation with Robert Dietz in *"G" Is for Gumshoe* and in her musings about her remodeled apartment in *"H" Is for Homicide*. When Dietz says he knows nothing about her, Kinsey's response is predictably couched in terms of the accident, as though the only way to know her is to know her loss. "I was raised by my mother's sister. My folks were killed in an accident and I went to live with her when I was five. *This is the first thing she ever said to me* . . . 'Rule number one, Kinsey . . . rule number one . . .'—and *here she pointed her finger right up in my face—'No sniveling'*" (emphasis added).

Dietz replies, "Jesus," to which Kinsey responds, "It wasn't so bad. I'm only slightly warped" (*G* 95). Kinsey may defend her aunt, but it still sounds pretty bad. Telling a child who has lost both parents and been trapped inside the car with their bodies for six hours not to cry—indeed, to trivialize such grief by calling it "sniveling"—is extremely tough. No depth of grief felt by Aunt Virginia can erase the impact on the newly orphaned Kinsey of being greeted by this directive and its accompaniment—a forefinger wagged in her face.

Later, in *Homicide*, Kinsey tells the reader why she loves her newly remodeled apartment, created by her landlord especially for her, and why she feels at home and secure for the first time in her life. She recalls going to live with her aunt: "Without ever actually saying so, she conveyed the impression that I was there on approval, like a mattress, subject to return if the lumps didn't smooth out. To give her credit, her notions of child raising, if eccentric, were sound, and what she taught me in the way of worldly truths has served me well. Still, for most of my life, I've felt like an intruder and a transient, merely marking time until I was asked to move on" (16–17). (We note with interest that Kinsey has lived most of her life in a series of trailer parks, and now, during the novels, she lives in an apartment converted from garage space, both settings associated with travel and impermanence.)

And what are these "worldly truths" imparted to Kinsey by her aunt? Some of them relate to the minutiae of daily life. There is a whole cadre of social no-nos: no pierced ears, no chewing gum in public, no red nail polish, no dingy bra straps (*H* 208), and no beauty care except for "an occasional swipe of cold cream" (*F* 12). And there are household hints galore: "Spring clean every three months. . . . Beat all the throw rugs. Line-dry the sheets" (*I* 125). Always use an upright vacuum cleaner, rather than a "useless" canister (*J* 105). The fact that Kinsey, in times of stress, will clean her apartment ("like Cinderella on uppers") is a direct consequence of her aunt's focus on cleanliness (*I* 207).

There were no cooking lessons, however, because cooking is boring, and it only encourages the cook to become fat (*D* 102). (Vir-

ginia's name for Kinsey's home ec class was "Home Ick," *D* 102.)
Instead, Kinsey's aunt taught her to knit (*A* 28) and crochet (*B* 149),
in order to learn "patience and an eye for detail" (*D* 102) and to
shoot a pistol, so that she might learn safety, accuracy, and good
hand-eye coordination (*D* 102). Her aunt considered reading, exercise, and good dental care to be essential, but since she believed that
"two out of three illnesses would cure themselves. . . . Doctors
could generally be ignored except in case of accident" (*D* 102).

Kinsey has a sense of having missed something important while
she was growing up. In *"C" Is for Corpse*, Bobby Callahan tells Kinsey
about the days following *his* near-fatal car crash. His mother virtually
willed him back to life, staying at his bedside twenty-four hours a day
and telling him he could not leave them. Kinsey thinks, "Jesus, what
must it be like to have a mother who could love you that way?" This
plaintive question is immediately followed by Kinsey's recall of her
parents' deaths. Reminded of what she has not had, she then feels
such "envy" for Bobby's having been the object of "a love of such
magnitude" that her eyes well up with tears (65).

Tiny things may trigger a fleeting sense of loss for Kinsey. Inside
Jorden's, a specialty kitchen shop, Kinsey observes, "The air smelled
of chocolate and made me wish I had a mother," who, unlike her
aunt, presumably would cook (*D* 83). The kindness of a woman physician makes tears come to Kinsey's eyes because it prompts a memory
of her own mother's compassion when Kinsey had a raw throat from
a tonsillectomy at the age of four (*E* 133). Another "one of the few
concrete memories" Kinsey has of her mother is also a picture of
maternal comfort during illness. For childhood colds, she remembers
her mother rubbing her chest "with Vicks VapoRub, then covering it
with a square of pink rose-sprigged flannel, secured to my pajama top
with safety pins" (*J* 41).

As an adult, Kinsey mothers herself in the same way she recalls her
mother's behavior. She relishes the luxury of staying home with a
cold, wrapped in a quilt, reading a book, and having a legitimate
excuse to take "NyQuil in fully authorized nightly doses" (*J* 36). She
keeps a "flannel nightie" just to wear when she's sick (*J* 37). In
addition, she knows where to go to get "mothering" from someone
else. When Kinsey is distraught because her car has been broken into

and her aunt's semiautomatic stolen, the first thing she does is go to Rosie's Tavern.

Ensconced in her favorite booth near the back, Kinsey opens the conversation with Rosie with a bald announcement of all of her bad news of the day. Like a beneficently dictatorial mother, Rosie immediately tells her in great detail exactly what she will eat for dinner, ending with a special dessert "If you're good and clean up your plate." She concludes her maternal diatribe with "If you had a good man in your life, this would never happen to you and that's all I'm gonna say." Kinsey's response is one of pure joy. She says, "I laughed for the first time in days" (*D* 104). The independent, grown-up Kinsey may not have any intention of putting a man in her life, but when she's hurting, she goes to the place where she knows she will be "mothered" shamelessly—even to the point of being told to eat her vegetables.

Kinsey is very aware of Rosie's place in her life. Just after she has solved the case and is heartsick over what she has discovered in *"E" Is for Evidence,* she plans to persuade Rosie to let her into the tavern early: "I needed a heavy Hungarian dinner, a glass of white wine, and someone to fuss at me like a mother" (217).

Interestingly, Kinsey appears to let a number of women, usually either older or bigger than she, "fuss at" her for some perceived inadequacy, usually involving her appearance. After Rosie, the most frequent scold is Vera Lipton, Kinsey's good friend and a claims adjustor at California Fidelity Insurance. Vera is always ragging her about her poor fashion sense and even lends her a dressy black silk jumpsuit and does her makeup for the retirement dinner in *"G" Is for Gumshoe.* Ida Ruth, Kingman and Ives' secretary, berates her about her failure to take vitamin C for her cold and for missing a local tourist attraction when she went to Mexico (*Judgment*). Lyda Case wants to do a complete makeover (*Evidence*). Danielle Rivers, a prostitute, thinks her hair is so bad that she gives Kinsey a haircut (*Killer*). Bibianna Diaz does a quick makeover of Kinsey's hair and dress in the restroom at the Meat Locker (*Homicide*). Olive Kohler is so afraid Kinsey won't have an appropriate dress for her New Year's Eve party that she gives her one from her own closet (*Evidence*).

Now, let's be realistic. Kinsey is an intelligent, grown woman, fully capable of learning about makeup and planning her own wardrobe, but she does not *choose* to do so. She also does not seem to mind all this motherly fussing over her. We could conclude that there must be something highly satisfying about all the attention, or Kinsey would not allow it to happen over and over. The implication that Kinsey is filling in the gaps from her childhood is strong.

Parental support is composed of more than food and fussing, of course, and to be fair to Aunt Virginia, what Kinsey gained from her guidance is a set of values far more important than dress codes and eating habits. The most detailed description of her aunt's core values and beliefs is given in *"D" Is for Deadbeat* when Kinsey discovers that her aunt's "no-brand semiautomatic" has been stolen (*B* 149). She is extremely upset because she treasures the pistol as Aunt Virginia's "legacy, representing the odd bond between us" (*D* 101). Apparently neither she nor her aunt owned much in the way of material things, and this was the only physical legacy from her aunt, whom she loved deeply whether or not either of them said so very often.

The loss reminds her of everything she misses about Aunt Virginia, who died ten years earlier, when Kinsey was twenty-two. She recalls some of the "dozens of . . . precepts" her aunt taught her. Some of them now seem amusing to her, but the most important lesson was one Kinsey took very seriously. It was about the value of earning one's own money. "Rule Number One [after the prohibition on sniveling], first and foremost, above and beyond all else, was financial independence. A woman should never, never, never be financially dependent on anyone, especially a man, because the minute you were dependent, you could be abused. Financially dependent persons (the young, the old, the indigent) were inevitably treated badly and had no recourse. A woman should *always* have recourse. My aunt believed that every woman should develop marketable skills, and the more money she was paid for them the better. Any feminine pursuit that did not have as its ultimate goal increased self-sufficiency could be disregarded" (*D* 102).

The need for financial independence and marketable skills is a lesson Kinsey still lives by. (This lesson will gain new meaning when we learn in *"J" Is for Judgment* about the Kinsey family wealth, which Virginia and Rita Kinsey turned their backs on for the sake of their own independence. Virginia knew intimately the power over others that money gives to its possessor.) Throughout the series, Kinsey maintains a successful one-person P.I. agency. She remains financially solvent and careful, always managing her career and her money to suit herself.

Kinsey also expanded the concept of independence beyond the financial to include personal, or emotional, independence. She chooses to remain single and carefully monitors how close she allows anyone to come. Certainly, the five-year-old who crawled inside a cardboard box and created her own world already had a streak of self-sufficiency, but this innate tendency was greatly encouraged by Aunt Virginia's passion for financial independence. The child's spark was fanned by her aunt into the fire that is the adult Kinsey.

Readers applaud Aunt Virginia's encouragement of financial autonomy and career goals for women, but they may be less comfortable with Kinsey's ambivalent attitude toward her aunt's distaste for makeup, fashion, and a whole range of "feminine" behaviors. If "increased self-sufficiency" is the goal for all activities, then, according to her aunt, " 'How to Get Your Man' didn't even appear on the list" (*D* 102). Apparently these lessons, too, were absorbed well. Kinsey wears no makeup most of the time, dresses comfortably in turtleneck sweaters and jeans, and owns only one "all-purpose dress" (*E* 39, 227, and lots of other places). She is uncomfortable in cocktail party settings and she seems totally clueless about the techniques of flirting.

These habits of dress and manner reflect deliberate choices by Kinsey, but she does not always seem happy with her ignorance about style and her lack of stereotypical feminine graces. "Of course, I was dressed wrong," she berates herself in the mirror when she misjudges and wears casual clothes to meet Ash and her mother at the wealthy Woods' home. Earlier, meeting Ash for lunch at the Edgewater Hotel, she had dressed *up* in her one dress—as a good detective, she always tries to disguise herself to blend into her setting—but Ash had surprised her by showing up in "an outfit suitable for bagging game." This time she thought she had it right by dressing *down,* but, to her dismay, she's gotten it wrong again. She continues to scold herself: "I never could guess right when it came to clothes" (*E* 66). She is irritated by her misjudgment, and she blames the fact that she has "no class" on her upbringing by an aunt whose "notion of 'day-core' was a pink plastic flamingo standing on one foot" (*E* 67).

A similar, but funnier, scene occurs in *"H" Is for Homicide,* when Kinsey goes to the raunchy Meat Locker to try to meet Bibianna Diaz. She wears what she thinks will be an appropriate disguise for this night spot: a rather outlandish outfit created around tight ankle-length black pants, lace-edged white socks, and a hair style that reminds her of a water spout. She finishes off the look with "gaudy red lipstick" and big dangling earrings with red stones (48). She's quite pleased with her creation of Kinsey-as-vamp until she shares the mirror in the women's room with Bibianna, whose sexy dress and manner have all the guys panting after her. Bibianna looks gravely at Kinsey's reflection and says: " 'I hope you don't mind my saying this, but that hair and the getup are completely wrong.'

" 'They are?' I looked down at myself, a feeling of despair washing over me. What is it about me that invites this kind of comment? Here I think of myself as a kick-ass private eye when other people apparently see me as a waif in need of mothering" (55).

Bibianna then redoes her hair, tells her to "dump the earrings," and does "some kind of tricky fold" thing with a hot pink scarf from her purse and ties it around Kinsey's neck, giving an instant boost to her color (55–56). Kinsey makes fun of all the fuss and calls Bibianna's hair mousse "some kind of bottled hair snot." But when she looks in the mirror, to her surprise, she actually likes the results. She would never have known to add a pink scarf to improve her coloring, but she can see that it does. "How do women know these things? More important, how come I don't?" (55).

She answers her own question in a number of scenes with something along the lines of her lament before the Kohlers' party in *"E" Is for Evidence:* "I'd never had a role model for this female stuff. . . . I'd been raised by a maiden aunt, no expert herself at things feminine. I'd spent the days of my childhood with cap guns and books, learning self-sufficiency" (126).

Kinsey is a complex and contradictory character. She is strong and self-sufficient and she has no intention of letting concern for trivial things like clothing and makeup run her life. She strongly agrees with her aunt's set of priorities. She does not define herself in relationship to a man in her life. She is her own person. She is a "kick-ass private eye." At the same time, probably like every other woman on the planet, she is not secure about how she looks and dresses. She knows other people place great value on looks, and she recognizes that she really does not know how to put on makeup or dress well. The dominant part of her character is amused by, and scornful of, the great value other people foolishly place on fashion and makeup, and she takes pride in her own disdain for dress and looks. The omission represents her commitment to more important values. At the same time, when Kinsey laughs about her social gaucheries, taking pleasure in the superficiality of those who might notice her social gaffs, we still sense a twinge of genuine embarrassment behind the laughter. She may deliberately choose not to develop social or fashion skills, but she can still be irritated or wistful about their absence on occasion.

Grafton gives us what literary critics call "a well-rounded character" in Kinsey; that is, she is capable of surprising us. She has richness, complexity, and contradictions. Just when we think we can pigeonhole her as a tough P.I. with a no-nonsense attitude toward fashion and looks, we see a sense of vulnerability about her appearance. In a second twist, then, Kinsey is not consistent even about that vulnerability. It is both a point of pride and a source of some discomfort.

In other words, Grafton has created a very human Kinsey with whom readers can easily identify. Who among us has not felt gauche and awkward at some social event? Kinsey simultaneously treasures what her aunt taught her ("a solid set of values," *E* 126) and laments what her aunt did not teach her ("I'm a social oaf," *E* 126). "My aunt, *for all her failings,* was a *perfect* guardian for me . . . brazen, remote, eccentric, independent" (*D* 129, emphasis added). If the combination of love, appreciation, and criticism sounds familiar to readers, it's probably because we ourselves have said something similar about our parent-figures more than once in our own lives.

Education

After the death of her parents and the consequent guardianship of her aunt, the second most important biographical fact to have an impact on Kinsey appears to be her early education. She emerged in the autumn from her cardboard retreat "like a little animal coming out of its lair" only because she had to enter kindergarten at Wood-

row Wilson Elementary School (*J* 133–34).* She recalls that first day
as the most threatening of her life (*G* 141), and of her early schooling
she says, "Nothing I've faced since has even come close to the horrors of grade school" (*J* 134).

Kinsey never uses these terms, but readers can see that she had no
chance to deal effectively with her grief and anger over her parents'
death before she had to face the regimented educational system, a
horde of noisy, unknown children who did not share her recent history, and "Mrs. Bowman, the teacher, in whose eyes I could read
both pity and disapproval" (*J* 134). She describes herself as "a timid
little child with skinny legs" (*B* 190), and "the kind of kid who, for no
apparent reason, wept piteously or threw up on myself" (*G* 42).

Perhaps the most detailed account of the agonies of elementary
school occurs in *"G" Is for Gumshoe,* when Kinsey goes to the Rio Vista
Convalescent Hospital to find Agnes Grey. Memories of grade school
are triggered by the building itself, which was originally a grammar
school: "The interior was nearly identical to the elementary school
I'd attended. High ceilings, wood floors, the sort of lighting fixtures
that look like small perfect moons. Across from me, a water fountain
was still mounted on the wall, white porcelain with shiny chrome
handles down low at kiddie height. Even the air smelled the same,
like vegetable soup. For a moment, the past was palpable, laid over
reality like a sheet of cellophane, blocking out everything. I experienced the same rush of anxiety I'd suffered every day of my youth. I
hadn't liked school" (42).

This laconic last statement is expanded elsewhere. She says she
"hated" school (*G* 162) with its "endless performances" and constant testing, judging, criticizing, grading, and reviewing. Her shyness
and small size made her an easy target for other children, and she
loathed being asked to do anything solo in front of the class (42). She
recalls the terror of having to be a bunny in the third grade dance
recital—alone, because Aunt Gin was ill (*M* 97). The only part of
grade school she liked was music (42), learning to nap on command
(196), and eating LePage's paste (*F* 47), not exactly a full day's schedule for an elementary school student.

---

* Kinsey is explicit about this point in *Judgment,* but earlier she had indicated that she
went to several Bible schools during the summer she was five (*F* 140). This is one of
the rare inconsistencies in the series.

Looking at Rio Vista, she thinks the conversion of the building is appropriate. "Maybe life is just a straight shot from the horrors of grade school to the horrors of the nursing home" (*G* 43).

As an adult, Kinsey looks back and feels some sympathy for the teachers, who must have worried about her (*J* 134 and *G* 42). Readers, however, are likely to have more sympathy for that young child whose reason for suddenly bursting into tears is only too obvious, especially since she had been forbidden to cry at home.

Kinsey promptly got into trouble at school. It was nothing big, passing notes in her first-grade class, but enough to frighten this already timid child and send her home in tears. Caught between the principal and her aunt, who marched her right back to school and "read everybody out" for the school's handling of the misdemeanor, Kinsey "sat on a little wooden chair in the hall and prayed for death. It's hard to keep passing myself off as a grown-up when a piece of me is still six years old and utterly at the mercy of authority" (*B* 190).

Kinsey's frustrations with systems of authority must have surfaced in other settings as well, because she tells us that she was asked to leave the summer vacation Bible schools by the Methodist, the Presbyterian, and finally the Baptist churches (*F* 140). She doesn't say exactly why. Nor does she ever indicate that any reprimands were issued for her tendency to bite other children when they bullied or frustrated her (*D* 19), a temptation she still feels, but does not yield to. At least, as far as we know.

By the fifth grade, she was in trouble constantly. Too timid for outright rebellion, she "did disobey the rules" by such actions as hiding "in the girls' rest room instead of going back to class" after lunch period (*G* 42). Apparently, none of the teachers thought to ask what would prompt a child to hide. They didn't try to deal with her underlying problems. Instead, Kinsey simply got sent to the principal, or put out in the hall again for "endless hours." Her aunt continued to behave like "an avenging angel," but to no avail (*G* 43). The fact that Kinsey knew her aunt was firmly on her side was a crucial security blanket for her, but even her strong aunt could not change the system.

Some help in the school hallways came from the one friend Kinsey mentions: Jimmy Tate, who befriended her in the fifth grade and later appears in *"H" Is for Homicide*. They were drawn to each other because they both liked to skip school. Jimmy had been bounced from foster home to foster home and labeled "incorrigible" by the age of eight for being rebellious and having fistfights. Kinsey says, "I was a timid child, but I had a wild streak of my own born of grief at the loss of my parents when I was five. My mutiny originated in fear, Jimmy's in rage, but the net result was the same." Kinsey says they loved the feeling of exhilaration "every time we raced away from the schoolyard, giddy with freedom, knowing how short-lived our libera- tion would be." Jimmy made himself her protector. "More than once he came to my defense, beating the snot out of some bullying fifth- grade boy who'd tried pushing me around." And he tried to teach Kinsey some valuable skills. "He introduced me to cigarettes, tried getting me high on aspirin and Coke, showed me the difference be- tween boys and girls" (H 58–59).

The initial experience of high school proved only a little better. Without Jimmy, the sixth grade must have been an especially tough year for Kinsey. That's when her "mortal enemy, Tommy Jancko," bullied her constantly. But since their major weapon of choice was the staring contest, there probably wasn't any physical damage done (C 29). That's also the year the little girls began to be teenagers and Kinsey went through the embarrassment of showing up for a party still dressed in "stupid white ankle socks" while the other girls wore hose (A 185). It was also a memorable year because Kinsey learned a useful new word: "Fuck" (A 212).

The initial experience of high school proved only a little better. Apparently Kinsey entered Santa Teresa High School with less trauma than elementary school, and she describes herself at fifteen as "full of hope, not yet into flunking, rebelling, and smoking dope" (I 264). The latter three proved to be her best subjects as high school pro- gressed (J 81), and Kinsey became "a screwup," as she describes herself to Guy Malek (M 67). She hated math and chemistry (I 82), and she never mentions a single teacher. The only girlfriend she names is Ash Wood, whom she dropped after only a short time be- cause she was so uncomfortable about the Woods' higher social and financial status (E 41). Her best friends were a group of "bad-ass boys," known as "low-wallers" because they "perched on a low wall that ran along the back of the school property" (M 67). They taught her to smoke marijuana and to add to an already substantial reper- toire of cuss words (E 126). (Her aunt objected to cursing only in front of those who might be offended, and she urged Kinsey to choose her audience carefully, *C* 191.) Ash and her sister Ebony remember Kinsey in high school as "a rebel" (*E* 42), full of "energy . . . fiery and defensive" (*E* 77). Kinsey remembers herself as "a complete misfit" (*E* 126) and "a wild thing" (*M* 67). On rainy nights, she "wandered the streets . . . barefoot, in a raincoat, feeling anxious and strange." At the time, she assumed her aunt was unaware of these nocturnal wanderings, but now she isn't so sure: "She had a restless streak of her own and she may have honored mine" (*D* 129). Certainly one of Virginia's great strengths as Kinsey's guardian was her rare ability to stand aside and let Kinsey learn for herself. For the small child this may have seemed occasionally nonsupportive, but for the teenager it was an enormously reinforcing, supportive, and generous gesture.

In trying to trace her education beyond high school, we run into some contradictory statements from Kinsey. In *"A" Is for Alibi,* a friend named Nell is identified as an old friend from "my college days" (146), but Kinsey tells Neil Hess at the California Fidelity retirement dinner in *"G" Is for Gumshoe,* "I didn't go to college" (161). We could speculate that Kinsey might be practicing her lying skills with Neil, just to twit him because he was so quick to assume she must have gone to college, but we also have Kinsey later thinking aloud, "I'd never gone to college. I was strictly blue-collar lineage" (252). We have to trust that Kinsey does not lie to readers.

The question of college becomes even more complicated with Kinsey's conversation with the hoodlum Raymond Maldonado in *"H" Is for Homicide.* As they work together inventing fictitious accidents and injuries for his insurance scam, Raymond is impressed with her writing skills. Kinsey thinks, "Raymond hadn't managed to graduate from high school, whereas I attended three whole semesters of junior college before I lost heart" (211). Now we have *junior* college thrown into the mix.

How do we reconcile these contradictions? Does Kinsey not think of "junior college" as "college," and therefore the truth is that she attended three semesters of junior college and no regular college? But Kinsey does not appear to make such a precise distinction between the two. We hear her refer to her attending "college" in the ensuing conversation with Raymond. Plus, we have the added complication that if we follow the clues about Kinsey's biography revealed in all the novels, there doesn't seem to be enough time for her to attend junior college between graduating from high school and entering the police academy. For graphic presentation of the problems with the years immediately following high school, see the Time Line at the end of this chapter.

Perhaps the only reconciliation possible is to acknowledge that there are problems inherent in writing a series of novels with one central character. If Grafton had known at the onset of *"A" Is for Alibi* that she would currently be engaged in the final stages of writing *N*, she might have given a lot more thought to casually identifying Nell as a college friend. Whether we like to admit it or not, Kinsey is a fictional character. And an author uses biographical detail only to help create that fictional character. In *Alibi*, the detail of college chums helps create warmth around the character of Kinsey. In several of the later novels, Grafton goes to some pains to paint Kinsey as working-class, a separate species from some of her wealthy clients or corrupt opponents. Not attending college is a detail that helps create that persona.

Career

Kinsey entered the police academy at either nineteen (*G* 150) or twenty (*B* 1), for training that lasted some months. Upon graduation at twenty, according to Kinsey in *"B" Is for Burglar* (1), she joined the Santa Teresa Police Department, where she worked for two years before quitting. But, according to Kinsey in *"G" Is for Gumshoe*, she was only *nineteen* when she finished the police academy, and since she had to wait until she was *twenty-one* to join the police department, she worked at California Fidelity as a receptionist until she was the requisite age (150).

The details about dates are small potatoes, though, compared to the larger portrait of Kinsey joining the police force and resigning after two years. That portrait is quite consistent.

Given the distaste for rules and regulations that lay behind her penchant for truancy, marijuana, and flunking in high school, a career choice in law enforcement may seem unlikely. But Kinsey says

she "straightened up [her] act" by the time she graduated from high
school (*E* 126). Although Kinsey never tells us precisely why she made
the decision to enter the police academy, random comments suggest
that her moral core was the primary cause. We might also speculate
that her lifelong curiosity about other people ("I'm an incurable
snoop and I search automatically," *C* 190) made the investigative side
of police work appealing.

Kinsey's distaste for regimentation never leaves her, however, and
this leads to problems with her work on the police force. All the
references to Kinsey's police days have these two themes in common:
her idealistic hopes for police work and the chipping away of those
hopes by the bureaucracy and the daily reality of police life.

"I don't even remember now how I pictured the job before I took
it on. I must have had vague, idealistic notions of law and order, the
good guys versus the bad, with occasional court appearances in which
I'd be asked to testify as to which was which. In my view, the bad guys
would all go to jail, thus making it safe for the rest of us to carry on.
After a while, I realized how naive I was. I was frustrated at the restric-
tions and frustrated because back then, policewomen were viewed
with a mixture of curiosity and scorn. I didn't want to spend my days
defending myself against 'good-natured' insults, or having to prove
how tough I was again and again. I wasn't getting paid enough to deal
with all that grief, so I got out" (*B* 1).

For someone she interviews in *"D" Is for Deadbeat,* she condenses
the story to, "I used to be a cop, but I didn't like it much. The law
enforcement part of it was fine, but not the bureaucracy. Now I'm
self-employed. I'm happier that way" (109). When she meets Sgt.
Jonah Robb, he asks if she too hadn't been a cop. She replies,
"Briefly. . . . But I couldn't make it work. Too rebellious I guess" (*B*
48).

Kinsey's willingness to assume responsibility—"I couldn't make it
work"—sounds amazingly like the generous comments about her
own responsibility for the problems in grade school. Surprisingly, she
shows no bitterness about the sexism or the bureaucracy of the police
force. She blames no one.

There was a third reason for her resignation, which she does not
reveal until she begins to open up to Dietz in *"G" Is for Gumshoe.*
Kinsey explains how she "got even" for her aunt's ban on "snivel-

ing." "She died ten years ago and I sniveled for months. It all came pouring out. I'd been a cop for two years and I gave that up. Turned in my uniform, turned in my nightstick" (95). The description sounds as if Kinsey took the time to retreat into grief once again after the death of a parent-figure. She even moved into her aunt's trailer, a small refuge that reminds us of the cardboard box, and for the second time in her life, Kinsey set about reinventing herself. For two years after quitting the police, she did a variety of jobs, including working again for California Fidelity Insurance, an association that goes back a long way, because her aunt had worked for them and arranged summer jobs there for Kinsey during high school (*G* 150).

Pulled back into investigative work by the "adrenal rush" and "the intermittent sick thrill of life on the edge" (*B* 1), Kinsey joined the small private investigative firm of Ben Byrd and Morley Shine. She spent "another two years learning the business" of being a private investigator (*B* 1), primarily from Ben, who taught her, among other things, the technique of putting her notes on index cards and studying them in varying sequences. She then obtained her license from the state of California and opened up her own office in the CF building. In exchange for office space, she handled two or three investigations each month, particularly arson and wrongful death, for the insurance company. In fact, she remembers that one of her first really big investigations after getting her licence was for California Fidelity (*G* 150).

Five years later, in May 1982, when Kinsey is thirty-two and in full swing as a detective, Grafton's series of novels opens with *"A" Is for Alibi.*

Marriages

In *"A" Is for Alibi,* Kinsey looks at the few papers and objects left by Libby Glass, who was murdered eight years before. She is initially saddened by the smallness of the collection, but then she realizes, "I didn't keep much myself, didn't hoard or save. Two divorce decrees. That was about the sum of it for me" (168).

Kinsey's two marriages (neither of which included a formal wedding, *J* 70) must have had less impact on her than the circumstances of her birth family and her early education, if we judge by the amount of attention they receive in Kinsey's references to her earlier life. We are told very little about her marriages. Of her two husbands, Kinsey says, "I dumped the first and the second one dumped me. With both, I did my share of suffering, but when I look back on it, I can't understand why I endured so long. It was dumb. It was a big waste of time and cost me a lot" (*D* 52). Kinsey has concluded that "Marriage is a mystery" (*B* 96).

Husband #1 is never even given a name. We learn practically zilch about this guy. All we know is that Kinsey married him within six months of her aunt's death and her resignation from the police force, and she now thinks of him as "a bum" (*G* 95). We don't know why she married him (we might speculate that it was part of her reinventing process after her aunt's death), what he was like, how long they were married, or why she divorced him.

We know more about Husband #2, even meeting him as a character in *"E" Is for Evidence*. Daniel Wade is a superb jazz musician, absolutely beautiful, and totally without moral scruples. Kinsey doesn't say how they met, but she initially ignored him because of his angelic good looks, falling for him only after hearing him play the piano. They married when Kinsey was twenty-three, apparently right on the heels of her first divorce, and "eleven months and six days" later—not that Kinsey was counting!—Daniel simply walked out and never came back (*E* 105). They divorced quickly, without ever seeing each other.

The marriage was a dizzying mix of play and pain. Kinsey says Daniel taught her how to have some fun in life, but he taught her more about how to endure loneliness. Daniel's order of priorities put music, drugs, sex, and parties well ahead of Kinsey, and she spent many nights waiting in vain for him to come home. Kinsey was deeply hurt by his behavior during their marriage and even more hurt by his leaving her, one more instance of being abandoned by someone she loved.

In *Evidence,* Daniel shows up on her doorstep eight years after walking out and seems genuinely bewildered that she might still bear a grudge. He claims he is clean now, no cigarettes, no drinking, and no drugs. He looks after Kinsey, even shopping and cooking for her, while she is recovering from being burned in an explosion. Kinsey adores hearing him play her landlord's piano, and she appreciates his listening to her worries about her current case, recalling that one of his good qualities she had liked so much was his ability to listen.

Just as Kinsey is beginning to think that Daniel might turn out to be at least an okay human being, she discovers that he has bugged her apartment. That was the reason for his showing up at her door, not any desire to set things straight between them. Once again he has betrayed her. This time she is more furious than hurt, and she quickly begins to refossilize any hint of feelings for her second husband. Daniel leaves with his lover at the end of the novel and we haven't seen him since. Which is fine with us.

Lovers

In the course of the novels, Kinsey sleeps with three men: Charlie Scorsoni in *Alibi,* Sgt. Jonah Robb in *Deadbeat,* and Robert Dietz in *Gumshoe* and *Malice.* Charlie is an attorney who turns out to be a murderer and Kinsey shoots him in self-defense. Jonah, with his boyish charm, is very appealing to Kinsey, but he remains tied to his wife, Camilla, and the relationship fizzles out. Strong-willed Dietz seems a perfect match for Kinsey in his competence, his self-control, and his toughness—plus, he's great in bed—but after several months together, he leaves for a job in private security work in Germany. When he returns in *"M" Is for Malice,* the relationship is resumed, but serious problems about commitment and direction surface, and readers are uncertain about their future. As are Kinsey and Dietz themselves.

Defense of Her History

One might look at Kinsey's biography thus far and consider it a rather grim, sad business. And, in many ways, it is. A painful childhood, a lousy time in school, two wretched marriages, and being forced to shoot a lover are not exactly the stuff of a *Brady Bunch* episode. To see her biography only in this light, however, is to do a serious disservice to Kinsey and to those around her. The title of this section, after all, is a direct quotation from Kinsey, "I like my history just as it is" (D 129).

To be sure, there were lighter moments in her history. Kinsey referred to her aunt by the playful pet name of "Gin Gin" (J 133). Her aunt appears to have had a number of friends, and Kinsey accompanied her to their homes, exploring the houses while the grown-ups talked and drank. In fact, she says that's how she became a detective—snooping in their bedrooms and bathrooms, wondering what that funny shaped doodad with the battery was for, or how the "marital artifacts between the mattress and box springs" were used (C 190). Since she couldn't ask her aunt, or she'd know her niece had been snooping, Kinsey just had to try to figure out the story on that doodad for herself.

Although she didn't like playing hide-and-seek because "the tension made me want to wet my pants" (A 274) and she dropped out of the Brownies after less than a week because she "thought it was dumb" (A 13), Kinsey enjoyed a number of typical childhood activities, including those all-time favorites of waxing the sliding board (M 31) and rolling pieces of bread into pellets and flicking them across the table at her unsuspecting aunt when she wasn't looking (L 37). Aunt Virginia taught Kinsey to play baseball. She doesn't say whether she liked playing, but given her successful swing of an impromptu bat at the murderer's head in the final scene of "C" Is for Corpse, we can assume she was good at the game and therefore probably enjoyed the sport. She also got past her initial distaste for summer camp enough to become a camp counselor by her sophomore year in high school.

Kinsey loved playing dress-up with her aunt's old clothes, and she describes in great detail the Halloween costume she wore in the second grade. In typical Kinseyesque contrariness, the costume was both beautiful and bloody. She went as the bride of Frankenstein, complete with "fangs and fake blood, and . . . clumsy black stitches up and down my face," drawn by her aunt. Her dress, however, was a vision of childhood loveliness: an ankle-length ballerina costume to which her aunt had added countless squiggles of "Elmer's glue . . . sprinkled with dime-store glitter. I'd never felt so glamorous." At the time, she considered it "the most beautiful dress I would ever own," and Kinsey still misses the feeling it gave her (J 70–71).

When Kinsey looks at her own life now, she sees much that she would defend. She likes her work and thinks she's good at what she does. She certainly solves all the cases she reports to us. She values her relationship with Dietz—just as she does for a short time with Jonah. Her closest and most constant friendships are with her landlord, Henry Pitts, a retired baker, and Rosie, who owns Rosie's Tavern. She also has a solid friendship with Vera Lipton, a claims representative at CF, for a number of the novels. There are other friendships appearing only in a single novel, for example, Bobby Callahan in *Corpse,* Danielle Rivers in *Killer,* and Guy Malek in *Malice.* These good relationships are clear signals of much that is positive and healthy about Kinsey's current life.

When Kinsey looks back at her life in the early novels, she sees the childhood we've described. And she thinks she knows all there is to know about her own early years with her strong-minded aunt Virginia, to whom she owes so much of her adult strength of character. But she is astonished by what she learns about her family in *"J" Is for Judgment.* It turns out there were huge gaps in the story she knew of her childhood and her family.

In *Judgment,* one of Kinsey's interviewees, Lena Irwin, thinks Kinsey looks a lot like the Burton Kinseys in Lompoc. Kinsey, who had thought she had no living relatives, checks her parents' marriage certificate (November 18, 1935) at the Hall of Records. She thinks about how little she really knows about either her mother's or her father's family, even how little she knows of her own early years. "I realized what a vacuum I'd been living in" (142). "Given my insatiable curiosity and my natural inclination to poke my nose in where it doesn't belong, it was odd to realize how little attention I'd paid to my own past" (133).

After Kinsey concludes that she probably does have relatives in Lompoc, her response is ambivalent. She has missed having a family, but now she says, "I could see in a flash what a strange pleasure I'd taken in being related to no one. I'd actually managed to feel superior about my isolation. I was subtle about it, but I could see that I'd turned it into a form of self-congratulation" (142). Later conversations with her cousins, Liza and Tasha, do nothing to reverse this position.

Liza shows up at Kinsey's office, Lena Irwin having called someone in the family without Kinsey's knowledge. Kinsey is astonished to learn that the family is extremely wealthy and that her mother, Rita, had made a debut on July 5, 1935. At that party, Rita earned the enmity of her mother, Cornelia LeGrand Kinsey (called "Grand" by the family), when she spoiled her hopes for a "proper match" by falling in love with one of the waiters. Liza proves as pretentious as their grandmother by explaining that "his real job was working for the post office here in Santa Teresa. It's not like he was really a waiter." Kinsey dryly interjects, " 'Oh, thank God,' . . . but the irony was lost on her" (171).

Rita Kinsey and Randy Millhone refused to be cowed by her family, and, only a few months later, they eloped to be married in Santa Teresa, with her sister Virginia serving as their only witness. The five Kinsey sisters tried unsuccessfully to patch up the quarrel between Grand and Rita, and Virginia maintained contact among all the family members. The remaining sisters and their children loved the family story of wild, rebellious Rita, who became their "patron saint of liberation" (170). While Grand would assign Rita's napkin ring as punishment for whoever was disobedient that day, the kids thought it was a great honor, and they fought over who got to be naughty enough to win the prize.

Kinsey is appalled by the story. How could an entire family live all those years a few miles away and never make any effort to contact her? Why did her aunt tell her none of this? Why did none of them contact her when Virginia died? In addition to these hard questions—which neither cousin can answer—Kinsey feels robbed of what she thought was her unique history. She thought she invented the pet name "Gin Gin" for her aunt, but she finds out all the kids called her that. She thought the peanut-butter-and-pickle sandwiches were her unique legacy from her mother, but her mother had taught all the kids how to make the sandwiches on a visit to Lompoc when Grand was away. She also hates the way in which the family turned Rita from a person into a family icon. "She was a ritual, a symbol, something to be fought over like a bunch of rowdy dogs with a bone" (173).

"In theory, I'd suddenly gained an entire family, cause for rejoicing if you happen to believe the ladies' magazines. In reality, I felt as if someone had just stolen everything I held dear, a common theme in all the books you read on burglary and theft" (174). What has been stolen is the *specialness* that each of us feels about the past that

has shaped us. Kinsey looks at the difficult circumstances of her childhood and, importantly, she really likes the person those circumstances made her become. She sees that she learned independence,
self-sufficiency, endurance, tolerance, adaptability, perseverance—a
host of valuable strengths. And she became this resilient person without any Hallmark scenes of a big family around the Christmas tree.
"At best, I was self-created; at worst, the hapless artifact of my aunt's
peculiar notions about raising little girls. In either event, I regarded
myself an outsider, a loner, which suited me to perfection" (142).

Kinsey may wonder what her life would have been like if her parents had lived, or if her aunt had been different, or if her Lompoc
family had contacted her (*J* 255). But she would not change the
person she has become and the life she has now. And she recognizes
that her character and personality are the result of her particular
history. "Had my parents lived, my life would have taken an altogether different route." Therefore, because she likes the person she
has become by traveling that route, she would not change the road
that got her here. She even goes so far as to suggest that "the death of
my parents may not have been as tragic as it seemed" because Aunt
Virginia, with her eccentricities, her independence, her determination not to let Kinsey ever see herself as a victim, and her respect for
Kinsey's emotional space, was such a perfect guardian for her (*D* 129).

Kinsey is not at all sure she *ever* wants to get to know the Lompoc
relatives. In *"L" Is for Lawless,* she is still resisting contact with the
family. She refuses cousin Tasha's invitation to Thanksgiving dinner.
She knows she does not want to be forced to rewrite her history, and
she fears that knowing the Kinsey family would make her see her own
life in a different way. And for what? "It's folly to think we can go
back and make it come out any different," Kinsey tells Tasha (28).

In spite of this reluctance, Kinsey is drawn into limited contact
with the family. By the end of *Lawless,* Kinsey runs out of people to
call for money when she's without funds in Kentucky, and she finally
calls her cousin Tasha for a loan in order to get home. In the next
novel, her case is the consequence of a luncheon with this cousin.
Tasha is an attorney handling the substantial estate of Bader Malek,
and she hires Kinsey to find Guy Malek, one of the sons, who hasn't
been heard from in eighteen years and who now stands to inherit up
to one quarter of the $40 million estate. Although Kinsey had gone to

the luncheon fully intending to say "no" and avoid further contact with her family, she promptly says "yes," but only because she loves doing missing person searches and this case sounds especially interesting.

Readers, eager to get every available scrap of information about Kinsey, do not share Kinsey's determination to avoid her Lompoc family. Grafton has given us a fictional character who seems totally real, and we are as curious about her as we would be about a flesh-and-blood friend. We remain hopeful that Grafton will tell us more about this irritating part of the Kinsey family. There's a story there. Why in the world has no one from the family contacted Kinsey before? Especially when her aunt died? Does this background explain Aunt Virginia's passionate insistence on women being financially independent? How do we reconcile Virginia's monied background with her plebeian tastes?

And, while we're on the subject of family, who and where are the Millhones? What are they like? And who was that first husband who was a bum?

TIME LINE FOR KINSEY MILLHONE

July 5, 1935

Rita Cynthia Kinsey makes her debut at 18 in Lompoc.

She meets Randy Millhone, working as waiter for her party.

The wealthy Kinseys, especially Rita's mother, Cornelia LeGrand, disapprove of the match.

November 18, 1935

Wedding of Terrence Randall Millhone, 33, of Santa Teresa, and Rita Cynthia Kinsey, 18, of Lompoc, takes place in Santa Teresa, witnessed by her sister Virginia Kinsey.

May 5, 1950

The Millhones' only child, Kinsey, is born in Santa Teresa at St. Terry's Hospital.

1954

Kinsey has a tonsillectomy.

The Millhones visit the Kinsey family when Grand is away. During the visit, Kinsey cuts her knee.

Memorial Day Weekend, 1955

Car accident kills Kinsey's parents on the way to a second visit
to the family in Lompoc.

Kinsey goes to live with her aunt Virginia in a trailer and lives
inside her cardboard box "cocoon of grief."

Summer 1955

She gets kicked out of three Bible schools, according to *"F" Is
for Fugitive.*

Fall 1955

She enters kindergarten at Woodrow Wilson Elementary School.

She dislikes school, her classmates, and her teacher, Mrs. Bowman.

She likes music and learning to nap on command.

When she's frustrated, she bites other children.

Fall 1956

She enters first grade.

Elementary school is terrifying.

She is a skinny, timid child who cries a lot and throws up a lot,
sometimes both on the same day.

She's sent to the principal for the first time—for passing notes
in class—and is disciplined by having to sit in the hallway.

She spends a lot of time in grade school in the hall.

1958

She witnesses a neighborhood playmate's death at his own
birthday party.

Summer 1958

Kinsey goes to summer camp.

She hates all the bugs and dust and nature.

Fall 1960

By fifth grade she's in frequent trouble at school, especially for
truancy and for hiding in the girls' rest room.

She's protected from bullies by Jimmy Tate, who also introduces
her to cigarettes and the difference between boys and girls.

1961

She's bullied in sixth grade by Tommy Jancko.

Fall 1964

Kinsey enters Santa Teresa High School.

She hangs out with tough guys who teach her to cuss and
smoke dope.

She especially dislikes math and chemistry.

She works summers at California Fidelity Insurance, where her
aunt works.

Summer 1965

She is a camp counselor for the Y.

Spring 1968

She graduates from high school, having cleaned up her act and
stopped playing with drugs.

Fall 1968–Fall 1969

Perhaps she goes to junior college for 18 months, according to
"H" Is for Homicide.

1969

Perhaps she enters the police academy, according to *"G" Is for
Gumshoe*.

She does well and gets in great physical shape.

She finishes at age 19 and cannot join police force until 21,
according to *Gumshoe*.

She works for California Fidelity Insurance as receptionist, again
according to *Gumshoe* timing.

1970

Perhaps she enters the police academy at this point, according
to *"B" Is for Burglar*.

1970–1972

Kinsey is a cop with Santa Teresa Police Department.

She likes the thrill and the investigations.

She dislikes the bureaucracy and the disdain for women cops.

February 1972

Her aunt Virginia dies at St. Terry's Hospital.

She moves into her aunt's trailer.

She quits the police force.

August 1972

Kinsey marries for the first time, husband's name not given.

After she ends that brief marriage, she moves back into her
aunt's trailer.

1972–1974

She works assorted unspecified jobs.

1973

She marries Daniel Wade, a jazz musician and drug user.

1974

Eleven months later Daniel leaves her, without explanation.

She learns later (in *"E" Is for Evidence*) that he left her for Bass
Wood, the brother of one of her high school friends.

1974–1976

Kinsey trains with the Byrd-Shine detective agency for the
4,000 hours required in order to obtain her license as
a P.I.

She begins living in a series of trailers.

1975

Kinsey starts jogging three miles, six days a week, a practice she
continues to the present.

1976

She handles her first homicide investigation, for the public defender's office.

1977

She begins to work on her own as a freelance P.I.

Her two-room office is supplied by California Fidelity Insurance
in exchange for two or three investigations per month, usually arson and wrongful death.

1979

Public defender's office hires her to find Tyrone Patty, wanted
for burglary and attempted murder. She finds him, and he
tries to get revenge by hiring a contract hit man to kill
Kinsey in *"G" Is for Gumshoe*.

March 1980

When her trailer park is converted to one for senior citizens,
she is evicted.

While everything is tied up in legal confusions, Kinsey goes
apartment hunting. She finds a studio apartment at Henry
Pitts' house, one block from the beach.

She discovers Rosie's Tavern—and Rosie—near her new apartment.

May 1982

"A" Is for Alibi takes place.

Case: Kinsey is hired by Nikki Fife to find out who really killed
her husband eight years ago, a murder for which she was
wrongfully convicted.

Travel: To do her investigation, Kinsey travels to Los Angeles
and Las Vegas.

Men: Kinsey sleeps with Charlie Scorsoni, one of the suspects.

Milestones: This novel contains the first time she kills anyone.

Injuries: She suffers partial hearing loss after firing her gun inside a garbage bin.

Rate of Pay: $30 per hour.

June 1982

"B" Is for Burglar takes place.

Case: Kinsey is hired by Beverly Danzinger, then by Mrs. Ochsner, to find out what has happened to Elaine Boldt, Beverly's missing sister.

Travel: She twice flies to Miami and drives to Boca Raton, Flor-
ida.

Men: She meets Jonah Robb.

Injuries: She's beaten up and shot in final scene. Her arm and
nose are also broken.

July 1982

"C" Is for Corpse takes place.

Case: Kinsey becomes friends with Bobby Callahan, who hires her
to find out who tried to kill him in a serious car accident.

Injuries: She's trying to regain strength in her broken left
arm.

October 1982

"D" Is for Deadbeat takes place.

Case: John Daggett hires her to deliver a check to Tony Gahan.
When Daggett turns up dead, his daughter hires Kinsey to
investigate his probable murder.

Travel: During the investigation, she drives to Los Angeles.

Men: She sleeps with Jonah Robb.

Milestones: She's bothered by her failure to prevent a suicide.

December 1982

"E" Is for Evidence takes place.

Case: She is her own client, because she has to prove that she
was framed in a charge of fraud made against her during an
arson case she's investigating for CF.

Men: Her second husband, Daniel Wade, pops back into her life
briefly.

Injuries: She sustains burns during a bomb explosion at the Kohlers' house.

A second bomb explosion at her apartment leaves her temporarily deaf.

Travel: Makes a quick flight to Dallas–Ft. Worth Airport to interview a witness.

Milestones: She has to work hard not to be lonesome during Christmas with Henry, Rosie, and Jonah all away for the holidays.

Her apartment is bombed—with her inside at the time. Most of her possessions and the apartment are destroyed.

February 1983

"F" Is for Fugitive takes place.

Case: Royce Fowler hires her to clear his son, Bailey, of murder charges by finding the real murderer of Jean Timberlake, killed years earlier.

Travel: She goes to Floral Beach and San Luis Obispo.

Milestones: While her apartment is being rebuilt, she lives in Henry's spare bedroom.

May 1983

"G" Is for Gumshoe takes place.

Case: Kinsey is hired by Irene Gersh to see if her missing mother, Agnes Grey, is all right. The search is complicated by the fact that Kinsey is the object of a contract killer.

Travel: To find Agnes Grey, she drives to an area of abandoned government property known as "The Slabs" in the Mojave Desert.

Men: She considers her relationship with Jonah to be over.

She sleeps with Robert Dietz.

Milestones: She returns to her newly remodeled apartment.

She's given a surprise birthday party at Rosie's Tavern.

Her beige '68 VW is totaled.

She hires a bodyguard, who moves into her apartment.

She's not the one who shoots the killer in the final confrontation.

October 1983

"H" Is for Homicide takes place.

Case: Kinsey gets caught up in a case involving the death of one of her fellow workers at CF, Parnell Perkins. Investigating one of Parnell's last insurance claims, Kinsey is virtually kidnaped by an insurance swindler, Raymond Maldonado. The LAPD and Santa Teresa police persuade her to work undercover for them against Maldonado.

Travel: Most of the novel takes place in Los Angeles.

Milestones: Kinsey has a new (used) '74 blue VW bug.

For the first time in her life she is arrested (for assaulting an officer) and put in jail overnight.

She works undercover for the first time.

Gordon Titus fires her from CF.

She is an attendant at the wedding of her best friend, Vera Lipton, on Halloween.

December 1983

"I" Is for Innocent takes place.

Case: Lonnie Kingman's client, Kenneth Voigt, wants to file a wrongful death suit against David Barney for the death of his wife, Isabelle, who was Voigt's first wife. Kinsey is hired to find proof of Barney's guilt. She is replacing the original detective on the case, Morley Shine, whose former partner trained Kinsey.

Injuries: She gets shot in the right hip.

Milestones: Kinsey has a new office arrangement with law firm of Kingman and Ives. This is her first investigation for Lonnie Kingman.

Henry's brother William comes to visit. He and Rosie are taken with each other.

Rate of pay: She increases her hourly rate from $30 to $55 when she finds out Morley had been charging $50.

July 1984

"J" Is for Judgment takes place.

Case: Mac Voorhies from CF hires her to do a job for the insurance company again. She is hired to find Wendell Jaffe, who was alleged to have committed suicide five years earlier.

Travel: Kinsey flies to Mexico, and she does a lot of driving to Perdido/Olvidado.

Milestones: A chance interview leads her to find out about her

mother's estranged family still living in Lompoc, about
whom she had known nothing.

Henry is unhappy that William and Rosie have fallen in
love.

Kinsey either fails to prevent a suicide or lets a murderer
escape—she doesn't know which is true.

Rate of pay: She goes to $50 per hour, a standard rate.

February 1985

"K" Is for Killer takes place.

Case: Kinsey is hired by Janice Kepler to find the murderer of
her daughter, Lorna, who died the previous April.

Travel: To interview someone, Kinsey flies to San Francisco and
drives home.

Milestones: William and Rosie are engaged.

For the first and only time Kinsey deliberately arranges for a
murderer to be killed, rather than killing in self-defense.

November 1985

"L" Is for Lawless takes place.

Case: Kinsey gets involved in a spontaneous cross-country chase
of stolen money in order to help out one of Henry's neighbors.

Travel: Kinsey flies to Dallas and then drives on a jaunt through
Arkansas and Tennessee, ending up in Louisville, Kentucky.

Injuries: She suffers a concussion after being hit on the head.

Milestones: Kinsey is not pursuing a killer.

William and Rosie get married.

For the first time Kinsey initiates contact with the Lompoc
family, in order to borrow money in an emergency.

January 1986

"M" Is for Malice takes place.

Case: Cousin Tasha hires Kinsey to find Guy Malek, a missing
heir to the wealthy Malek estate. When he is killed and his
brother Jack arrested for the murder, Kinsey suggests Lonnie Kingman as his lawyer; in turn, Lonnie hires Kinsey to
locate the killer.

Men: Robert Dietz returns. Their mutual attraction is still strong
and they make love twice, but the relationship is problematic.

Travel: Kinsey drives to Marcella, California, to find Guy Malek.

Milestones: Kinsey has stopped carrying a gun.

She is not under great personal threat in the confrontation with the murderer.

She voluntarily gets a salon haircut *and* she tips the stylist.

She suspects she sees a ghost.

Kinsey's Personality

"I have my little quirks."

In the opening of *"H" Is for Homicide,* Kinsey is concluding a three-week investigation for California Fidelity in San Diego. At her motel, she wakes up "at 3:00 a.m. with a primal longing for home." By 3:30 she is in her "new (used) VW bug," a part of the light, but growing, traffic on the Los Angeles freeway system as the predawn rush hour begins. She watches the other drivers with pleasure. "I always feel an affinity for others traveling at such an hour, as if we are all engaged in some form of clandestine activity." Some are juggling "oversize Styrofoam cups of coffee" and some are wolfing down fast food. Cars pass with "bursts of booming music." Kinsey notices that the woman behind her is "belting out a lip-sync solo as the wind whipped through her hair." The moment is a perfect one for Kinsey (2).

She says, "I felt a jolt of pure joy. It was one of those occasions when I suddenly realized how happy I was. Life was good. I was female, single, with money in my pocket and enough gas to get home. I had nobody to answer to and no ties to speak of. I was healthy, physically fit, filled with energy. I flipped on the radio and chimed in on a chorus of 'Amazing Grace,' which didn't quite suit the occasion but was the only station I could find. An early morning evangelist began to make his pitch, and by the time I reached Ventura, I was nearly redeemed" (2–3).

The scene is striking for its sense of Kinsey's joy in life—her pleasure in being alone and autonomous, yet interested in other people, her financial and personal independence, her physical strength, her fondness for music, her adaptability, and her great sense of humor.

The final scene of the same novel could not offer a more stark contrast in its depiction of another Kinsey. At St. John's Hospital in Los Angeles, Raymond Maldonado, the hoodlum who has kept Kinsey and Bibianna Diaz prisoner for almost the entire novel, shoots Jimmy Tate, Kinsey's old grade-school chum. Kinsey is unable to prevent the shooting because the hospital hallway is too crowded for her to fire her gun safely. Furious that Raymond has almost killed Bibianna and now may have killed Jimmy, she is determined to keep him from getting away. He runs out of the hospital and onto the grounds, heading for the street. Gun in hand and "wheezing, lungs on fire," Kinsey chases after him.

"Raymond took a quick look behind him, gauging the distance between us. He got off a shot that smacked into a palm tree to my left. He tried to goose up his pace, but he really didn't have it in him. I was close enough now that the sound of his heavy breathing seemed in concert with mine and the heels of his shoes nearly touched my pumping knees. I had a tight grip on the gun. I reached out and pushed him hard in the back. He stumbled, arms flailing as he tried to regain his balance. He went down in a sprawl and I landed, knees first, in the middle of his back. His breath left him in a *whoosh* and the gun flew out of his hand. I was up and on my feet, panting heavily. He turned over as I raised the barrel of the gun and placed it between his eyes. Raymond had his hands up, inching away from me. For ten cents I would have blown that motherfucker away. My rage was white hot and I was out of control, screaming *"I'll kill your ass! I'll kill your ass, you son of a bitch!!"* (253).

This second scene is striking in its depiction of the violent, angry Kinsey who is capable of outrunning a murderer and, apparently, shooting him between the eyes for what he has done to her friends. Her language is crude and she completely gives in to a desire for personal revenge. She has lost all self-control.

The opening and closing scenes of *Homicide* nicely capture the adult Kinsey Millhone with all her contradictions. She's a tough private eye with no hesitation about shooting a murderer and she's very much a person of action, but she's also thoughtful, quirky, vulnerable, and funny. She's brave enough to take risks in spite of experiencing such fear that her eyes well with tears. Rational, observant, and analytical, she's also perfectly willing to admit that she has emotions and hunches. More than anything else, she wants self-control and autonomy, yet she sometimes loses control. A loner who likes a few people intensely and a noncook who eats an enormous variety of foods, Kinsey is a bundle of contradictions. She drinks her coffee black, remember? Except when she uses cream, that is, or milk. And sugar, or Equal.

In sum, while Kinsey may be larger than life in her ability to defeat the bad guys and dodge disaster again and again, she still seems a real person to her readers precisely because she is so much like the flesh-and-blood human beings we all live and work with—complex, inconsistent, and endlessly interesting.

Independence

From what we know about her life after her parents' deaths, we are not surprised to find Kinsey in the opening scene happily driving *home*, driving *alone,* and driving in a *small* car. Typically, she is interested in the other people on the road and what they are doing. She sees herself as part of the humanity "pouring north to work" (*H* 2), but she observes and speculates about individuals from a safe distance inside her own car. Throughout the novels she tells us about her "exaggerated desire for independence" (*D* 1, *A* 188 and 222–26, *B* 64, *G* 58, *G* 150, *I* 222, *J* 142 and 84) and her "layers of caution" in dealing with other people (*E* 125 and *M* 87). "I'm an expert," she says, "at using words to keep other people at bay" (*M* 49).

That caution is understandable, in light of both her biography and her current job as a private investigator. "Since my principle means of employment involved exposure to the underside of human nature, I tended . . . to keep other people at a distance" (*K* 21). In several novels, she says something along the lines of "most homicide victims are killed by close relatives, friends, or acquaintances. Reason enough to keep your distance, if you're asking me" (*K* 1). She once goes so far as to call herself a "misanthrope" (*K* 20), but this characterization does not seem borne out by her friendships with Henry or Rosie, or, to a lesser extent, Vera, and by her fondness for a number of people she meets during her investigations. She does not dislike people. She simply does not want them too close, and, above all, she does not want them telling her what to do.

Henry Pitts, Kinsey's landlord and closest friend, is the person throughout the series with whom Kinsey is most open about her feelings. But even this relationship is fragile and takes a long time to become secure. Her relationship with him in *'F' Is for Fugitive* is a good illustration of the cautionary approach Kinsey takes to people in general. Because her garage apartment was destroyed by a bomb at the end of *Evidence,* she is living in Henry's spare room while her apartment is being rebuilt. Kinsey is grateful, but uncomfortable.

She says, "I had my own key to the house and I came and went as I pleased, but there were times when the emotional claustrophobia got to me. I like Henry. A lot. There couldn't be anyone better-natured than he, but I've been on my own for eight years plus, and I'm not used to having anyone at such close range. It was making me edgy, as if he might have some expectation of me that I could never meet" (11).

The situation also worries Kinsey because she suspects she may be becoming *too* fond of Henry. "This man was eighty-two. Who knew how long he'd live? Just about the time I let myself get attached to him, he'd drop dead. Ha, ha, the joke's on you, again" (14). As Kinsey knows only too well, people close to us can die without warning. To avoid the pain accompanying that loss, Kinsey tries—not always successfully—to avoid emotional attachments and dependence on other people.

Clearly, Kinsey was not successful in keeping her second husband, Daniel Wade, outside her emotional fortress. The pain and anger she still feels about his leaving her only intensified her natural caution about attachments. Adding her personal experience to what she sees of marriage in her investigations, Kinsey has come to think of marriage as the most intense form of "emotional claustrophobia." She agrees completely with Charlie Scorsoni's distaste for the confinements of marriage: "I don't like the idea of giving someone else the right to make demands. In exchange for what?" (*A* 188). When she interviews the Snyders, she is appalled by Mr. Snyder's "minor tyrannies" of his wife, shuffling endlessly along on her walker. She thinks, "maybe it is all the same clash of wills behind closed doors. . . . Personally, I'd rather grow old alone than in the company of anyone I've met so far. I don't experience myself as lonely, incomplete, or unfulfilled, but I don't talk about that much. It seems to piss people off—especially men" (*B* 64).

Despite her disclaimer, Kinsey *does* often talk—at least to us readers—about how much she likes living and working alone. "I needed . . . space between me and the world" (*A* 233). "I like being alone" (*C* 1). "Anyone who knows me will tell you that I cherish my unmarried state" (*E* 3–4). "The virtue of being single is you get to make up all the rules" (*G* 29). "I love being single. It's almost like being rich" (*D* 20).

It's interesting that Kinsey connects being single with being rich, because, as Aunt Virginia kept drumming into her head, the person who chooses to be her own boss, personally and at work, had better know how to make and manage money. In the earlier description of Kinsey driving home in the opening of *Homicide,* it's worth noting that she is delighted to have "money in [her] pocket and enough gas to get home." Kinsey is proud of her financial autonomy as a freelance private investigator and she frequently comments on the rates she charges, the bills she collects, and the taxes she pays. Charging from $30 to $55 an hour, Kinsey never makes big bucks, but by careful management of her expenses she gets by, and her small savings in CDs, plus the reward money earned in *"I" Is for Innocent,* have even given her a cushion of $25,000 by the time of *"M" Is for Malice,* so she can afford to be a little more choosy about her cases and clients (*M* 2). She thus firmly maintains control of her financial and professional life. This is a source of great satisfaction to Kinsey.

Sense of Humor

Kinsey's joke in the opening of *Homicide* about the radio evangelist is typical of her sense of humor. She has a fine appreciation for the absurdities of life. Incongruity, pomposity, and exaggeration all receive verbal jabs from Kinsey, who likes to face life in its harshness without falling prey to sentimentality or other false protections for the ego. Humor becomes one of her primary weapons in her fight for self-control, her fight against the bad guys, and her acceptance of life's realities.

Thus, she jokes about organized religion, which she sees as one of those systems offering too easy comfort. It may look good, but she is highly suspicious of its validity, especially for herself. In fact, she is downright snide about organized religions until she meets Guy Malek and the Antles in *"M" Is for Malice.*

The balloon of religious pomposity is especially full of hot air when the church service is a funeral for someone virtually everyone hated. The hypocrisy of ritualized mourning for a jerk brings out Kinsey's humor at its best and most stinging. In *"D" Is for Deadbeat,* she goes to the funeral of John Daggett, a bigamist, wife-beater, and alcoholic who killed five people in a hit-and-run accident.* The funeral takes place at "some obscure outpost of the Christian church" (139). From the pained expression of the funeral home director ("His manner suggested that the services were spiritually second-rate, this being the K Mart of churches"), Kinsey expects the worst. And she is delightedly correct. The interminable hymns make her apprehensive that she will be publicly denounced for bad singing as well as bad faith. Pastor Bowen, "who looked like he would suffer from denture breath," begins a sermon that is fortunately completely unrelated to the character of the deceased (140). The congregation settles in, Kinsey says, for "an energetic discourse on the temptations of the flesh, which put me in mind of the numerous and varied occasions on which I'd succumbed. That was entertaining" (140). After the sermon, everyone gets caught up in swaying to the music of the final hymn and calling out hosannas and amens. Kinsey thinks, "This was beginning to feel like soul-aerobics" (141). The emotional shouters include the widow, Essie, wearing a broad black straw hat with veil that reminds Kinsey of a beekeeper. "Stung by the Holy Spirit, I thought" (142).

---

* We are indebted to Rachel Shaffer for calling our attention to the richness of this particular scene. Her paper at the Popular Culture Association in 1996, "Grafton's Black Humor," is forthcoming in *The Armchair Detective.*

Kinsey's jokes continue as the recessional moves out into the churchyard and goes to the cemetery. But the impetus behind the humor shifts somewhat. Inside the church Kinsey was laughing at the hypocrisy of all the exaggerated mourning for a man everyone disliked. At the cemetery she seems to use humor as a way to distance herself from *real* grief as the headstones remind her of death in general, not just Daggett's death.

Keeping the pain of her own encounters with death and loss at bay, Kinsey quips that the new cemetery is "a wide flat field planted to an odd crop." Then she tries another way of looking at it. Noticing all the winding roads, she wonders "if cemeteries, like golf courses, had to be designed by experts for maximum aesthetic effect. This one felt like a cut-rate country club, low membership fees for the upstart dead" (142).

Kinsey's effort to see the cemetery as a planted field or a golf course is a distancing device. "Why is it that grief always seems edged with absurdity?" Kinsey asks (143). She herself has shown us the answer, because if she can make herself and us see the pain-laden cemetery as a line of newly planted corn or beans, then none of us is likely to be moved to tears by the sight.

Emotional control is frequently the goal when Kinsey cracks a joke. The horror of a murder scene, or the fright brought on by a killer in pursuit of her, will not dominate her emotions (and keep her from acting) if she can prevent it. And, like so many whose professions mean they must face blood on a daily basis, she stops it with a put-down, a joke, a verbal lunge that keeps revulsion, or fear, in its place. We see this in *"E" Is for Evidence*, when Terry Kohler breaks into her apartment. Kinsey is stunned to see him emerge from her bathroom and circle the couch, a gun in one hand "pointed right at my gut" (217). She stalls for time and bright ideas. "There was nothing in his manner to indicate how nuts he was. How nuts is he? I thought. How far gone? How amenable to reason? Would I trade my life for bizarre sexual favors if he asked? Oh sure, why not?" (218).

Kinsey also uses dismissive laughter when she is awakened in the middle of the night by a threatening phone call. She gets out her .32 but insists, "I didn't take the death-and-dismemberment talk very seriously. Where could you rent a chain saw at this time of night?" (*F* 193). Nervous laughter likewise helps her handle the unpleasant experience of moving a corpse in a morgue. She makes the experience bearable by talking to the body as if he were still alive. "Sorry to disturb you, Frank . . . but you have to go next door for some tests. You're not looking so good" (*C* 232).

All the novels, except *"M" Is for Malice,* conclude with Kinsey facing some kind of personal physical threat, either from the killer or from the situation into which the killer has placed her. In some terrifying final scenes, killers confront her on a darkened beach, in a water treatment tunnel, in a dark, bug-infested basement, in a morgue, across an airport tarmac, in a client's bedroom, in a cemetery, or even in her own living room or office. They are ready to kill her with guns, axe handles, tasers, butcher knives, or their fists. Kinsey doesn't pretend she's unafraid. She may be clammy with fear, but that does not keep her from using her resources—humor, anger, analysis, action, and, on occasion, luck—to save herself and subdue the killer. In other, perhaps equally terrifying, confrontation scenes, it is Kinsey who does the pursuing. She chases killers by swimming dangerously far into the ocean, or by hanging onto the parapet of an eight-story building. Importantly, in every confrontation scene, even the ones in which she is trying to prevent the murderer from committing suicide, humor is a primary tool for Kinsey to maintain control of herself and the situation.

Typical is the confrontation scene in *"F" Is for Fugitive.* Facing Ann Fowler, a psychotic killer armed with a shotgun aimed at her chest, Kinsey thinks, "Why you have chats with killers in circumstances like these is because you hope against hope you can (1) talk them out of it, (2) stall until help arrives, or (3) enjoy a few more moments of this precious commodity we call life, which consists (in large part) of breathing in and out. Hard to do with your lungs blown out your back" (254).

The commentary is vintage Kinsey. She can see the duality of things (life is precious, but it consists primarily of breathing in and out), she can analyze and itemize even in a crisis, and she can keep fear at a manageable distance by laughing at it, in this instance through laconic understatement.

In her passion for independence, Kinsey also uses humor to keep other people at a distance. A joke is her protection against letting anyone get too close or become too real. She is attracted to Charlie, who, in his beige shirt and dark vest, "reminded me of a Reese's Peanut Butter Cup with a bite taken out and I wanted the rest" (*A* 208). She finds Kitty Wenner's anorexia and obvious drug addiction frightening, and she keeps an emotional distance by thinking, "It reminded me of Hansel and Gretel. Maybe Kitty was worried that if she got fat, they'd put her in the cooking pot" (*C* 28).

She also uses humor to keep from taking herself too seriously. Although she takes her work as a private eye very seriously, she does not let her own ego become too precious. Kinsey is engagingly self-deprecating throughout the series. Because she is anxious about a case, she drinks too much one night. "I'd be sick in the morning, but I didn't care at this point. Maybe I could carve out a quiet life for myself on the bathroom floor, head hanging over the toilet bowl" (*H* 180–81). Upon meeting a woman who is trim, delicate, and gorgeous, she says, "In her presence, I felt as dainty and feminine as a side of beef. When I opened my mouth, I was worried I would moo" (*G* 230). Noticing that she needs to shave her legs, she remarks, "It looked as if I had taken to wearing angora knee socks" (*J* 166).

Kinsey not only doesn't take herself too seriously—she doesn't take life too seriously. She sees a basic absurdity in the human condition and is quick to make fun of the illogical or silly. When Tillie Ahlberg doesn't want Kinsey to search her vandalized condo carrying a gun because guns are dangerous, Kinsey snaps, "Of course, they're dangerous! That's the point. What do you want me to do? Go in there with a hunk of rolled-up newspaper?" (*B* 43).

At the more abstract end of the absurdity scale, Kinsey recognizes a basic incongruity in the way in which somber and silly intertwine and interact through life. She is keenly attuned to this slight tilt to the universe. In the Rio Vista Convalescent Home, she talks with Agnes Grey, trying to decide how lucid the elderly woman really is. Agnes seems periodically disoriented and disconnected from what her visitor wants to discuss. Finally, when Agnes is quiet, Kinsey asks, "Uh, Agnes? Do you have any idea where you are?" Agnes shoots back, "No. Do you?" "I laughed," Kinsey says. "I couldn't help myself" (*G* 66). "Life itself is a peculiar outing," Kinsey concludes. "Sometimes I still feel like I need a note from my mother" (*E* 167).

Anger

Her usual defense against being overwhelmed by the deaths she encounters in her work, Kinsey says, are "action, anger, and a tendency to gallows humor" (*H* 8). Kinsey uses both action and anger in the same way she uses humor: they are weapons in her determined struggle to be autonomous and self-sufficient and to keep the bad guys at bay.

Kinsey has a healthy acceptance of anger as a part of her emotional repertoire. The social conditioning of women to deny their anger and appease the anger of others appears not to constrain her and she doesn't hide behind cute euphemisms. She just flat out says, "I was getting in touch with some anger" (*C* 133), "I could feel my temper snapping" (*D* 226), or "I was feeling a deadly rage" (*F* 127).

Kinsey's willingness to announce her anger does not mean that she is an angry person. Her anger is always triggered by specific events.

What elicits her anger? People who frustrate her need for information trigger a low level of anger, which manifests itself in some small gesture of annoyance. For example, when Bibianna Diaz's employer refuses to answer Kinsey's questions and hangs up the phone, Kinsey responds by making faces at the phone in her hand. She becomes more frustrated by a clerk in the sheriff's department who has made nonresponsiveness into an art form. "Situations like this bring up an ancient and fundamental desire to bite. I could envision a half-moon of my teeth marks on the flesh on her forearm, which would swell and turn all colors of the rainbow. She'd have to have tetanus and rabies shots. Maybe her owner would elect to put her to sleep" (*H* 31). Highly satisfied by her imaginary biting of the obstreperous clerk, Kinsey takes no further action against her.

At the next level of anger, Kinsey may take verbal or physical action against someone who is offensive. The triggering offense could be anything from rudeness to criminal activity. In *"A" Is for Alibi*, Kinsey gets angry at Andy Motycka because he won't fight Marcia Threadgill's fraudulent insurance claim. In response to Andy's request to see the incriminating photos anyway because Marcia's "tits are huge," Kinsey says, "Screw you," and walks out of the office

(200). Investigating the death of Lorna Kepler, Kinsey questions the sister, Berlyn. To Kinsey's shock, Berlyn reveals that she had discovered her sister's body, but instead of reporting it to anyone, she had just walked away, taking Lorna's bank statements and jewelry with her. Kinsey is furious over this unfilial and illegal behavior. "What kind of fuckin' twit are you?" she shouts at Berlyn and throws her out of the car. "I started the car and backed out, so mad I nearly ran her down in the process" (*K* 258).

Kinsey becomes increasingly angry with Nola Fraker for her continued refusal to admit she was having an affair with Bobby Callahan, the young son of one of her friends. "She was pissing me off" (*C* 193). The confrontation escalates verbally to the point that Kinsey grabs Nola by the wrist "so fast she gasped. She gave a little jerk and I released her, but I could feel myself expand with anger like a hot-air balloon" (194). As if the anger has cleared her head, Kinsey suddenly realizes the identity of Nola's first husband, a key to solving the entire case, and the scene concludes without violence.

Kinsey, in fact, seldom *initiates* violent action. In her gutsy approach to a case, she often asks questions that she knows will anger the person she's interrogating, but she does not take physical action against a suspect or witness. On the other hand, if she or anyone with her is under physical attack, Kinsey is quick to defend herself with whatever level of violence is needed. She typically responds in kind. Lila Sams, Henry's manipulative lady friend, gives Kinsey a ring-crushing handshake, for which Kinsey retaliates by crunching Lila's foot with her shoe, all cleverly done with a smile in full view of unsuspecting Henry. Likewise, when Gordon Titus, the new CF efficiency expert, presses all of Kinsey's antibureaucracy buttons and raises his voice to her, Kinsey shouts back, "I don't see why I have to put up with this bureaucratic bullshit. I don't work for you" (*H* 25–26). She continues to face him down, glare for glare, knowing full well she might be fired, but refusing to "take any guff" (27). She will not allow herself to be under someone else's control. "I hate to be bullied" (110).

Instinctive responses against being bullied occasionally get Kinsey into more than a verbal fight. When Elva Dunne suddenly uses her tennis racket like a samurai sword against Kinsey, she tries in vain to dodge the blows. The racket hits Kinsey on the arm. She responds immediately and enthusiastically: "I can't say I felt pain. It was more like a jolt to my psyche, unleashing aggression" (F 166). Kinsey promptly punches her out and relishes a feeling of victory.

Only rarely does Kinsey lose control of her anger. Most of the time, she keeps it in check in order to get her work done. A good judge of people, she recognizes young Brian Jaffe as someone who would "strike out if he were pressed." She has found him hiding in his motel room and he is "nearly cross-eyed with rage" at her. Rather than respond in kind, she deliberately calms herself, slows her breathing, holds absolutely still, and even becomes obsequious, saying, "Don't hit me. Don't hit" (J 240). The technique works. Jaffe's anger subsides, and he is arrested without anyone getting hurt.

Kinsey can also redirect her anger from violence into other activities, such as eating a meal of comfort foods or engaging in some physical activity. Cleaning her apartment and jogging are routine ways she works up a sweat while avoiding punching out someone. Other, less frequent, opportunities to let off steam also come along. Kinsey finds it satisfying, for instance, to do all the drilling and hammering required to install locks on Agnes Grey's abandoned trailer. She's been angry about a number of aspects of the case, including her client's insistence on installing locks on an already vandalized trailer, but "the physical labor improved my mood. It felt good to smash things. It felt good to sweat. It felt good to be in control of one small corner of the universe" (G 55).

The most threatening situations, the ones generating the highest level of anger and retaliation from Kinsey, are, of course, those in which a killer is prepared to add Kinsey to the list of his or her victims. She responds to lethal weapons pointed at her with a healthy mix of fear, anger, and action. At the end of "I" Is for Innocent, David Barney traps her in Kingman and Ives' darkened law offices, alone, at night, and shoots her in the hip. As she hides from him, trying to keep her breathing, her wits, and her anger under control, he toys with her, treating the situation as a game in which he has the best pieces and the strategic advantage. Confident that she doesn't have another shot, he comes into the copy room, where she is crouched beside the Xerox machine. She shoots Barney, wounding him, but not seriously. He's pleased that she has *certainly* used her last bullet by now. He asks, "Are you prepared to die?" (282).

Kinsey replies, "I wouldn't say prepared exactly, but I wouldn't be surprised." She spotlights Barney with her small flashlight. "How about you? . . . Surprised?" she asks as she fires point-blank at him (282). She studies him as he slides down the wall, a wet red stain forming on his shirt and his expression shifting from "smug superiority to consternation." She says, "I told you I had a ten-shot" (283). Kinsey has won. And she's won by playing Barney's own game of bluff better than he.

Anyone—even her good friend Henry and certainly an unfaithful ex-husband—can be the recipient of anger from Kinsey if she thinks she is being manipulated. Once, Kinsey even punches a cop in the face. But, as might be expected in detective fiction, the people who receive the most intense anger and the most physical response are those who violate legal and moral codes by committing murder. In the big confrontation scenes concluding the novels, Kinsey typically subdues the killer.

One novel, however, is very different from this format.

At the conclusion of *"K" Is for Killer*, Kinsey is convinced that Roger Bonney is the killer of Lorna Kepler and the assailant of Danielle Rivers, but Lt. Phillips says there is not enough legal evidence for him to arrest Roger. Everyone assumes Danielle will recover from her beating. When Kinsey learns that the girl has died instead and the police still will do nothing, she loses all control. She says, "What I experienced wasn't grief, but a mounting fury. Like some ancient creature hurtling up from the deep, my rage broke the surface and I struck" (278).

The strike is a phone call to some Mafia men working for Lorna's fiancé. Kinsey names Roger Bonney as Lorna Kepler's murderer, knowing full well that they will kill Bonney. Throughout the series, Kinsey has bent the rules a bit. She's proud of her lying skills, she relishes the fun of a little breaking-and-entering—she is very fond of her set of lock-picks for just such occasions—and she's been known to steal people's mail. She's even killed people. But those killings were always done in self-defense. But *"K" Is for Killer* takes her a giant step beyond as Kinsey tries to get justice by arranging a hit on a murderer.

Within two minutes of the call, she realizes the enormity of what she has done, and she immediately tries to undo her action, but it is too late to stop what she has set in motion. She goes to warn Roger and almost gets herself killed in the process. The hitmen arrive and take Roger away. His body is never found. Kinsey accepts her responsibility for the deliberate and cold-blooded killing of another person. In a way, justice was served: Roger was a murderer whom the legal system could not punish. But Kinsey worries about her own morality. "Having strayed into the shadows, can I find my way back?" (285).

Kinsey is concerned that she may now be a different person because of that act. In her defense, we note that Kinsey only loses control of her anger when someone close to her has been abused, not when she herself is threatened. Anger was not an issue when she killed Charlie at the end of *"A" Is for Alibi*. Kinsey fired her gun only in self-defense, not as a result of losing control of her anger. Similarly, she was able to kill David Barney at the conclusion of *"I" Is for Innocent* only because she maintained her wits. In contrast, at the conclusion of *"H" Is for Homicide*, Kinsey is out of control. She is so furious she is ready to shoot Raymond between the eyes because he has tried to kill both Bibianna and Jimmy Tate. In the same way, she orders a hit on Bonney at the conclusion of *"K" Is for Killer* because he is about to get away with killing Lorna and Danielle, to whom she's become close in the course of the investigation. The fact that Kinsey loses control of her anger on behalf of a friend, rather than on her own behalf, makes her vigilante action a bit more palatable to most readers.

Compassion

Kinsey may be a "kick-ass private eye" (*H* 55), but she has a rich capacity for compassion, even tenderness. Her compassion is not an automatic response to people or situations that might popularly appear to call for it. Just because Ori Fowler is ill, Kinsey does not jump to sympathize with her—the woman is also domineering, egocentric, and manipulative. Being ill does not give her a license to be rude (*Fugitive*). Raymond Maldonado has Tourette Syndrome, but this does not excuse his immoral and illegal behavior (*Homicide*). Automatic sympathy is not part of Kinsey's personality.

Knee-jerk gestures of sympathy can be meaningless. Kinsey's sympathy is selective and genuine. Her reaction to meeting Bobby Callahan, nearly killed during a car crash several months earlier, reveals her response to the pain of others. She sees his scars, wonders what caused them, admires his tenacity and the effort he must put into every activity. During the morning in which he hires her, she does not patronize him or offer platitudes. She listens seriously to his fears and she looks him directly in the eye as they talk, actions he greatly appreciates because he is so often ignored by other people now. She talks matter-of-factly about his injuries and what he wants her to investigate. Afterward, Kinsey says, "We walked back to my car slowly and I was conscious of the stares of the curious, faces averted with pity and uneasiness. It made me want to punch somebody out" (*C* 10).

While we may smile at the Kinseyesque reaction (punching someone out), we can still see that it is prompted by a real sensitivity to how Bobby must feel as the object of an automatic pity from strangers for whom he is only a collection of scars and not a person. She shows the same kind of sensitivity dealing with elderly, frail Royce Fowler, dying of pancreatic cancer, in *'F" Is for Fugitive*. As they enter the courtroom for his son's arraignment, Kinsey thinks, "I controlled an urge to give him physical support, sensing that he might take offense" (75). Throughout the series, she often comments on how a situation must feel to the other person and she is fully capable of being moved to tears by another's pain or grief or powerful emotion. And her own grief can be overwhelming, for example, when Bobby is killed. There, although she tries to maintain control in order to help his mother, Glen, survive the crisis, she says, "Something in her face spilled over me like light through a swinging door. Sorrow shot through the gap, catching me off-guard, and I burst into tears" (*C* 101).

Organization

Part of Kinsey's success as a private eye is due to her sense of organization. She wants everything in its place. The approach is obvious in her organized handling of investigative work and in keeping her apartment clean and tidy.

Perhaps less obvious is the same approach to her personal life: she even tries to organize her own emotions. She neatly compartmentalizes them in order to get on with her job and her life. For example, Kinsey talks very openly with Henry about her feelings about killing Charlie Scorsoni and then she goes for a jog. She says, "Once outside, I had to put it out of my mind again. Back the subject went, into its own little box" (*B* 84). The topic of "Killing, responsibility for" is not being erased or ignored by Kinsey. She's merely putting it away, where she knows she can look at it again whenever she's ready to do so. Meanwhile, she turns to physical action—jogging—and the current case. In a similar fashion, she organizes her response to the heated confrontation with Gordon Titus at CF. Stomping away from his office, she says, "I put the entire exchange in a mental box and filed it away" (*H* 26). When she momentarily breaks down in grief for Guy at the police station, she painfully regains control and puts her "emotions back in the box again" in order to continue with the interview (*M* 199).

Control, control, control.

Phobias

Kinsey considers herself an optimist and pretty easygoing. At the same time she admits she's stubborn, sometimes downright bitchy and cranky. And, goodness knows, we hear a *long* list of things Kinsey doesn't like, especially getting shots ("I'm a bad-ass private eye who swoons in the same room with a needle," *F* 203) and having dental work ("My semiannual visit to the dentist is as masochistic as I care to get," *H* 129). Other things such as garlic salt, instant coffee, cake mixes, heights, and spelunking come in for at least one denunciation each in the series.

Topping the list of "Things Kinsey Dislikes" are dogs. "Dogs and I do not get along" (36), she says in the first novel, and her basic opinion that they are surly, rude, and clumsy creatures does not change throughout the series, although she occasionally meets a dog that elicits a minimal flicker of tolerance. The reason for Kinsey's distaste is simple. "I'm hardly ever smitten with a beast that looks like it's prepared to rip out my carotid artery" (*H* 136). This prompts Kinsey to view a disc jockey's pet, Beauty, with considerable apprehension. Beauty is "a big reddish yellow dog with a thick head, heavy

chest, and powerful shoulders" (K38). Unmoved by Beauty's interest
in her shoe (she knows a puppy peed on it last week), Kinsey speculates, "She probably had a tendency to sulk when she wasn't allowed
to feast on human flesh" (39–40). As Kinsey and the disc jockey talk,
she anxiously observes that Beauty "kept her eyes straight ahead,
gazing intently at the flesh on my hip, possibly with an eye toward a
late evening snack" (44). On her way out, Kinsey says, "Next time I'll
bring her a bone," and mutters to herself, "Preferably not mine"
(44).

Grafton proves she has a wicked sense of humor, then, by placing
a pit bull named Perro inside the Maldonado apartment, where Kinsey is kept for days in *"H" Is for Homicide*. Kinsey's basic fear of all dogs
is fed by one of the guys telling her not to make sudden moves
around this brindled dog with a spiked collar and bat ears, and, above
all, not to touch his head, or "He'll tear your arm off" (136). The
dog lunges toward Kinsey as far as his chain will let him reach, bark-
ing ferociously, and, in general, confirming her fears that he's capable of swallowing her up in three easy gulps. So, it is with
considerable amusement—at Kinsey's expense—that we watch as she
is suddenly awakened by a strange noise in her room one night. She's
nice and calm when she thinks it's one of the guys. That she can
handle. But when she hears "the sound of metal being trailed across
the floor," she almost loses it. She knows *the dog* is there and she is
frozen in terror. For over a page Kinsey waits in the dark to be de-
voured by this ravening, slobbering monster. Finally, Perro props
himself on the couch and pushes his head under Kinsey's hand. She
tries to withdraw her hand, but the dog growls her into immobility.
He whines a bit and then climbs into bed with her! Having little
choice, Kinsey begins to pet his head, very tentatively. The dog responds, not by tearing her arm off, but by licking the palm of her
hand.

"I didn't dare complain, even though he did exude a rich cloud
of doggie B.O. It was the first time I'd ever had a bed partner who
smelled like hot pork" (154). We're glad Kinsey can finally laugh,
because we have been doing it for the last two pages.

Dogs are not the only part of the natural world that Kinsey does
not like. "I don't look to Nature for comfort or serenity" (D131).
She hates bugs, worms, and all crawly things. She doesn't care much

for horses or birds. Being attacked by guard geese makes her add geese to her list. She doesn't like swimming in the ocean or wading in tidal pools because of all the potentially lethal creatures in the water. In fact, when you get down to it, there's not much about nature that Kinsey does like. Not even house plants. She cannot believe that some people, like Ida Ruth, a secretary at her second office, actually choose to go hiking into the local mountains. Camp at the age of eight only convinced Kinsey that nature is "straight uphill, dusty and hot and itchy" (*H* 213). "The outdoors, as far as I can see, is made up almost entirely of copulating creatures who eat one another afterward" (*M* 151). There is no doubt that Kinsey is utterly and completely an urban creature.

She's also utterly and completely intriguing to her readers. Most of us would be happy to share a peanut-butter-and-pickle sandwich, as yucky as that sounds, if it meant we could just have a nice, long conversation with this blunt, funny, capable, tough, quirky private eye.

KINSEY LAUGHS AT:

Dogs: "People always love it when you say their dogs are nice. Just shows you how out of touch they are." (*C* 189)

Fear: "I wanted to be on my feet, in motion, taking action instead of crouching down with my hands held over my face hoping God had rendered me transparent." (*C* 239)

Herself: "It was hard for me to mind my own business when I had someone else's business within range of me." (*I* 36)

"I'm not that fast at subtraction so it's probably fortunate that I don't lie about how old I am." (*C* 193)

"I could tell I was ruining her day, which improved my appetite." (*E* 51)

Life: "As long as you have sufficient toilet paper, how far wrong can life go?" (*M* 114)

Kinsey's Daily Life

"In my own skin again": *Kinsey's Appearance*

Everything about the way Kinsey looks and lives reflects her concern for function before appearance. Her work is the most important part of her life, and whatever she does in her personal life, from the places she chooses to live to the way she wears her hair, supports the primacy of her job.

Early in every book Kinsey gives us a few facts that help us *see* her. Typically these basic details sound more like the description a witness to a crime might give to the cop on the beat than a friend describing a proposed blind date. There's no salesmanship going on here. Kinsey is 5' 6" and weighs 118 pounds; she has dark hair and hazel eyes. As the novels unfold, we gradually fill in some blanks as we learn a little more about the shape of the hair or the condition of the body. She usually wears no makeup, but she sometimes uses cologne. Her hair is thick and unruly, usually worn short. Her teeth are "very white and square" (*J* 169). But we never have Kinsey's face or body given descriptive adjectives, such as "pretty" or "ugly" or "bland." Function rather than looks.

Kinsey's trim body must be in good physical shape for her to do all the dangerous and difficult physical activities she engages in during her cases. She does a lot of running, she balances on the parapet of an eight-story building, she changes tires, she swims after a killer, and she engages in physical fights, punching and kicking to good effect. Her body shows the effects of her demanding life. Her nose has been broken twice, her left arm once. She grinds her teeth during her sleep. Tinnitus bothers her after she fires her gun from inside a garbage can in *Alibi*. She frequently has bruises and skinned knuckles from her work, and in *Evidence* she is burned on the hands and face by an explosion. Sunbathing in a bikini for surveillance work in *Judgment,* she says she is "boldly exposing a body riddled with old bullet holes and crisscrossed with pale scars from the assorted injuries that had been inflicted on me over the years" (15).

Kinsey doesn't *say* she is opposing stereotypical expectations that women focus on being attractive and sexy. She just *does* it. She counters the stereotype by accepting the physical scars that come with her job, instead of bemoaning them or hiding them. They're "no big deal" to Kinsey (*E* 149). When her left arm is shot and broken, she works hard to regain strength in the arm, because her job requires the use of a good arm, but she never refers to trying to make it look better. Her nose may have been broken twice, but it "blows real good" (*F* 12). She counters the stereotype by not wearing makeup on a daily basis, because "it's a waste of time" (*F* 12). (She'll make an exception if makeup is needed for a disguise for her job, or if a friend badgers her into makeup for a special event, or if she's nervous about meeting her cousin Tasha for lunch.) She counters the stereotype by accepting the smallness of her bust without lamentation or wholesale purchase of Wonderbras. She counters the stereotype by telling us nothing descriptive about her physical appearance. In fact, she is emphatic about this point. "If I were asked to rate my looks on a scale of one to ten, I wouldn't" (*G* 2). The one time we think she's about to give a description, she veers right back into function over form: "We could not call mine a beautiful puss, but it does the job well enough, distinguishing the front of my head from the back" (*F* 12).

Perhaps our first clue that appearance is not a top priority is the understated information that she cuts her dark, thick, unruly hair herself, every six weeks, with nail scissors. In a comment that in no way explains the method of the cut, she simply tells us, "I keep my hair short because I don't like to fool with it" (*B* 31). She also explains that she's "too cheap to pay twenty-eight bucks in a beauty salon" (*G* 2). The difference between not having to fool with it and a constant bad hair day is not apparent until we hear from someone else about how dismally Kinsey wields those nail scissors. One of her interviewees, Lyda Case, repairs her own makeup and then studies Kinsey. "I could make you over in a minute. You ought to do a little more with yourself. That hair of yours looks like a dog's back end" (*E* 96).

In *"G" Is for Gumshoe* Kinsey decides to let her hair grow out "just to see what it would look like"(1) and it reaches shoulder length, "just the teeniest bit uneven" (*H* 22). By the time of *"I" Is for Innocent,* Kinsey's hair looks so scraggly that, during an interview, a beautician mistakenly thinks Kinsey has come into her shop for an appointment. She jumps to look after Kinsey. "Boy oh boy. You sure do have a hair emergency. Take a seat." The beautician wonders if this is a new Los Angeles mod cut. She points out that kind of cut is "Asymmetrical. . . . Usually looks like it's been whacked off with a ceiling fan" (34). Kinsey glances in the mirror. "It did look kind of weird. I'd been growing my hair for several months now and it was definitely longer on one side than it was on the other. It also seemed to have a few ragged places and a stick-up part near the crown" (36). Kinsey asks the beautician if she thinks a cut is needed: "She hooted out a laugh. 'Well I should hope to shout. It looks like some lunatic hacked your hair off with a pair of nail clippers' " (36). The lunatic in question only fleetingly considers professional help.

During her investigation into Lorna Kepler's death, Kinsey meets Lorna's friend and fellow sex-worker, Danielle Rivers. They become friends. Danielle tries to break it gently to Kinsey, but she finally blurts out, "That haircut of yours is gross" (167). She talks Kinsey into letting her cut her hair. "Now don't get scared. I know it looks like a lot [being cut off], but it's just because the whole thing's uneven. You got great hair, nice and thick, with just the tiniest touch of curl. Well, I wouldn't call it curl so much as body, which is even better" (168).

Kinsey's satisfied response reveals how superior Danielle's skills are to Kinsey's. "The difference was remarkable. All the choppiness was gone. All the blunt stick-out parts that seemed to go every which way were now tamed and subdued. The hair feathered away from my face in perfect layers. It even fell into place again if I shook my head" (170).

The haircut sounds great. But even after Lyda's insult (which must have bothered Kinsey because she remembers it in several later novels), the beautician's amusement, and Danielle's good haircut, Kinsey continues to cut her own hair. It's quick and cheap, two qualities that are worth more to Kinsey than feathered hair falling in perfect layers away from her face. The only time she succumbs to a salon cut is in preparation for lunch with her cousin Tasha in "M" Is for Malice. She pays $35 for a cut and then tips the stylist $5, both astonishing acts from tightfisted Kinsey (15). The two gestures unmistakably declare the depth of Kinsey's nervousness about the impending luncheon.

Oh, yes, we almost forgot.

What do most of us do in order to picture Kinsey's facial features, since Kinsey consistently resists telling us? Turn the novel over and look at the photo of Sue Grafton on the back of the book, of course. Hmmmm. Can't tell about the hazel eyes, but the thick, dark, unruly hair and the square white teeth are right there. And in many she's wearing Kinsey's signature clothes of jeans and turtleneck. Better haircut, though.

Kinsey derives such pleasure from her comfortable daily attire that we wonder how she ever thought she could spend eight hours a day in a police uniform or business suit. She dons dress and pantyhose only with grumbles, growls, and whines. It isn't that she doesn't care about how she looks, but her first priority is comfort, the second, ease of movement. It's pretty hard to chase a killer up seven flights of stairs in high heels. Function over fashion could be a lifestyle rule for Kinsey.

Kinsey's standard garb is a uniform itself, but a totally comfortable, functional one: jeans, T-shirt, and tennis shoes, with slight adjustments to turtleneck and boots as the season demands. Even a professional interview doesn't lead Kinsey to dress up. Negative reactions to her clothes cause her to make no more changes than do remarks about her hair.

"He surveyed me for a moment, taking in the boots, the faded

jeans, the wool sweater beginning to pill at the elbows. I was determined not to let his disapproval get through to me, but it required an
effort on my part. I stared at him impassively and warded off his
withering assessment by picturing him on the toilet with his knickers
down around his ankles" (D 115).

And she interprets the disdainful look from a lawyer's secretary as
suggesting that she "probably looked like someone [her boss] might
represent on a charge of welfare fraud" (F 150). This look doesn't
send her back to rummage in her closet either.

Only with great reluctance does Kinsey respond to an occasional
call for less casual attire. At these times, out comes the little all-
purpose black dress, everywoman's dream dress. It fits, stays clean,
and never needs ironing, no matter what. It's often left in the back
seat of her car and resists destruction even when her car is totaled
and the dress lies in stagnant ditch water for hours. Kinsey describes
this impressive garment: "It can be squashed down to the size of a
rain hat and shoved in the bottom of my handbag without harm. It
can also be rinsed out in any bathroom sink and hung to dry overnight. It's black, lightweight, has long sleeves, zips up the back, and
should probably be 'accessorized,' a women's clothing concept I've
never understood" (D 88). By the time of Vera's wedding in "H" Is for
Homicide, she has had the dress for six years (13) and has no intention
of giving it up at anyone's urging.

On rare occasions Kinsey likes the way she feels when she dresses
up. The black silk jumpsuit with spaghetti straps borrowed from Vera
(Gumshoe) and the green evening dress from Olive Kohler (Evidence)
make Kinsey feel festive and attractive, like a grown-up, as she puts it.
But the feeling doesn't last, and she always looks forward to the lovely
moment after changing clothes. "Once in my jeans and turtleneck, I
felt like I was back in my own skin again" (K 140). "My whole body
[was] sighing with relief" (E 48). Or she may describe this feeling as
simply "Heaven" (I 236).

Her footwear preferences are distributed along a comfort continuum ranging from Nikes and Reeboks, to boots, sandals, and all the
way to fuzzy slippers. Heels of all sorts are off the scale, partly because
they're so uncomfortable and partly because they require panty hose,
which is always a downer. "Even with low-heeled pumps, my feet hurt
and my pantyhose made me feel like I was walking around with a hot,

moist hand in my crotch" (*D* 132). Kinsey sums up her feelings about high heels, fashion, comfort, and power when she observes: "I have friends who adore high heels, but I can't see the point. I figure if high heels were so wonderful, men would be wearing them" (*I* 216).

Other pieces of clothing appear as she needs them for weather, a minimum of wardrobe variety, or her health. She wears a windbreaker (preferably one she hasn't just used to wipe the windshield), rain slicker, denim vest, and, as a reward for successful completion of a case, she surprises us by buying herself a tweed blazer. In *"M" Is for Malice,* she also surprises us by wearing a short cotton skirt. Once.

After she loses almost everything in the explosion at her apartment, she enjoys fooling around with the clothing Vera gives her from her own wardrobe. The long skirts and scarves are not really her style, but she thinks they look rather dashing. She also admires the swashbuckling look of a hat she wears in *"B" Is for Burglar* and the "devil-may-care" look of a "long crocheted runner" her aunt had made for a dresser top that she loops around her neck à la Isadora Duncan (*J* 74).

Her underwear comes in for more attention than one might expect. Although she routinely sleeps naked, she keeps a "flannel nightie" and sweat socks to wear when she's sick (*J* 37). In keeping with her cleanliness and tidiness, Kinsey keeps clean underpants (no elegant terms like "lingerie" for Kinsey) in her oversized shoulder bag. Sometimes she keeps another clean pair in an overnight bag in the back seat of her car. In that way, she is always prepared to travel whenever a case requires it. She often tells us when she rinses out her underpants; she laments that her underwear drawer is uncharacteristically messy, and on her extensive journey in *"L" Is for Lawless,* she *really* wants a clean pair of underpants, so much so, in fact, that she considers stealing a pair. Only her toothbrush seems as important.

She can improvise in a hurry when she needs to, assembling bits and pieces in a manner reminiscent of a Sherlock Holmes disguise. In *"C" Is for Corpse,* she realizes that her pants and tunic are a bit casual for a party with her client's wealthy family. She trades the pants for panty hose from the back seat of her car (kept for use as an emergency filter), and, tossing her sandals aside, digs out black spike heels, bought so she could pass herself off as a hooker. For a final touch, she ties the tunic's belt around her neck in "an exotic knot," and she's ready for cocktails with the money crowd (19).

In addition to the "hooker heels," she keeps a variety of clothing to wear in connection with her job. Of real utility is the generic Southern California blue-gray shirt and pants, which she wears with the black shoes she kept from her time on traffic detail when she was a police officer. When she wears these together and carries a clipboard, she can impersonate any general service employee and be virtually invisible to neighbors and passersby.

Kinsey typically carries a leather or canvas shoulder bag large enough to hold her travel supplies, a gun and ammunition, driver's license, P.I. license, credit cards, birth control pills, a set of lock picks, Swiss Army knife, assorted rarely used makeup, notecards for her work observations, and, according to a single remark in *"F" Is for Fugitive,* even "a voice-activated tape recorder" (193). The bag is multipurpose, amazingly so: it even saved her from broken ribs by acting as an air bag when her car was run off the road (*G* 72). Understandably, she regrets having to leave it behind in a hotel fire in *"L" Is for Lawless:* "My handbag was a talisman, as comforting as a security blanket. Its bulk and heft were familiar, its contents assurance that certain totem items were always within reach. The bag had served as both pillow and weapon" (189).

"Pulling up the drawbridge":
Kinsey's Lifestyle

Apartments

Given Kinsey's childhood retreat to a cardboard box after her parents' deaths, there is little surprise in Kinsey's preference for "small, enclosed spaces" (*I* 48) and in her considering home an important refuge. Home for Kinsey is a 15′ × 15′ studio apartment she rents from Henry Pitts, initially for the low rate of $200 a month, later for a still reasonable $400, an increase insisted upon by Henry's accountant when local property taxes zoom up (*I* 2). She sighs with relief when she returns home, often speaking of the pleasure of "pulling up the drawbridge" (*D* 36), and she longs for home when she's on the road. "Of all the places I've lived in Santa Teresa, my current cubbyhole is the best" (*A* 17).

In 1980 Kinsey was living in a trailer in the Mountain View Mobile Home Estates in Colgate. When the trailer park was converted to "seniors, 55 and older only," she was served with eviction papers. Tired of waiting for all the lawsuits to be settled, she began to look for an apartment in her price range of "very cheap to extremely modest" (*K* 19). She admits she was also motivated by a desire to get away from the imposed closeness of neighbors in a trailer park (*M* 82). She was just about to give up in despair when she saw Henry Pitts' ad for a "bachelorette" posted at the laundromat. As she parked her car in front of Henry's house, she liked the look and smell of the flowering trees in the neighborhood after the rain. She liked the smells of "yeast, cinnamon, and simmering spaghetti" drifting out from his kitchen. One look at the compact space inside the converted garage "was all it took to know I was home" (*K* 20).

Kinsey's apartment is on Albanil, "a modest palm-lined street" (*C* 13) that parallels Cabana, the wide boulevard along the beach, with its bicycle path, where Kinsey takes her morning runs. The area is residential, most of its houses owned by retired persons, although Rosie's Tavern, a laundromat, and an appliance repair shop operate only half a block away (*B* 90). As the series develops, Kinsey increasingly finds herself growing closer to Henry and she develops a sense of being part of a neighborhood.

When Kinsey first rents the apartment, it is a small "cozy den" with a "completely nondescript" aluminum-siding exterior. The fifteen-foot-square interior is "outfitted as living room, bedroom, kitchen, bathroom, closet, and laundry facility" (*A* 17–18). A narrow extension on one side contains "the kitchenette, separated from the living area by a counter." Kinsey likes the cleverness with which so much is contained in so little. "Bookshelves, drawers and storage compartments [are] built into the wall. . . . My bathroom is one of those preformed fiberglass units with everything molded into it, including a towel bar, a soap holder, and a cutout for a window that looks out at the street" (*D* 20). Kinsey sometimes munches a sandwich while standing in the tub, looking out the window at the people and cars on Albanil. She apparently prefers watching her window to watching TV.

Kinsey never refers to the way the furniture *looks* in this first incarnation of her apartment. Instead, in typical Kinsey fashion, she is interested in how it *functions*. She likes things that are "multipurpose and petite." She has "a combination refrigerator, sink, and stovette, a doll-sized stacking washer/dryer unit, a sofa that becomes a bed (though I seldom bother to unfold it), and a desk that I sometimes use as a dining-room table" (*C* 12).

The multipurpose nature of so many fixtures and the tightly organized floor plan assist Kinsey in her passion for organization. She likes to keep her apartment extremely clean and orderly. She picks up after herself as she goes, explaining she finds it depressing to come home to a mess after work, as usual connecting her personal habits to the demands of her job (*B* 114). Plus, cleaning is a major form of recreation for Kinsey.

Her apartment faces the rear of Henry's fenced-in property, which gives her "a picturesque little bit of scenery. Henry has a patch of grass back there, a weeping willow, rosebushes, two dwarf citrus trees, and a small flagstone patio" (*C* 13). Her apartment, which used to be Henry's garage, is connected to her landlord's house by a glass-enclosed breezeway. During dry weather, Henry proofs his rising bread dough in the breezeway, sending delicious smells Kinsey's way and often drawing her into his kitchen for talk and food.

There are two threats in the series to Kinsey's well-being in her "tiny kingdom" (*E* 8). The first one is Lila Sams, a plastic-braceleted simperer who seduces Henry, much to Kinsey's surprise and dismay. The woman irritates Kinsey from the moment they meet on Henry's patio early in *"C" Is for Corpse,* but she really scares Kinsey when she accuses her of taking advantage of "an old softie like Henry" by paying too little rent (132). Kinsey is distressed that Henry might share that opinion. He says he doesn't, but by now Kinsey is seriously worried about this middle-aged Delilah. She gets busy pronto and finds the proof that Lila is a con artist. She recovers $20,000 that Henry had given to Lila for one of her real estate "investments," and Lila is arrested. Both Kinsey and Henry are now out of harm's way, although Kinsey continues to worry about the impact of all this on Henry.

The second threat comes at the end of *"E" Is for Evidence* when a bomb explodes in her apartment, reducing the building to a crater.

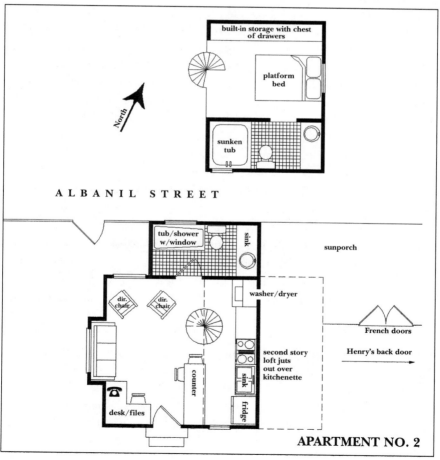

Henry, true to his nature, is more concerned about possible damage to Kinsey than about his insured garage apartment, and he promptly meets with an architect to begin drawing up plans for an apartment he thinks will fit Kinsey's specific needs and tastes. Henry refuses to let Kinsey see the plans. She worries that his good cheer about the project signals too much opulence or too large a space. She frets, "I don't want an apartment too fancy for my pocketbook" (*F* 9). This rebuilding continues throughout *"F" Is for Fugitive,* during which Kinsey works primarily in Floral Beach and lives in Henry's spare bedroom when she's in Santa Teresa.

"G" Is for Gumshoe begins on Kinsey's birthday, May 5. Henry's presents to her include the key to her new apartment. Her apprehensions disappear the minute Henry opens the front door, "with its porthole-shaped window," for a guided tour of her new home (4). The new apartment is "a perfect little hideaway" (*I* 53), so right for her that she is speechless. "The entire apartment had the feel of a ship's interior. The walls were highly polished teak and oak, with shelves and cubbyholes on every side" (*G* 4). Perhaps Henry remembered that Kinsey at five thought of her cardboard box as a sailing ship; perhaps the similarity is coincidental. In any case, the self-contained, highly organized, small nautical world is just what Kinsey likes.

The basic floor plan for the new apartment is much the same as the first one. The kitchenette is still located on the right, now galley-style, with a tiny stove and refrigerator, plus a microwave oven and a trash compactor. Beside the kitchen is a stacking washer/dryer and nearby is a tiny bathroom. The living area has a window bay with the sofa built in and a trundle bed underneath. Pleased with the *looks* of her new home, Kinsey even notes that "two royal blue canvas director's chairs" flank the sofa and there is blue carpeting. She was never prompted to tell us colors in the old apartment. Perhaps the most delicious part of the new apartment is the bedroom loft that has been added to what is essentially still a fifteen-foot-square box. A small spiral staircase leads to a sleeping loft, with a double platform bed, topped by a blue-and-white coverlet, and a cedar-lined wall forming a closet by clever placement of rods, pegs, and drawers. There is a skylight overhead and loft windows looking out to the beach and to the mountains. Just off the loft is a small bathroom featuring a sunken bathtub, with shower, and "a window right at tub level . . . [so] I could bathe among the treetops" (4–5). The color scheme continues in the bathroom. The towels and the cotton shag carpet are also royal blue.

"The apartment has the feel of an adult-size playhouse" (*J* 54). It sounds like a splendid combination of function and fun. She continues to enjoy this new sanctuary through the rest of the series, often telling us what she sees through the domed skylight or how comfortable the bed is. (She still likes to sleep naked, but she does sleep on the bed now, rather than wrapped in a quilt on the sofa, as she did in the first apartment.)

The only touch that doesn't seem perfect for Kinsey is the row of plants Henry has placed on the bathroom windowsill. Kinsey has said repeatedly she's no good with plants. Perhaps Henry thought his gift of an air fern (in *Evidence*), which requires no attention whatsoever, not even water, had generated at least a tolerance for house plants. It was, after all, one of the few things to survive the bomb blast at the earlier apartment. At any rate, Kinsey does not comment negatively about the row of plants. She seems utterly delighted with the apartment and so touched by Henry's caring that she can say nothing at the end of the tour. She is close to tears as she hugs him, and waits until she's recovered a bit to thank him. "I couldn't ask for a better friend" (*G* 5).

Considering the great care Henry has taken to create exactly the kind of home Kinsey likes and that he has not raised her rent in spite of what must have been considerable expense (*teak* walls and a *sunken* bathtub were probably not covered by the insurance money), we'd say Kinsey is absolutely right.

Car and Driver

Kinsey is proud of her small, cheap, but functional VW bug. It starts out as a battered beige, but by her fourth report we learn that the fourteen-year-old car (1968 model) has more rust than paint. Never sentimental, Kinsey nonetheless does have affection for the car, patting the dashboard when it starts up easily (*D* 107). She is also proud of the fact that the car is cheap to own and run. "The damn thing is paid for and only costs me ten bucks a week in gas" (*E* 47). She acknowledges that her bug is not ideal for a car chase, but P.I.s are more likely to do surveillance and process-serving than high speed chases anyway (D 6). Although she worries about being conspicuous on stakeouts in some of Santa Teresa's more elegant neighborhoods, her car usually blends right in for tailing or surveillance, and it's nice to have a car she's not afraid will be ripped off.

She confesses, "Every time I think about a new car, it makes my stomach do a flip-flop. I don't want to be saddled with car payments, a jump in insurance premiums, and hefty registration fees. My current registration costs me twenty-five dollars a year" (D 107). As careful and responsible with her car as with her business in general, she belongs to AAA for emergency road assistance (J 211).

Kinsey always gives precise directions about where she drives, whether in Santa Teresa or elsewhere, and when she enters unfamiliar territory, the first thing she does is buy a good map. And she keeps maps of Santa Teresa and California in her car, her office, and her apartment—she *likes* the efficiency of maps. As she drives, she names the street, says whether she turns right or left, or gives the compass point. We note with interest that she has never gotten lost in any of the novels. Since much of her work involves driving—for surveillance, to locate crime sites, to collect evidence, or to interview suspects and witnesses, or to time a certain drive integral to the crime—Kinsey is a careful and deliberate driver. Efficient driving is part of her job effectiveness. Even coming back on a deserted straight highway from Las Vegas early in the morning, Kinsey still drives a sedate 55 miles per hour (A 134).

Very rarely do we hear of a bad mood or a crisis pushing Kinsey to speed or recklessness. *"B" Is for Burglar* offers one of those atypical moments—and it's pretty mild stuff—when Kinsey is desperate to get to the Grices' burned-out house and remove the murder weapon before Marty and Leonard Grice can recover it and escape. She is delayed by taking the time to convince Leonard's sister to seek protection at a neighbor's house before she drives to the Grices' as fast as she can. "I got in my car and squealed out, burning rubber as I skidded around the corner two blocks down. I drove tensely, sliding around stop signs, bypassing traffic any way I could" (217). Even in this high-pressure moment, she doesn't actually run any stop signs or traffic lights. No wild and dangerous high-speed car chases in this detective series—from Kinsey, that is. As Raymond Maldonado speeds after Bibianna in *"H" Is for Homicide,* Kinsey, an unwilling passenger, is absolutely terrified by his manic driving (227). And Kinsey spends much of her time in *"G" Is for Gumshoe* jamming her foot almost through the floorboard in Dietz's car, trying to press imaginary brakes for him as he drives them around in his little red Porsche after her VW has been totaled. He is one of those aggressive drivers, "impatient every time he found himself behind another vehicle" (88). Going up the pass to the gun club, Dietz drives "like a man pursued." Kinsey says, "I was wishing I believed in an afterlife, as I was about to enjoy mine" (147).

Kinsey likes her car and she appears to enjoy driving, especially at night and in the very early morning hours (*A* 112 and *H* 2). She enjoys sitting in her car, "a favorite occupation of mine" (*A* 264), to make notes about her case or just to think. Given her fondness for personal autonomy, for blending into the landscape, exploration, and getting to destinations, we can understand her affection for her car.

When her car is totaled by a hit man in *"G" Is for Gumshoe,* Kinsey only reluctantly abandons it. "I felt like I was leaving a much-loved pet behind" (*G* 74). She unhesitatingly replaces it with another used beetle, a 1974 model, pale blue rather than beige, with only one small ding in the left rear fender (*H* 2). The only problems with this second car are the erratic nature of the radio (*J* 122) and the heater (*M* 107). In keeping with Kinsey's frugal nature, she pays cash for the car.

She cares no more about what others think of her car's looks than about her own looks. The car's function is what counts. Like so much in her life, it is multipurpose and petite. Her car is "a traveling office, a surveillance vehicle, the observation post for a nightlong stakeout, even a temporary motel if your travel funds run short" (*I* 179).

She keeps an entire workshop of useful junk in the back seat, including notecards and pen to keep track of her case observations, files, law books, a small suitcase with a change of clothes, a locked briefcase where she keeps her gun, motor oil, rubber gloves, all sorts of clothes for disguises, and an old cotton shirt for emergencies. She also has a 35-millimeter camera on hand in the glove compartment for her work. Unlike her apartment, the back seat of her car is a mess. Her euphemism is, "I like my cars cramped" (*A* 6), and she tells us frankly that "while I tend to maintain an admirable level of tidiness in the apartment, my organizational skills have never extended to my car" (*D* 123).

Food

The importance of food in women's lives has received much attention by social commentators. Although women in our culture are the primary preparers of food for themselves, their families, and their communities, they are also under strong cultural pressure to refrain from eating and enjoying food. The most obvious sign of this pressure is a preoccupation with dieting and weight. The cover of a typical checkout-line magazine for women highlights luscious high-calorie dessert recipes, side by side with articles on products and programs guaranteed to make readers as skinny as today's extremely thin high-fashion models. Some readers of female detective fiction have indicated that one of the reasons they enjoy these books is that the protagonists do many things the readers feel they cannot—and one of these secret and guilt-ridden pleasures is eating.

On these grounds alone, Kinsey was destined for popularity.

Kinsey does *a lot* of eating and drinking. She keeps a coffee pot going in her office and she typically has a glass of wine when she arrives home. Eating on the run, she'll choose Quarter Pounders, Egg McMuffins, and whatever the local dive offers—whether it's black bean soup, killer burritos, badly fried chicken, spareribs with sourdough bread, or Cajun popcorn. Wealthy clients serve her delicate meals of "Plump quartered chicken served cold with a mustard sauce, tiny flaky tarts filled with spinach and a smoky cheddar cheese, . . . [and] an icy tomato soup with fresh dill clipped across the surface and a little dollop of crème fraîche" (*C* 38). Lovers treat her to sensual meals of spicy hot chili verde topped with cilantro pesto, or "sand dabs sautéed in butter and served with succulent green grapes" (*A* 186). Rosie feeds her meal after meal of heavy Hungarian dishes whose names have "lots of accent marks and *z*'s and double dots, suggesting that the dishes would be fierce and emphatic" (*B* 90). And, then, there are Henry's delicious baked goodies—breads, cinnamon rolls, and brownies, plus plenty of lunches and dinners in his great-smelling kitchen.

Even the bad food sounds good. And the good food sounds "as close to heaven as a sinner could get without repenting first," to quote Kinsey herself (*G* 149).

When it comes to food, Kinsey is strictly a consumer. With very few exceptions, she is not interested in either buying or preparing food. She often finds the cupboard and refrigerator bare when she suddenly realizes that she is hungry. "All I have at the back of my kitchen cupboard is an old box of cornmeal with bugs" (*C* 14). Dietz is dismayed that he can never find any food in her apartment and he always has to go out and buy groceries for them. No wonder, since the only items we ever see her buy at a grocery store are milk, bread, and toilet paper (*C* 97 and *L* 29). Well, okay, she *once* expands this grocery list to include Diet Pepsi and eggs (*D* 36). Her firmly held belief is that "the only reason for cooking is to keep your hands busy while you think about something else" (*I* 191). Her aunt's refusal to teach her to cook—because it's boring and likely to make one fat—has clearly had an impact.

She seems to eat primarily to satisfy hunger, not because social custom dictates that it's time for lunch or dinner. She frequently forgets meal time entirely and continues hard at work until her stomach calls. We get used to her dawning awareness that "as nearly as I could remember, I hadn't eaten lunch" (*B* 72), or "Belatedly, I realized I'd never eaten lunch" (*F* 176). "Sometimes I get so wired that I forget to eat at all" (*A* 186).

As for most of us, eating can sometimes be an emotional experience for Kinsey. After spending a night in bed thinking she is getting sick, she awakens feeling wonderful. "I felt whole again. I ate a big breakfast in a little diner across the road from the motel, washing down bacon, scrambled eggs, and rye toast with fresh orange juice and three cups of coffee" (*A* 134). Quite simply, she feels good and wants to eat. Conversely, to counter a bad mood, she also eats. The morning after an argument with Henry, Kinsey eats her favorite breakfast out, explaining that she is "loading up on fats and carbohydrates, nature's anti-depressants" (*J* 166). She, like so many of us, can find eating a more appealing choice than being angry, or depressed, or nervous. Just before meeting Cousin Tasha for lunch, Kinsey is so nervous she eats *three* of Henry's cinnamon rolls (*M* 4). And when she is scared while tracking a killer, she thinks, "I desperately longed for a glass of wine'' (*A* 265). At an emotional extreme, the act of preparing and consuming a favorite food may be replete with evocative memories. The cheese-and-pickle sandwiches and peanut-butter-and-pickle sandwiches, which she loves to make, are a link to her mother, who made these sandwiches for her (*I* 48–49).

Most often, though, Kinsey eats fast food on the run simply to be able to keep going. She seems drawn to her favorite meal of a Quarter Pounder with cheese, fries, and a Coke. It's filling, fast, and cheap—all great values for a P.I. who just needs to refuel and get back to work. Not atypical is her visit to a generic fast-food place which feels more like a pit stop than a dining experience. "I pulled into a fast-food restaurant, parked, and went in. . . . I wolfed down a cheeseburger, fries, and a Coke for a dollar sixty-nine and was back on the streets again in seven minutes flat" (*B* 72).

When Kinsey does eat at home on her own, it is usually a sandwich and some empty calories on the side—"a sliced hard-boiled egg sandwich, which I ate hot on wheat bread with a lot of mayonnaise and salt, popping open a Pepsi and a package of corn chips" (*A* 221). Her idea of a gourmet touch is Lawry's Seasoning Salt on the egg. The only food we see her prepare, in fact, is a variety of sandwiches, although she tells us she can pour canned cream soups over anything "baked at 350 for an hour . . . scramble eggs and make a fair tuna salad, but that's about it" (*I* 190–91). We never see her prepare food for anyone else, although she does offer a bite of her sandwich to Henry, holding it carefully so he won't take too much (*M* 115). When she volunteers to make peanut-butter-and-pickle sandwiches for herself and Dietz, he merely glares at her as if she had suggested "cooking up a mess of garden slugs" (*M* 232).

While she at least once complains about eating alone (*D* 158), this complaint feels like the exception that proves the rule, so often does Kinsey sing the praises of the solitary meal. In fact, one of the attractions of living alone is that she can eat whenever she wants to. She takes great pleasure from the privacy and informality of her meals. "My notion of setting an elegant table is you don't leave the knife sticking out of the mayonnaise jar" (*D* 158). In the first version of her apartment with her bathroom at ground level, she often ate her meal standing in the bathtub, arms resting on the windowsill, watching the world go by.

She routinely eats her food from a paper towel, which she then discards with satisfaction over an effortless cleanup. Cleanup is an important component of her eating alone. On one occasion, she eats cereal and then soup, washing the bowl and spoon after each course. She observes, "If I kept up this cycle of cereal and soup, I could eat for a week without dirtying another dish" (*I* 191).

If she's sitting down for a meal, the food is normally prepared for her by one of her friends, Rosie or Henry. In fact, a Rosie-dictated dinner sounds wonderful. Here's a typical meal: a green pepper salad, tejfeles sult ponty, pike baked in cream, and deep-fried cherries with an Austrian wine (*B* 91). Usually Henry's homemade rolls are also included. Henry, whose career was as a commercial baker, frequently offers Kinsey cinnamon rolls, chocolate-chip cookies, and brownies. In addition, when Kinsey has had a difficult time, Henry can be counted on to provide a delicious and nurturing meal of comfort foods. We see a good illustration of this in *Gumshoe,* where Kinsey has been pursued by a hit man. Henry brings dinner for her and her bodyguard, and the three of them sit down to eat "succulent meatloaf with mushroom gravy, mashed potatoes, fresh green beans, homemade rolls, fresh lemon meringue pie, and coffee" (*G* 139).

As much as Kinsey likes to eat alone, she clearly loves having someone else prepare food. "What could smell better than supper being cooked by someone else?" (*E* 160). For some reason that she doesn't completely understand, she is frequently in the company of men who are preparing food. She enjoys watching Henry cook and she is often in his kitchen for talk and food. For instance, their serious conversation about the impact on Kinsey of having killed someone takes place while he is making napoleons (*B* 82–84), and she tells him about her newly discovered relatives over a pan of his brownies fresh from the oven (*J* 163). The pattern begins as early as *"A" Is for Alibi,* when Kinsey goes to interview Nikki Fife and is engaged by watching her young son, Colin, knead bread, an activity requiring impressive concentration and skill (177–79). Daniel Wade makes an omelet from the scraps in Kinsey's refrigerator (*E* 160) and later assembles a picnic of "wine, pâté, cheeses, French bread, cold salads, fresh raspberries, and sugar cookies the size of Frisbees" (172). Luis prepares two meals of Mexican food, including an omelet that Kinsey is "forced to report . . . was one of the best I've ever eaten" (*H* 191). Harris Brown fries chicken "mahogany brown with spice-speckled crust," but, to her regret, it isn't done before she leaves (*J* 274). J. D. Burke starts cooking ground beef, which Kinsey thinks unappetizing until he begins to add tomato, onion, and garlic, and the smells get to her (*K* 60–63). Wim Hoover prepares eggs and bacon for his lover, while Kinsey questions him, "starving to death just watching this stuff" (*B* 102). The newly returned Dietz prepares a one-skillet meal of "fried onions, fried potatoes, and fried sausages with liberal doses of garlic and red pepper flakes, all served with a side of drab, grainy mustard that set your tongue aflame" for Kinsey and himself (*M* 74).

The smells and the look of the food—and often the skills of the cook—are very appealing to a famished Kinsey. Standing on a murder suspect's front porch, she is brought to the verge of whimpering aloud by the sounds and smells of frying chicken: "If he would just offer me some chicken, I wouldn't care what he'd done. Food first, then justice. That's the proper ordering of world events" (*J* 272). Her stomach is so much in control of her judgment that, if it is not being prepared for her or offered to her, she may just ask to have some of the guy's food. Watching Chester Lee fry bologna for sandwiches, she becomes so "dizzy from the sensory overload," she blurts out, "I'll pay you four hundred dollars if you fix me one of those" (*L* 37).

"Somehow in my profession I seem to spend a lot of time in kitchens looking on while men make sandwiches, and I can state categorically, they do it better than women" (*L* 36). (Of course, she explains what she means by that is men have a total disregard for nutrition and will put anything into a sandwich.) A great account of sandwich-making by a man occurs when she goes to interview Phil Bergen in *"C" Is for Corpse*. The food would sound appealing only to someone of Kinsey's famous "low appetites" (*E* 79, *J* 112). Kinsey says, "I could see his sandwich preparations laid out . . . an assortment of processed cheese slices and a lunchmeat laced with olives and ominous chunks of animal snout. . . . He was already slathering Miracle Whip on that brand of soft white bread that can double as foam sponge. I kept my eyes discreetly averted as if he were engaged in pornographic practices. He laid a thin slice of onion on the bread and then peeled the cellophane wrap from the cheese, finishing with layers of lettuce, dill pickles, mustard, and meat" (*C* 91–92).

Within minutes, Kinsey is practically drooling on the kitchen table. Bergen takes pity on her and divides his sandwich, giving her half, then makes another "more lavish than the first" and divides it as well. They sit "in silence, wolfing down lunch" (92).

When the occasion arises, Kinsey thoroughly savors the subtle flavors of a gourmet meal at a good restaurant. For instance, she and Charlie Scorsoni linger over an erotic meal, during which her intuitive suspicions of him seem to disappear along with dessert: "The meal that followed was one of the most sensual I ever experienced: fresh, tender bread with a crust of flaky layers, spread with a buttery pâté, Boston lettuce with a delicate vinaigrette, sand dabs sautéed in butter and served with succulent green grapes. There were fresh raspberries for dessert with a dollop of tart cream, and all the time Charlie's face across the table from me, shadowed by that suggestion of caution, that hint of something stark and fearful held back, pulling me forward even while I felt myself kept in check" (A 186–87).

But it doesn't take gourmet foods to make Kinsey whimper and moan. Cherry pies, whether the carefully homemade or the fast-food variety filled with "glue," bring sounds of pleasure from Kinsey, who remembers how much she liked cherry pie as a child. A visit to a "dumpy" Mexican restaurant leads her to enjoy a combination plate with "the sort of flavors that make you whimper" (G 92). She gets so hungry that she even eats a bland sandwich at a hospital cafeteria, "nearly weeping, it tasted so good. I moaned" (K 211). After a scary visit from the Mafia, cinnamon rolls at a coffee shop bring on similar moans (K 182). Kinsey's fondness for chocolate is fully indulged by one of Henry's warm brownies: "If I moaned aloud, Henry was too polite to call attention" (J 163).

Obviously, the sensual pleasures of food and drink are not lost on Kinsey. She herself comments on this in such scenes as her dinner with Bibianna Diaz and Jimmy Tate at Bourbon Street. The two are draped all over each other in barely contained sexuality, so Kinsey turns to other satisfactions. "I concentrated on the meal in front of me with the kind of gusto that can only be thought of as sexual sublimation" (H 74). We do hear moans of satisfaction over indulging her gastronomical appetite far more often than over her sexual one. And her expressions of pleasure are quite uninhibited. One illustration is her response to a martini—enough to tempt a temperance worker: "Mine was silky and cold with that whisper of vermouth that makes me shudder automatically. I always eat the olive early because it blends so nicely with the taste of gin. He [Aubrey] caught sight of the shiver. 'I can leave the room if you want to be alone with that' " (*B* 143).

Kinsey also drinks screwdrivers, margaritas, bourbon, and brandy, whenever the choice seems appropriate for her work. Well-made cocktails, though, are the exception to her regular consumption of white wine, preferably Chardonnay or Zinfandel, occasionally Chablis. In the early novels, in which she appears to drink more than in the later books, she even keeps a bottle in her office. Although she can appreciate a good wine, she seems to take pride in her consumption of the less expensive versions often sold in cardboard boxes (*C* 22 and *D* 20), only occasionally in the later novels splurging with a corked bottle. Francesca Voigt serves hors d'oeuvres and a lovely white wine when Kinsey goes to interview her. "I tried a sip of the wine, a silky blend of apple and oak. Kick-ass private eyes hardly ever live like this. We're the Gallo aficionados of the jug-wine set" (*I* 56–57).

She consumes beverages and food alike without a trace of the guilt women typically experience at such indulgence. Even when she does give a passing thought to her weight, the entire process of controlling it seems haphazard and more a result of the demands of her job than careful planning on her part. "I have a hard time eating meals when I should. Either I'm not hungry when I'm supposed to be or I'm hungry and not in a place where I can stop and eat. It becomes a weight-control maneuver, but I'm not sure it's good for my health" (*C* 88).

That health concern lasts about a nanosecond.

Kinsey doesn't worry about the nutritional value of what she eats. She lets us know that she's aware of healthy food guidelines and enjoys ignoring them. Chowing down on her favorite Quarter Pounder with cheese, she considers the impact on her body: "I could feel my arteries hardening, plaques piling up in my veins like a logjam in a river, blood pressure going up from all the sodium" (*G* 196). She likes salt and has no intention of reducing her use, "I don't care what they say" (*D* 39). And after a tough episode, she thinks, "this was no time to torment my cells with good nutrition" (*E* 80). She eschews trendy California health foods and even national health trends, favoring instead, for example, a complete breakfast of eggs, bacon, and coffee. "It's the only meal I'm consistently fond of as it contains every element I crave: caffeine, salt, sugar, cholesterol, and fat" (*B* 188). In later case reports, we find Kinsey eating breakfast at home more, where cereal with skim milk is the main course, but she still loves to indulge in the restaurant cholesterol special (*L* 123).

Perhaps the ease with which she maintains her own slenderness in spite of lousy eating habits partially explains Kinsey's very critical attitude toward people who are overweight. She often comments about overweight people, selecting their size as the distinguishing characteristic worthy of note. Arlette, the manager at a motel Kinsey uses when in Los Angeles, is described by her as "a very fat woman" (*A* 83) and her mother is "twice as fat" (*A* 246). She also shows far less tolerance for others' consumption of fatty foods than she does for her own. Observing a receptionist's breakfast of sausage and eggs, she considers, "She was in her twenties and apparently hadn't yet heard about the hazards of cholesterol and fat. She would find the latter on her fanny one day soon" (*E* 2). It's revealing that Kinsey is sexually attracted to Charlie and Jonah only after they both lose some weight. And she likes Henry's lean looks in his eighties much better than his fuller looks in the old photos of him as a young man.

She often jokes about her unhealthy food consumption. The only things she won't eat are jelly doughnuts (*A* 173) and tripe (*G* 89). And she doesn't really like marshmallows on sweet potatoes, either (*B* 95), but just about anything else is fair game. Eating when, what, where, and how *she* chooses is just one more way that Kinsey creates herself and shows the world, including all of us who avidly read her reports, that she is emphatically her own person.

Exercise

For many women, diet and exercise are the two components that keep their weight in check. They exercise in order to stay slender and look good. Gaining physical fitness is only a nice bonus, rather than the goal. Kinsey, who exercises regularly, may occasionally refer to working off a Quarter Pounder, but she offers many more reasons than a simple desire to stay slim, and most relate to her work.

Kinsey describes her exercises in every novel. After all, she has been jogging three miles, six days a week, since she was twenty-five (*L* 49–50). In her first case, she explains her jogging routine when she is at home. Late in the afternoon, she runs along the mile-and-a-half bicycle path on Cabana that parallels the beach near her apartment. Beginning with her third report, she switches to a regular 6:00 a.m. jog, without comment about the reason for the change. Perhaps it is a consequence of her being "addicted to early rising and morning sunshine" (*K* 95). Her daily routine, in fact, is amazingly regular, considering her line of work. Except in *"K" Is for Killer,* in which she stays up night after night, she likes to be home early in the evening and asleep by eleven o'clock (95). This gives her seven hours of sleep and she seems to sleep well most of the time in the early novels, or in her words, "like a stone" (*E* 122). By the time of *Killer,* her sleep is often troubled by dreams of the dead.

Jogging is Kinsey's regular exercise in every novel, but in a few of the novels, she also works out at a local no-frills gym. We first encounter her weight lifting in *"C" Is for Corpse,* where she is on a rigorous work-out schedule to restore the damage to her arm, which was broken and shot in a fight at the end of the previous novel. In addition to rebuilding the strength and flexibility of her arm, she finds weights mentally satisfying. "Lifting weights is like a meditation: intermittent periods of concentrated activity, with intervals of rest. It's a good time for thinking, as one can do little else" (*E* 49). After her burn injuries in *"E" Is for Evidence,* Kinsey discontinues lifting weights. She says she's stopping only "temporarily" (*F* 15), and she continues to refer occasionally to weights, but we don't actually see her working out with weights again. She keeps instead to her regular jogging routine.

Early in the series, she gives us two reasons for her running. First, running is a physical challenge that she struggles to conquer. "I'm really not a physical fitness advocate . . . but there's something about running that satisfies a masochistic streak. It hurts and I'm slow but I have good shoes and I like the smell of my own sweat" (*A* 60). She likes the self-discipline of responding to the alarm clock and pushing herself to meet personal standards. It is "a way of asserting the will in the face of life's little setbacks" (*M* 87).

Her second motivation, mentioned throughout the series, is that she runs to stay prepared for the physical demands of her job. "I run for the same reasons I learned to drive a car with a stick shift and drink my coffee black, imagining that a day might come when some amazing emergency would require such a test" (*A* 109). Her job does frequently require her to run: from a villain, like Charlie Scorsoni in *A;* and from the police, as in *F;* from attack geese in *A;* and after killers, like Raymond Maldonado in *H.* Kinsey concludes, "Sometimes I end up running for my life, so it will never do to get out of shape" ("Falling off the Roof," *Kinsey and Me,* 113). Also, daily exercise gives her the endurance needed to save her own life in crises, such as being drugged (*Corpse*), wounded (*Innocent*), entrapped with a bomb (*Evidence*), and run off the road (*Gumshoe*). As she sums it up, "I try to run every day not from passion, but because it's saved my life more than once" (*F* 15). Less threatening emergencies also vindicate her commitment to exercise. When changing a flat tire, she comments: "This is why I jog and bust my hump lifting weights, so I can cope with life's little inconveniences" (*G* 52). Running up seven flights of stairs after Tony Gahan, she says, "I don't keep fit for nothin', folks" (*D* 216).

In fact, Kinsey reveals a whole gym bag of reasons for exercising as the series progresses. The emphasis changes with her mood and the situation. Recalling her aunt's dictum that "Exercise was important. Fashion was not" (*D* 102), she usually discounts jogging as a way to improve her appearance. Once in a while, however, she tells us that she *does* exercise to look good. "I've never rhapsodized about exercise and I'd avoid it if I could, but I notice the older I get, the more my body seems to soften, like butter left out at room temp" (*D* 28). She also exercises to restore her body to health after injuries. And sometimes Kinsey takes advantage of her running time to take her mind off her case, especially if she is worried about the investigation. "I needed to clear away the dregs of nagging anxiety. . . . Running is the only relief I can find short of drink and drugs, which at 6:00 a.m. don't appeal" (*D* 131). "I kept moving, working out hard, as though physical pain might blot out its emotional counterpart" (*C* 119). On the other hand, there are times when she makes use of the jog to apply her mind *to* the case. She uses the time and the rhythm to go "through the mental gymnastics of getting the case organized" (*C* 67).

And let's not forget the moment when the married Jonah asks her in *"D" Is for Deadbeat* what she does for sex; Kinsey replies, "Jog on the beach. How about you?" Jonah laughs, so she insists, "I'm telling the truth" (51). These varying impulses, related to her mood, only make her more like us—different days, very different motivators.

The pain of running stays much the same, though. Kinsey never claims to like exercise. In fact, she outright complains about it a lot, especially in the early novels. She runs in spite of the pain it consistently brings on, even after she hits her stride. "Running always hurts—I don't care what they say—but it does acquaint one with all of one's body parts. This time I could feel my thighs protest and I noticed a mild aching in my shins, which I ignored, plodding on gamely" (A 161–62). Rain or shine, she runs even though she doesn't experience the so-called runner's high. "I find exercise loathsome. . . . I've never thrilled to it. . . . I'm still waiting for the rumored 'euphoria' that apparently infuses everyone but me" (B 84). Perhaps continuing to run past the pain is part of the self-discipline of running that makes Kinsey feel so good. And we note that by the time of "C" Is for Corpse, Kinsey begins to refer to the endorphins kicking in (15) and throughout the later novels she does seem to feel the pleasant high that can come with exercise (M 150).

We are so used to Kinsey's regular running date with herself that we notice when she skips it, and she does too. We learn a lot about how much the run means to her on the rare occasions when she is too hurt, too tired, too drained, or too sick to take her daily jog. Or when her bodyguard says it's too dangerous (Gumshoe). She feels it, for example, when she has gone undercover to help Bibianna and she has to skip her jogs; at the conclusion of the case, she chases Raymond Maldonado through a hospital and out onto the street: "I was . . . calling on the last of my physical reserves. I had to be in better shape than Raymond, but I could feel myself wheezing, lungs on fire. Six days without exercise had taken the edge off, but I still had some juice" (H 253).

In spite of the many adventures that lead us to respect her strength and endurance, she doesn't think of herself as achieving a high level of fitness. "I've been in shape maybe once in my life, when I qualified for the police academy" (A 60). Her idea of fit appears to be the incredible condition of an aerobics instructor she admires in "C" Is for Corpse, a standard far above what most of us would consider fit. The standard she does achieve gives her competence for the physical demands of her job, and, in the midst of all the motivators she lists, that remains her ultimate goal.

Recreation

Cleaning

What does Kinsey do in her spare time to relieve the stress of her high-pressure job or just for fun? Clean the house, of course. She spends a great deal of time and energy in concentrated, committed, and unremitting cleanups that restore the apartment and herself to a state of normalcy.

To those of us whose favorite household pets are dust bunnies, this may seem an odd form of recreation, but it works for Kinsey. Cleaning helps her to relax and recharge her mental batteries. (Remember this is a woman with such a high-stress job that she grinds her teeth in her sleep, *A* 186.) Kinsey sounds like any sports fanatic explaining the joys of a chosen sport: "As a way of unwinding, I tidied up the living room and scrubbed the downstairs bath. Cleaning house is therapeutic—all those right-brain activities, dusting and vacuuming, washing dishes, changing sheets. I've come up with many a personal insight with a toilet brush in hand, watching the Comet swirl around in the bowl" (*I* 93).

She just prefers a toilet brush to a tennis racket.

Later in the same report she's cleaning again as a way of redirecting her determination to wipe out the bad guys. "It was the only thing I could think of to offset my anxiety. I grabbed some sponges and the cleanser and attacked the bathroom off the loft. I don't know how men cope with life's little stresses. Maybe they play golf or fix autos or drink beer and watch TV. The women I know (the ones who aren't addicted to junk food or shopping) turn to cleaning house. I went to town with a rag and a johnny mop, mowing down germs with copious applications of disinfectants, variously sprayed and foamed across every visible surface" (*I* 207).

Similarly, after Dietz leaves in *"M" Is for Malice*, Kinsey is both angry and hurt, and she substitutes anger against dirt for her anger against Dietz. She skips lunch and cleans her office even though it is regularly maintained by a professional cleaning crew. "I found a

plastic bucket, sponges, cleansers, a toilet brush, and mop and entertained myself mightily killing imaginary germs. . . . By three
o'clock, I smelled of sweat and household bleach and I'd forgotten
what I was so unhappy about. Well, actually, I remembered, but I
didn't give a shit" (89–90).

Amazingly, Kinsey also cleans everyone else's space. When she
finds Shana Timberlake drunk and sick, she cleans up her kitchen. "I
squirted dish-washing liquid into the tumbling water and watched
with satisfaction as a cloud of bubbles began to form" (F 108). Later
in the same report we find her washing dishes again, this time for the
Fowlers, in order to escape the self-centered, whining Ori. But the
cleaning goes on, case after case. She always makes her own place
sparkle, and she at least keeps tetanus at bay in the Maldonado apartment (H). She helps Tillie Ahlberg clean up after her apartment is
vandalized (B 42). She makes a comforting homecoming possible for
Danielle Rivers (which death sadly prevents, K 227–28), she fulfills
her undercover role as a hotel maid so well that she gets a generous
tip (L 115), and she cleans Helen Rawson's house after the older
woman shoots Gilbert Hays with shotgun pellets (L 245).

Kinsey is most comfortable with small litter-free spaces. "I do love
tidiness," she tells us (B 106), and we believe her as we experience
one clean-up after another, at all hours of the day and night, mental
or physical injuries notwithstanding. The process of taking care of
her living space is a way of taking care of herself, and she inevitably is
more comfortable with her world as a result.

Books

Books are an important part of Kinsey's life. She says they are often
"stacked up on my desk" (A 61). Her aunt considered reading an
essential activity for children and adults. Kinsey reads fiction and nonfiction with no clear rules about how she decides what and when to
read, with one exception: her favorite response to the luxury of a rare
rainy day in Santa Teresa is to curl up in her quilt and read a good
book (D 28).

She must enjoy the adventures of her fictional colleagues in crime
solving. She mentions Nancy Drew (H 233), Sherlock Holmes (B 196,
H 178), Len Deighton (D 29), Dick Francis (H 48), Elmore Leonard

(*L* 68), and Agatha Christie (*H* 10). Kinsey seems to read nonfiction, job-related books with as much frequency and enthusiasm as novels. She specifically mentions "the abridged California Penal Code" (*F* 179), books on auto theft (*F* 179 and *A* 62), fingerprint mechanics (*B* 151), burglary and theft (*C* 71, *J* 174), and tidal pools (*M* 151), and says "a prime source of entertainment is a textbook on practical aspects of ballistics, firearms, and forensic techniques" (*E* 12).

We know that her reading of a "paperback romance novel" in *"L" Is for Lawless* is merely a consequence of what was available at the hotel store. It is unlike her usual taste and she had earlier laughed at the Victoria Holt–Georgette Heyer tradition (*A* 169).

Target Practice

Along with reading books on ballistics, Kinsey enjoys trips to the firing range. As a young girl, she was taken there by her aunt, who taught her to shoot, and she has strong positive memories of the trips. She loves the smell of gunpowder and used to explode caps on her front steps as a little girl, just to get a whiff. A fun afternoon for Kinsey can be spent in target practice (*B* 149–50), and, as she tells us, it "is what I do for laughs" (*D* 2). In *"C" Is for Corpse,* she says, "If I have any hobbies at all, they consist of cleaning my little semiautomatic and reading up on evidential documents" (12).

Kinsey enjoys everything about the experience at the firing range. "The wind had picked up and mist was being blown across concrete bunkers like something in a horror movie. I set up the target at a range of twenty-five yards. I inserted soft plastic earplugs and then put on hearing protectors over them. All outside noises were damped down to a mild hush, my breathing audible in my own head as though I were swimming. I loaded eight cartridges into the clip of my .32 and began to fire. Each round sounded like a balloon popping somewhere close by, followed by the characteristic whiff of gunpowder I so love" (*E* 64).

She's struck by a similar feeling in *"G" Is for Gumshoe,* when she and Dietz go to the range after she is shot at by a hit man. With the "smell of gunpowder perfuming the air," she imagines the hit man as the target (*G* 149). Through this stratagem, she banishes her fears and restores her confidence. For themselves, many readers might prefer ice cream and a good detective novel, or a quiet walk in the woods, but target practice is what restores Kinsey's "old self." That sense of restoration is, after all, the point of what we call "recreation." And even after the hit man is killed, we note that Kinsey and Dietz continue to enjoy target practice together (*M* 15).

Kinsey also enjoys cleaning her gun. "I sat on the couch and cleaned my gun, taking in the smell of oil, finding it restful to dismantle and wipe and put it all back together again" (*B* 150). Tidy Kinsey, in control of her world again. She has a healthy respect for the gun, not treating it as a toy, and she normally keeps it secured in what she considers a safe place in her car, her apartment, or on her person.

Music

Kinsey tells us that the only subject she liked in elementary school was music (*G* 42–43), but in keeping with her avoidance of possessions, she doesn't seem to have records, tapes, or CDs in her apartment. She does enjoy listening to the car radio, and misses it when it's broken, as it often is in her second car (*J* 122 and *K* 33). As with food, Kinsey is a consumer, rather than a maker, of music. She says she has a bad singing voice (*D* 140), and she doesn't refer to being able to play any musical instrument.

Her taste is eclectic. She likes James Taylor and Kitaro's *Silk Road* (*I* 39 and 82). She recognizes dueling jukeboxes in two neighboring bars, one playing Helen Reddy and the other Linda Ronstadt (*L* 63). In *Evidence,* she fondly recalls the schmaltzy Johnny Mathis tunes, which seemed to play a role, along with a number of margaritas, in relaxing her inhibitions and persuading her to go to bed with Jonah (*E* 37). In *"M" Is for Malice,* she's caught in a birthday tribute to the King, and at least initially, she finds herself singing and dancing along with Elvis (14). Kinsey particularly enjoys jazz, especially tenor sax (*K* 33), yet classical music also appeals to her (*K* 144 and *E* 172).

She tells us that it was Daniel's musical expertise that first drew her to him. We understand her attraction when he plays Henry's piano for her. Because he was classically trained, he begins with Chopin, Liszt, and Bach, then moves into variations and improvisations that Kinsey fully appreciates (*E* 172). She loves his jazz pieces as well. She has definite taste in music, rejecting out of hand Robert Dietz's love of country music (*G* 104), yet she herself must listen to it because she often identifies the singers when she goes into bars ("A Willie Nelson single was playing, but it wasn't one I knew," *D* 70). And even as she is being stalked by a killer, she can complain that the murderer's version of "Someone to Watch Over Me" "didn't do the Gershwins justice" (*C* 238).

Movies

Although Kinsey never mentions attending a single movie (she tries unsuccessfully to go to one in *"L" Is for Lawless*), we know that movies are important reference points in her life. Throughout the series, Kinsey makes comparisons between the current scene and the world of movies, especially horror movies. For instance, she says "fear is contagious . . . which is why horror movies are so potent in a crowded theater" (*G* 191). Or, she regrets that life doesn't have a musical score so that we could know when the scary part is coming the way we do in frightening movies (*H* 133).

She has seen everything from the Alfred Hitchcock classics, such as *Vertigo,* to B-grade sci-fi of the *Godzilla Meets Bambi* sort. She's familiar with the Hollywood classics of the '30s and '40s, making comparisons to Jean Harlow's outfits (*C* 171), a Joan Crawford pose (*E* 107), Marlene Dietrich's voice (*B* 103), a kiss between Jean Simmons and Stewart Granger in *Young Bess* (*A* 145), June Allyson's long-suffering wifely roles (*B* 74), and the light dancing of Ginger Rogers (*H* 68). She also knows European films, if we can judge by her reference to someone looking as world-worn as Anna Magnani, Jeanne Moreau, or Simone Signoret (*B* 86). She is familiar enough with Andy Warhol films to recognize the resemblance of a bank of security TVs all showing the same scene (*H* 92). She refers to such popular icons as John Wayne (*I* 214), *The Wizard of Oz* (*C* 218), and Walt Disney (*C* 174 and elsewhere).

While we never hear of a visit to a movie theater, we might remember that she does have a life outside and between the novels. Or she could be watching old movies on television. She has a portable black-and-white television set with a VCR, which she says she turns on primarily to keep her company while she cleans or eats breakfast. There was one unnamed television program she got hooked on: it

featured a male-and-female duo in a spoof of other detective series
("A Little Missionary Work, *K & M* 179). She's watched *M*A*S*H* (*C*
129), *The Twilight Zone* (*M* 58), *My Favorite Martian* (*C* 69), and some
soap operas, but that's about the limit of her interest in TV programs.

Interest in California History

Kinsey has "an affection for early California history" (*F* 38). This
prompts her to make a visit to the local mission and some of the old
adobes in Floral Beach while she is there on a case (38). Her interest
gives us a frequent opportunity to learn about the state and town
through her bemused eyes. For instance, she admires the Santa Teresa Courthouse, which "looks like a Moorish castle." "One courtroom sports a cycloramic mural that depicts the settling of Santa
Teresa by the early Spanish missionaries. It's sort of the Walt Disney
version of what really went on as the artist has omitted the introduction of syphilis and the corruption of the Indians. I prefer it myself, if
the truth be known. It would be hard to concentrate on justice if you
had to stare up at some poor bunch of Indians in the last stages of
paresis" (*C* 203).

This interest may also be the impetus for her repeated desire to
take Spanish lessons, which she finally does in *"J" Is for Judgment.* She
and Vera take a night course in Spanish at the local community college.

Staying Close to Home

By far the best place for Kinsey to "re-create" herself is her own cozy,
private apartment. We never hear of her inviting friends in for parties
or casual visits, and she tells us she doesn't entertain (*C* 12). Clearly,
she enjoys having her own space and keeping it free from foreign
bodies of all sorts. When she does venture out for entertainment, her
favorite spot is the neighborhood bar, Rosie's Tavern. Kinsey often
eats there, but she tells us it's also her favorite place to hang out. "I'm
embarrassed to say how much I like the place" (*B* 92). Although the
nature of the bar changes as the sports crowd discovers the place and
it becomes too noisy and crowded to suit Kinsey, she continues to
consider it her second place of retreat, after her apartment.

What She Doesn't Do

Kinsey doesn't take vacations. By that, we mean she doesn't travel for fun (*M* 47); she will occasionally not work for a few days between cases.

Kinsey says in the early reports that she doesn't usually read the newspaper or news magazines (*B* 19). When she does attack *Time,* she says she starts "with the sections on books and cinema, losing interest by the time I reach Economy & Business" (*D* 158). (It's difficult to know how much credence to give this assertion; by the time of *"E" Is for Evidence,* she is regularly reading the *Los Angeles Times* with her breakfast cereal and coffee, and many of her comparisons draw on the way life is portrayed in *GQ,* women's magazines, interior-design magazines, and science magazines. Maybe she reads them during her hospital stays.) Kinsey doesn't swim in the ocean and avoids nature adventures at all costs. Although she used to smoke, she'd "rather drive off a bridge than light up" (*K* 144).

She doesn't keep house plants or pets (*C* 12). When Henry gives her an air fern—the perfect plant for her because it needs absolutely no care, she says: "I held the little pot up and inspected the fern from all sides, experiencing this worrisome spark of possessiveness" (*E* 7). She doesn't like possessions of any sort and is practically un-American in her resistance to shopping and owning things. We never see her spend leisure time or money at a shopping mall or boutique. Her income is modest, and she doesn't "like working just to pay a bunch of bills every month" (*I* 247). In fact, when a bomb destroys her apartment, she reflects on her good luck in not owning much (*E* 225).

Finally, with a rare exception or two, Kinsey enjoys just being alone. "I like being by myself. I find solitude healing . . ." (*E* 180). Appropriately enough, she enjoys playing solitaire (*M* 3 and 88). In a society in which a woman without a man is considered incomplete, many of us enjoy Kinsey's deep and satisfying pleasure at being single and alone. She doesn't rush around, filling her calendar with activities, or in other ways attempting to avoid coming home to an empty apartment. Once she's finished cleaning, she seems to relish the quiet and peace of solitary living.

KINSEY LAUGHS AT:

Bad restaurants:

"I stopped at a fast-food place and ate some brown and yellow things that I washed down with a carton of orange juice. All of it tasted like something the astronauts would have to reconstitute." (*B* 21)

A restaurant near the Hacienda Motor Lodge "seems to change nationalities every time I'm there. . . . This time it was Greek: turdlike lumps wrapped in leaves. I'd seen things in roadside parks that looked about that good but I washed them down with a glass of wine that tasted like lighter fluid and who knew the difference?" (*A* 85)

"The sandwich was filled with preservatives, which might be just what I needed to keep my body from going bad." (*C* 92)

"I didn't see any flies, but the ghosts of Flies Past seemed to hover in the air." (*L* 196)

Good restaurants:

The Ranch House in Ojai is "one of those elegant restaurants where the waiter stands at your table and recites the menu like a narrative poem." (*A* 184)

The waiter "told us about the specials as if we might want to take notes." (*E* 43)

Cleanliness in motels/hotels:

"The room was serviceable, though it smelled faintly of eau de bug." (*G* 31)

"This was the kind of hotel that generates worries about exotic new strains of Legionnaires' disease." (*J* 25)

Clothes:

"Now I'm an haute couture ignoramus, but today she was wearing an outfit even I recognized. The two-piece 'ensemble' (to use fashion magazine talk) was the work of a designer who'd amassed a fortune making women look ill-shapen, over-dressed and foolish." (*I* 223–24)

Kinsey looks in her drawer for a pair of panty hose "that didn't look like kittens had been climbing up the legs." (*I* 215)

"Vera's into these Annie Hall ensembles that look like you're preparing for a life sleeping on sewer grates." (*J* 73)

About Dana Jaffe's casual good looks: "When I wear the same outfit, it looks like I'm all set to change the oil in my car." (*J* 64)

"She wore a pale-yellow sweater about the hue of certain urine samples I've seen where the prognosis isn't keen." (*E* 51)

Clothes for weddings:

"I thought a black dress would be perfect for Halloween nuptials [Vera's wedding for which Vera wants her to buy a new dress]. Once the reception was over we could go trick-or-treating together and maybe pool the take. I wanted dibs on the Hershey's Kisses and Tootsie Rolls." (*H* 13)

For William and Rosie's wedding: "I'd actually hoped to serve as the oldest living flower girl on record, but Rosie had decided to dispense with the role." Instead, all three attendants will be dressed in matching dresses of bright cabbage roses on a green background: "I was certain that, once assembled, the three of us would resemble nothing so much as a set of ambulatory bedroom drapes." (*L* 3)

Her fondness for food:

Ash says she can't decide which is better, sex or a warm chocolate-chip cookie. Kinsey's answer: "Go for the cookies. You can bake 'em yourself." (*E* 44)

"Even on the porch, I could smell bacon and eggs and the scent of maple syrup. My whimper probably wasn't audible above the sound of the mower two doors down." (*M* 253)

Her bust size:

Bibianna lends her clothes to wear and Kinsey gives back the bra: "No point in putting apples in a sack meant for canta-loupes." (*H* 140)

Interior design:

"A painting of Jesus hung on the wall at the foot of the bed. He had his palms open, eyes lifted toward heaven—pained, no doubt, by Ori's home decorating taste." (*F* 22–23)

"Renata had chosen the kind of wallpaper only decorators find attractive: a poisonous Chinese yellow with vines and puff-balls exploding across the surface. There was expensive fabric to match, drapes and upholstery continuing the pattern. It was possible that a fungus had got loose in the room, replicating like a virus until every corner had been invaded. I'd seen pic-tures of something like this in a science magazine, mold spores blown up to nineteen hundred times their actual size." (*J* 129)

Messiness in someone else's house:

"I was trying to think of something nice to say about her house, but I was secretly worried about my tetanus shots being out of date." (*C* 166)

Kinsey's Personal Relationships

"I don't socialize much."

K insey's self-proclaimed insistence on "keeping her distance" from other people does not prevent her from establishing a few warm relationships: with her landlord, with the proprietor of her favorite bar, with a coworker, with a client, and occasionally with someone she meets in the course of an investigation. Still, Kinsey's native caution about relationships, her strong drive for autonomy, and the nature of her work combine to make her essentially a loner who permits friendships and romantic attachments to get only so close and no closer. Some of them are extremely important to her, and she will take risks on behalf of the other person in that relationship, but none of them will be allowed to become all-consuming.

Major Friends Appearing Throughout the Series

Kinsey has two older friends who appear throughout the series, sometimes figuring in the action of the novel, sometimes only a voice on the phone, or the recipient of a postcard from Kinsey, but always a stable and important part of Kinsey's world.

Henry Pitts (and His Siblings)

Henry is Kinsey's landlord and most trusted friend. They met prior to the first novel, when Kinsey was apartment hunting in 1980. By the time the first novel opens, they are good friends, and the relationship grows stronger as the series continues until Kinsey can describe him in *"M" Is for Malice* as "perfection—smart, good-natured, and responsible—with the cutest legs I've ever seen" (82).

Henry is eighty-one (b. February 14, 1901) in *"A" Is for Alibi.* He has thick white hair, periwinkle-blue eyes, those great legs, and a year-round tan. Kinsey looks at photos of him over the years and sees that he had a fuller face as a young man. The pictures show him becoming thinner, "growing lean and fierce, until now he seems totally concentrated, like a basic stock boiled down to a rich elixir" (191).

Early in the series, Kinsey freely admits to a hint of sexual attraction between the two of them: "We simply eye one another across that half a century with a lively and considerable sexual interest that neither of us would *dream* of acting out" (*B* 82). In *"C" Is for Corpse,* she sees Lila Sams simpering at Henry, patting him on the arm, calling him pet names. When Henry surprises Kinsey by lapping this up, she recognizes that what she feels is garden-variety jealousy. She wonders "if this was how he felt on those rare occasions in the past when he'd spotted some guy rolling out of my place at six a.m." (16).

Later in the series, Kinsey begins to see Henry as a father substitute, but this is not a recognition she comes to easily, and she never drops her awareness that Henry is sexy and the best friend anyone could ask for. In the opening of *"F" Is for Fugitive,* Kinsey—staying in Henry's spare bedroom while her apartment is being rebuilt—is made uncomfortable by their daily contact. She is even bothered by Henry's gestures of kindness, such as doing her laundry. She fusses at him for fussing over her, saying, "Would you quit? I don't need a mother."

Henry laughingly and vehemently agrees. "You need a *keeper.* I've said so for months. You don't have a clue how to take care of yourself. You eat junk. Get beat up. Place gets blown to bits. I told you to get a dog, but you refuse. So now you got me, and if you ask me, it serves you right" (14). Only Henry can talk this way to Kinsey and get her to listen, but she is still irritated by his smothering attention. "I felt like one of those ducklings inexplicably bonded to a mother cat" (14). And she is afraid to bond too much with him, because she knows from her own experience how easy it is to lose someone you care for. So it is with considerable relief that Kinsey accepts a case in Floral Beach, pleased that she can get away from Henry, his solicitude, and his spare bedroom for several weeks.

The case involves the nasty, dysfunctional Fowler family (the name couldn't be more perfect). Kinsey is sickened by the twisted family relationships. The bedridden mother, Ori, is a manipulative dictator who uses her illness to control the family, and the daughter, Ann, is even worse. She proves to be a maniac who kills several people, including her mother, frames her own brother, and would have killed Kinsey if she had not been stopped by her father, Royce. The father is no saint either. Throughout Ann's life, Royce has been so obsessed with his son that he was barely aware of his daughter's existence. Once this ugly case is over and Ann is arrested, Kinsey is glad to return to Santa Teresa—and to her own sane home with Henry. The brutality of the Fowler family, her own escape from death, and Ann's final tirade against her father have given Kinsey a new willingness to risk emotional attachment to Henry. "I find that I'm looking at Henry Pitts differently these days. He may be the closest thing to a father I'll ever have. Instead of viewing him with suspicion, I think I'll enjoy him for the time we have left, whatever that may be. He's only eighty-two, and God knows, my life is more hazardous than his" (261).

Henry is a retired commercial baker who "used to run that little bakery at the corner of State and Purdue" (*B* 133). He continues to cook for himself, often inviting Kinsey to join him. In fact, it was the delicious smell of cinnamon rolls and spaghetti sauce that first attracted Kinsey to the advantages of renting Henry's studio apartment. He "supplements his income now by turning out breads and pastries that he trades with local merchants for goods and services. He caters tea parties for the little old ladies in the neighborhood, and in his spare time, he writes crossword puzzles that are a bitch to figure out" (*C* 13). He also stretches his income "by clipping coupons avidly" (*D*

38). Henry enjoys one glass of Jack Daniels before dinner (*I* 78), and he drives "a 1932 Chevrolet that he's had since it was new. It's been meticulously maintained. . . . With Henry at the wheel, there was something rakish and sexy about the vehicle" (*I* 228). In *"L" Is for Lawless* we learn that the Chevrolet is bright yellow, and Henry also has a station wagon for daily driving, saving the "five-window coupe" for "special occasions" (7). His living room contains a piano, which he plays with considerable gusto (*L* 45). He tends his yard and patio garden with great care.

Kinsey describes Henry as "caring, compassionate, and sweet" (*C* 13). "His overriding intelligence is tempered with warmth, and his curiosity hasn't diminished a whit with age" (*F* 10). Henry and Kinsey hit it off from the beginning. They are both self-sufficient souls who know how to respect each other's strengths. Henry finds Kinsey a constant source of adventure, and, in turn, Kinsey finds Henry to be the one reliable person in her life. He is the only person to whom she turns when she is grappling with moral dilemmas. For instance, she looks back on her first killing with more than a little discomfort. She firmly believes that she had no other option but to shoot Charlie Scorsoni at the end of *Alibi*, when he held a butcher knife on her. Yet, the fact that she has killed a fellow human being bothers her more than she is willing to admit, even to herself. In Henry's kitchen, she talks with him about it while he is making napoleons. She tries to rationalize the shooting. Henry is almost sharp with her, finally telling her just to accept what she did and stop trying "to turn it into a philosophical statement" (*B* 83). Only with Henry is Kinsey ever willing to be so open and vulnerable.

The strength of their friendship is shown in ways large and small. They exchange thoughtfully selected, or handmade, Christmas and birthday presents. Kinsey even knits Henry a "periwinkle-blue mohair muffler" to match his blue eyes (*E* 6). They share meals, talk, and laughter. They worry about each other. Henry "never goes to bed without peering out his window to see if I'm safely home" (*I* 21). They help each other in times of crisis. Examples of mutual support include Kinsey's retrieval of $20,000 that Lila Sams conned out of Henry, his incredibly perfect rebuilding of the studio apartment especially for her after the first one was bombed out of existence, and her willingness to investigate something at Henry's request in *"L" Is for Lawless.*

We learn a lot about Henry's family also. In *"E" Is for Evidence* Kinsey fights off loneliness when Henry excitedly flies to Michigan to spend Christmas with his older—yes, older—brothers and sister. His sister, Nell, is nine years older; his brother Charlie eight years older; his brother Lewis three years older; and his brother William two years older. They are all active, feisty people, and Kinsey becomes fond of them, most of them, that is. She never does completely take to William. In *"I" Is for Innocent,* Grafton focuses a lot of time and attention on Henry and William, as if to make up for our not seeing Henry at all in *"H" Is for Homicide,* when Kinsey worked undercover in Los Angeles. After William suffers a heart attack back in Michigan, he becomes so insufferable because of depression and hypochondria that Henry suspects brother Lewis of palming off William on him to get even with Henry for stealing his girl back in 1926. As Henry tells Kinsey, Lewis has "a long memory and not a shred of beneficence," so retaliation from him is probably behind William's unexpected two-week visit (*I* 79).

Henry is quickly driven crazy by William's obsession with his heart rate and blood pressure and with his refusal to eat anything Henry prepares. William's idea of fun is to go to strangers' funerals—apparently to reassure himself that it's not him in the casket. Henry takes William to Rosie's Tavern, where he sends distress signals to Kinsey to beg her to rescue him by joining them. She does, and both Kinsey and Henry can hardly wait to introduce William to Rosie. They figure that bossy, tyrannical Rosie will "take care of William and no two ways about it." Kinsey says, "I found myself almost feeling sorry for the man" (*I* 211). They wait, gleefully, for Rosie to demolish William, but to their utter amazement, Rosie bullies, charms, and flirts with William to the point that he drinks her sherry, eats her heavy Hungarian dinner, and pronounces, "That's remarkable. . . . I believe I can actually feel my blood pressure drop" (214).

By the time of the next novel, *"J" Is for Judgment,* William's two-week visit has turned into seven months, and Henry is dumbfounded that William is heavily into a "geriatric fling with Rosie" (23). Love has turned these two opinionated, cantankerous souls "rather kittenish, and it was nearly more than Henry could bear." Kinsey thinks it's "cute" (24). The affair steadily progresses: first, William starts helping out at Rosie's Tavern. Then he moves in with Rosie, and, conventional to the core, he promptly proposes marriage (*J* 86–87). In *"L" Is for Lawless,* the two are getting married, with Kinsey and Nell as the bridesmaids, and the brothers as ushers. In *"M" Is for Malice,* William and Rosie, like so many characters in the series, have mellowed somewhat. The sharp edges have been blunted. "William had given up some of his imaginary illnesses and she'd surrendered some of her authoritarianism" (252). William has been successful in persuading penny-pinching Rosie to pay better salaries; consequently, they have been able to employ better staff to whom more work can be delegated and they have more time together. Both the marriage and the business partnership appear to have settled into a comfortable routine.

Henry and his siblings extend their family circle to include Kinsey, at least to the extent that she will let them. She is amused and charmed by their closeness, their squabbles, and their family traditions. She participates in one such tradition in *"L" Is for Lawless.* She joins "the tribe" (48) at Henry's house for a birthday party for Lewis, who, according to family custom, has asked that his favorite meal be prepared. Kinsey's gift for Lewis is a sterling-silver shaving set, "more 'collectible' than antique" (46), she says, but we still assume this is a significant purchase for a cheapskate like Kinsey. The event is jolly and convivial, with Henry playing the piano while everyone engages in a sing-along. Kinsey seems much more at home with this birthday party—and more at ease with these people—than she did for her own birthday party at the beginning of *"G" Is for Gumshoe.* There she said, "Truly, the best moment of the day came when I was finally by myself" (28).

Kinsey especially admires the vigor and the independence of Henry's only sister, Nell, who returns the affection and admiration. In *"J" Is for Judgment,* we notice, for instance, that Nell made a "hand-stitched quilt" for Kinsey for her birthday (37), presumably the birthday she celebrated in *"G" Is for Gumshoe.*

From the vantage point of *"M" Is for Malice,* Kinsey considers her friendship with Henry: "From the outset, Henry and I established just enough of a relationship to suit us both. Over the years, he's managed to civilize me to some extent and I'm certainly more agreeable now than I was back then. Little by little, we forged the bond between us until now I consider him the exemplary mix of friend and generic family member" (82). In fact, when Henry laments that none of the sibs have children to leave the family photographs to, Kinsey says, "Why don't you put 'em in an album and pass them on to me? I'll pretend they're mine" (83).

Rosie

Just about the same time Kinsey met Henry, she also met Rosie, the owner and despot of Rosie's Tavern. We don't know her last name, because Kinsey says it's a name "I don't pronounce and couldn't spell on a dare" (G 17). The scruffy neighborhood bar, only half a block from Kinsey's apartment, is her favorite hangout.

"Like" may not always be the right word for Kinsey's feelings toward Rosie. Early in the series, Kinsey says, "Half the time, I don't like her much, but she never ceases to fascinate" (C 68). "Like your best friend's cranky grandmother, she's someone you endure for the sake of peace" (D 103). Kinsey's friendship with Rosie grows throughout the series, although this relationship never becomes as comfortable or as important as her relationship with Henry. One of the few times we see Rosie outside of the bar occurs when she delivers one of her nut strudels to Kinsey's apartment for her birthday. Kinsey invites her in, and they eat the strudel and drink tea. The scene is an uneasy one for all participants, including the reader, because both Kinsey and Rosie are out of their usual setting. Kinsey is distinctly uncomfortable by the end of the visit. "We didn't have that much to talk about and I found myself manufacturing chitchat, trying to ward off any awkward pauses in the conversation" (G 19). We can't imagine her ever having the heart-to-heart talks with Rosie that she does with Henry. Rosie is just too opinionated and intimidating.

Rosie is a colorful figure. Literally. Kinsey struggles to find the right word to describe the color Rosie dyes her hair: in *Alibi,* it is "a remarkable shade of rust, rather like the color of cheap redwood furniture" (19). It's "the color of dried tangerine peels" in *Burglar* (91). It's "a cross between terra cotta floor tile and canned pumpkin pie filling" in *Deadbeat* (103). In *Gumshoe,* her hair is "dyed the utterly faux orange-red of new bricks" (18). As for dress, she shows up on Kinsey's doorstep to deliver the nut strudel wearing an olive-green muumuu "printed with islands, palm trees, and parrots in hot pink and chartreuse" (17). For Lewis' birthday party in *"L" Is for Lawless,* Rosie is "decked out in a dark red muumuu with a purple-and-navy paisley shawl, the rich colors adding a note of drama to her vibrantly dyed red hair" (48).

Rosie's looks are distinctive, all right. She is almost a caricature. Henry may sound like a gorgeous, swashbuckling pirate; Rosie sounds like the Wicked Witch of the West. Kinsey describes her as "probably sixty-five, Hungarian, short, and top-heavy, a creature of muumuus and hennaed hair growing low on her forehead. She wears lipstick in a burnt-orange shade that usually exceeds the actual shape of her mouth, giving the impression that she once had a much larger set of lips. She uses a brown eyebrow pencil lavishly, making her eyes look stern and reproachful. The tip of her nose comes close to meeting her upper lip" (*B* 90). Rosie wears her hair "parted down the center and plastered into place with sprays that have sat on the grocery-store shelves since the beehive hairdo bumbled out of fashion in 1966." Because she smokes, there is usually "a halo of nicotine and hair spray" swirling around her head (*C* 68).

From the first of her meals at Rosie's, Kinsey—like the other patrons—is at Rosie's mercy. She is "a merciless enforcer for the food Mafia" (*I* 80) and the "dominatrix" of the bar (*G* 19). If you go to her bar and she likes you, she will tell you exactly what you will eat. If she doesn't like you or doesn't know you, she'll completely ignore you and talk only to the person at the table she does know. Jonah Robb surprises Kinsey by joining her at the tavern one night. Rosie is clearly pleased to see a good-looking guy with her (she's always telling Kinsey to get a man in her life), but, even then, she will not address Jonah directly. "[S]o we were forced to go through this little playlet in which I interpreted as though suddenly employed by the U.N." (*B* 93).

For some reason—perhaps because of Henry's friendship with them both, perhaps because Rosie responded to Kinsey as another strong woman—Rosie immediately took Kinsey under her wing. She orders Kinsey around like a culinary Attila the Hun. When Kinsey has not been in the bar for a entire week, Rosie pouts and glares, tells

Kinsey in no uncertain terms what she may and may not have to eat and concludes, "If you clean your plate, I could give you deep-fried cherries if I think you deserve it, which you don't" (*B* 91). Kinsey is properly chastened.

Like a naughty kid, Kinsey is also caught by Rosie's perceptive eye when she and Dietz go to the tavern after making love in *"M" Is for Malice.* Kinsey has tried to cover up whisker burns on her chin and cheek, but she sees that Rosie has noticed them. "She seemed to take in at a glance both the source of satisfaction and our avid interest in food. . . . She was visibly smirking as she recited the meal she intended to prepare for us." Enjoying herself, Rosie describes an elaborate meal. "Is guaranteed to perk up tired senses of which you look like you got a lot." She then refuses to serve them coffee, because, she says with a straight face, "You need sleep" (112). Few secrets can be kept from this woman.

Kinsey knows the rules: "Usually Rosie waited until I tasted a dish and gave elaborate restaurant-reviewer-type raves" (*B* 95). "You ate it the way she served it or you went somewhere else" (*C* 69–70). If Rosie stands by the table and folds "her hands in front of her, wiggling slightly in place," this means "she wants your attention or feels you haven't lauded her with quite enough praise for some culinary accomplishment" (*C* 70). "She hated anyone intruding on her kitchen, probably because she violated health codes" (*C* 133). It's better to keep quiet whenever Rosie turns on someone, "lest Rosie turn on [you] inexplicably and eighty-six [you] for life" (*C* 70).

Normally Kinsey chooses to abide by Rosie's rules. She may laugh at Rosie's domineering ways and she may claim to be intimidated by them ("I'd never had the nerve to stand up to her," *L* 48), but she keeps coming back for more. By the time of *"G" Is for Gumshoe,* Kinsey is able to characterize the relationship in much stronger terms than we heard in the early novels, although it's still a qualified description. She says about Rosie, "I suppose she's a mother substitute, but only if you favor being browbeaten by a member of your own sex" (17).

Kinsey actually seems to like, or at least tolerate, being browbeaten by other women. When she is having a bad time with a case, she heads straight for Rosie's, knowing full well she will be bullied, told what to eat, told to get a man and a dog for protection, but told first to buy a dress in order to attract the man. Presumably she should also buy the dog. She laughs at Rosie, and she doesn't buy the dress, the dog, or get the man, but she clearly likes the attention and the caring that lie behind the bullying.

As with Henry, Kinsey gets to know Rosie's family. Unlike Henry's family, though, Kinsey never feels close to Rosie's sister, whom Kinsey meets between *"F" Is for Fugitive* and *"G" Is for Gumshoe*. In the opening of *Gumshoe*, Kinsey tells us that she has "spent the last two weeks helping [Rosie] find a board-and-care facility for her sister Klotilde, who'd recently moved to Santa Teresa from Pittsburgh" (18). In marked contrast to Henry's warm and teasing family, this is not a family unit of which Kinsey wants to be a part. "Theirs was a bickering relationship and after an afternoon in their presence, I was cranky and impatient myself" (18). There appears to be little chance of an enveloping family circle here.

Most of the time, Rosie appears only as an abrasive maternal figure for Kinsey to return to when she needs an emotional fix, but in one novel she plays a key role in determining the outcome of the subplot action. In *"C" Is for Corpse*, Rosie shares Kinsey's distaste for Henry's girlfriend, Lila Sams. Kinsey watches Rosie spot Henry and Lila as they enter her bar. "Rosie's antennae had apparently gone up automatically, like My Favorite Martian in drag" (69). She sat bolt upright, put aside the evening paper, and "left her stool, gliding through the bar like a shark" (69). Kinsey watches the ensuing conversation in pantomime, since she is too far away to hear the words. Rosie does what Rosie always does—order pad in hand, she ignores Lila and stares at Henry. Lila flutters all over Henry, apparently explaining some specific dietary needs, none of which appears to suit Rosie. Finally, Lila pushes back her chair and delivering what looks like a scathing remark, marches out the door. Henry scrambles after her. Instead of being unhappy over the loss of customers, Rosie just smiles "secretly as cats do in the midst of mouse dreams" (70).

Kinsey congratulates Rosie: "Looks like you took care of *her*."

Rosie replies, "Is vulgar woman. Terrible creature. She was in once before and I don't like her a bit. Henry must be crazy nuts to come in my place with a hussy like that. Who is she?" (70).

The two women agree completely that Lila is up to no good. Rosie is even more suspicious of Lila's character than Kinsey, who thought her only irritating because of her flirtatious, simpering manner. Rosie thinks she is a "little snake" out to get something from Henry (71). Neither of them knows where she came from, or why Moza Lowenstein, who doesn't normally rent rooms, would have made an exception to rent this woman a room.

Later in the novel, Lila accuses Kinsey of cheating Henry by deliberately paying too low a rent on her apartment. Kinsey is dismayed by the intensity and irrationality of the accusation, and she heads straight to Rosie for consultation, even daring to go into the forbidden kitchen to find her. Without comment, Rosie listens to Kinsey's account of Lila's verbal attack. Kinsey concludes, "Rosie, the woman is crazy as a loon" (133). Rosie immediately responds by pouring each of them a coffee cup full of vodka. Then she calls Moza Lowenstein and tells her to come over to the bar "right this minute" (134). Moza is so afraid of Rosie—"as anyone with good sense would be" (134)—that she rushes right over, dish towel in hand, to report as directed. Rosie proceeds to terrorize a thoroughly intimidated Moza, a task made easier by the fact that she continues to chop leeks with a wicked-looking meat cleaver while they talk. Rosie quickly gets Moza to agree to spy on Lila. "You find out where she comes from and Kinsey can take care of the rest" (136).

Kinsey does take care of the rest. She discovers that "Lila Sams" is an alias for a con artist wanted in several states for real-estate fraud. She arranges for Lila's arrest and, before the police arrive, retrieves $20,000 Henry had given Lila to invest, but she continues, even into the next novel, to worry about Henry's reaction to learning that Lila was a fraud.

This subplot running throughout *"C" Is for Corpse* is given major impetus by the instincts and decisive actions of Rosie. In the other novels, Rosie is less integral to the plot and more important in creating character and background for Kinsey.

In some ways, Rosie seems an exaggeration of Kinsey herself. If Kinsey is independent and strong-willed, Rosie is an autocrat and a bully; if Kinsey is frugal, Rosie is a skinflint, even having her wedding on Thanksgiving Day so she won't lose any business; if Kinsey is brave, Rosie is fearless; if Kinsey acts decisively, Rosie makes snap decisions; if Kinsey's choice of dress and hairstyle is eccentric, Rosie's is bizarre.

They have both struggled to make their own way in careers dominated by men. They are both loyal, determined, outspoken survivors in life.

No wonder they feel a connection.

Significant Friends Appearing in Several Novels

Lt. Con Dolan

Dolan is a lieutenant in the Homicide Department of the Santa Teresa Police Department, someone with whom Kinsey worked when she was a cop. Because Dolan is a good resource for her own cases, she has maintained a relationship with him, a relationship characterized by adversarial posturing from Dolan and a grudging mutual respect, even affection.

In *"A" Is for Alibi,* Kinsey describes Dolan as "in his late fifties with the aura of the unkempt: bags under his eyes, gray stubble or its illusion, a pouchy face, and hair that's been coated with some kind of men's product and combed across a shiny place on top" (10–11). Kinsey says, "I feel an ornery kind of kinship with him, which I never can quite identify. He's tough, emotionless, withdrawn, calculating, harsh. I've heard he's mean, too, but what I see in him is the overriding competence. He knows his business and he takes no guff and despite the fact he gives me a hard time whenever he can, I know he likes me, though grudgingly" (193). His success as an investigator, according to Kinsey, is based on "his powers of concentration" and his "clear and pitiless" memory. "Few people can outthink him" (11). Later Kinsey describes him as "smart, meticulous, tireless, and very shrewd." "He's a man I admire, though our relationship has had its antagonistic moments over the years" (*H* 5).

Lt. Dolan does not like private investigators as a breed, or women as a gender, but he too appreciates competence, and he sees that trait in Kinsey. "Believe it or not," he tells her, "I don't think you're a bad investigator. Young yet, and sometimes off the wall, but basically honest at any rate" (*A* 15). In that first report, Kinsey realizes that Dolan has actually fed her information, hoping she would be able to solve a case that had stymied him and his men eight years ago.

In addition to their professional relationship, Dolan belongs here in the friends category because of Kinsey's firm respect for him and because of his role as a stable entity in her life. He appears in or is referred to by characters in all the novels through *"L" Is for Lawless.* By *"M" Is for Malice,* he has retired from the police force.

Kinsey seems to prefer that Dolan stay within his designated role as gruff adversary. Whenever he moves outside those bounds—for example, when he asks her how she is recovering from the experience of killing a man—she feels distinctly uncomfortable (*B* 48–49). The question is too personal. In turn, Kinsey recognizes that he is uncomfortable with her when he shows up in her hospital room after the first bomb explosion in *"E" Is for Evidence.* It may be part of his job to question her about the bombing, but Kinsey sees that her unusually subdued manner after the event throws him for a loop. She is scared and quiet, and Dolan seems awkward in the face of her pain and fright. He doesn't know what to do or say to a Kinsey Millhone lacking her usual sassiness toward life and toward him.

Kinsey returns the hospital visit in *"K" Is for Killer* when Dolan has a heart attack and is in the cardiac care unit at St. Terry's Hospital. Kinsey hears the news from another policeman, Cheney Phillips, to whom she has gone for help with her case. "So startled" by the news that she almost knocks over her wine glass, Kinsey asks about his condition and vows, "I'll try to get over there first chance I have" (31). As genuinely concerned as she seems at the time, though, Kinsey does not go to the hospital to visit Dolan until she has "about four hours to kill" (70) before Cheney is scheduled to pick her up for a drive through the prostitutes' territory to search for a witness.

Two seemingly disparate things strike us about her visit: Kinsey is touched by the vulnerability so apparent in Dolan's thin stringy arms and overall frail appearance, and, in spite of that human sympathy, she conducts some business with him. Because Dolan was responsible for the original investigation of the Lorna Kepler death, Kinsey asks him if he will authorize her access to the photographs of the scene and body.

Does this leap to a business request mean that Kinsey is not humanely concerned about Dolan, or that there is not a spark of real

friendship connecting the two? No, more likely, both Kinsey and Dolan behave the way many of us do during hospital visits to friends or
relatives. The experience is a reminder of all human mortality (Kinsey recalls her aunt's death at St. Terry's) and helplessness in the face
of another person's illness. Most of us are tongue-tied, unsure about
what to say to patients stuck in inadequate hospital gowns and
propped up on accordion beds, surrounded by buzzers and dangling
equipment. Especially if the patients are friends, rather than family
members, we are unaccustomed to having them greet us from their
beds. To see them do so when they are incredibly vulnerable because
of an accident or disease is especially unnatural. When Kinsey and
Dolan turn away from forced chitchat and begin to talk police business, the entire conversation begins to feel comfortable to both of
them. It is their normal relationship.

Dolan returns to his work at the police department after his heart
attack. In the Epilogue, Kinsey reports that she told him the entire
truth about her part in the disappearance of Roger Bonney, but Dolan does not press any charges against her because Bonney's body is
never found. She, Dolan, and Cheney may *assume* that the Mafia guys
killed Bonney thanks to a tip from Kinsey, but there is no proof of
Bonney's death, much less Kinsey's part in it. Dolan clearly trusts her
enough—or likes her enough—to accept her account of events.

Dolan and Kinsey understand each other well. In *"H" Is for Homicide,* Dolan immediately recognizes that a colleague, Lt. Santos from
the LAPD, is taking the wrong approach to get Kinsey to work undercover for them in the Maldonado insurance-fraud ring. Santos is bullying and threatening. Dolan stops him and uses instead a rational
argument and an appeal to her friendship with one of the victims.
His approach works perfectly and Kinsey agrees to take the assignment.

There is little surprise, then, in Dolan's strong defense of her in
"L" Is for Lawless. When Kinsey's account of the story was doubted by
the Kentucky police, they placed a call to Dolan, who "spoke up in
my behalf and defended my somewhat sullied honor" (287) so persuasively that the Kentucky police reversed themselves and accepted
her story as valid. Kinsey also calls on Dolan for help in an instance
he never even learns about. In *"I" Is for Innocent,* Kinsey interviews
Curtis McIntyre in jail and he tries to hit on her. Nothing seems to

rebuff him. Finally, he asks if she has a boyfriend. She identifies Lt. Dolan in Homicide as her boyfriend and claims he is so jealous, "he'd rip your head right off your neck if he found out you were hustling me" (44). Curtis temporarily drops the macho posturing and Kinsey gets some answers to her questions.

In its place—as a professional relationship tinged with friendship—the relationship between Kinsey and Dolan is important to Kinsey. With his retirement in *"M" Is for Malice,* we don't know whether their contact will be maintained in some altered form.

Lonnie Kingman

Lonnie Kingman is Kinsey's attorney and landlord for her second office space.

After Kinsey's relationship with CF is terminated by Gordon Titus at the end of *"H" Is for Homicide,* she looks for new work and a new space for her office. Before the opening of *"I" Is for Innocent* she finds the space with the law firm of Kingman and Ives, located in the Kingman Building, which Lonnie owns, in downtown Santa Teresa. The rental arrangement is similar to the one she had with CF: she is an independent contractor who is given office space in exchange for being available to undertake occasional investigations for the law firm.

"Lonnie Kingman is in his early forties, five foot four, 205 pounds, a weight-lifting fanatic, perpetually pumped up on steroids [a rumor Kinsey denies in *Malice*], testosterone, vitamin B^{12}, and caffeine. He's got a shaggy head of dark hair, like a pony in the process of shedding a winter coat. His nose looks like it's been busted about as often as mine has" (*I* 3). "His speech is staccato and he's generally amped up on coffee, anxiety, or lack of sleep" (*M* 207). He has a BA from Harvard and an MBA from Columbia (*I* 4). He is a summa cum laude graduate of Stanford Law School (*E* 36) and he's married to a woman with a black belt in karate (*M* 207) whom he had successfully defended on an assault charge (*I* 141).

Lonnie's cases are as colorful as he is. "He's best known for his criminal defense work, but his passion is complex trials in any case involving accident injury or wrongful death" (*I* 4), which makes Kinsey's office rental a good business opportunity for both of them. Kinsey especially likes the new situation, because Lonnie gets "all the flashy cases" in Santa Teresa (4) and he screens out all the deadbeats before calling on Kinsey.

We first hear about Lonnie in *"E" Is for Evidence,* when Kinsey is accused of insurance fraud in an arson investigation. At that time she had done some investigative work for him and admired his skills, so he is the logical choice for her to employ on her own behalf. She hates having to call on any attorneys because they typically have only bad news to tell their clients. Lonnie does not disappoint her. He paints a dismal picture of the several ways she could be charged and sighs "like he was going to hate to see me in a shapeless prison dress" (36). He does, however, give her sound advice, which she follows and remembers gratefully.

Their later working and rental arrangement appears to be mutually beneficial. Kinsey's investigation in *"I" Is for Innocent* is triggered by Lonnie's hiring her to investigate one of his cases: Kenneth Voigt is pressing a wrongful death suit in civil court against David Barney for the murder of Isabelle Barney, David's wife and Kenneth's ex-wife. In spite of some difficulties, Kinsey solves the case for Lonnie, plus two other cases—the poisoning murder of the previous investigator hired by Lonnie and a hit-and-run—along the way.

As with Con Dolan, calling Lonnie a friend may be stretching the use of the word. Lonnie and Kinsey are business colleagues who respect each other's expertise. Lonnie is supremely confident about his own legal abilities. He is a workaholic who appreciates Kinsey's no-nonsense directness. In the middle of his elaborate explanation of the case in *Innocent,* Kinsey stops Lonnie and says, "Just tell me what you need and I'll go out and get it for you." Lonnie laughs, "This is why I like her. No bullshit" (12).

The four novels that follow refer to the continuation of the rental arrangement and Lonnie continues to be involved with Kinsey's work; in *"M" Is for Malice,* Kinsey asks Lonnie to see Jack Malek, who's been arrested for Guy's murder. Lonnie takes the case and immediately hires Kinsey to investigate Guy's murder and find the real killer, since it couldn't be his client. Their relationship is strong enough that when Paul Trasatti, someone she interviewed, calls Lonnie to complain about Kinsey's aggressive questioning and demand that she be removed from the case, Lonnie tells her, "Forget it. The guy's a prick. . . . I'll take care of him" (*M* 263).

Vera Lipton

Kinsey describes Vera Lipton as "probably as close to a best friend as I'll ever have," but, as always, Kinsey further qualifies her already qualified statement by adding, "though I don't really know what such a relationship entails" (*J* 120). Similarly, Kinsey tells Dietz that Vera is "the closest thing to a friend I've got and even then, I can't claim we know each other very well" (*G* 150). There's an important friendship there, but expressed in very tentative terms by Kinsey, who doesn't "socialize much" (150) and who trusts no relationship to be lasting.

Vera either appears, or is referred to, in most of the novels, although she is more prominent in the early books when Kinsey is still associated with CF, where Vera is employed, first as a claims adjuster, later as claims manager (*G*). Understandably, the two women see more of each other then. After Kinsey leaves CF, they have to work at maintaining their "catch as catch can" friendship, planning such shared activities as taking a Spanish course together at the local community college (*J* 11, 120–22). Gone are the casual opportunities to talk that were available when Kinsey worked out of the same building.

In *"A" Is for Alibi*, Vera is simply referred to as one of the claims adjusters at CF, but by *"B" Is for Burglar*, we see Kinsey going out of her way to drop by Vera's cubicle, perhaps for some business information, but also just to talk. Vera is "thirty-six, single, and she collects men with ease, though none of them seems to suit her" (*B* 67). About men, Vera says, "I figure guys are like Whitman's Samplers. I like to take a little bite out of each and then move on before the whole box gets stale" (71). Kinsey is intrigued by "the air of total confidence she exudes" (*G* 20)—she smokes like a fiend (until *Gumshoe*, when she quits cold turkey), drinks Cokes all the time, dyes her hair a different color each month, and, in general, drives men crazy. "Her glasses today had tortoiseshell rims and big round lenses tinted the color of iced tea. She wore glasses so well it made other women wish their eyesight would fail" (*B* 68). "I do admire her. She's smart. She's got style. She doesn't take any guff" (*G* 151).

By the time of *"G" Is for Gumshoe* and *"H" Is for Homicide,* the chats have developed into a real friendship. Their conversations are full of the teasing jabs only close friends can give each other. Stopping by Vera's desk, Kinsey offers to treat her to dinner, but she refuses, saying, "I don't *want* a Quarter Pounder with cheese" (*H* 14). Like Rosie, Vera wants Kinsey to get a new dress and she offers to go shopping with her to prevent her from buying the dress at K Mart.

Vera knows all about the affair between Kinsey and Jonah. She thinks it is high time Kinsey moved on to someone who is available, instead of a married man who will never leave his wife. (Kinsey observes, "People like to take charge of my personal life. Many seem to feel I don't do things right," *H* 14.) So Vera offers Kinsey one of her discards, a good-looking physician named Neil Hess. Knowing that Vera miraculously manages to stay friends with all her lovers, Kinsey is willing to consider this referral if Vera will tell her why she doesn't want him. Vera says he's too short for her: she's five nine and Neil is only five four. Kinsey thinks this is a ridiculous reason to dump an otherwise great guy, but she lets herself be set up to meet Neil at a CF retirement dinner.

Vera doesn't trust Kinsey's fashion sense for two seconds. (She considers Kinsey "a complete fashion nerd," *J* 73.) For the dinner Vera brings one of her own outfits for Kinsey to wear, alters it to fit Kinsey perfectly, and does Kinsey's makeup herself. Kinsey looks smashing in the black silk jumpsuit and she meets Neil with an open mind. He turns out to be a genuinely nice guy, but there is no chemistry between the two of them. She notices how his face brightens whenever he looks at Vera. Naughty Kinsey can't resist temptation. She tells Neil that Vera is "completely smitten with you. She just hasn't figured it out yet" (*G* 163).

The next day, in the ladies' room at CF, Vera is more distraught than Kinsey has ever seen her. She is furious with Kinsey: "I don't appreciate the crap you told Neil last night" (204). And she bursts into tears. Kinsey finally gets the story out of her. It turns out Vera surprised herself by becoming livid with jealousy when she saw Neil appear to be interested in Kinsey, so she drank too much. When Kinsey and Dietz left the banquet, Neil came over to Vera and, instead of being interested in Kinsey, he told her what Kinsey had said, and then he *proposed* to her. They rushed up to Vera's room in the hotel.

They were so eager that they didn't even reach the bed for their lovemaking. Neil was absolutely horrified when the maid walked in on them *"grappling* on the floor'' (206)—and the maid turned out to be one of his patients.

Kinsey is so tickled by the story that she almost pees in her pants. Over the cubicle walls she tries to convince Vera that she certainly should marry Neil. They're perfect for each other. Forget the stupid two inch—Vera had exaggerated it into five—difference in their heights. Vera seems somewhat reassured by Kinsey's words and her surprisingly maternal pats on the back.

In *"H" Is for Homicide,* Vera and Neil get married. On Halloween. With Kinsey as the sole bridesmaid. Wearing her all-purpose black dress, in spite of Vera's determination to get her into a new dress. As Kinsey would say, what a hoot.

The marriage seems to agree with Vera. We don't see her in *"I" Is for Innocent;* Kinsey just refers to not having seen her since the wedding. But we do see her in *"J" Is for Judgment* at the Spanish class, and she looks great. Since getting married, she has stopped dyeing her hair and it is now "a honeyed brown" (121). She and Neil have been working out together and she has dropped fifteen pounds from her generous build, always a good move as far as Kinsey is concerned. She's still dressing in her flashy aviator suits and is as irrepressible as ever.

Vera is an appealing character, and we hope she does not drift out of Kinsey's life completely, but that seems to be a distinct possibility. At the end of *"L" Is for Lawless,* we find Kinsey thinking of Vera as one of the few people (after Henry and Rosie) she can call for help, but there is no answer when she does. Kinsey speculates that Vera must be on vacation with Neil. But we haven't seen her throughout the novel, and she is not mentioned at all in *"M" Is for Malice.*

Darcy Pascoe

Darcy Pascoe is a secretary/receptionist at California Fidelity who appears in a limited role in *Evidence, Gumshoe, Homicide,* and *Malice.* Distinctly not a friend at first, Darcy becomes closer to Kinsey when they work together on an investigation, although they never bond to the extent of Vera and Kinsey.

In *"E" Is for Evidence,* Kinsey is suspended from her work at CF because she is accused of taking money to falsify records in an arson case. Becoming her own client, she must find out who is framing her and why. She realizes that the frame was probably arranged from within California Fidelity itself. She considers and rejects several possibilities before settling on Andy Motycka, the claims manager, a slimeball who dislikes her as much as she dislikes him, as the most likely suspect. In order to search his home and his office, Kinsey solicits the help of Darcy.

Kinsey approaches Darcy at a diner near the office and just about spoils Darcy's meal. Kinsey describes Darcy as having "baby-fine hair that defies styling, a high, bulging forehead, pale-blue eyes. Her skin is milky white and translucent, with a tracery of veins showing through like faded laundry marks" (51). Darcy behaves just as prissily as her description leads us to expect. She has been told not to talk to Kinsey during her suspension, but Darcy and Kinsey have never hit it off anyway. She tries in vain to escape to another table, but Kinsey is relentless. Darcy is stunned by Kinsey's direct request for help. "You don't even like me," Darcy protests. Kinsey replies, "You don't like me either. What's that got to do with it? We both hate Andy. *That's* the point" (53).

In the process of spying on Andy together, Darcy and Kinsey become cordial, even friendly. Kinsey always responds to competence in others, and Darcy proves to be very good at finding out information about Andy's home life, searching his office, and even talking to Kinsey in code while Mac Voorhies is standing right by her desk. Kinsey's growing respect for Darcy's skill is mirrored by Darcy's growing appreciation of Kinsey's gutsiness and drive. And they discover they have things in common. For example, they laugh heartily together at the drafts of graphic love letters that Kinsey finds during a search of Andy's apartment.

Darcy's increasing pleasure in working on the case with Kinsey means we are not surprised that by *"G" Is for Gumshoe,* Kinsey says of her: "She had helped me on a couple of cases and was thinking about changing fields. I thought she'd be a good investigator and I was encouraging her" (20). Darcy, a literature major at the University of Nevada, Las Vegas, appears later in the novel and gives Kinsey a vital clue by telling her that the name "Agnes Grey" was the title of a novel by Anne Brontë (207), but the plot line of Kinsey as mentor to Darcy the Detective is not pursued further.

By *"M" Is for Malice,* Darcy is still working at CF, where she is now readily assisting Kinsey. Unable to get information quickly from the Division of Motor Vehicles about Guy Malek's driver's license or address, Kinsey asks Darcy to use the resources of the insurance company to help her out. In less than a day, Darcy obtains Guy's home address. The two women banter over the phone and sign off, swearing to have lunch soon. Kinsey later protects Darcy, who bent a few rules to get the information, by not telling anyone how she obtained the data. There is enough friendship for each woman to take risks to help the other.

Ida Ruth

Ida Ruth is Lonnie Kingman's secretary in the law firm of Kingman and Ives. She is another figure with whom Kinsey has a cordial and friendly relationship based on proximity at work. *"I" Is for Innocent* begins Kinsey's arrangement with Kingman and Ives, and it's there that we first hear about Ida Ruth. She never figures significantly in the action of a novel.

One of the reasons Kinsey likes the new office arrangement is that there are people with whom she can touch base during the tough cases. She likes having "people who were aware of my whereabouts, and I could check in with them if I needed any mothering" (*J* 2–3). Ida Ruth is the primary figure to whom she turns for supportive human contact.

Ida Ruth is "thirty-five and unmarried, a robust vegetarian, with windswept blond hair and brows bleached by the sun. Her cheekbones are wide, her ruddy complexion unsoftened by makeup. While she's always dressed well, she looks like she'd prefer wearing flannel shirts, chinos, and hiking boots" (*I* 22).

The differences between the two women go beyond Ida Ruth's vegetarianism vs. Kinsey's preference for Quarter Pounders, or Ida Ruth's inclination to wear official "straight medium-length skirts, boxy jackets in muted tones," and "a boring succession of . . . long-sleeved, button-down" blouses versus Kinsey's casual turtlenecks and jeans. The real difference between the two women is huge: Ida Ruth actually *likes* one of Kinsey's Top Ten Phobias, the out-of-doors. Kinsey says, "She looks like she'd prefer to be paddling a kayak or climbing the face of a rock in some national park. I've heard that in her spare time she does precisely that—backpacking trips to the High Sierras, fifteen-mile hikes in the local mountain range" (*J* 43). Kinsey is both astonished and impressed by the nerve of this woman. "She's undeterred by ticks, steep inclines, venomous snakes, poison oak, sticks, sharp rocks, mosquitoes, or any of the other joyous aspects of nature I avoid at all costs" (*J* 43).

As always, Kinsey admires competence and skill in others. Though she would never dream of attempting to scale the face of a cliff herself, she admires Ida Ruth's ability to do so. At the same time, she is genuinely puzzled why anyone would *want* to do it. In turn, Ida Ruth finds Kinsey an interesting specimen, brave and daring, but also in need of some serious mothering about the daily minutiae of life. Like Rosie and Vera, Ida Ruth seems to feel that Kinsey is someone she should look after. When Kinsey returns from Mexico in *"J" Is for Judgment,* Ida Ruth asks about Kinsey's fading tan-from-a-bottle (part of her disguise as a tourist), gives her vitamin C tablets to take for her cold, and wants to know why she didn't go to the famous ruins near Viento Negro.

The relationship is cordial, but it is not developed beyond warm, casual conversations at Ida Ruth's desk.

Mac Voorhies

Maclin Voorhies, one of the vice presidents at California Fidelity, is Kinsey's boss from the time she starts at CF until she is fired. He figures prominently in two novels: *"E" Is for Evidence* and *"J" Is for Judgment.*

Kinsey calls Mac "lean and humorless, with sparse, flyaway white hair and a perpetual cigar clamped between his teeth. He's smart and fair-minded, honorable, conservative, ill-tempered sometimes, but a very capable executive" (*G* 163). He is in his sixties, married to Marie, and they have eight grown children, "all of them married with countless children of their own" (*J* 6).

As an independent contractor, Kinsey is given specific jobs by Mac, usually involving arson or wrongful death, and she reports her results directly to him. The first novel in which Mac plays a significant part is *"E" Is for Evidence,* when he asks Kinsey to look into a burned warehouse at "Wood/Warren, a local company manufacturing hydrogen furnaces for industrial use" (2). Trouble starts before Kinsey can complete her report. Mac calls her into his office and catches her completely off-guard by saying her preliminary report contradicts the police report and he has received a phone call suggesting that she is "on the take" (29). Kinsey is suspended until the Wood/Warren matter can be cleared up.

Kinsey is dismayed that Mac doesn't know she would never do something like this. He seems prepared to believe her claim of a frame-up, but he will do nothing to stand up for her to his colleagues. To try to make up for any inadequacies in their treatment of Kinsey, Mac later persuades the company to refurbish Kinsey's office when she is reinstated at the end of *"E" Is for Evidence.* In her typically generous way, Kinsey seems to think that Mac did what he had to do and she holds no grudges.

In *"G" Is for Gumshoe,* Mac appears only to speak at a CF retirement dinner at the Edgewater Hotel. By the time *"H" Is for Homicide* begins, CF has brought in Gordon Titus, "an 'efficiency expert' from the Palm Springs office . . . to bolster profits" (1). Titus quickly earns the epithet "s.o.b. extraordinaire" from Kinsey (1), an opinion widely shared throughout the company. Kinsey's independent status, her arrangement of conducting a number of investigations per month in exchange for her office, plus, let's face it, Kinsey's refusal to be cowed by him—all these "problems" are neatly eliminated when, at the end of the novel, he fires Kinsey, primarily for what she sees as a failure to kiss ass. Again, Mac, who seems to have learned the technique of puckering up, appears unable to help Kinsey.

To Kinsey's surprise, Mac appears at her new office at Kingman and Ives in the beginning of *"J" Is for Judgment* to hire her for an investigation. Kinsey is so happy to see him that she rushes up to him and hugs him. But Mac has changed since she last saw him, and she is saddened by what she sees as the loss of his former "spark," "a passion for getting the job done right". He seems "tired and uncertain, which was completely uncharacteristic" (5). He is even considering retirement, because, as he puts it, "They're taking all the fun out of the job" (5). He misses the old sense of CF as a family. Instead, the new executives now focus only on the bottom line, rapid turnover, and cost containment. Mac says he would like to close his career with this big case he wants Kinsey to handle. Someone thinks he has spotted Wendell Jaffe, a man alleged to have committed suicide five years ago and for whom CF has just paid the presumed widow half a million dollars. Retrieving that money would make a nice conclusion to Mac's career. He assures Kinsey he will take care of any objections from Titus.

Sadly, Mac lets Kinsey—and himself—down.

Kinsey locates Wendell, only to lose him, and she suspects he has been murdered. Gordon Titus sends for Kinsey. It's the first time they've met since he fired her and she's interested to see that he chooses to ignore their last encounter. She also understands the implication behind Titus's occupying Mac's chair in his old office, while Mac sits in one of the visitors' chairs. When Titus hands Kinsey a check for a "final payment" (261), she objects because she doesn't consider the case closed. Wendell's boat has been found, empty, and she has good reason to think he has been killed. Don't they want her to pursue this investigation to its conclusion? Apparently not. As Titus points out, all she needed to do was prove that Wendell was alive when the so-called widow collected his insurance. She proved this, and the insurance company can now reclaim the money. If it turns out that Wendell is really dead now, the widow can always refile her claim. "But aren't we in business to see that claims are settled fairly?" Kinsey cries. "Isn't anybody interested in the truth?" (262).

Kinsey looks from one man to the other. Titus's face is calculatedly blank. "Mac's expression was tinged with guilt. He was never going to stand up to Gordon Titus. He was never going to complain. He was never going to take a stand" (262). Titus offers a final sarcastic jab to Kinsey and leaves Mac to tidy up the scene. "After he left, Mac and I sat in silence for a moment, not looking at each other. Then I got up and walked out myself" (262).

Mac's lack of moral courage is the death knell to any friendship between Kinsey and him. Kinsey responds to competence—of any kind—as well as to courage and strength. She is amazingly generous about frailties or eccentricities in others if they have that strong center. She excused Mac as long as she could, but his moral flabbiness and cowardice are finally undeniable. She does not berate him for this. She just has nothing else to say to him. Then, or ever.

Significant Friends Appearing in a Single Novel

Bobby Callahan

In *"C" Is for Corpse,* the friendship between Bobby Callahan and Kinsey lasts all of four days before Bobby is killed. The briefness of the time does not reflect the depth of the bond between these two fighters.

Kinsey meets Bobby at Santa Teresa Fitness, "a real no-nonsense place: the brand X of health clubs" (2), where they are both working out regularly in order to recover from severe injuries. Kinsey has only a broken arm, an unpleasant residue from the conclusion of her previous case, but Bobby's injuries are more extensive. "He was probably just short of six feet tall, with a football player's physique: big head, thick neck, brawny shoulders, heavy legs. Now the shaggy blond head was held to one side, the left half of his face pulled down in a permanent grimace. His mouth leaked saliva as though he'd just been shot up with Novocain and couldn't quite feel his own lips. . . . There was a terrible welt of dark red across the bridge of his nose, a second across his chest, and his knees were crisscrossed with scars as though a swordsman had slashed at him. He walked with a lilting gait, his left Achilles tendon apparently shortened, pulling his left heel up" (2).

Bobby's determination and courage are what draws Kinsey to him. "Working out must have cost him everything he had, yet he never failed to appear. There was a doggedness about him that I admired" (2). She watches him work on the machines, somewhat ashamed of her own complaints about her own recoverable problems in contrast to his more debilitating, probably permanent, injuries. Always curious, Kinsey is interested in the story behind the scars and impressed by his bravery.

One Monday morning they have the gym to themselves. While

Kinsey watches Bobby on the leg-curl machine, he strikes up a conversation, asking her if she is a private detective. He wants to hire her to find out who tried to kill him by running him off the road nine months before. Everyone else thinks it was an accident, but he is convinced otherwise. "He held his hand out and we shook, sealing an unspoken bargain. I knew even then I'd work for him whatever the circumstances" (4). His case is the basis for the novel.

Kinsey learns that Bobby is convinced someone tried to kill him because of something he knew, but the injuries have taken away much of his memory, and now he doesn't know the reason for the attack. He wants Kinsey to figure out what he knew at the time and find the person who tried to kill him.

Kinsey begins work on the case promptly, starting with a visit to Bobby's home in order to meet his family. She gets Bobby to go with her to the site of the crash. Kinsey doesn't get any sudden insights there, but she's glad they went because "I'd seen the miry pit into which he had been flung and I'd felt the bond between us strengthened" (65). The two of them have faced and survived catastrophic losses that would have felled many people.

Bobby and Kinsey can talk openly and honestly to each other. If Kinsey responds to Bobby's bravery, he responds to her acceptance of him as a person rather than an object of pity. At one point, Bobby tells Kinsey, "When I'm with you, I don't feel self-conscious or like I'm crippled or ugly. I don't know how you do that, but it's nice." Feeling "oddly self-conscious" herself, Kinsey replies, "You remind me of a birthday present somebody's sent through the mail. The paper's torn and the box is damaged, but there's still something terrific in there. I enjoy your company" (66).

Just as their friendship becomes a solid bond and Kinsey's investigation begins to stir things up, she is stunned to receive a phone call from Bobby's stepfather, Derek Wenner, telling her that Bobby is dead. A second car crash has proved fatal. The bad-news phone call awakening one in the middle of the night is everyone's nightmare. Kinsey reacts with the typical human response: it can't be true. She just saw him. They are friends. She's making progress on his case. "No way. Nuh-un. How could Bobby be gone? Not true" (99). We share her disbelief. We have liked and respected Bobby. How can he be a character who's killed? It's not fair.

Albanil Street (Mason
Street in Santa Barbara)
(Carol McGinnis Kay)

Kinsey's first office, at
907 State Street
(Carol McGinnis Kay)

Kinsey's second office, on Capillo (210 Carillo Street in Santa Barbara)
(Carol McGinnis Kay)

Santa Teresa Courthouse viewed from the sunken garden at the rear
(Carol McGinnis Kay)

The marina breakwater *(Carol McGinnis Kay)*

Entrance to the Edgewater Hotel (Four Seasons Biltmore in Santa Barbara)
(Carol McGinnis Kay)

The public library *(Carter Blackmar)*

Kinsey's car in front of the police station *(Carter Blackmar)*

The police station *(Carter Blackmar)*

The jogging path *(Carter Blackmar)*

Kinsey does the only things she can do for her deceased friend. She helps Bobby's mother, Glen, cope with his death, she attends Bobby's funeral, and she finds out the identity of his killer. Doggedly pursuing things even after her client's death, which has been falsely reported as the consequence of a stroke, she solves the case, types up her findings as if they were a report to Bobby, and returns the unused portion of his advance to his attorney "to be factored into his estate. The rest of the report is a personal letter. Much of my last message to Bobby is devoted to the simple fact that I miss him" (243).

So do we.

Bibianna Diaz

Bibianna Diaz is a suspect who becomes a friend, of sorts, in *"H" Is for Homicide*. Kinsey is given her name and CFI claim file early in the novel, because her file was flagged as needing investigation.

Kinsey sets up a chance meeting with Bibianna at the Meat Locker, a rowdy bar. Bibianna, with her long dark hair, smooth olive skin, and low-cut tight fitting red dress "pulled taut across the flat belly, slim hips, and trim thighs" (53), just about has to beat guys away with a stick. She has a warm easy manner with everyone, including Kinsey. The conversation, drink, and food with Bibianna and her boyfriend, Jimmy Tate, give Kinsey a good start on investigating the legitimacy of Bibianna's car accident claim against CF, but the night suddenly turns ugly when Bibianna is kidnapped by people working for her old boss and boyfriend, Raymond Maldonado. There is a gunfight in the street and Jimmy kills Maldonado's brother. Bibianna, Jimmy, and Kinsey are arrested and jailed.

Because Kinsey has established a relationship with Bibianna by their being arrested and jailed together, "a form of female bonding not commonly recognized" (*H* 99), she is asked by the Santa Teresa and Los Angeles Police Departments to work undercover to investigate Maldonado's insurance-fraud ring. She reluctantly agrees and accompanies Bibianna when she is picked up from jail by Maldonado and his men the next morning. For the remainder of the novel, the two women are prisoners of Raymond Maldonado in his apartment in Los Angeles.

Shared danger brings the women together. So do some shared

traits. Kinsey likes Bibianna's courage in standing up to Raymond and her intelligence in handling his difficult personality. Bibianna responds to the same self-confident strengths in Kinsey, and she appreciates her willingness to take personal risks to help her in a tough spot. They come to sound like old friends, exchanging whispered confidences when they can and planning ways to circumvent Raymond's craziness. Bibianna even gives Kinsey some of her clothes to wear—full colorful skirts and peasant blouses that sound very un-Kinseyesque, but Kinsey is in no position to complain.

Kinsey comes to have such respect for Bibianna's gutsiness in trying to escape from Raymond that she takes an enormous personal risk, at least partially on her behalf, at the end of the novel. Bibianna flees in one of Raymond's cars and he responds by sending a henchman to kill her by running her off the road. When he almost succeeds, Bibianna is hospitalized with serious injuries. Raymond comes to the hospital and goes berserk when he learns that Jimmy Tate and Bibianna are married. He shoots at Jimmy. Kinsey chases Raymond out of the hospital, almost shooting him in retaliation for his actions against Bibianna and Jimmy. She is prevented only by the timely arrival of another undercover cop.

Respect, trust, affection, willingness to take risks on behalf of the other person—all the essentials of friendship are here in the brief relationship between Kinsey and Bibianna.

Guy Malek

Kinsey's relationship with Guy Malek echoes her relationship with Bobby Callahan. Both are men who are considered by others to be maimed, Bobby physically and Guy morally. Kinsey sees the reality of the person behind the scars or the old bad-boy reputation. With both, Kinsey forms a warm friendship based on mutual respect; both are killed midway through their novels, *"C" Is for Corpse* and *"M" Is for Malice*. The two books end with Kinsey saying farewell to men she liked and admired and will miss.

Guy is one of four sons in the wealthy Malek family, the black sheep who left home eighteen years before at the age of twenty-six and has not been heard from since. At the opening of *"M" Is for Malice*, Kinsey's cousin Tasha hires her to locate Guy, who stands to inherit one-quarter of the $40 million estate left by his recently deceased father, Bader.

Having been told about all the scrapes—some pranks and some more serious—Guy had gotten into as a kid, Kinsey is startled by his appearance once she tracks him down in Marcella, California. He looks younger, healthier, and more gentle than she had expected. "Now his good angel had apparently taken up residence, bestowing on his countenance the look of serenity. . . . Already, I liked this man better than his siblings" (59).

Guy has turned his life around, thanks to the firm encouragement of Peter Antle, the pastor of Jubilee Evangelical Church, and his wife, Winnie, who picked up Guy hitchhiking on the day he left home eighteen years earlier. They helped Guy to find the moral compass he says he never had at home, and they helped him back on his feet through several drug episodes. He now works as a janitor and handyman for the church and for anyone in the small town of Marcella who needs assistance, and he hasn't touched drugs or hard liquor for fifteen years. Kinsey's usual distrust of organized religion is countered by the genuineness of Guy, Peter, and Winnie. Although she remains leery that one of them may suddenly give in to an impulse to convert her, she accepts the apparent goodness of all three people.

As always, Kinsey admires strength in others, and she sees much of it in Guy. In turn, Guy sees Kinsey as a kindred soul when he learns that she too was "a screwup" at Santa Teresa High before turning her own life around (67). Their friendship is immediate and important to both of them.

When Donovan, the eldest Malek son, invites Guy to come back home to talk, Guy asks Kinsey's advice. Her strong counsel is not to go. Get an attorney to handle everything, she urges. She knows that all three brothers resent the idea that Guy will inherit equally. She has seen them drunk and belligerent and she considers Guy, who is sweet and naive in comparison with his brothers, to be unprepared to withstand their onslaught. Guy, however, feels he should settle old grievances and he longs to be part of a family.

The family reunion is emotionally brutal for Guy, who soon asks Kinsey to meet him for a brief respite of sane conversation in her car outside the estate one night. There is a hint of sexual attraction between the two of them, and later Kinsey finds a letter left in the car by

Guy, which asks her to take a trip to Disneyland with him after all this is over—he says they both need a little silliness in their lives. She says she would "have accepted in a flash" (268), but, shockingly, Guy is killed that night.

Had Guy lived, would the relationship have developed romantically? Kinsey thinks it unlikely. "Kinsey Millhone and a born-again was probably not a combination that would have gone anywhere. But we might have been friends. We might have gone to Disneyland once a year to experience some silliness" (268). The power of the attachment that already exists is evidenced in several ways. Kinsey is stunned and outraged by his murder, and she swears to find out who killed him whether anyone hires her or not. One of the reasons Kinsey makes love so passionately with Dietz that night is that she is thinking of Guy (and unsure about which man she is betraying in the process). When she returns to the Malek house, there is some kind of presence, which Kinsey keeps denying is Guy's ghost, dismissing it as "woo-woo stuff" even as it almost takes her breath away (284). And in the Epilogue, Kinsey tells us about Guy returning to her in a dream to say good-bye. This is all a bit more irrational and emotional from Kinsey than we are accustomed to and it attests to the closeness of these two people.

Cheney Phillips

Lt. Cheney Phillips, recently moved from Homicide to Vice in the Santa Teresa Police Department, assists Kinsey in *"K" Is for Killer*. They discover ideas and feelings in common and establish a brief friendship.

"Cheney was probably in his early thirties: a white guy with a disheveled mop of dark curly hair, dark eyes, good chin, prickly two-day growth of beard. His was the sort of face you might see in a men's fashion magazine or the society section of the local papers, escorting some debutante decked out like a bride. He was slim, of medium height, wearing a tobacco-brown silk sport coat over a white dress shirt, his pants a pleated cream-colored gabardine" (27–28). Everything about Cheney suggests old money and a privileged background to Kinsey. Given her usual distaste for the rich, we may be a little surprised to see how willing Kinsey is to like Cheney.

Part of her willingness may be explained by the open way in which he helps her with the investigation of Lorna's death, but it's probably more important that they both have problematic families. And they feel the same way about them. Cheney is from great wealth, but his father has neglected him all his life. Kinsey tells Cheney about her newly discovered family in Lompoc, who ignored her for thirty years and now want to make contact. They laughingly agree that they are both cynical about their families and want to stay as far away from them as possible (81–82). From this beginning, a friendship grows throughout the novel.

Thus far, the friendship is not explored further. One might argue that Cheney's refusal to arrest Bonney halted the friendship, but there is no indication that Kinsey considered his action the end of their relationship.

Danielle Rivers

A strong friendship unexpectedly develops between Kinsey and Danielle Rivers, a sex-worker interviewed by Kinsey in *"K" Is for Killer.*

Kinsey meets Danielle through Lt. Cheney Phillips, who knows that Danielle was a friend of Lorna Kepler, the subject of Kinsey's murder investigation. At first she sees Danielle only as a "little twerp" (85), "probably in her late teens . . . [with] dark hair long enough to sit on and long legs that seemed to go on forever . . . slim hips, a flat belly, and the breasts of early adolescence. . . . She was wearing lime-green satin hot pants and a halter top with a lime-green bomber jacket over it" (84). Her nails are bitten to the quick, and she is sullen and rude.

But connections are quickly made. Danielle is feisty, funny, and strong—she even sounds like a streetwise version of Kinsey's aunt: "you got money, you're independent. You can do anything you want. Some guy mistreats you, you get the fuck out. You can walk. Know what I'm saying?" Kinsey does. "That's my philosophy," she says (88). To their mutual amazement, their lives are a lot alike—they're both in unconventional dangerous jobs, they've both had their noses broken on the job, they both like independence, their success depends on their ability to read people and to keep their mouths shut, they both work by the hour, and so on. But there is one big difference they discover—Kinsey's income last year was $25,000, while Danielle's was more than double that at $52,000. (Danielle's coworker, Lorna, typically had an annual income of over $200,000.) To Kinsey's great amusement, the younger woman counsels her to change her career to one that pays more and specifically recommends hooking.

Danielle next does something very unusual in the Grafton novels: she visits Kinsey at her apartment. The two women spend the evening together, sounding like a couple of old high school buddies—they even order pizza, and Danielle persuades Kinsey to let her cut her hair. Unfortunately, this warm visit is soon followed by Danielle's being beaten so severely that she is hospitalized.

Kinsey visits her at St. Terry's. She is furious with the unknown assailant and appalled by the extent of Danielle's injuries. Unable to take any action against the assailant, Kinsey does the only thing she knows to be helpful. She goes to clean up Danielle's blood-soaked apartment. Considering the extent of the damage and the blood, this proves to be quite a chore, but Kinsey thinks it is important for Danielle not to come home to a mess. The homecoming does not happen because Danielle dies. The depth of Kinsey's feeling for her new friend is evidenced in her act of revenge for Danielle's murder.

Lovers and Ex-husbands

Kinsey is sexually attracted to a number of men: Jonah Robb, Robert Dietz, several she interviews, and, disturbingly, even her would-be killers, Charlie Scorsoni, Mark Messinger, and Roger Bonney. During the course of the novels, she has three lovers (plus, one of her ex-husbands also reappears briefly). As good as the sex is, none of the men becomes a daily fixture in her life, at least not for more than a few months. The word "love" and the associated interdependence it implies are not stressed in Kinsey's accounts of these relationships. The bond might deserve that label in at least a couple of instances, but Kinsey shies away from the confinement of such definitions.

Kinsey's sense of humor is nowhere more keen than when she observes the sexual side of the human equation. "I'm always startled at what fools men and women make of themselves in the pursuit of sex" (*C* 71). Including herself in that observation, she typically expresses her attraction to a man with a self-deprecating laugh. She looks at Brian Jaffe, stretched out on a motel bed, and wryly observes, "I wondered if I was reaching an age where all young boys with hard bodies would seem sexual to me. I wondered if I'd been that age all my life" (*J* 238).

Kinsey can be very funny about other people having sex. Witness the scene in *"G" Is for Gumshoe* in which Kinsey can't sleep because of the noises from the motel room next door. A drunk couple arrives at one a.m.; the bed starts thumping immediately, almost knocking a picture of a moose off Kinsey's wall. Noisy couplings ("she uttered a little yelp of astonishment, but I couldn't tell if she came or fell off the bed") alternate with the smoke of postcoital cigarettes seeping through the walls for the rest of the night. The noise ultimately drives Kinsey to try for some quiet by stuffing her bra with rolled-up socks to create earmuffs. "I lay there, a cone over each ear like an alien, wondering at the peculiarities of human sex practices. I would have much to report when I returned to my planet" (68).

Kinsey is cautious about acting on her own attraction to a man. As she phrases it, "After two unsuccessful marriages, I find myself keeping my guard up, along with my underpants" (*C* 13). "About every six or eight months, I run into a man who astounds me sexually, but between escapades I'm celibate, which I don't think is any big deal" (13).

Who are these men who "astound" Kinsey "sexually"?

Robert Dietz

Only a voice on the phone in *"A" Is for Alibi*, Robert Dietz becomes a major figure in *"G" Is for Gumshoe* and *"M" Is for Malice*. He is a fellow private investigator, from Carson City, Nevada, who helps Kinsey in the first novel by locating Sharon Napier in Nevada. In *Gumshoe*, Kinsey hires him as her bodyguard when she is the target of a hit man. Dietz moves into her apartment, drives her everywhere because her car has been totaled, and, because he is constantly at her side, assists with her case. The two eventually fall into bed, perhaps into love.

In *"G" Is for Gumshoe,* after she's been run off the road, Kinsey calls Dietz from her hospital bed to hire him. She wakes up to find him "leaning against the wall, arms folded across his chest. Dietz. Late forties. Five ten, maybe 170, in jeans, cowboy boots, and a tweed sport coat with a blue toothbrush protruding from the breast pocket like a ballpoint pen. He was clean-shaven, his hair medium length and showing gray around the ears. He was watching me with expressionless gray eyes. 'I'm Dietz.' Husky voice in the middle range" (84).

Kinsey and Dietz begin to exchange information about themselves simply because they will be working together. These conversations—in the car and over meals—sound more like first date exchanges about family background and personal interests than plans to keep a hit man away from the apartment.

Compared to her reactions to the other men in her life, Kinsey seems slow in recognizing what a perfect match the two of them are. Dietz's laconic, cool competence is much like Kinsey's laconic, cool competence, perhaps a touch harder and certainly more restless, but clearly made from the same mold. They are both tough, shrewd, brave, independent, and constantly testing themselves. They both had unorthodox childhoods, Dietz having been brought up essentially by his granny in the back seat of the family van as his brawling father moved them from town to town. They both disliked school. Even their idea of packing is identical: grab the toothbrush first.

We see the kinship as early as the drive back to Kinsey's apartment from the hospital in Brawley, when Dietz starts to light a cigarette and asks if it will bother Kinsey. She replies, "Probably," and Dietz tosses the lighter and the pack of cigarettes out the window.

> I stared at him, laughing uncomfortably. "What are you *doing*?"
> "I quit smoking."
> "Just like that?"
> He said, "I can do anything."
> It sounded like bragging, but I could tell he was serious.
> We drove ten miles before either of us said another word (88).

We see the appropriateness of the match even more when they arrive at Kinsey's apartment and she compares the looks of Dietz and

Henry Pitts. Henry is her touchstone for judging men. They are not alike (Henry's lean asceticism is contrasted by Dietz's compact, muscular, brazen energy), but the fact that Kinsey considers them together, both here and later in *"M" Is for Malice*, is significant in signaling Dietz's importance.

Kinsey adjusts to having Dietz around all the time better than she, or the reader, expects. (In fact, some readers may be dismayed by Kinsey's dependence on Dietz for protection and for emotional pats on the back in this novel, but she *is* being pursued by a killer. That gives her a pretty legitimate excuse for being willing to accept help.) Dietz insists that she buy a better gun, insists that she join him for some serious target practice in order to regain her confidence, makes her temporarily suspend her jogging, and accompanies her on her current case involving the search for elderly Agnes Grey.

Halfway into the novel, on the evening Kinsey and Dietz evade the hit man at the Edgewater Hotel, Kinsey is called to the hospital. There she and Dietz learn that Agnes Grey has died. As Agnes' daughter, Irene Gersh, sobs in her husband's arms, Kinsey and Dietz suddenly make eye contact. "I saw Dietz through the open doorway, leaning against the wall. His posture was identical to my first sight of him. Cowboy boots, his tweed coat. . . . His gaze moved casually to mine, moved to Irene, came back to mine and held. The look in his eyes was quizzical, perplexed. . . . I felt an unexpected flash of heat. I broke off eye contact, feeling flushed. My gaze drifted back. He was still looking at me, with a wistfulness I hadn't seen before" (174–75).

Finally, the sexual attraction between them—about which only Kinsey has seemed to be unaware—is acted upon. The two return to Kinsey's apartment where they move into each other's arms and up the spiral staircase to the loft. "All the danger, all the tension had been converted into this mute longing" that is "humankind's only antidote to death" (178).

Their lovemaking is intense, and Dietz stays with Kinsey past the time of his employment as her bodyguard. Dietz has been a private eye for ten years and is now bored with the "cerebral" side of it, the endless paperwork, which his partner used to do. Like Kinsey, he prefers the physical side of detection, the toying with danger. His partner's death ten months ago has caused Dietz to rethink his career. Following his job for Kinsey, he stays for a few months until a job he's been waiting for materializes in Germany, where he will be setting up antiterrorist training programs.

In the next two novels, Kinsey will worry if she should have gone with Dietz, as he urged her to do; she will wonder what he is doing and regret they are both too cheap to telephone each other very often. "The hard part about love [there, she finally said it] is the hole it leaves when it's gone," Kinsey observes, but then she undercuts the seriousness of her own statement by adding, "which is the substance of every country-and-western song you ever heard" (*H* 19).

Robert Dietz returns in *"M" Is for Malice.* Early in the novel Kinsey is studying a map and lip-synching to an Elvis marathon when a knock at the door produces Dietz. Understandably surprised, Kinsey blurts out, "Well, look who's here. . . . It's only been two years, four months, and ten days" (14). Bored with the antiterrorist training exercises in Germany, for which the funding was drying up anyway, Dietz has returned to the U.S. and is on his way to see his two sons in Santa Cruz as soon as they finish some college work. (The sons, Nick, twenty-one, and Graham, nineteen, are the result of a long-ago relationship with "a woman named Naomi who had steadfastly refused to marry him," 16.)

Dietz is now fifty, grayer, a little heavier, and he looks tired, perhaps from the discomfort of "a bum knee" damaged when he stumbled into a pothole during night maneuvers (16). He asks Kinsey if he can sleep on her couch for four days until he can visit the boys. Kinsey feels thoroughly deflated by the whole situation. "I'd imagined his return a hundred times, but never this way. Now the flatness of it was inside and all of my past feelings for him had shifted from passionate involvement to mild interest, if that" (17).

Agreeing that Dietz can stay, Kinsey leaves to work on her current case, locating Guy Malek. For a couple of days they struggle to define this new-old relationship. Ever cautious, Kinsey wants to understand what they did have, what they have now, and what they might have in the future. She is extremely hesitant about releasing her emotions again when he has already said he'll leave in four days. "Why get enmeshed when all it means is I get to have my heart ripped out?" (76).

Dietz is bewildered by her blank response to his arrival. He's the same nomadic loner who was perfect for her before—her twin, in fact—so what is her problem now? He can't understand what she wants. After all, the two of them have said repeatedly that they do not want the entanglement of marriage, so why does Kinsey want to define the relationship? Since she was the one who refused to go with him to Germany, why does she now say she felt "abandoned" (17)? Kinsey doesn't seem much more clear about all this than he does, but we note she had opened this novel with the description of a New Year's personal assessment. "I usually don't pay much attention to the passing of time, but this year, for some reason, I was taking a good hard look at myself. Who was I, really, in the scheme of things, and what did it all add up to?" (1–2) Dietz returns in the middle of this soul-searching, and she promptly adds him to her list of things to puzzle over.

In *"G" Is for Gumshoe*, she—and the readers—had observed all the ways in which she and Dietz were alike. Throughout *Malice* she focuses on the *differences* between the two of them, and she observes details about him that are less than engaging—his watching television in his underwear, his wearing reading glasses (although she had said they looked good on him in *G* 201), his snapping his fingers in restlessness, and his always looking tired. The major differences she now sees are that he is willing to take risks and to be satisfied with the moment, while she is innately cautious and, especially right now, wants to consider implications for the future. She finally sums it up: "His basic attitude was 'What are you saving yourself for?' My basic attitude was 'Let's not jump into things' " (*M* 46).

Kinsey, however, can remember with pleasure how they used to make love as if they were racing, "like some contest to see who could get there first" (47). "We'd spent the last three months of our relationship in bed together when we weren't up at the firing range doing Mozambique pistol drills. Romance between private eyes is a strange and wondrous thing" (15).

The fiery nature of those memories is shared by the reader, too, so it is painful to listen to Kinsey and Dietz now talk as if they are terribly polite office coworkers, making superficial inquiries about each other's family, recent events, and work. Dietz brings in groceries he's bought and cooks meals. Kinsey washes the dishes, wondering if this empty domesticity is what most married couples degenerate into.

Dietz sleeps downstairs and Kinsey sleeps upstairs, each being ultra careful not to disturb the other. Leaving for work the first morning, she says, "See you later," to which he replies, "Have a good one" (50). It's all impersonal and blah enough to make a grown reader cry.

Thinking that it might be easier on Kinsey if he just left, Dietz packs up after two days and heads for Santa Cruz. Kinsey is surprised by the anger and disappointment she feels at his premature "abandonment." "Under the fury was the old familiar pain. Why does everyone end up leaving me?" (88). But that night she is astonished to find Dietz back in her apartment. He had gotten no more than a block away before he had turned around and come back.

Kinsey looks at Dietz, "thinking about the fearful risks of intimacy, the potential for loss, the tender pain implicit in any bond between two creatures. . . . In me, the instinct for survival and the need for love had been at war for years. My caution was like a wall I'd built to keep me safe. But safety was an illusion and the danger of feeling too much is no worse than the danger of being numb" (108–09).

Kinsey chooses feeling over numbness and, accepting the feelings of this moment, she and Dietz make love. At last. Enthusiastically. And with a great deal of laughter as they maneuver around the problems of Dietz's bad knee. Kinsey had forgotten just how much Dietz could arouse her. This evening of renewed passion seems to signal a reestablishment of their old relationship.

But this expectation does not exactly pan out.

Dietz departs for his scheduled visit with his sons, returning after only one week's absence because he had seen newspaper accounts of Guy Malek's murder and wanted to be with Kinsey, but, curiously, the effect of his return has more to do with the case than with Kinsey personally. Dietz is interested in everything Kinsey tells him about Guy's murder and finally asks, "You want some help with the grunt work?" (235). For the remainder of the novel (approximately one-fifth of it), Dietz serves as Kinsey's assistant, looking up information at the public library, the newspaper morgue at the *Santa Teresa Dispatch,* and the Hall of Records. Although we can give him credit for finding the key bit of evidence that links the identities of Claire Maddison and Myrna Sweetzer, he is essentially a minor player in her

investigation. For those readers who objected to Kinsey's being sub-
servient to Dietz in *Gumshoe*, there is more than adequate role rever-
sal in this novel as Dietz does all the paperwork he normally hates,
while Kinsey goes out on the adventurous work in the case. Dietz even
acts as her receptionist, answering Kinsey's phone for her and giving
her messages.

On the whole, the personal and passionate relationship between
Dietz and Kinsey seems stalled by the end of this novel. The only part
of their relationship that appears to work well is the professional
partnership they slip into. There are a number of subtle hints that the
romantic affair may end soon: unlike the deep postcoital slumber
Kinsey enjoyed in *Gumshoe*, she finds it difficult to sleep with Dietz on
her sofa in *Malice* (only part of the problem is his bad knee) (112); as
she tells Henry about Dietz's return, she puts quotation marks
around "romance" (115), and as she leaves the apartment for jogging, she says she is "thankful for the opportunity to spend time
alone" (251), the same sentiment she had uttered after refusing to
let Jonah stay the night after her birthday party in *Gumshoe*, when that
affair was over. Her emotional attachment in this novel appears to be
less with her lover Dietz, who is her alter ego in toughness, than with
her friend Guy, who is her alter ego in gentleness and compassion.
On the second of their two sexual encounters in the novel, Kinsey
even thinks of Guy during her lovemaking with Dietz. After this, his
knee becomes so bad that they resume sleeping in separate beds.
Kinsey concludes the Epilogue with her emotional account of saying
good-bye to Guy in a dream, but she is completely silent on the subject of Robert Dietz.

Jonah Robb

Sergeant Robb works in the Missing Persons Division and is later
promoted to lieutenant in the Homicide Division of the Santa Teresa
Police Department. He is attracted to Kinsey from the time they meet
in *Burglar*, when she comes to his desk at the police station for routine information about her missing client, but Kinsey seems no more
attracted to him than she is to a number of men she meets in her
work. In addition, she has no interest in affairs with married men and
she immediately notices the "dent in his left ring finger where he'd

recently worn a wedding ring" (*B* 47). They are both subject to an attack of the pheromones in *Corpse,* and they finally succumb in *Deadbeat.* By the time of *Gumshoe,* Kinsey has decided to end the dwindling affair. By *Malice,* Kinsey speaks of him with detachment; in fact, she can even laugh at the way he steadfastly stays in a marriage designed by Medusa on a bad hair day.

Two things keep the relationship from developing in the novel in which they meet. When Jonah surprises Kinsey one night by showing up at Rosie's and joining her for dinner, about all he can talk about is his separation from his wife, Camilla, his high school sweetheart, who made a year's worth of frozen dinners for him before leaving with their two daughters. In addition to this ill-chosen conversational gambit, Jonah is some twenty pounds overweight, always a turn-off for Kinsey. She thinks he's "a nice guy with a bland face" (*C* 201), and they talk like old friends, even sharing a pleasant afternoon of target shooting, but friendship is all the relationship appears headed toward in its early days.

The relationship takes a sudden turn in the next novel. Kinsey is people-watching in the sunken gardens behind the Santa Teresa Courthouse while she waits for Jonah to join her for a business lunch. She's not seen him for several months, in part because she was miffed that he and his wife had gotten back together again in spite of the fact that "he'd exhibited a bit of healthy male interest" (*C* 201) in Kinsey. "Idly, I catalogued the merits of a good-looking man coming toward me in a pale blue short-sleeved shirt. I was doing one of those visual surveys that starts at the bottom and moves up. Uh-hun, nice hips, dressing left . . . uh-hun, flat belly, great arms, I thought. He'd almost reached me when I checked out the face and realized it was Jonah" (204). Kinsey stops "dead in [her] tracks" (204). Diet and exercise have trimmed the extra twenty pounds. "His face, which in the past I'd labeled 'harmless,' was now nicely honed. His dark hair was longer and he'd picked up a tan so that his blue eyes now blazed in a face the color of maple sugar" (204).

Sounds like a young Henry Pitts, doesn't he?

Never one to mince words, Kinsey says, "Oh, God. . . . You look great" (204). Jonah, who's been attracted to Kinsey from the beginning, stares back. After some abortive attempts to talk about the subs and Pepsis he brought with him for their picnic lunch, he says, "Kinsey, I don't remember going through this before. . . . Why don't we fuckin' skip lunch and go over there behind that bush?" (205).

Their laughter allows them to pull themselves together enough to deal with the business Kinsey wanted to discuss. Kinsey keeps hands off because she believes "The only thing worse than a man just out of marriage is a man who's still *in* one" (204). But they, and the readers, now suspect it's just a matter of the right opportunity coming along for Kinsey and Jonah.

The opportunity finally appears in *"D" Is for Deadbeat,* when once again Kinsey calls on Jonah for some help with a case. One night Jonah pulls up beside her car and they stop for a drink at a nearby bar, the Crow's Nest. Kinsey's subsequent account of sex with Jonah is appealing. She gives a spare description of the sexual tension building between the two of them. "Jonah was looking good" (174). They have several margaritas, slow dance, listen to Johnny Mathis, run out of business to discuss, and generally eye each other with an awareness of their long-standing attraction. Kinsey muses, "Most of the time, the chemistry is kept in check by a bone-deep caution on my part, ambivalence about his marital status, by circumstance, by his own uneasiness, by the knowledge on both our parts that once certain lines are crossed, there's no going back and no way to predict consequences" (174).

On this slow rainy night, though, Kinsey, who is always susceptible to the languor of rain, studies Jonah for a moment and then asks, "What would Camilla do if you didn't come home tonight?" They kiss, and Kinsey says simply, "We left soon afterward" (175).

Kinsey skips any description of their actual lovemaking. At the beginning of the next chapter, Kinsey wakes up alone, observing "good sex transforms and I was feeling energized" (176). As she drives to work—and misses her exit ramp because she is so preoccupied—she thinks about the night in a way that sounds very much in keeping with her character. ("We'd behaved like bad kids, eating snacks, telling ghost stories, returning now and then to a lovemaking which was, at the same time, intense and comfortable," 177.) Nonspecific in detail, Kinsey says, "He was so generous and affectionate, so amazed at being with someone who didn't criticize or withhold, who didn't withdraw from his touch as though from a slug's" (177). The experience sounds like fun—warm and sexy and obviously exhilarating.

At the beginning of the next novel, *"E" Is for Evidence,* Kinsey describes Jonah and herself "at that stage in a new relationship where both parties are tentative, reluctant to presume, quick to feel injured, eager to know and be known as long as the true frailties of character are concealed" (37). She promptly demonstrates the problem with the affair, as well as her own vulnerable position, by calling Jonah at his office for some help when she is falsely accused of taking bribes. He's not at the office. One of his fellow policemen tells her that he has taken his family skiing for the Christmas holidays, something she had not known anything about. "I have to confess that in the privacy of my own home, I burst into tears and wept with frustration for six minutes flat" (38). We notice that she gives Jonah only six, precisely six, minutes of crying time, before she says, "Then I went to work" (38). And we never see Jonah in this novel or in the next. Not until the opening of *"G" Is for Gumshoe* do we pick him up again, and by now Kinsey has realized that the affair can go nowhere.

Jonah attends the surprise birthday party for Kinsey given by Henry and Rosie, and he takes Kinsey home afterward, but she does not let him stay for the night. In fact, she moves away from his good night kiss. She has told Vera "the high had long since worn off" this relationship (22) and now she says, "I really wasn't sure what I felt for him at this point. He's kind, confused, a good man who wants to do the right thing, whatever that is" (27). He just can't seem to get his push-pull relationship with Camilla settled, and Kinsey feels distinctly left out. "While I didn't want much from the relationship, I found it disquieting that I never knew where I stood" (27).

Obviously, the affair has almost fizzled out. It's at this point Kinsey meets Robert Dietz and we hear no more about any attraction to Jonah. By the time of *"J" Is for Judgment,* Kinsey has a hard time remembering why she was ever interested in him. When she calls him on business and he says how much he has missed her, she feigns the arrival of a client in order to end the conversation. A few days later they run into each other in the same garden in which they had met for lunch in *Corpse,* and Kinsey is both amused and irritated that Jonah wants her to stay so he can introduce her to Camilla. "Jesus,

Jonah, get a clue," Kinsey thinks. "No wonder Camilla was always mad at him. What wife wants to meet the woman her husband was boffing during past marital separations?" (180–81).

The awkwardness of a dead affair colors their conversations as Kinsey continues to call on Jonah for information she needs in her cases. They struggle through the husk of their affair with an admirable level of civility. By the time Kinsey sees Lt. Robb in his new role as the head of the Homicide Division and chief investigator into Guy Malek's death in *"M" Is for Malice*, she is able to say of Jonah, Camilla, and herself, "Occasionally now, the three of us crossed paths out in public and I'd become an expert at pretending I'd never dallied with him between my Wonder Woman sheets" (138).

Jonah remains as clueless as ever about relationships. When Jonah questions Kinsey about what she knows of Guy's murderer, Kinsey is surprised to notice some of the old attraction still smoldering between them. Perhaps as a defensive move, she politely inquires, "How's Camilla?"

Jonah replies, "She's pregnant."

Kinsey's automatic response, "Congratulations," receives an unexpected rejoinder from Jonah.

"It's not mine."

"Ah," says Kinsey (178).

Her verbal reaction may be noncommittal, but we suspect that Kinsey quickly finds a nearby door behind which to guffaw. Poor, good-looking, naive Jonah. And as if that's not funny enough, Kinsey later finds herself giving advice to Lt. Betsy Bower, a policewoman attracted to Jonah, about the dangers of "the dread Camilla" and her irrational hold on Jonah (201).

Charlie Scorsoni

Charlie Scorsoni is Kinsey's most serious erotic mistake. They become lovers in *"A" Is for Alibi*, in spite of the fact Charlie is one of Kinsey's suspects in the murder case she is investigating. It turns out that Charlie is indeed a killer, in fact, a triple killer, and Kinsey is forced to shoot him to keep him from murdering her in the novel's final scene.

Charlie Scorsoni is the former law partner of Laurence Fife, the man whose murder eight years before Kinsey is now investigating. Kinsey remembers him from the original case, but when she visits him now she notices that he has lost weight (another man who's attractive after a weight loss), and she finds him incredibly sexy. "He had thick, sandy hair, receding at the temples, a solid jaw, cleft chin, his blue eyes magnified by big rimless glasses. His collar was open, his tie askew, sleeves rolled up as far as his muscular forearms would permit. He was tilted back in his swivel chair with his feet propped up against the edge of the desk, and his smile was slow to form and smoldered with suppressed sexuality" (29).

There are clues galore to his inappropriateness as Kinsey's lover, even if it takes a while longer to figure out that he is a murderer. From the beginning he bosses Kinsey around, something we would not think she would accept, but she does. (At least, she does in this first novel. It would be interesting to see how the more fully developed Kinsey, say in *Killer* or *Judgment,* would respond to a Charlie.) From the very first scene when he makes Kinsey wait to be admitted to his office and then has his feet propped on his desk, we see him as arrogant and selfish. His smoldering sexuality seems to be something he can turn on and off, rather than an honest, open part of his nature. He arrives unannounced at her apartment and reads through her books and magazines without her permission. He tells her to change clothes and get ready to go out to dinner. He orders the meal for both of them. He dominates everything about their relationship, including the sex. And Kinsey seems to like it, even as she says, "My early-warning system was clanging away like crazy and I wasn't sure how to interpret it" (65).

Kinsey knows that getting involved with anyone in a case—especially a suspect—is stupid. "As a rule, I scrupulously avoid personal contact with anyone connected with a case. My sexual wrangling with Charlie was foolish, unprofessional, and in theory, possibly dangerous. In some little nagging part of my head, it didn't feel right to me, but I did love his *moves*" (226). He's a snake who hypnotizes Kinsey, but not the readers.

We don't know, though, that Charlie is the murderer of three women until the night that Kinsey gets the last clue she needs to figure it out. Kinsey locates the final evidence at the Powers' beach house proving Charlie guilty of murder. But, to her horror, Charlie pulls up at just that moment and gets out of his car. He chases her down the cliff and across the empty beach until she hides in a garbage can. When Charlie pulls off the lid, she sees the butcher knife in his hand and she shoots him.

We knew the relationship was doomed from the beginning, but this is a spectacular ending to the affair.

Daniel Wade

In a different, but more profoundly disturbing way for Kinsey, Daniel Wade is another romantic mistake. Daniel is Kinsey's second husband, the one who left her. He is mentioned by Kinsey in several novels, and, to her astonishment, he appears at her door in *"E" Is for Evidence,* where he betrays her a second time.

The first time Kinsey tells us anything about him occurs in *"C" Is for Corpse.* She is questioning Kelly Borden, an assistant in the morgue, who says he plays jazz guitar. Suddenly, from out of nowhere, Kinsey asks if he's ever heard of Daniel Wade. Kelly says everyone knows him; he was a great local jazz pianist and Kelly wonders where he's gone now. Kinsey confides that she was once married to Daniel, a personal revelation that appears to be prompted by a combination of hearing Kelly's avocation and seeing the jars that line the morgue walls, any one of which might have "a pickled heart tucked in among all the livers, kidneys, and spleens" (86).

Kinsey and Kelly talk about Daniel's great talent and his equally great drug problem. She thinks of their brief marriage as "the best few months of my life. Daniel had the face of an angel back then . . . clear blue eyes, a cloud of yellow curls. He always reminded me of some artist's rendering of a Catholic saint—lean and beautiful, ascetic-looking, with elegant hands and an unassuming air. He exuded innocence" (86). Ash Wood, Kinsey's friend from high school, remembers seeing Kinsey and Daniel together and thinking he was "the most beautiful boy I ever saw in my life" (*E* 42). Kinsey agrees. "Daniel Wade is quite possibly the most beautiful man I've ever seen . . . straight, well-proportioned nose, high cheekbones, strong jawline, sturdy chin. . . . His teeth were straight and very white, his

smile slightly crooked. Get the picture, troops? . . . Good voice, too
. . . just in case his other virtues fail to excite. Reedy and low. He
sings like an angel, plays six instruments" (*E* 103–04).

Kinsey tells us repeatedly throughout the novels that pretty men
do not attract her. We might attribute some of that response to her
having been treated so shabbily by Daniel, but this seems to have
been her initial reaction even when she met Daniel. She was attracted
to him in spite of her long-standing suspicion that beautiful men tend
to be either gay or narcissistic. She immediately wrote him off precisely because of those good looks. Then she heard him play the
piano. "I did a long double-take, astonished, and I was hooked"
(163). "I fell in love with his hands first and then worked my way up"
(103).

We don't know exactly how they met, or how long it was before
they married, but we do know the marriage lasted "eleven months
and six days" before Daniel walked out and never came back (105).
Kinsey was twenty-three when they married and twenty-four when he
left. A divorce was effected without their ever seeing each other
again. Then Daniel arrives on Kinsey's doorstep one morning, eight
years later, prompting Kinsey to respond, "Shit," and after a few
more well-chosen words, slam the door in his face.

Kinsey says, "I really thought I'd made my peace with the past
until I came face to face with it" (105). "It was amazingly painful just
to be in his company. . . . There's nothing more infuriating than a
man who's manipulated your emotions once and now thinks he can
do it again" (119).

Earlier Kinsey may have recalled the happiness of their brief marriage, but actually seeing Daniel again prompts her to recall all the
pain of living with a man without a conscience (162). He "was married to his music, to freedom, to drugs, and briefly, to me. I was about
that far down on the list" (162). Daniel's sexual attraction, his incredible musicianship, and his great sense of fun may have touched an
intensity of emotional response Kinsey had not felt before, but Daniel
also gave her countless miserable nights when he was away, without
explanation, using cocaine or engaging in "chronic infidelity." "Being married to a doper is as close to loneliness as you can get" (164).

"Lying in bed, you tell yourself you're worried that he's wrecked the car again, that he's drunk or in jail. You tell yourself you're worried he's been rolled, mugged, or maimed, that he's overdosed. What really worries you is he might be with someone else. The hours creep by. From time to time, you hear a car approaching, but it's never his. By 4:00 a.m. it's a toss-up which is uppermost in your mind—wishing he would come home or wishing he were dead" (164).

Daniel seems genuinely bewildered that Kinsey is angry after all this time. All he did was walk out, what's she so steamed about? Kinsey is outraged that he doesn't understand the depth of pain he caused her by simply disappearing, without explanation. But he claims he is now clean and, on the advice of his therapist, trying to make amends. He asks for one little favor: he'd like to leave a valuable guitar with Kinsey for a few days because the lock to his car trunk is broken. Kinsey begins to berate him for his obtuseness, but she runs out of steam. "I might as well save my breath. I might as well give him what he wanted and get it over with" (120).

Daniel's guitar is propped in a corner of Kinsey's apartment. Contact between the two of them continues, primarily because Kinsey needs help after she is injured in an explosion. To her surprise, Daniel buys her groceries, prepares food, and plays Henry's piano for her. Daniel listens with great interest to her account of becoming a private detective and of investigating her current case. "Daniel was a good audience, asking just the right questions. It felt like old times, the good times, when we talked on for hours about whatever suited us" (162).

Kinsey finally asks Daniel why he left her. Astonishingly, Daniel replies, "It wasn't you, babe. It wasn't anything personal. . . . It wasn't that I didn't want you. I wanted something else more, that's all."

Kinsey asks, "What?"

"Anything. Everything. Whatever came down the pike," is Daniel's uninformative response (162).

Kinsey may know little more about why Daniel behaved as he did, but his reappearance touches old feelings she had tried to bury. "Being with him had brought back the pain in fossil form, evidence of ancient emotional life, embedded now in rock" (164).

Fortunately for Kinsey, she does not go beyond a scrutiny of those earlier sensations. She does not appear to be ready to *revive* those emotions with Daniel's reappearance, especially after Daniel tells her he really wants to return to drugs in order to play the piano with soul again. ("Get out of my life, Daniel. Would you just do that?" 174.) We say *fortunately* Kinsey does not want to revive their relationship because Daniel betrays Kinsey yet again.

Kinsey discovers that her apartment has been bugged and to her horror, the surveillance device is inside the guitar left by Daniel. Kinsey is shocked that he has set up a way to spy on her during her current case, but she's in for another order of shock when she goes to his motel room to confront him about the bug.

Kinsey shouts at him, "It took a lot of fuckin' nerve to come waltzing back in my life and betray me again" (189). She had seen Ash Wood's car in the motel parking lot. Now she notes Daniel's bare chest, the closed bathroom door, and the "musky smell of sex still [hanging] in the air like ozone after a rainstorm" (189). Before Daniel can say anything, Kinsey opens the bathroom door to surprise the person she thinks must be there—Ash—but she is the one who's surprised. It is Ash's brother, Bass Wood, standing in the bathroom. Things click in Kinsey's brain. It was two weeks after Daniel played for Bass' birthday party that he walked out of Kinsey's life. This must be what he left her for.

Kinsey learns later that the men's affair had ended, but when Terry Kohler needed help to oust Lance Wood from the family business, Bass had agreed to locate Daniel again. When asked, Daniel had agreed to spy on Kinsey, in hopes that he and Bass would get together again. Which they did. And they leave town together shortly after the motel scene.

Kinsey says little, then or later, about Daniel's being gay or bisexual. When she finds Bass in Daniel's room, she checks "out the body Daniel found preferable to mine" (190). Watching the two light up a joint, she says, "The two men locked eyes, exchanging a look so filled with tenderness I had to drop my gaze" (190). Nowhere does she condemn the relationship as inappropriate because it involves two men.

We have the impression that Kinsey will try to refossilize the intense feelings she once felt for Daniel. And the relationship leaves her more determined than ever to be careful of romantic involvements. Love is demanding under the best of circumstances, but caring for the wrong person can be crippling. The scar tissue Kinsey forms may be thick, but it covers a still painful wound named Daniel Wade.

Finally, if we want to have a sense of the degrees of closeness Kinsey feels in the stable relationships of her current life, we might note the order in which she calls people for help when she needs money to get home from Kentucky in *"L" Is for Lawless*. First she calls Henry, then Rosie, then Vera, then "my old friend Jonah," and "even" Darcy. "Finally, in desperation," she calls her cousin Tasha, who is the only one she can reach (288).

KINSEY LAUGHS AT:

Celibacy:

"I lay there, trying to think back to when I'd last had sex. I couldn't even remember, which was *really* worrisome. I fell asleep wondering if there was a cause-and-effect relationship between memory loss and abstinence." (*K* 44)

"There's something about love that brings a sense of focus to life. I wouldn't complain about the sex, either, if I could remember how it went. I'd have to get out the instructor's manual if I ever managed to get laid again." (*L* 68)

Sex:

"The air smelled of desire, like the sweet perfume of wet grass after a rainstorm. That or cat spray." (*H* 67)

"There is nothing quite as smug as the self-congratulation that abounds when one has been thoroughly and proficiently screwed." (*A* 226)

"I can still remember the mix of mirth and pity I felt when I realized all boys were afflicted with a doo-dad that looked like an ill-placed thumb stuck between their legs." (*H* 59)

Marriage:

Regarding Rosie's leaving a sports fan's jockstrap on the spike of the marlin over her bar: "Apparently her impending nuptials had lowered her IQ several critical points." (*K* 68)

Women:

"Women don't want to sit around listening to guys talk about themselves. Women like to have conversations about real things, like feelings—namely, theirs." (*H* 163)

The Scene of
the Action

"White adobe and red tile roofs":
Santa Teresa and Environs

Kinsey lives and works in Santa Teresa, California, a coastal town of approximately eighty thousand (eighty-five thousand by the time of *"M" Is for Malice*), some ninety-five miles northwest of Los Angeles. The name is fictitious, but the town is quite real. "Santa Teresa" was the geographical pseudonym Ross Macdonald used for his hometown, Santa Barbara, in many of his Lew Archer mysteries. Sue Grafton now lives in Santa Barbara and continues using the town and the name as a tribute to Macdonald, whose novels she greatly admires.

From the beginning of the series we get a picture of the prettiness and money that is Santa Teresa, qualities that sometimes amuse, sometimes irritate, and occasionally please Kinsey. The town is "artfully arranged between the Sierra Madres [actually the Santa Ynez Mountains] and the Pacific Ocean—a haven for the abject rich. The public buildings look like old Spanish missions, the private homes look like magazine illustrations, the palm trees are trimmed of unsightly brown fronds, and the marina is as perfect as a picture postcard with the blue-gray hills forming a backdrop and white boats bobbing in the sunlight. Most of the downtown area consists of two- and three-story structures of white stucco and red tile, with wide soft curves and trellises wound with gaudy maroon bougainvillea. Even the frame bungalows of the poor could hardly be called squalid" (*A* 10).

Kinsey says there are three styles of building in the town: "the Spanish, the Victorian, and the pointless" (*D* 187). Although she gets tired of all the stucco and red tile roofs, longing for more of the Victorian bungalows left from Santa Teresa's earlier days, she likes the absence of neon and factories and clutter. The very perfection of the "look" may be "unsettling" but it is "so lush and refined that it ruins you for anyplace else" (*B* 7).

In keeping with the perfection of the town is the perfection of the moderate weather in Santa Teresa, where "The days are blanketed with sunlight" (*A* 35). Kinsey comments often on the constant sunlight, the temperature in the fifties to the seventies, the very occasional rain—so rare that the town "takes on a festive air when it comes" (*D* 28)—or haze or cool weather, and the near absence of changing seasons. "It was technically winter, which, in California means the perfect days are cut from fourteen hours to ten" (*F* 230). The only conceivable adverse weather comes in the winter, when the dryness sometimes triggers fires, followed by mud slides when the rain does arrive (*A* 10). But we have had neither fire nor mud in any of the novels thus far.

The other big scare for the California coast—earthquakes—doesn't seem to be as much of a threat as in the San Francisco or Los Angeles areas. "Actually, the only quakes I've experienced have been minor temblors that rattle dishes on the shelf or set the coat hangers in the closet to tinkling merrily. . . . In Santa Teresa (aside from the Big One in 1925) we've had mild, friendly earthquakes that do little more than slop some of the water out of our swimming pools" (*F* 18).

Despite all the natural and mandated beauty of Santa Teresa, Kinsey's reports still have the gritty atmosphere typical of the hard-boiled detective genre. How does Grafton achieve this dark perspective on a sunny town? By taking Kinsey into the scruffy suburb of Colgate or nearby Elton or residential areas of town that belie her claim that even the poor houses are not squalid; for example, Bibianna Diaz lives in "a dank-looking brown cottage at the back of a dank brown house, located in a midtown neighborhood distinctly down at the heel" (*H* 35), and Coral's trailer in *"D" Is for Deadbeat* is run-down, dirty, littered with junk inside and out, and the area is noisy and unkempt (64–66). And by taking Kinsey inside a *great* number of dark, seedy spots, such as the Hub, "a bar with all the ambience of a converted warehouse" (*D* 70), or the raunchy Meat Locker (*H* 52– 53), or even her favorite hangout, Rosie's Tavern. Finally, if Grafton runs out of shabbiness in pretty Santa Teresa, she can always send Kinsey to Los Angeles.

The town of Santa Teresa is defined to the north by the Sierra Madre Mountains* and to the south by the Pacific Ocean in a gentle curve of beach sometimes abutting rocky cliffs, sometimes rolling quietly inland. Visible from shore are channel islands twenty-six miles out, and oil derricks closer to land. "It's worrisome, but true, that the oil rigs have taken on an eerie beauty of their own, as natural to the eye now as orbiting satellites" (*F* 15). The eastern and western borders are the two wealthy residential areas of Montebello (old money)—where, for example, Glen Callahan in *"C" Is for Corpse* owns a house on a street named for her, and Horton Ravine (new money), where the Barneys and the Voigts live in *"I" Is for Innocent* and the Frakers have a house in *"C" Is for Corpse*. According to local rumor, Montebello can boast more millionaires per square mile than anywhere else in the country (*A* 45 and *C* 17). Ten miles northwest lies the bedroom community of Colgate, where the Wood/Warren plant is (*Evidence*) and where Morley Shine lived (*Innocent*), and where Kinsey lived in a trailer park before finding Henry's studio apartment (*K* 19). Previously farmland and citrus groves, "the uninhabited countryside has now given way to service stations, bowling alleys, funeral homes, drive-in theaters, motels, fast-food restaurants, carpet outlets, and supermarkets, with no visible attention paid to aesthetics or architectural unity" (*I* 28). Kinsey wryly observes that Colgate is known as the Frostee-Freeze capital of the world (*D* 81).

Santa Teresa's streets and landmarks are laid out exactly like those of Santa Barbara, with the names changed by Grafton for everything except the main avenue, State Street, and Highway 101, which are

---

* Grafton slips once and calls them the Santa Ynez Mountains (*I* 47).

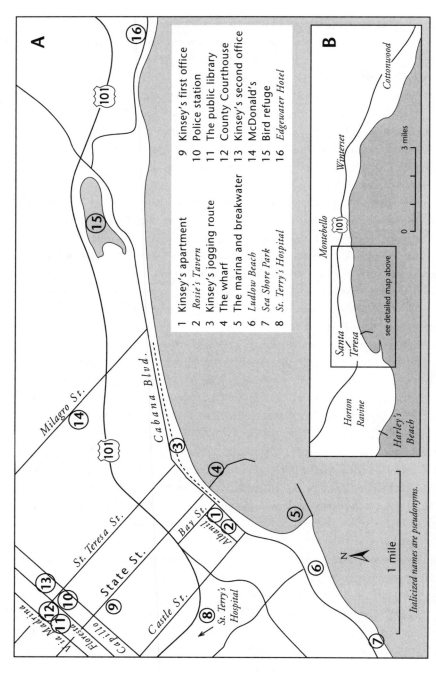

A

1 Kinsey's apartment
2 *Rosie's Tavern*
3 Kinsey's jogging route
4 *The wharf*
5 *The marina and breakwater*
6 *Ludlow Beach*
7 *Sea Shore Park*
8 *St. Terry's Hospital*
9 Kinsey's first office
10 Police station
11 The public library
12 County Courthouse
13 Kinsey's second office
14 McDonald's
15 Bird refuge
16 *Edgewater Hotel*

Italicized names are pseudonyms.

Milagro St.
St. Teresa St.
Bay St.
Albanil
State St.
Castle St.
Cabana Blvd.
Via Madrina
Floresta
Capillo
St. Terry's Hospital
101
N
1 mile

B

Santa Teresa
Montebello
Winterset
Cottonwood
Horton Ravine
Harley's Beach
101
see detailed map above
0   3 miles

Designed by Patricia Gilmartin/produced by Ellen White

A

CANADA

UNITED STATES

- San Francisco
- Las Vegas
- Salton Sea
- Brawley
  see inset below
- Louisville
- Dallas

MEXICO

- Viento Negro
- Boca Raton

B

- San Luis Obispo
- Floral Beach
- Sierra Madre Mountains
- 101
- Marcella
- Lompoc
- Colgate
- Elton
- Santa Teresa
- Perdido
- Olvidado
- Los Angeles
- Claremont
- 101

Pacific Ocean

35 miles

Italicized city names are pseudonyms.

Designed by Patricia Gilmartin/produced by Ellen White

identical in both towns. The Santa Teresa names often retain the same initials as the Santa Barbara names; for example, the real Hope Ranch becomes the fictitious Horton Ravine. Or Grafton plays with the meaning of the original name: Summerland becomes Winterset and Montecito becomes Montebello. We especially like the fun of Arroyo Burro Beach in Santa Barbara becoming Harley's Beach in Santa Teresa.

Landmarks

The map of Santa Teresa in this chapter includes major locations that are a routine part of Kinsey's life in almost every novel. (In the following descriptions, the numbers correspond to those on the map.)

1. Kinsey's Apartment

Throughout the novels Kinsey lives alone in a 15′ × 15′ studio apartment converted from a garage behind the home of Henry Pitts, her landlord, on tree-lined Albanil Street one block from the ocean. "Albanil" is the fictional name given Santa Barbara's Mason Street by Grafton. (In addition, she has moved it one block over—in Santa Barbara, it would be Yanonali Street. Grafton has laughingly said that as "the goddess of Santa Teresa," she can move real estate around all she wants.) Bombed out of existence by a killer at the conclusion of "E" Is for Evidence, the apartment is rebuilt by Henry into a snug little kingdom that reminds Kinsey of living in a ship. She moves into the new apartment at the beginning of "G" Is for Gumshoe. There is no exact model for her apartment on either Mason or Yanonali—one street just has the right feel and the other the right location.

Kinsey loves everything about her living quarters. Given her childhood and her fondness for order, autonomy, and frugality, it is understandable that she likes the smallness of the space, the clever dual function of everything in the apartment, and the modest rent.

2. Rosie's Tavern

Half a block down Albanil Street from Kinsey's apartment is Rosie's Tavern, a bar ruled over by Rosie, whose surname we never learn because Kinsey can't spell the complicated Hungarian name (*G* 17). The Tavern is "a cross between a neighborhood bar and an old-fashioned beanery" (*B* 90).

Unlike the other buildings in the novels, there is no real-life equivalent of Rosie's Tavern in Santa Barbara. Grafton modeled Rosie's on a neighborhood bar in Columbus, Ohio, called Schiller's. Anyone looking along either Mason or Yanonali Street for Rosie's Tavern will be frustrated, because the real streets are completely residential.

"The building that houses Rosie's looks as if it might once have been a grocer's. The exterior is plain and narrow, the plate-glass windows obscured by peeling beer ads and buzzing neon signs" (*I* 79–80).

The interior of the bar, which becomes Kinsey's home away from home, is a dark contrast to all the sunny prettiness of Santa Teresa. As early as *"A" Is for Alibi*, Kinsey describes it as a wonderfully scruffy, no-frills, nontourist hangout. "It's the sort of place where you look to see if the chair needs brushing off before you sit down. The plastic seats have little rips in them that leave curls of nylon on the underside of your stockings and the tables have black Formica tops hand-etched with words like *hi*" (19). "The walls are paneled in construction-grade plywood sheets, stained dark, with a matte finish of cooking fumes and cigarette smoke" (*B* 91). Ever sensitive to smells, Kinsey says the bar "will always smell like spilled beer, paprika, and hot grease" (92). The light is dim, making everyone look sallow or ill. Booths lining the walls are "stiff, high-backed pews sawed out of construction-grade plywood, stained dark brown to disguise all the knot-holes and splinters" (*K* 68). Kinsey has her favorite booth in the back, where she can have her treasured privacy and a good view of the room. The menu, a mimeographed sheet inside a plastic cover, stands between the ketchup bottle and the napkin box (*B* 90).

Of course, the menu is pointless for Kinsey, because Rosie treats her the way she treats all her favorite regular customers. Rosie simply tells her what she will have to eat, regardless of what the menu—or Kinsey—might say. Rosie herself does the cooking, refusing to let anyone else come into her kitchen, probably because she cuts so many corners with most public health regulations. Kinsey laughingly describes the bar as "always feel[ing] as though it's on the verge of being raided by the food police" (*K* 68).

Rosie usually perches on a stool behind the bar, reading the newspaper and smoking a cigarette. On the bar sits a color television, which is turned on, but mute, in the early novels. "To the left above the bar, there's a dusty marlin, and when people get drunk, Rosie lets them shoot rubber-tipped arrows at it with a toy gun, thus averting aggressions that might otherwise erupt into vicious barroom snits" (*A* 19). Near the door to the kitchen is a pay phone, which everyone, including Rosie, must use for calls.

"The place appeals to me for a couple of reasons," says Kinsey. "Not only is it close to my home but it is never attractive to tourists, which means that most of the time it's half-empty and perfect for private conversations" (19).

In spite of her early insistence that "No one will ever 'discover' " Rosie's or "award it even half a star" (*B* 92), in *"J" Is for Judgment,* we learn that the bar has inexplicably become a favorite place for "sports nuts." A "variety of teams seem to use it as a hangout, especially on occasions when they've just won a trophy and feel the need for a parade" (84). Now, the sound on the television blares out, and Rosie has even started displaying sports insignia above the bar. In the next novel, some of the "sports nuts" invent a game called "Toss the Jockstrap," which leaves a jockstrap caught on the spike of the marlin over the bar (*K* 68). Both Henry and Kinsey are dismayed by all the new "testosterone and hysteria"—which Rosie actually appears to like—but they continue to patronize the place, and Henry continues to barter his baked goods to Rosie in exchange for meals (*J* 84). Kinsey admits, "If it weren't for my fondness for Rosie and the close proximity to my apartment, I might have moved on to some new eatery" (*L* 69).

The tavern undergoes a second change after Rosie and William get married and he assumes some responsibility for the running of the bar. Rosie's becomes more humane in its salary scale for employees and probably safer from exotic germs in the kitchen, but the tameness is a bit of a letdown to those readers who enjoyed the eccentric funkiness of its original incarnation.

3. Kinsey's Jogging Route

Afternoons in the first three novels, mornings thereafter, Kinsey jogs three miles on a bicycle path (or occasionally the sidewalk) lining Cabana Boulevard, the wide street paralleling the beach. In Santa Barbara, the real Cabrillo Boulevard, on which Cabana is based, is in fact bordered by exactly such a bicycle path. Kinsey lives only one block inland from Cabana. When she reaches the concrete path and turns to the left to run southeast, she has the ocean on her right and to her left a boulevard lined with palm trees, restaurants, and businesses. She will occasionally see other joggers—some with dogs, much to her dismay—and homeless persons who have slept on the beach the night before.

Most of the novels include a description of the vivid sunrise she sees on these morning runs. Just in case anyone wants to quibble about the feasibility of someone on the West Coast seeing the sun rise over the ocean, please refer to the map and note the curve of the California coast that indeed puts this stretch of beach facing southeast.

4. The Wharf

A wooden wharf with a few shops and a restaurant projects into the ocean, forming one of the arms of the harbor. "The wharf on one side is like the crook of a thumb with the breakwater curling toward it in a nearly completed circle in which the boats are nestled" (*J* 79). The entrance to the wharf, accessible to both cars and people, is off Cabana, almost opposite Bay Street. The wharf is identified often as one of the landmarks Kinsey passes. It and the adjacent marina figure prominently in the action of *"D" Is for Deadbeat:* Daggett's body is found at the marina and a key witness, Dinah, works at the restaurant on the wharf, as does Tippy Parsons in *"I" Is for Innocent.*

5. The Marina and Breakwater

The Naval Reserve Building and a parking lot are adjacent to the harbor's four marinas with "eighty-four acres of slips for eleven hundred boats. A wooden pier, two lanes wide, juts out into the water topped with a crane and pulleys for hoisting boats" (*D* 108). On the right of the pier is "a row of waterfront businesses—a fish market with a seafood restaurant above, a shop selling marine and fishing supplies, a commercial diving center, two yacht brokers. The building fronts are all weathered gray wood, with bright royal blue awnings that echo the blue canvas sail covers on boats all through the harbor" (108). In *"J" Is for Judgment,* Wendell Jaffe's former boat, now belonging to Carl Eckert, the *Captain Stanley Lord,* is visited a couple of times by Kinsey. It is kept in Marina 1, its locked gate accessed only by card key (79).

The walkway along the curve of the marina extends over the rocks of the breakwater creating the harbor. "The curving wall along the breakwater is about eighteen inches wide, a ledge of hip-high concrete. The ocean crashes perpetually against the barrier, water shooting straight up. A line of spray is forced along the wall and around the bend, which is marked by a row of flagpoles" (*J* 280). In the final scene of *"J" Is for Judgment,* Renata Huff walks along this concrete ledge and, after confessing to Jaffe's murder, jumps into the churning ocean in an apparent suicide attempt.

6. Ludlow Beach

When Kinsey tries to escape the pursuing Charlie Scorsoni in *"A" Is for Alibi,* she scrambles down the rocky cliff from the Powers' house and runs east toward Ludlow Beach, Grafton's name for Leadbetter Beach. She chooses this destination over Harley Beach to the west because it is less isolated and will be more likely to have people around. She climbs over rocks, wades through waves and kelp, and reaches the wide expanse of beach that will take her in the direction of streetlights and people. "I could make out lights now, dark patches of palm against gray sky. . . . This stretch of beach was gentle and clean, looking pale gray, widening to the left where the high cliff finally dwindled away into sloping hillside, slipping down to the flat of the sand" (271). Kinsey heads toward the lights of the parking lot and takes refuge in a garbage bin by the small cinder-block concession stand.

7. *Sea Shore Park*

Just above Ludlow Beach, Sea Shore Park (Grafton's name for Shore-line Park), runs along the bluff overlooking the curve of beach in Santa Teresa. Although there has not yet been major action there in any of the novels, the park is sometimes used as a reference point.

8. *St. Terry's Hospital*

The nickname for Santa Teresa Hospital makes it sound a lot warmer and cozier than Kinsey's descriptions of it, but she clearly has respect for the work taking place in this building. Her aunt died here years before the novels begin and she thinks of that February night when-ever she comes to the hospital (*K* 71); she visits her friendly antago-nist, Lt. Con Dolan, here after his heart attack (*Killer*); she visits her new friend, Danielle Rivers, here after she is severely beaten (*Killer*); and she comes to the hospital to interview several people, for exam-ple, Serena Bonney, night nurse in the emergency room (*Killer*), Kitty Wenner, the anoretic step-sister of Bobby Callahan (*Corpse*), and Dr. James Fraker, pathologist (*Corpse*). She herself is taken to St. Terry's Emergency Room, then to a regular room for patients, fol-lowing the bomb blast at the Kohler house in *Evidence*. We can as-sume the hospital to which she was taken after being beaten and shot in *Burglar* is also St. Terry's, but her reference to the stay is only a sentence or two in the Epilogue and says nothing about her ex-perience there. The same assumption could be made after the bomb blast at her apartment concluding *Evidence* and after she is shot at the end of *Innocent,* but, again, she says nothing about the experience.

In *Corpse,* the hospital is important to the plot, and Kinsey has lots to say about it. "Santa Teresa Hospital, by night, looks like an enor-mous art deco wedding cake, iced with exterior lights: three tiers of creamy white, with a square missing in front where the entranceway has been cut out. . . . There was a large portico and covered walk leading up to double doors that shushed open as I approached. In-side, the lobby lights had been dimmed like the interior of an air-plane on a night flight. To my left was the deserted coffee shop, one waitress still at work, dressed in a white uniform almost like a nurse's.

To my right was the gift shop with a window display done up with the hospital equivalent of naughty lingerie. The whole place smelled like cold carnations in a florist's refrigerated case. The decor had been designed to soothe and pacify, especially over in the area marked 'cashier' " (*C* 49).

Each place Kinsey goes in the hospital has its own character: the orange carpeted psychiatric ward where the walls are "hung with Van Gogh reproductions; a curious choice for the psycho ward, if you ask me" (*C* 50); the miles of underground corridors and small offices that house the Pathology Department and all the nonmedical departments, such as maintenance and housekeeping (*C* 75); the glass doors, cool southwestern colors, and quiet efficiency of the Coronary Care Unit (*K* 72–73); and the crowd of machines and personnel hovering in the Intensive Care Unit (*K* 215–16). The overall impression throughout the hospital is of great efficiency and quiet reassurance. Except for the inevitable out-of-date magazines in the waiting rooms (*K* 95–96).

9. Kinsey's First Office

In *"A" Is for Alibi*, Kinsey returns to her second-floor office at the end of a work day and opens a bottle of Chablis, which she keeps in a small refrigerator. Pouring the wine into a coffee mug left from the morning, which she has quickly rinsed out, Kinsey steps onto the balcony and looks down at State Street, watching the pedestrians below and smelling the ocean breeze (16).

This first office, part of the California Fidelity Insurance building at 903 State (*I* 20), is only a ten-minute drive from her apartment and suits her nicely. She has a great view of the main street of Santa Teresa: all "Spanish tile and stucco arches and bougainvillea growing everywhere" (*A* 16–17). The private balcony has French doors and a waist-high wall and the two-room office has its own separate entrance. Best of all for Kinsey, she pays no rent. She has it gratis in exchange for being available to investigate two or three cases each month for CF. From everything we know of Kinsey, we can assume the office has a neat appearance. In *"A" Is for Alibi*, she has an answering service, which she drops by the time of *"B" Is for Burglar* in favor of an answering machine on her phone. Because she employs no secretary, she maintains all her records herself. In addition to the refrigerator, there is a coffeepot (kept in constant use), a Sparklett's watercooler behind the door, and such standard office essentials as a desk (near the French doors), file cabinets, telephone, Rolodex, chairs for clients, and portable Smith-Corona typewriter. At her desk she uses a swivel chair, which she likes to roll in while she thinks. A parking lot behind the office offers plenty of space for Kinsey's VW.

In compensation for suspending Kinsey when she was framed in *"E" Is for Evidence*, Mac Voorhies of CF has her office refurbished at the end of that novel so that, at the beginning of the next, we learn the walls have been painted "a fresh white" and a new, expensive short-pile slate-blue carpet has been installed. A new Sparklett's watercooler with both hot and cold water has replaced the old one. Kinsey considers all this "classy stuff" and she's quite happy with the office and her arrangement with CF (*F* 3).

It is with real dismay, then, that Kinsey tells us in the Epilogue to *"H" Is for Homicide* that the new efficiency expert at CF, a real jerk who has earned everyone's enmity, has terminated her association with the insurance company. Kinsey couldn't tolerate the man. Since their first encounter was mutually hostile, she was prepared for some kind of retaliation. But eviction and dismissal are more than she was expecting. This strikes a real blow—she had been in the office and associated with CF for seven years. (Actually, longer than that because of her aunt's employment there.) She is also astonished by the dismissal because she has just busted up an automobile-insurance scam ring and saved the company millions. The only things she recovers from her office are her client files, packed into cardboard boxes and unceremoniously handed to her on her way out the door (*I* 2).

10. Police Station

The Santa Teresa Police Department on Floresta Street "is located near the heart of town on a side street lined with cottages painted mint green with low stone walls and jacaranda trees dripping lavender blossoms" (*A* 10). Although Kinsey goes often to the police station to talk with cops or other staff, she apparently thinks the building itself is unremarkable because she says virtually nothing about its external appearance. From the scant details we pick up about the interior, we know there is linoleum on the floor, the furniture is a standard collection of wooden desks, chairs, and benches, and the air smells of cigarette smoke. The coffee is wretched because it's been sitting too long and comes in Styrofoam cups. Into the coffee Kinsey can put packets of Cremora or Equal. "Just what I needed, a cup of hot chemicals" (*D* 50).

11. Santa Teresa Public Library

Kinsey uses the resources of the library in many novels, depending on its reference department, telephone directories, city directories, and the crisscross for help in tracing suspects and witnesses. The library is on State Street, an easy walk from each of Kinsey's offices. As with the police station, Kinsey says little about the library's exterior, probably because she is so dependent on its interior, about which she comments a bit more. "The periodicals room . . . is down a flight of stairs, a spacious expanse of burnt-orange carpeting and royal blue upholstered chairs, with slanted shelves holding row after row of magazines and newspapers. A border of windows admits ample sunshine and recessed lighting heightens the overall illumination" (*G* 210).

The staff are invariably helpful, looking up references for Kinsey, directing her to the correct resource, and showing her how to use the microfilm. They even keep their cool when Deitz gives Kinsey a passionate kiss in celebration of finding a key bit of evidence, although the librarian at the counter "pulled his glasses down and peered at us over the rims" (*G* 214).

12. Santa Teresa County Courthouse

"The Santa Teresa Courthouse looks like a Moorish Castle: hand-carved wooden doors, towers, and wrought-iron balconies. Inside, there's so much mosaic tile on the walls, it looks like someone's covered them with patchwork quilts" (*C* 203). A great archway leads to large sunken gardens, where many people like to bring their lunches and eat on the lawn, as Kinsey and Jonah Robb do in *"C" Is for Corpse*.

Kinsey often uses the resources of the courthouse, going to the Hall of Records to check such things as birth certificates, marriage licenses, and other official records.

13. Kinsey's Second Office

Within a month of her eviction from CF and by the time *"I" Is for Innocent* opens, Kinsey has located a second office with a similar arrangement for the rent and also only a ten-minute drive from her apartment. She is now an independent contractor for attorney Lonnie Kingman, of Kingman and Ives. Kinsey's new office is in the Kingman Building, a three-story stucco on Capillo Street (210 Carillo Street in Santa Barbara), is not far from her first office and convenient to both the courthouse and the police station.

"Across the facade, there are six pairs of floor-to-ceiling French doors that open inward for ventilation, each flanked by tall wooden shutters painted the soft verdigris of a greening copper roof. A shallow wrought-iron bracket is secured across the lower half of each set of doors. The effect is largely decorative, but in a pinch might prevent a suicidal dog or a client's sulky child from flinging itself out the window in a fit of pique" (*I* 5). There is an elevator, but it gives the impression of always being on the verge of getting stuck, so Kinsey usually takes the stairs (*M* 51).

Kinsey's third-floor office had originally "served as a combination conference room and kitchen, and was outfitted now with my desk and swivel chair, file cabinets, a small flop-out couch that could double as a bed in an emergency, a telephone, and my answering machine" (*I* 6). There is "a full 'executive' bathroom attached" (*M* 89). "The room wasn't large, but I had my own window, lots of clean white wall space, and burnt orange carpeting in an expensive wool shag" (*J* 4). She continues most of her habits from the previous office, keeping a coffeepot going, meeting clients, working late if she needs to, cleaning up her office as therapy in spite of the fact Lonnie has a cleaning service every Friday, and maintaining her own files. She keeps handy a good light, a magnifying glass, a map of California, and a fingerprint kit to help her with her work. She keeps a chain on her office door in case she wants to refuse to let someone in. We also know the office has three framed watercolors and a large artificial ficus plant (*J* 4); given her distaste for house plants, we need not expect her ever to put up with the demands of a live plant.

One of the aspects of the new office that appeals greatly to Kinsey is the presence of several other people, especially Ida Ruth, Lonnie's secretary, with whom Kinsey can check in from time to time.

The only drawback to this new office is the parking situation. The ground level of the Kingman Building is only a facade behind which a twelve-car parking lot is accessed by driving through an arched drive on the right of the building. As a new tenant, Kinsey has no claim on any of the slots and must find a parking place on the street. With only 90-minute parking for most of the town's spaces, Kinsey is always scrambling for a safe place to park and always complaining about it (*I* 5). She could, of course, pay for a place in a nearby parking lot, but that would cost money—and we know how Kinsey feels about spending money.

14. McDonald's

We trust there's no need to describe a typical McDonald's. Kinsey, who loves fast food, goes to several McDonald's, but the one she frequents most often is on Milagro (Milpas), near Highway 101. For example, on her way home in *"J" Is for Judgment,* she "stopped off at the McDonald's on Milagro and picked up a Quarter Pounder and an order of fries. For the remainder of the drive home, the air in the car was moist with the smell of steamed onions and hot pickles, meat patty nestled in melted cheese and condiments" (130–31).

15. Bird Refuge

"The bird refuge is a landscaped preserve near the beach, established to protect geese, swans, and other fowl. The forty-three-acre property abuts the zoo and consists of an irregular-shaped freshwater lagoon, surrounded by a wide lane of clipped grass through which a bike trail runs. There's a small parking lot at one end where parents bring little children with their plastic bags of old popcorn and stale bread. Male pigeons puff and posture in jerky pursuit of their inattentive female counterparts, who manage to strut along just one step away from conception" (*E* 170).

The refuge is a meeting place for Kinsey in several books. She and Dolan are supposed to meet Lyda Case there in *"E" Is for Evidence,* and she asks Jonah Robb to back her up when she plans to meet a suspect there in *"I" Is for Innocent.*

16. Edgewater Hotel

Referred to in a number of novels, the Edgewater Hotel (The Four Seasons Biltmore in Santa Barbara) comes in for the most attention in *"E" Is for Evidence,* when Kinsey joins Ash Woods for lunch there, and in *"G" Is for Gumshoe,* when Kinsey goes there for a CF retirement dinner.

As Kinsey and Dietz arrive for the retirement dinner, Kinsey describes the setting for the Edgewater Hotel on its "twenty-three acres of ocean-front property" (*E* 40). "The grass was close-cropped, a dense green, the lawn bordered with pink and white impatiens and clumps of lobelia, which glowed an intense, electric blue. On the far side of the road, the surf battered at the seawall, clouding the air with the briny smell of the thundering Pacific. In addition to the Edgewater's sprawling main building, there were a line of bungalows at the rear of the property, each the size of the average single-family dwelling in my neighborhood. The architecture was Spanish-style, white stucco exterior, heavy beams, age-faded red tile roofs, interior courtyards" (*G* 153).

Inside the hotel is a "spacious lobby, which was flanked by two oversize imported rose marble desks" (*G* 154), "little shops where rich people browsed, looking for ways to spend money without having to leave the premises" (*G* 117–18), a vast glass-enclosed restaurant with polished red tile floors, white wicker furniture, and a menu on parchment with prices and descriptions that immobilize Kinsey. The guest room taken by Vera for the night of the dinner is enormous, elegant, and color-coordinated down to the silk flowers in the bathroom (*G* 156). Even the air smells like money. It reminds Kinsey "of one of those movie-star perfumes that cost a hundred and twenty bucks an ounce" (*G* 118).

"Stuck a toothbrush and toothpaste in my purse and called it packing": Outside Santa Teresa

Except for the occasional trip to nearby Los Angeles on a case, Kinsey does not travel regularly outside the Santa Teresa area, but she stays prepared for any impromptu travel demanded by her job. She tries to keep a change of clothes, or at least fresh underpants and a toothbrush, available to grab at a moment's notice. The travel is always associated with her investigations, never a vacation, and she is impatient to get there, get the job done, and get home.

Most of her travel is done by car, although she will fly if the distance or the time saved warrants the expense to the client. When she flies, she typically says more about the airport than about the city, and when she drives, she says little about the countryside. In keeping with her self-assessment that she is not a process person, she likes "the arrival instead of the journey itself" (*C* 72), and she says she has little interest in looking at the scenery outside the car windows. "I'm not a sightseer at heart and in travels across the country, I'm never tempted by detours to scenic wonders. I'm not interested in hundred-foot rocks shaped like crookneck squash. I'm not keen on staring down into gullies formed by rivers now defunct and I do not marvel at great holes in the ground where meteors once fell to earth. Driving anywhere looks much the same to me. I stare at the concrete roadway. I watch the yellow line. I keep track of large trucks and passenger vehicles with little children asleep in the backseat and I keep my foot pressed flat to the floor until I reach my destination" (*A* 112). (Given her insistence elsewhere on maintaining the speed limit, we assume the latter statement refers only to her focus on driving, not to speeding.)

Despite this disclaimer of interest, Kinsey is *always* caught up in observing and analyzing whatever is around her. This extends to the places she travels during her investigations.

Southern California

Floral Beach

Kinsey spends most of *"F" Is for Fugitive* in this small fictitious town, based on Avila Beach, twelve miles south of San Luis Obispo (28). "Floral Beach has a population so modest the number isn't even posted on a sign anywhere. The town is six streets long and three streets deep, all bunched up against a steep hill largely covered with weeds. There may be as many as ten businesses along Ocean: three restaurants, a gift shop, a pool hall, a grocery store, a T-shirt shop that rents boogie boards, a Frostee-Freeze, and an art gallery. . . . Everything closes down after five o'clock except the restaurants. . . . The whole town resembles the backside of some other town, but it has a vaguely familiar feel to it, like a shabby resort where you might have spent a summer as a kid" (1–2).

The wide beach has few trees (2). "Public access is afforded by a set of concrete stairs with a metal rail. A wooden fishing pier, built out into the water, is anchored at the near end by the office of the Port Harbor Authority, which is painted a virulent blue" (1).

Behind its extremely ordinary facade hide some of the most repugnant and hypocritical people Kinsey ever deals with—a married church minister who seduces a teenaged girl, a married high school teacher who gets one of his students pregnant, and a daughter who kills her mother (*Fugitive*).

San Luis Obispo

Also in *"F" Is for Fugitive*, Kinsey goes to San Luis Obispo to interview several people during her investigation of Bailey Fowler's possible murder of Jean Timberlake. "This is clearly a museum town, with Spanish and Victorian structures restored and adapted to current use. The storefronts are painted in handsome dark shades, many with awnings arching over the windows. The establishments seem to be divided just about equally between trendy clothing stores and trendy restaurants. Carrotwood trees border most avenues, with strings of tiny Italian lights woven into branches bursting with green" (*F* 28). The main street has lines painted on it as a Path of History that

Kinsey, with her interest in early California history, hopes to have time to follow later in the case.

Kinsey is amused that none of the brochures extolling the virtues and the history of the town ever mention the prison just outside of it. Like Floral Beach, this town also has two faces. The nearby California Men's Colony holds six thousand prisoners in an idyllic setting of green and gray rolling hills (44). This is the prison where Bailey Fowler had been incarcerated before his escape in *"F" Is for Fugitive,* as well as the place of John Daggett and Billy Polo's imprisonment in *"D" Is for Deadbeat.*

Lompoc

Kinsey has not yet been to Lompoc in any of the novels, but the town is important because it is the home of the Burton Kinseys, her mother's family. She learns about the existence of this family in *"J" Is for Judgment,* and in *"M" Is for Malice,* she is hired by her cousin Tasha, who is an attorney with offices in Lompoc and San Francisco.

Marcella

In *"M" Is for Malice* Kinsey locates the missing Guy Malek in Marcella (Grafton's fictitious name for Cuyama), approximately eighty miles north of Santa Teresa, with a population of under fifteen hundred (55). "The town of Marcella was situated in the shadow of the Los Cochas Mountain. . . . The streets were six lanes wide and sparsely traveled. An occasional palm or juniper had been planted near the curb. There were no buildings over two stories high and the structures I saw consisted of a general store with iron bars across the front windows, a hotel, three motels, a real estate office, and a large Victorian house surrounded by scaffolding. The only bar was located in a building that looked like it might have been a post office once, stripped now of any official function. . . . There wasn't another town for miles and the businesses in this one seemed weighted toward drinking beer and going to bed soon afterward. . . . The land surrounding the town seemed barren" (56–57).

It seems an unlikely place for resurrection, yet this is the setting in which Guy has gotten clean of drugs, found a moral compass, and discovered his own gentle nature.

Elton

Elton is the small town adjacent to Colgate (real name: Ellwood), where the slimeball Andy Motycka has an apartment. Mentioned in several novels, Elton is most often visited by Kinsey in *"E" Is for Evidence* as she goes back and forth between Colgate, where the Wood/Warren hydrogen-furnace manufacturing company is, and Andy's apartment in Elton, trying to stir up something that would clear her of the conspiracy charges with which she has been framed.

Perdido and Olvidado

"I was beginning to think the real definition of Hell was this endless loop between Santa Teresa and Perdido," Kinsey groans in *"J" Is for Judgment* (185). "Perdido" and "Olvidado" are the fictitious names Grafton gives to Ventura and Oxnard in this novel, although in other novels both towns are referred to by their real names. In this instance, Grafton invents not only new names, but also an elaborate history for the dual township (123).

Dana Jaffe, the presumed widow of Wendell Jaffe, lives in a tract house in Perdido. Their son Brian escapes from Connaught, a Perdido County prison for juveniles, and later is briefly incarcerated in the Perdido County Jail, "a sprawling mass of pale concrete" (107). Their other son, Michael, his wife, Juliet, and baby, Brandon, also live in Perdido. During the novel, they move out of Dana's house into a tiny stucco bungalow in a residential section known as the Boulevards (99). Kinsey interviews all of them and fully expects to be able to catch Wendell when he contacts his family; she is convinced he left Mexico because he read the newspaper account of Brian's escape from Connaught. She therefore keeps the road to Perdido well-traveled and even spends the night there in a typically nondescript motel when her car is damaged by gunshots.

"The wide main street was edged with diagonal head-in parking—lots of pickup trucks and recreational vehicles in evidence" (63). "The architecture in the town itself was a mix of boxy, blocky modern buildings interspersed with Victorian structures. On the far side of 101, between the freeway and the ocean, there were sections of the land entirely covered with blacktop, a series of interconnecting parking lots for supermarkets, gas stations, and fast-food establishments. . . . Closer to the ocean, the houses seemed to take on the look of a little beach town—board-and-batten with big decks, painted sea blue and gray, the yards filled with impossibly bright purple, yellow, and orange flowers" (123–24).

Kinsey finds Renata Huff's house on the Perdido Keys, "long fingers of seawater stretching back from the ocean" (124). Since Renata is the woman with whom Wendell Jaffe left five years ago, Kinsey also keeps this location under close watch. Her "two-story dark blue stucco with white trim" has a dock with access to a deep channel behind the house (124), a feature that has allowed Renata and Wendell to use her boat to come and go unnoticed.

Los Angeles

Kinsey drives to L.A. during several investigations (she keeps handy a copy of the detailed *Thomas Guide to Los Angeles Streets, D* 7), but her longest stay in the city occurs in *"H" Is for Homicide,* where Kinsey, working undercover for the cops, is kept for days in Raymond Maldonado's apartment.

Maldonado grabs Kinsey and Bibianna Diaz when they are released from jail and takes them to his place in Los Angeles. His assistant, Luis, begins the drive on the freeway and then joins the coastal highway, taking them through the prosperous community of Malibu before reaching Maldonado's apartment in "a beach town a few miles south of the airport in an area tainted with poverty. . . . Here, there were only endless drab buildings decorated with angular territorial declarations thrown up by the taggers with cans of black spray paint. . . . Even the passing city buses were defaced, mobile messengers bearing insults from one gang to the next. The streets were littered with trash and old tires. . . . On the island side of the four-lane boulevard, every third storefront had been boarded up" (131).

Kinsey is marginally relieved when they park outside Maldonado's "three-story apartment building, across the street from an automobile salvage yard" because it's not quite as "impoverished as some we'd traversed" (132). In the few instances when Kinsey leaves the apartment to participate in the car accident scam, she sees that the nearby area is weedy, shabby, and full of dust and despair. The scam takes them into more prosperous neighborhoods, but Kinsey is so engaged by learning how to fake accidents that she says little about the places they go. She does, however, complain often and loudly about the famous L.A. rush-hour traffic, or as she describes it, "six lanes of the Indy 500, featuring business execs and other control freaks" (209).

Whenever Kinsey goes to L.A. on business and stays overnight, her usual motel is the Hacienda Motor Lodge on Wilshire, near Bundy, where she usually has room # 2. It has one virtue: it's cheap. $11.95 plus tax. For this lavish expenditure, she gets such amenities as a paper shower mat and a lamp with a football helmet for a shade sporting "UCLA" on the side. "It is the sort of place where you are likely to find someone else's underpanties beneath the bed" (A 84). She says little about L.A. during these visits except to comment on either the exhaust fumes bothering her while she jogs (A 84) or the shabby character of the places she goes. For example, in *"D" Is for Deadbeat,* she locates John Daggett's apartment building, garishly painted, covered in graffiti, and surrounded by spiky weeds. "I had noted the building because it seemed so typical of L.A.: bald, cheaply constructed, badly defaced" (D 8). Much of the L.A. she visits is "as torn and deserted as a war zone" (H 143).

The areas around Kinsey's motel and Maldonado's apartment might as well be on a separate planet from Beverly Hills, or Brentwood, the wealthy neighborhoods in L.A. yet to be visited by Kinsey for anything more than a quick drive-through. Granted, Westwood Village is near Kinsey's motel and, in the first book in the series, she goes to the Avco Embassy Building in Westwood to interview people at the CPA firm of Haycraft and McNeice, but she comments on nothing about the area, only about her amusement over the forced Western motif of the office (A 106 and 156). Nor does she say much about downtown, which she describes as "a tangle" of converging highways "with high-rise buildings caught in the knot" (G 26). Anyway, Kinsey says she's never actually known "anyone who had business in downtown Los Angeles" (26).

Frustrated in "A" Is for Alibi, Kinsey stops at the Santa Monica pier and jogs "south along the promenade, a stretch of asphalt walk that parallels the beach" to Venice Boulevard (108–09). She studies the remnants of the sixties' drug culture with interest. The people and the animals are so entertaining that Kinsey runs farther than usual.

Brawley

In "G" Is for Gumshoe, Irene Gersh hires Kinsey to check on her mother, Agnes Grey, living on a deserted Marine base called "The Slabs" in the Mojave Desert near Brawley, California. Kinsey meticulously lays out her route to the Mojave and describes much of what she drives through. "The national forests were tinted a paler green, while the Mojave itself was a pale beige, mountain ranges shaded in the palest brushstrokes. Much of the desert would never be civilized and that was cheering somehow. While I'm not a big fan of nature, its intractability amuses me no end" (29).

The abandoned government facility is a remarkable place, where remnants of the military base contend with efforts by squatters to impose the character of a town (inhabitants invent such street names as "Rusted-out Chevy Road," 34). Both human endeavors—the base and the "town"—are clearly losing a battle against stronger natural forces. The intractable desert is busily reclaiming its own. "Here, in the endless stretch of gravel and dirt, I could see numerous vans, a few automobiles, many with doors hanging open to dispel the heat. Trailers, RVs, tents, and pickup trucks with camper shells were set up in makeshift neighborhoods. The wide avenues were defined by clumps of creosote and mesquite" (32).

The closest town is Brawley, where Kinsey rents a room at the Vagabond Motel for several days during her search for Agnes. The motel is boringly generic (except for the lively entertainment offered by listening to the couple having sex next door) and the town unremarkable. This is the site of the Rio Vista Convalescent Home, where Agnes was brought after collapsing near a downtown coffee shop (40), and Kinsey visits her there before reporting her findings to Irene. Kinsey drives to the Slabs a couple more times. The last drive ends with a guy in a red Dodge pickup running her off the road and heading toward her with a tire iron in his hand. Over the top of her totaled car, she takes aim with her .32 Davis semiautomatic and, miraculously, the man flees. Passersby help her and take her to the hospital in Brawley. From her hospital bed, she calls Robert Dietz, hiring him as her bodyguard, and he drives her home to Santa Teresa.

Salton Sea

On the way back from Las Vegas in *"A" Is for Alibi*, Kinsey stops "outside Durmid on the eastern shore of the Salton Sea" to interview Greg Fife (135). Greg lives in an aluminum trailer in treeless desert about two hundred yards from the edge of the water. "The Salton Sea has a mild to nonexistent surf, like an ocean that has been totally tamed. There is no vegetation visible in the water and few if any fish. It gives the shore a curious air, as thought the tides had been brought to heel, becalmed, the life forms leeched away" (137). Because Kinsey is interested, Greg gives her a quick history of the formation of this freshwater sea formed from the Colorado River and explains that it is now extremely salty because of gradual absorption of the salt in the ground from the prehistoric periods when the entire area was under the ocean (138).

Claremont

After leaving Greg Fife at the Salton Sea in *"A" Is for Alibi*, Kinsey goes to Claremont, California, to interview his sister, Diane Fife. "I reached Claremont at 6:00, driving through Ontario, Montclair, and Pomona; all townships without real towns, a peculiar California phenomenon in which a series of shopping malls and acres of tract houses acquire a zip code and become realities on the map. Claremont is an oddity in that it resembles a trim little midwestern hamlet with elms and picket fences. . . . Except for the smog, Claremont could even be considered 'picturesque' with Mount Baldy forming a raw backdrop" (146).

Outside Southern California

Las Vegas

In *"A" Is for Alibi,* Kinsey drives to Las Vegas in order to locate Sharon Napier, a possible witness in her investigation. Kinsey's travels usually occur because she needs to interview someone and she says little about any interest in the place she's headed, but she definitely does *not* want to go to Las Vegas. She has no interest in gambling and the demi-life that surrounds it. "Life in Las Vegas exactly suits my notion of some eventual life in cities under the sea. Day and night mean nothing. People ebb and surge aimlessly as though pulled by invisible thermal currents that are swift and disagreeably close. Everything is made of plaster of paris, imitative, larger than life, profoundly impersonal. The whole town smells of $1.89 fried shrimp dinners" (113).

The glitter of Glitter Gulch, as the main casino strip is known, is faintly mimicked by Kinsey's motel. Always choosing a cheap one, she stays in the Bagdad, near the airport. It looks "like a foreign legion post made of marzipan" (113) and features a night manager in gold and orange satin—and a fez—who offers her a paper cup of nickels for the slot machine by the door.

The glitter is flatly contradicted by the pale gray of the desert surrounding the town in daylight and by the worn character of Sharon Napier's apartment complex with its "salmon-pink stucco eroding around the edges as though animals had crept up in the night to gnaw the corners away" (116). When Sharon is murdered, Kinsey is glad to get away from a city she didn't like in the first place. "After Las Vegas, the desert drive was a pleasure" (134). Despite her earlier insistence that she is not a sightseer, she describes the spare land and its subdued colors with obvious pleasure. "There was something appealing about all that country unconquered yet, miles and miles of terrain without neon signs" (134).

Boca Raton

In *"B" Is for Burglar,* Kinsey twice flies to Miami and drives a rental car to Boca Raton, where Elaine Boldt owns a condominium. Kinsey says little about either place. All she sees of Miami is the airport, which, since she arrives at 4:45 a.m., is "sparsely populated" and has "lighting as subdued as a funeral home's" (21). On her second trip she just says the air smells of "rain and jet exhaust" (164). Both trips last only a few hours and she does not stay overnight.

The dawn drive to Boca Raton reveals vegetation that is different from California's. Here she sees "patches of saw grass and stunted cypress" (21). Even the beach where Kinsey stops to walk after writing up her interview notes is different: "the sand was littered with exotic shells. All I'd ever seen on the California beaches were tangles of kelp and occasional Coke-bottle bottoms worn smooth by the sea" (33).

Dallas

In *"E" Is for Evidence,* Kinsey makes a quick trip to Dallas to interview Lyda Case, who works at a bar at the airport; consequently, she doesn't even get out of the airport on that trip. In *"L" Is for Lawless,* Kinsey spends more time in Dallas as she is following Laura (she of the many aliases: Huckaby, Hudson, Rawson, Hays). The neutrals and beiges of the Dallas–Fort Worth airport are generic airport stuff (92–93), but the hotel Laura heads for is distinctive: "a big commercial hotel" with red neon lettering that empties and fills. Just below the name "The Desert Castle" is "Where You're Guaranteed a Good Knight's Sleep (94)." Its public face offers two sides: a disconcerting mix of "merrie aulde England" (95) and a "wild and woolly West" decor from some earlier incarnation (96).

Louisville

In *"L" Is for Lawless,* against her better judgment, Kinsey winds up accompanying Laura and her father, Ray Rawson, from Dallas to Louisville, Kentucky, in search of stolen money and jewels. They drive through Little Rock and Memphis without comment (beyond Kinsey's repeated desire to be dropped off at an airport), and Nashville is noteworthy only because they stop at a McDonald's, much to Kinsey's relief. By the time they reach western Kentucky, Kinsey sees "rolling hills, carpeted in dull November green" with lots of hemlock and pines (210). When they reach Louisville, Ray—pleased to see his home after so many years in prison—points out the Portland Canal, the Ohio River, and the "clusters of tall buildings, sturdy blocks of concrete, most of them squared off on top" forming downtown Louisville (212). They head for his mother's place in an older residential neighborhood of modest houses and overgrown shrubs that Kinsey thinks must have looked exactly the same in the 1940s (213).

Kinsey, Ray, and his mother, Helen, head for the Twelve Fountains Memorial Park (Grafton's name for Cave Hill National Cemetery in Louisville), a handsome old cemetery of stone headstones, iron gates, and fountains "against a backdrop of cypress and weeping willow" (278). The cache of money they seek is in a mausoleum vault for the Lawless family. This final confrontation scene includes a gun battle between Ray and Gilbert Hays, Laura's abusive live-in boyfriend, during which Kinsey is hit over the head, leaving her with a concussion and a lot of explanations needed for the police before she can fly back to Santa Teresa.

Viento Negro

On the eastern coast of the Baja Peninsula in Mexico is the fictitious town of Viento Negro, where Kinsey goes for several days in *"J" Is for Judgment* to locate Wendell Jaffe. The name "means 'black wind,' a fair description of the blizzard of dark lava soot that swirled up from the beach late every afternoon" (14). Kinsey stays at the Hacienda Grande de Viento Negro, a three-story modest resort hotel in apricot yellow with balconies across the front, a restaurant, two bars, a swimming pool, and lots of wind and black sand every evening.

In her efforts to spot Wendell, who was allegedly seen at this hotel, she hangs around the place and tries typical tourist attractions— "the sunset cruise, a snorkeling expedition, a bumpy ass-agonizing jaunt on a rented all-terrain vehicle, roaring up and down dusty mountain trails" (14). The small town is a ten-minute taxi ride "down a dusty two-lane road" (15). Its "once stunning view of the harbor was obscured now by condominiums" and the streets are full of billboards, shoddy merchandise, and abandoned construction (15). The cafés in town offer mediocre food whose best charms are that it is filling and cheap (19).

This is not exactly what Kinsey had hoped for when she took the Mexicana flight to Cabo San Lucas within a few hours of being hired by Mac. She had liked the spur-of-the-moment nature of the trip, the "heightened sense of self-awareness that traveling engenders" (11), and the margarita at the LAX cocktail lounge. This was a rare instance in which she envisioned turning a business trip into a bit of a vacation and a nice opportunity to test her language skills (she's been studying Spanish). The investigative purpose is fulfilled as Kinsey locates Wendell Jaffe, but as a pleasure trip, it's a fizzle. Except for the fun of breaking and entering Wendell's hotel room, that is—Kinsey does always enjoy a little B & E.

San Francisco

In *"K" Is for Killer,* Kinsey flies on a commuter plane to San Francisco. Of the trip, she says more about the home she goes to than about the city. Kinsey does her usual rental car and city map routine and soon arrives at the home of Joseph Ayers, a porno producer, in Pacific Heights. The neighborhood is dark, quiet, and wealthy. The Ayers are giving a party and their "looming" three-story house is alight with laughter, "alcohol-amplified voices," indirect lighting, servants, elegant food, and a three-piece combo. "The house was surrounded by a narrow band of yard, generous by San Francisco standards, where houses were usually constructed smack up against each other" (126).

After meeting with Ayers, Kinsey heads for Haight Street, where Russell Turpin, one of the porno actors, lives in a very different world. "The sidewalks were crowded with pedestrians. Remnants of the past glories of Haight-Ashbury were still in evidence: vintage dress shops and bookstores, funky-looking restaurants, a storefront clinic. The street was well lighted, and there was still quite a bit of traffic. The street people were decked out like flower children of old, still wearing bell-bottoms, nose rings, dreadlocks, torn blue jeans, leather, face paints, multiple earrings, backpacks, and knee-high boots. Music tumbled out of bars. In half the doorways, kids loitered, looking stoned, though perhaps on drugs more exotic than grass or 'ludes" (131–32).

KINSEY LAUGHS AT:

Airport protocol:

"One immutable law of travel is that one's arrival or departure gate is always at the extreme outer limit of the terminal, especially if your bag is heavy or your shoes have just begun to pinch." (*J* 12)

At the luggage carousel: "The moving bag was spirited through a small opening like a coffin on its way to the flames." (*L* 80)

Flying:

"While the engines were being revved up with all the high whine of racing mopeds, the flight attendant recited last rites." (*K* 123–124)

"It was one of those lurching flights with sudden inexplicable drops in altitude that make napping tough. Most of us were too worried about how they'd collect and identify all the body parts once we'd crashed and burned." (*B* 181)

Kinsey at Work

6

"Hooked on the adrenal rush."

Kinsey Millhone is a highly successful private eye if we apply the two basic criteria for success as a fictional detective: does she identify (and defeat, contain, or arrest) the murderer and is she still alive at the novel's end? Her work as an investigator demands that she be physically resilient and intellectually sharp. She has come to this work, which she loves, through a logical evolution in her personal and professional life, and she has developed an impressive variety of skills that assure success in her quest for some semblance of justice in a world that often seems devoid of it.

"Too rebellious, I guess": *Training and Job History*

Formal Training: Police Academy

Kinsey's formal training for her career began with the police academy, probably at the age of nineteen, almost immediately after she finished high school. We learn little about the academy or her reaction to it. She does say she liked being in good physical condition, a requirement for entrance. But we have only a few tidbits about her actual training. For example, she learned what she knows about electronic surveillance in a crash course there, but by *"E" Is for Evidence,* when she needs to use such technology, her limited information is ten years old.

Formal Training: Santa Teresa Police Department

A second phase of training, about which we learn a bit more, took place during her two-year service in the Santa Teresa Police Department. In addition to learning the basic police procedures at a crime scene and the major players on the police force and in many city and county agencies, she developed a number of skills that have come in handy for her current job, including: identifying specific violations of the California criminal and civil code, getting through an autopsy without losing her lunch, how to talk with jumpers, how to lift fingerprints, the importance of having backup, and the ins and outs of debugging a room. She also learned to respect the basic routine established to protect the line of evidence. "Having spent two years as a cop myself, I know better than to withhold information or tamper with evidence" ("Between the Sheets," *K & M* 33). Especially useful was learning the procedures by which all the public agencies operate, so that she now knows whom to call and what buttons to push to get information. Also absolutely essential for Kinsey's current work was her police training in ballistics, guns, and shooting.

Training and Use of Weapons

Her work at the police academy and on the force gave Kinsey formal training in the care and use of guns, training that built on the skills she already had from her aunt Virginia who taught her to shoot.*

---

* According to Daniel Fuller, in a paper presented at the 1997 meeting of the Popular Culture Association ("Is That Cordite I Smell, or Just a Red Herring: Firearm Facts and Follies in Detection"), Kinsey Millhone is one of the few fictional detectives who really knows guns. Fuller identified several authors who make egregious errors, against whom he placed Grafton as the lone good example. For example, Grafton doesn't make the mistakes of many of her colleagues by misnaming the caliber or the ammunition, by referring to the kick of a small weapon, or by having anyone claim to smell cordite after a gun battle (cordite has not been used in the manufacture of gunpowder since 1905).

Virginia also gave Kinsey the no-brand semiautomatic she carries in the early novels, rather than any handgun issued by the police. She keeps this gun in an old sock in the top drawer of her desk and transports it in a briefcase, canvas duffel bag, or her purse, depending on her destination (car travel, target range, work, respectively). When Kinsey goes for target practice in *"B" Is for Burglar,* she tries out another gun, but, she tells us "it was still a distinct and familiar treat when I took up my .32 again, like holding hands with an old friend" (150). She is heartbroken in *"D" Is for Deadbeat* when her aunt's gun is stolen from her car. Tony Gahan uses it to kill two people and then casually returns it to her while they are perched precariously high on a building ledge in the novel's final scene.

Unfortunately, the gun is not very accurate, especially at long range. Near the end of *"E" Is for Evidence,* she confronts this problem. Despite her emotional attachment to the gun, she acknowledges, "It worried me that the sights were off. A gun is no protection if you can't control what it does. I stuck it in my handbag. I was going to have to leave it at a gun shop in the morning. Grimly I wondered if a gunsmith supplied loaners" (193).

Kinsey is fortunate that she put the gun in her purse because it comes in handy when she's facing her assailant, Terry Kohler, in the final scene of *Evidence.* After that, the gun, along with most of the rest of Kinsey's belongings, is "blown sky-high" by the bomb explosion concluding the novel (*G* 2).

Although Kinsey regrets the loss of her aunt's gun, she is extremely happy in the next novel with its replacement, a "Davis .32, chrome and walnut, with a five-and-a-quarter-inch barrel. . . . This one weighed a tidy twenty-two ounces and already felt like an old friend, with the added virtue that the sights were accurate" (*F* 127). She practices with the new gun at the target range and can "hit damn near anything" (*F* 193), and she treats herself to an Alessi shoulder holster to make her weapon more accessible (*F* 228).

Kinsey is irate when Robert Dietz, in *"G" Is for Gumshoe,* dismisses the new Davis she likes so much. He tells her to "dump" it because it is "useless" against the professional killer they are facing. He calls it "cheap and unreliable" and unsafe "to carry with a round in the chamber" ready to shoot, all in all not very helpful for emergencies (141). Although Kinsey is "stubborn and argumentative," she is the object of a contract killer's assignment and therefore very frightened, so she yields to Dietz's pressure. He is her hired bodyguard, after all, and Kinsey always respects the professional expertise of others. Of course, yielding on the big decision doesn't prevent her from putting up a fight about all the subsequent decisions. They argue for an hour at the gun store before closing a deal on a Heckler & Koch P7 in 9 millimeter, the one Dietz recommended in the first place. In *"I" Is for Innocent,* we discover that one point of dispute between Kinsey and Dietz was the size of the magazine. He persuades her to get a nine-round magazine. The nine shot plus one in the chamber gains her the ten rounds that save her life in the final scene.

Kinsey doesn't romanticize the place of guns in her life's work. They can be useful. She sometimes saves her own life by shooting another person, for example, Charlie Scorsoni (*Alibi*), Terry Kohler (*Evidence*), and David Barney (*Innocent*). On other occasions she uses a gun as a threat to prevent trouble, as she does in *Gumshoe,* when she aims her gun across the top of her car to scare away the hit man who's run her off the road. Guns may not be the primary tool in her investigative repertoire ("I spend more time practicing my skills with a Smith-Corona than a Smith & Wesson," *M* 149), but when they are needed, nothing else will do. When she is being held at gun point by the murderer in *Fugitive,* she thinks longingly, "My little Davis was still in the holster tucked up against my left breast. What I wanted to do was take it out and plug her right between the eyes—or someplace fatal" (256). "The life of a private eye is short on gun battles, long on basic research, but there are times when a ball-point pen just doesn't get it" (*B* 42–43). She's realistic about the physical danger she may encounter and she takes steps to be prepared. That means cleaning and reassembling her gun on a regular basis and maintaining her shooting skills by frequent target practice. Maintaining both the gun and her skills gives her pleasure.

Kinsey does not explain why she has discontinued carrying a handgun with her at all times in *"M" Is for Malice* (192). There are, however, a number of suggestions in this most recent novel that Kinsey is changing. We note also that, unlike its predecessors, this novel does not conclude with a violent physical confrontation. Kinsey may be mellowing somewhat.

Life on the Police Force

Talking to her ex-husband, Daniel, Kinsey describes her private investigator's job as very similar to her police job, but with one big difference. "I'm not part of the bureaucracy, that's all. Don't wear a uniform or punch a time clock. I get paid more, but not as regularly" (*E* 161). She also doesn't think that her new career is any more dangerous than police work. "Traffic detail, every time you pull someone over, you wonder if the car's stolen, if the driver's got a gun. Domestic violence is worse. People drinking, doing drugs. Half the time they'd just as soon waste you as one another. Knock on the door, you never know what you're dealing with" (*E* 161).

What did she like about that job? All we really know is: "Whatever else is true of police work, it does entail the intermittent sick thrill of life on the edge. I was hooked on the adrenal rush" (*B* 1). In spite of the periodic excitement, though, she left the force after two years primarily because she couldn't stand to be so much under the control of others. Lieutenant Dolan reads her well. He tells Kinsey, "That's why you didn't like being a cop yourself, Kinsey. Working with a leash around your neck" (*A* 15). She tells Jonah Robb that she left because she was too rebellious (*B* 48). She hated the bureaucracy (*D* 109), the boring routine, and the paperwork (*D* 176). Her private investigation business also requires extensive paperwork, but at least she gets to choose when and how she will do it. For Kinsey, that autonomy is important. Desire for personal control may have been part of her distaste for having to wear a uniform as a cop, but she also says she hated wearing something that made her "look like a camel from the rear" (*F* 206). Given Kinsey's disregard for looks, though, we scarcely need give this latter observation much credit as a reason for leaving the force.

She did become disillusioned with her job on the police force. In spite of her wild teenage years, she has a strong moral core, and one of the reasons she went into law enforcement was that she really wanted to be one of the good guys defeating the forces of evil. She had originally believed that the law enforcement system could be summed up easily: "The bad guys would all go to jail, thus making it safe for the rest of us to carry on. After a while, I realized how naive I was" (*B* 1).

Another reason Kinsey left the police force was the pervasive sexism. "I was frustrated . . . because back then, policewomen were viewed with a mixture of curiosity and scorn. I didn't want to spend my days defending myself against 'good-natured' insults, or having to prove how tough I was again and again. I wasn't getting paid enough to deal with all that grief, so I got out" (*B* 1).

There are hints of other reasons for Kinsey's departure as well. She tells Dietz in *"G" Is for Gumshoe* that she left the police force right after her aunt died, implying this was at least one of the precipitating factors in her decision to leave the force (95). In *"M" Is for Malice* Kinsey tantalizes us by saying of her departure: "life intervened," a story "I don't intend to tell (yet)" (2).

Regardless of the reasons for her resignation, it is clear that she left on good terms with her fellow officers, judging by the courtesy with which she is treated during such encounters as Lt. Feldman's questioning of her after Billy Polo's death (*D* 202), Officers Guittierez and Pettigrew inviting her to accompany them to question's Billy's sister (*D* 204), as well as a whole series of other police officers who are efficient and collegial with Kinsey.

After the Police Department: Training with the Byrd-Shine Detective Agency

After leaving the police force, Kinsey tried a number of unspecified jobs for two years before realizing that the lure of the "adrenal rush" was too strong to resist. Knowing she did not like working for someone else, she decided this time to go out on her own as a private investigator. To learn the skills needed in order to be licensed by the state of California, she apprenticed herself to the Byrd-Shine Detective Agency. Ben Byrd and Morley Shine sound like stereotypical private eyes of the thirties. Kinsey calls them "two old-fashioned gumshoes with whiskey bottles in their desk drawers and endless hands of gin rummy" (*I* 236). Although we know little about this period of her life, we do learn that her primary tutor was Ben, who taught her many investigative techniques, including how to put her notes on index cards and study them in various sequences.

Self-employed as a Private Investigator

Once Kinsey completed the requisite 4,000 hours to obtain her license as a private investigator, she opened her own office and devoted herself wholeheartedly to her work. "Private investigation is my whole life," she says in *"A" Is for Alibi* (233). Her first big investigation was for her former employer, California Fidelity Insurance. As a result of her success, she was hired by them to work full time investigating fire and wrongful-death claims. This work gave her valuable skills in detecting arson and recognizing the behavior of any large fire, as well as in the use of photography to prove arson or fraud.

Later she was able to negotiate an ongoing informal arrangement with CF: in exchange for office space, she would investigate as they needed her. She maintained an independent status, handling her own cases, and reporting to CF's vice president, Mac Voorhies, only when he hired her for a specific job. This suited her perfectly, giving her independence and requiring no payment of rent. All of this occurs before the series begins.

The comfortable arrangement with California Fidelity ends when an efficiency expert, Gordon Titus, challenges it. In spite of her extraordinarily good work for CF in *"H" Is for Homicide,* Titus ends the arrangement and throws her out of her office space. As she tells Dietz in her typical delicate fashion, "I got my ass fired because I wouldn't kiss someone else's" (*M* 44). She soon works out a similar office-sharing arrangement with a pair of law partners, Lonnie Kingman and John Ives.

One of the many engaging features of the series is the realism of Kinsey's self-employed status. She is sometimes enticed through a sense of thwarted justice, curiosity, or friendship to take on a non-paying job, but most of the time we know she is a paid professional. She hates getting "stiffed" and will work on her own time to track down clients who don't pay their bills (*C* 199, among others). One such instance occurs in *"D" Is for Deadbeat,* where she drives to Los Angeles to get her client to make good on his bounced check.

As a self-employed P.I., she tells us that she is careful to keep her medical insurance up to date "to cover the hazards of my trade" (*C* 12). With all the injuries she incurs, we may wonder that she is still insurable. She is also meticulous about keeping her disability insurance current, paying the premium before she pays her rent (*F* 3). She pays her other bills on time and keeps good up-to-date records. She is less meticulous with her tax receipts, but we at least get the impression that they are all there. Even if her accountant despairs because they are not neatly filed in the appropriate tax categories, they are at least all in one shoebox (*K* 2).

Before beginning work, Kinsey normally asks clients for a retainer, and she sends them weekly status reports. The final report comes with an itemized bill, including a refund if due. She began by charging $30 an hour plus mileage and expenses (*A* 22). In *"G" Is for Gumshoe* she tells Neil Hess that she thinks people hire her believing that they can pay a woman less (161). Neil thinks she's joking, but she's not. Even so, she is startled when she finds out just how wide the gender pay gap really is. In *"I" Is for Innocent,* Lonnie casually refers to paying Morley Shine, her predecessor on the case, $50 an hour. "Morley was getting fifty? I couldn't believe it. Either men are outrageous or women are fools. Guess which, I thought" (23). She proceeds to ask for—and get—$55 an hour from Lonnie Kingman, her new landlord-employer. She later calms down and charges a standard rate of $50 per hour from then on.

Unconventional Training

Kinsey has also acquired the skills of her profession from a plethora of other sources on both sides of the law. From her aunt's intentional and unintentional lessons and her favorite childhood game of remembering everything she saw briefly displayed on a tray (*G* 21) to her formal police academy instruction, Kinsey has been learning all her life how to be a good detective. She speculates that she learned a lifelong habit of eavesdropping by listening to her parents talk in the front seat on car trips (*L* 209–10). As early as *"A" Is for Alibi,* she tells us humorously that her entire socialization as a woman has contributed fundamentally to her career preparation: "Most of my days are the same: checking and cross-checking, filling in blanks, detail work that was absolutely essential to the job but scarcely dramatic stuff. The basic characteristics of any good investigator are a plodding nature and infinite patience. Society has inadvertently been grooming women to this end for years" (*A* 33–34). Similarly, Kinsey says,

"There's no place in a P.I.'s life for impatience, faintheartedness, or sloppiness. I understand the same qualifications apply for house-wives" (*B* 34).

Kinsey's innate curiosity and fondness for risks lie behind her confession that with only a slight difference or two in her life experi-ence she might have been equally happy on the wrong side of the law. Although her strong moral convictions would make life as a criminal difficult, if not impossible, for her, we know what she means as we watch her joyously pick a lock, spontaneously reel off credible lies, happily steal mail, and gleefully rummage through possessions when left alone in a room. No wonder, then, that she occasionally befriends and learns from unconventional citizens.

An unnamed ranking member of the burglar elite taught her everything she needs to know about picking locks in appreciation for some work she did for him (*B* 123). He also provided her with an excellent set of lock picks, one of Kinsey's few prized possessions. "I had a set of five picks with me on a key ring and a second more elaborate set at home in a nice leather case. They'd been given to me by a nonresidential burglar who was currently serving ten months in the county jail" (*B* 123). Kinsey had agreed to check up on his wife for him while he was in jail and found that she was faithfully waiting. "He was so grateful for the good news that he gave me the key picks and taught me how to use them" (*B* 123). The combination of dan-ger and expertise makes picking locks especially exciting for Kinsey. Having successfully opened a lock in *"C" Is for Corpse,* she exclaims: "It's this sort of shit that makes my job fun" (231).

Kinsey stays in touch with her criminous pals, and one, Harry Hovey, helps her to foil a kidnapping con in "A Little Missionary Work" (*K & M*). Hovey gives Kinsey directions to locate half a million dollars from his hidden stash in order to ransom the husband of a TV star he adores. Kinsey finds the money, pays the ransom, and is stupe-fied to discover she's been conned. The kidnapping was staged and the famous TV couple make off with the money. The money from Hovey, however, was some of his own counterfeit work, so the two of them trump up a charge of counterfeiting against the couple and get them arrested for that.

Kinsey also continues to learn from every case she takes on. Some-times she picks up a small scrap, almost in passing, such as Mike with the Mohawk teaching her a few things about drug dealing in *Burglar*, Dietz showing her a night-vision scope in *Gumshoe*, and learning about safe-cracking in *Lawless*. Sometimes the lesson is more overt and more extensive, such as learning about automobile accident insurance scams in *Homicide*, Ponzi schemes in *Judgment*, water-treatment plants and real estate manipulation in *Killer*, or the production of gravel in *Malice*.

"I want quick results": How She Operates as a Private Investigator

We all have our own idea of how a detective should detect, probably based on how our favorite detectives operate. Is it the slow, careful observer drawing strictly rational conclusions, or the joyfully spontaneous enthusiast who plunges ahead based on "gut feeling"? Or even the shoot-first-ask-questions-later-if-anyone-survives detective? Kinsey integrates some of the very best from each of these schools, using her analytical skills, but also remaining open to the hunches that spring apparently unbidden from unknown recesses of her mind, and she is always prepared to respond with physical action.

Methods of Investigation

Kinsey's personal skills and habits of thought have combined with her training and experience to give her some unique and adaptive strategies for crime solving. She seems to feel that she is in a three-dimensional puzzle, striving physically and mentally to create her own way of working it out. The essence of her work is asking the right questions and not giving up until she finds the right answers. As in scientific research, keeping the questions coming may be more important than coming up with quick answers. Kinsey muses that a particular interview "had generated more questions than it answered, but that was fine with me. As long as there are threads to unravel, I'm in business" (*E* 102). "Sometimes the noes are just as important as the yeses because they represent cul-de-sacs, allowing you to narrow

your field of inquiry until you stumble into the heart of the maze"
(*C* 88).

Like most real-life detectives, Kinsey is working on a number of
cases concurrently (in *"M" Is for Malice,* she says fifteen to twenty
cases, 147–48), but, of course, she reports on only one or two for each
novel. She does a lot of "routine snooping for a divorce attorney
down the street" (148), skip tracing, background checks, financial
research, and preemployment investigations for local businesses.
Much of it is not pressing, serving subpoenas for example, and she
says little about her routine cases while she focuses on the more
interesting primary investigation in each novel. These main cases may
begin routinely enough—she is hired to find a missing person, investigate a charge of arson, deliver a check, and so forth—but the case
typically becomes entangled with a murder, and Kinsey must find the
killer. She becomes passionately committed to each search and she
works hard to find the answers.

Step One: Information Gathering

So how does Kinsey acquire the information she needs? By a variety
of methods, almost all of which require long hours of hard work,
attention to detail, and cultivation of numerous resources, both human and technical. Kinsey combines office work and leg work. In *"D"
Is for Deadbeat,* she asserts, "I prefer fieldwork" (176), but she recognizes the essential nature of the paperwork. "I conduct maybe 40
percent of all business in my swivel chair, telephone in the crook of
my neck, files close at hand. Sixty percent of the time I'm probably on
the road, but I don't like feeling cut off from my reference points. It
puts me at a subtle disadvantage" (*E* 55). She keeps her office as tidy
and organized as her apartment. Needed tools of her trade, such as a
magnifying glass or her fingerprint kit, are kept handy.

We see some combination of Kinsey's holistic approach to detecting in all of her reports, but the full range of training, resource-
fulness, hard work, and imagination is perhaps most apparent in *"I"
Is for Innocent.* On this case report, her ninth in the series, Kinsey,
recently terminated from her association with California Fidelity, is
surviving financially by serving subpoenas, not her favorite job, but it

will keep her afloat for a while. She happily accepts Lonnie Kingman's first request for her services: take over an investigation begun
by one of Kinsey's former mentors, Morley Shine, who died while
working on the case. Lonnie's client is a plaintiff in a wrongful death
suit. David Barney was acquitted of the murder of his wife, Isabelle, in
the criminal trial, but Isabelle's family is suing to prevent him from
keeping the money he inherited upon her death. In the course of the
investigation, Kinsey not only solves the murder of Isabelle Barney,
but also the previously unsuspected poisoning of Morley Shine and
an unsolved hit-and-run manslaughter case.

Her investigation begins with the normal information gathering
that is the foundation of any serious detection effort. First, she does
her own on-site observations of the people and the location of the
murder. Shortly after taking the case, she goes to the scene of the
crime—Isabelle Barney's home, where she was murdered in the middle of the night in an especially gruesome method. (She was shot in
the eye as she looked through the peephole in the front door.) Kinsey personally makes a detailed scrutiny of the house, grounds, and
neighborhood. She times the walk from the road up the driveway and
thence, up to the house. She notes the placement of the bushes as
potential hiding places if a surprise visitor arrived. She takes down
the addresses of the neighbors, planning to go door to door to make
inquiries about events on the night of the murder (*I* 61–62). She
carefully conducts these investigations in spite of the fact she doesn't
like this part of her work. Such "dogged patience and a fondness for
repetition . . . doesn't really come naturally" (*D* 107).

Kinsey's favorite childhood memory game appears to have prepared her well. She has excellent powers of observation and memory.
In her keen reading of tiny details, Kinsey can seem as clever as the
British detectives of the Sherlock Holmes mold. For instance, during
an interview in *"C" Is for Corpse,* she notices that Nola Fraker's fingertips leave marks of perspiration on a glass coffee table. From this,
Kinsey concludes that Nola's current poised demeanor is just a
facade, and she is encouraged to press the woman further with questioning than she had intended at the beginning of their conversation
(192). When she returns to her motel room in *"F" Is for Fugitive,* she
immediately knows someone has broken in because she spots the
fresh indentation of a single shoe heel in the carpet by the sliding

glass door (123). Seeing blue towels used for a homemade silencer among some evidence at the police station in *"D" Is for Deadbeat,* she immediately remembers that those towels were with a number of other items in a laundry basket carried by Tony Gahan's aunt Ramona during an interview several scenes earlier (181 and 212).

Kinsey is shrewd about how to physically make observations. In *"G" Is for Gumshoe,* she wants to see what evidence she can find of an old murder at the home of Patrick Bronfen. She suspects that when Irene was a child she witnessed a murder there. Knowing that Irene was only four at the time, she stoops down to what she thinks would be the right height for a four-year-old child in order to see exactly what the child would have seen. She follows this process of using the right perspective—literally—and finds old blood behind the current wallpaper near the baseboard (243).

Insight plays a large role in her work. Sometimes the insight is clearly tied to her gender. It's hard to imagine those "Magnum, P.I. guys" figuring out that Laura must be faking her pregnancy by noticing tampons in the jumble of items in her purse (*L* 152). In Kinsey's first appearance in a short story, she uncovers a murderous husband because of a similar error. The man packs his wife's overnight case, which is found in her office. The husband claims she ran away from home. Unfortunately for him, when he packed the case, he put in her diaphragm to make it appear she was running away with a lover, but Kinsey learns that the wife has secretly had a tubal ligation and therefore would have had no need for birth control devices ("Long Gone," *K & M* 62).

As we are well aware, Kinsey normally isn't very scrupulous about how she gets information from personal observation. Sometimes we get the impression that her rule might be: the less legal, the more fun. How then does she feel about working for a lawyer and being required to gather material in proper ways from traceable sources? Not good. Going to Morley's office to pick up files, Kinsey finds herself casing the place. "Without even thinking about it, I walked around to the rear and tried the window back there. Then I remembered I was playing by the rules. What a bummer, I thought." (*I* 34).

In contrast, Kinsey hates having to make her observations by surveillance of a witness or suspect. She hates doing any kind of surveillance, whether she's moving or sitting still. She explains that many detective firms routinely charge a higher rate for such work because it is so boring (*H* 39). She doesn't choose to charge extra, but she fully understands the desire to do so. Kinsey takes food and coffee or Pepsi on these jobs whenever she has the chance to plan ahead, but nothing helps much. And then there is always the tug-of-war between the demands of a full bladder and the need to keep the subject in sight at all times. This is the only time Kinsey hints that being a female is a handicap: she remembers a comment from an old cohort "that men are the only suitable candidates for surveillance work because they can sit in a parked car and pee discreetly into a tennis-ball can, thus avoiding unnecessary absences" (*A* 33).

Interviewing

With so much technology available to conduct investigations, it may appear that detectives no longer need to talk to real people. Kinsey acknowledges that some people conduct all their work by phone or computer, but such impersonality is hardly her style. She believes that there is much to be gained by face-to-face interviews. Although many of them may be unproductive, the personally conducted interview "always pays unexpected dividends. I didn't want to bypass the possibility of surprise, as that's half the fun" (*D* 30). "Unless you're dealing with people face-to-face, there are too many ways to be deceived and too many things to miss" (*B* 20).

Kinsey has an impressive ability to get people to talk to her. When she is not on the job, we often sense that she is ill at ease making small talk or getting to know new people. But once she is in her detecting persona, Kinsey is skilled at reading people and sensing the best approach to them, whether to be direct or circuitous, brutal or gentle, quick or slow. "You better be good at reading human nature" (*J* 119). The result is that she usually gets others to tell her what she needs them to. Unless it's a bank clerk. In that case, forget it. Kinsey can never seem to get one of the minor minions in the bank bureaucracy to budge.

When interviewing a father whose son was killed in a car accident, Kinsey goes slowly, respectfully, eating lunch with him, and gently guiding the conversation toward what she wants to know (*C* 91–95).

Impressively, she knows when to back off entirely. Attempting to interview a young man who is both shy and suspicious, Kinsey decides to wait for him to come to her. "You can always push people around, but it's not a good idea. Better to let them volunteer information for reasons of their own. You get more that way" (*C* 129).

One resistant interviewee is Lyda Case, finally tracked down at her bartending job at the Dallas-Fort Worth airport. We watch Lyda's attitude change under Kinsey's persistent and determined goodwill from hostility to "sullenness to simple impatience" to downright friendliness (*E* 94).

Kinsey uses a different technique with Ava Daugherty, the office manager at Wood/Warren. Reading her carefully, Kinsey hooks Ava by telling her all the gory facts about Lyda Case's murder and her bloated body found in a car outside Kinsey's apartment. "I told her the details, sparing little. Ordinarily I'd downplay the particulars, not wanting to pander to the public appetite for the gruesome specifics of violent death. With Ava, I felt the reality of the situation might loosen her tongue" (*E* 95).

In perhaps the ultimate test of her abilities, Kinsey gets Terry Kohler to talk to her as a way of distracting him from killing her. "I wanted him to talk. I didn't want him to tie me up because then I'd be dead for sure" (*E* 219). The chat works; he eventually lowers his guard and Kinsey is able to get off a shot at him, which leads to her eventual escape.

Whenever Kinsey needs information that cannot be obtained by personal and direct observation of people or places, she resorts to other methods. She maintains a wide variety of contacts in public and private agencies who can often be called on to help her track down information about suspects or potential witnesses.

Resources

We are all vaguely and uncomfortably aware that information about us is more available than we'd like. But these sources are Kinsey's bread and butter. "It's hard to remain anonymous these days. Information is available on just about anyone: credit files on microfiche, service records, lawsuits, marriages, divorces, wills, births, deaths, licenses, permits, vehicles registered. If you want to remain invisible, pay cash for everything and if you err, don't get caught. Otherwise, any good P.I. or even a curious and persistent private citizen can find you out. It amazes me that the average person isn't more paranoid. Most of our personal data is a matter of public record. All you have to know is how to look it up" (*B* 34).

Kinsey is a regular visitor to the public library, the courthouse, and the police station. She also cultivates a large number of private sources who help her acquire much of the rest of the information that her job requires. "I have contacts at the telephone company, the credit bureau, Southern California Gas, Southern Cal Edison, and the DMV. Occasionally I can make a raid on certain government offices, but only if I have something worthwhile to trade. As for information of a more personal sort, I can usually depend on people's tendencies to rat on one another at the drop of a hat" (*D* 30).

Kinsey is, of course, better than most at getting people to rat on each other.

A buddy at the credit bureau lets her secretly look at files to which she would otherwise have no access (*A* 33, *E* 123). Dr. Laura Palchak in the Pathology Division at St. Teresa Hospital calls her about her case in *"G" Is for Gumshoe*. Darcy Pascoe does a search through the records of the Department of Motor Vehicles using CF's computers, although she is not supposed to do this without authorization (*M* 52). A friend at the telephone company gets information for her, also contrary to company policy (*C* 200). And Kelly Borden, the morgue attendant in *Corpse*, later helps her with information in *Deadbeat* (44). In *Innocent* she gets crucial information from Detective Burt Walker of the coroner's bureau. He provides psychological support to Kinsey when he takes seriously her suspicion that Morley Shine was poisoned and he works overtime to get the evidence needed to prove that Morley had indeed been murdered. A male friend at the Department of Motor Vehicles sometimes helps her track down license tags ("Full Circle," *K & M* 169) and another friend in the District Attorney's office will sometimes offer assistance on insurance-fraud suspects.

"Any competent detective quickly learns how to follow the trail of paper bread crumbs left by the private citizen wandering in the bureaucratic forest" (*J* 119). Kinsey's regular sources in the forest, without which she could not operate, include:

Police files
Autopsy reports
Dental records
Voter registration records
Tax rolls
Local phone books, city directories, and the "crisscross"
      (phone numbers cross-referenced with addresses)
The newspaper morgue at the *Santa Teresa Dispatch*
Real property records
Utility companies
Local labor unions
Social Security
Licenses for guns, driving, fishing, hunting, marriage
Birth and death certificates
Wills

She frequently laments the fact that police officers have access to national databases for criminal records that she does not. She does not seem to turn to bank records as a routine resource, as many detectives do through various necessarily illegal stratagems, nor does she use trial transcripts. (The transcript for the trial of David Barney in *"I" Is for Innocent* is the exception.) Nonetheless, she maintains an impressive array of resources, human and nonhuman.

Although she occasionally complains about the repetition of information searches, most of the time Kinsey seems to delight in the data-collecting process. "There's something restful about a morning spent cruising through the marriage licenses and death records in pursuit of genealogical connections, or an afternoon picking through probated wills, property transfers, and tax and mechanics' liens. . . . Sometimes I can't believe my good fortune, working in a business where I'm paid to uncover matters people would prefer to keep under wraps" (*M* 148). She says, "My notion of heaven is being accidentally locked in the Hall of Records overnight" (*L* 19).

An interesting sidelight to her work is that, regardless of the method or source used to obtain information, regardless of the utility of the facts discovered, competitive Kinsey appears to delight in the *finding* of the information itself—a search successfully concluded is its own reward. In *"G" Is for Gumshoe,* she describes such joy after some work in the newspaper archives pays off. "I could feel my brain cells doing a little tap dance of delight. I was half-skipping, excitement bubbling out of me as we crossed the street. 'I love information. I love information. Isn't this great? God, it's fun' " (220). Even finding an address is cause for joy. For that, Kinsey does "a quick dance, complete with butt wiggles, thanking the universe for small favors" (*J* 122). Likewise, Kinsey's "backside [is] dancing" while she studies a city map for information in *"M" Is for Malice* (14).

In addition to these regular sources, Kinsey has an array of sometimes highly *irregular* skills to help her generate information in even more surreptitious ways.

Lying

One of her less conventional skills is her incredible talent for lying. Whether it's falsely identifying herself to a cabby (*C* 211), telling a sick woman who looks awful that she looks fine (*F* 22), or deceiving a bar full of patrons about who she really is (*F* 61–72), Kinsey is completely at home in her falsehoods. As she "creates" a father who is not only a criminal, but also one who has robbed at gunpoint and done time for it, she congratulates herself. "Oh, I liked that. The lie rolled right off my tongue without a moment's thought" (*F* 66).

Kinsey appropriately thinks of herself as a world-class liar. She knows just how much detail to give, how much truth to weave in, how to select the best details for effect, and how to appear nonchalant about it all (*B* 30). She says she lies "with a certain breezy insolence that dares the listener to refute or contradict" (*A* 121). Most of us are willing to engage in the polite lie to avoid hurting someone's feelings, but Kinsey finds her skill a useful part of any disguise she assumes during an investigation, and she is so well versed in the practice that the falsehoods come trippingly, often spontaneously, off her tongue even when there doesn't appear to be a need for a lie. At a cemetery office, when approached by a clerk, she immediately responds, "I wasn't really up on the fine points of cemetery ethics so, of course, I told a lie" (*G* 236). Once when making a trial phone call, her party unexpectedly turns out to be home; she instantly launches into a telemarketing routine that she had just experienced herself, without preparation or glitches, and even manages to turn it into an opportunity to gain information from the other person (*J* 147–49).

Kinsey sometimes surprises even herself with the success of her lies; for example, while pretending to be a new member at a women's club, she frets, "I lied so well, I worried I'd be elected to office" ("Falling Off the Roof," *K & M* 120). And with one of her suspects, she says, "The fib I cooked up for Susie Grissom wasn't far from the truth and I sounded so sincere that I half believed it myself" ("Falling Off the Roof," *K & M* 117).

Her own skill at lying makes it easier for her to tell when she is being lied to by her interview subject or a witness, certainly a valuable skill for an investigator. "I love bad liars. They work so hard at it and the effort is so transparent" (*F* 242). Questioning Tippy Parsons about her activities on the night of the murder, she is completely convinced Tippy is lying (*I* 175), and she is proven correct.

Breaking and Entering

Kinsey loves a little spot of breaking and entering. "Actually, it's fun to horse around with danger. It's fun to snoop in people's dresser drawers. I might have turned to burgling houses if law enforcement hadn't beckoned to me first" (*C* 153–54). Early in *"E" Is for Evidence,* she breaks into the apartment of Andy Motycka, the person at California Fidelity whom she suspects of framing her on charges of insurance fraud. "I dearly love being in places I'm not supposed to be. I can empathize with cat burglars, housebreakers, and second-story men, experiencing as I've heard some do, adrenaline raised to a nearly sexual pitch. My heart was thudding and I felt extraordinarily alert" (59). She has the same reaction to breaking into Wendell Jaffe's hotel room: "I love this stuff. I was born to snoop. Nothing's as exhilarating as a night of breaking and entering. . . . If I didn't work in behalf of law enforcement, I'd be in jail, I'm sure" (*J* 28).

Like the rest of her job, breaking and entering is also hard work. "In TV shows, people pick locks with remarkable ease. Not so in real life, where you have to have the patience of a saint. I was working in the dark, clamping the penlight in my mouth like a cigar while I used the rocker pick in my left hand and the wire in my right. . . . This time it took forever, and I was sweating from the tension when the lock finally gave" (*F* 252).

Reading Upside Down

An unusual skill perfected by Kinsey is her ability to read upside down, an ability of great value in her chosen career. When Dolan is interviewing her about the explosion at the Kohlers', she can recite details about the package containing the bomb that she read upside down (*E* 135). And in *"F" Is for Fugitive,* she reads important legal documents from the wrong side of a legal secretary's desk (150).

Assuming Disguises

Kinsey is also good at assuming disguises, although she uses them infrequently. She has a blue-gray shirt and pants outfit with a Velcro patch on the sleeve to which she can apply any symbol she wants. Made for her by an ex-con, this "generic uniform" worn with her black traffic-officer shoes and a clipboard enables her to be "invisible" for her surveillance work, or for breaking and entering (*H* 33). For the clipboard she keeps "a supply of all-purpose forms. . . . They look like a cross between a job application and an insurance claim" ("Long Gone," *K & M* 52). She can pretend to be reading the water meter, checking for a gas leak, or delivering flowers as the need arises. And she keeps several sets of false IDs in her briefcase in her car (*H* 36).

Kinsey does not always resort to an outright disguise in order to go unnoticed. Sometimes she does little things to blend into her surroundings and observe others while going unobserved herself. Pretending to be a tourist for surveillance work in a Mexican resort hotel, she applies tan-in-a-can, reluctantly dons a bikini, and stretches out by the pool for some sunbathing, an activity she personally loathes as a waste of time (*Judgment*). Although she has little interest in fashion, she dresses up (although not without complaint) if she must attend a formal occasion, such as a funeral, and she dresses down and funky for such dives as the Meat Locker. As with all good detectives, she does whatever she needs to in order not to attract attention from other people on the scene.

Step Two: Recording the Information

Using index cards or her portable Smith-Corona, Kinsey is very careful about recording all the information she finds in her observations and her interviews. By keeping track, she realizes she is more likely to match her conclusions to the information rather than fit a selection of facts to a predetermined conclusion. Thus, she doesn't make guesses at the start of the case, because, as she explains in *"A" Is for Alibi*, "I didn't want to form a hypothesis too early for fear it would color the entire course of the investigation" (25).

She is well organized and accepts the responsibility to her client and herself to keep up with the paperwork. Since she employs no office help, she herself maintains the file for each case, plus her general office and personal files, keeping everything accurate, thorough, and up-to-date. She records facts and impressions as soon as possible after a stakeout, an interview, or a search through print sources, sitting in the car after an interview or staying up late at night if she must. She needs accurate reports both to solve the crime and to earn her money. In addition, especially since she is working for a lawyer on the case in *"I" Is for Innocent* and *"M" Is for Malice*, she needs to be credible in court. "In some ways, the measure of a good investigation is the attention to the paperwork. Without meticulous documentation, you can end up looking like a fool on the witness stand" (*I* 33). Interestingly enough, even after she begins to work with a law firm, we do not see Kinsey in court. Throughout the series we have seen her in court only once, for the arraignment of Bailey Fowler in *"F" Is for Fugitive*, for which she had no official responsibilities. She does refer to spending "most of the day over at the courthouse sitting in on the trial of a man accused of embezzlement" in *"M" Is for Malice*, but we have not gone into the courtroom with her. And that case wasn't even one of hers. She was not there to testify, but to watch "the legal system grind away" at someone she had known for years was dishonest (165).

The seriousness of Kinsey's attention to accurate paperwork is apparent in all her cases. As she puts it: "It's all detail; facts accumulated painstakingly" (*B* 34). Even when she chooses to work beyond the case for which she was hired, after she's been officially paid off, she continues to maintain careful records. Although her client in *"C"*

Is for Corpse, Bobby Callahan, has died, she writes up her report just as she would have done for him and files it away.

Step Three: Understanding What She Has Observed

When Kinsey has made her varied observations, she often has the technical knowledge needed for an immediate understanding of what she has seen. For example, she has acquired enough scientific knowledge to understand the process by which the medical examiner in *"I" Is for Innocent* determines the likely time of death. "Using the Moritz formula and adjusting for the temperature in the foyer, her body weight, clothing, and the temperature and conductivity of the marble floor on which she lay, the medical examiner placed the time of death roughly between 1:00 a.m. and 2:00 a.m." (*I* 19).

In almost every book, the next step is to record her observations on index cards. She was taught this technique by Ben Byrd of the Byrd-Shine Detective Agency, and Ben probably learned the technique from Morley Shine, his partner (*I* 236). Using an endless supply of 3″ × 5″ cards, she painstakingly records all the information she has gathered, one key fact per card. Fact or impression, but not interpretation.

In *"I" Is for Innocent* she describes the method: "I opened the first pack of index cards and started making notes of my own, laying out the story as I understood it. . . . The index cards permitted a variety of approaches: timetables, relationships, the known and the unknown, motives and speculations. Sometimes I shuffled the pack and laid the cards out like solitaire. . . . It was restful, reassuring, a welcomed time-out in which to get the facts down" (236).

At this point Kinsey begins to pin up the cards on her bulletin board. As she does, she thinks, "I censor nothing. There's no game plan. I simply try to record all the information, writing down everything I can think of in the moment. All the cards for Isabelle's murder were green. Tippy's accident was on the orange cards, the players on the white. I found the box of pushpins and began to tack the cards up on the board. . . . I sat on a kitchen stool, elbows propped on the counter, my chin in my hands. I studied the effect, which really didn't look like much . . . a jumble of colors, forming no particular pattern" (237).

Kinsey cleverly disengages any preconceived notions by creating a chaos of factual details, a colorful anarchy of impressions. And she just stares at the pattern made by the cards. "What was I looking for? The link. The contradiction. Anything out of place. The known seen in a new light, the unknown rising to the surface. At intervals, I took all the cards down and put them up again, ordered or random, arranging them according to various schemes. I thought idly about Isabelle's murder, letting my mind wander. . . . There was something here. I was almost sure of it. Maybe it was the angle of approach, some elusive piece of information, some new interpretation of the facts as I knew them" (237–38).

Kinsey surprises us sometimes with her intuition and never more startlingly than in *Innocent*. Having carefully accumulated and recorded an enormous amount of information and having sorted and shuffled her index cards, she has positioned herself to come up with insights into Isabelle's murder. Instead of fixating any longer on the cards, stalled in her efforts to deduce the answer rationally, she takes a mental break. "I made my mind a blank, erasing the day's events in a cloud of chalk dust. I was still troubled about Tippy [whom she suspects of having been out that night driving her dad's pickup and perhaps witnessing something she's now trying to hide], but there was no point in trying to force the issue. I turned the whole business over to my subconscious for review. Whatever was bugging me would surface in time" (152).

And she isn't let down. She wakes up in the early morning hours "with a telegram from my subconscious." The message is a single word: "pickup." Where has she seen the word "pickup" recently? With some rechecking of the newspaper files she's already consulted, she finds that the unsolved hit-and-run on the night of the murder involved a pickup. Was this possibly Tippy's truck? Through some clever maneuvering, she is able to prove that this was the case.

The message from her subconscious might be called intuition or inspiration or a hunch, yet it clearly arose from the hard work she had put in on the investigation at a conscious level before turning the problem over to her subconscious mind. Kinsey knows that her job requires "ingenuity, patience, and systematic routine, but success sometimes hinges on pure luck and a touch of magic." She adds dryly, "Try billing a client on the basis of *that*" (*M* 14).

Persistence

Once she takes on a job, she will not stop trying to decipher the evidence and find the murderer. She is single-minded in seeking a resolution. "I'm like a terrier pup. Somebody tells me to do something and it gets done. I'll worry the damn thing to death" (*B* 160). Or as she says in *"G" Is for Gumshoe,* people "hire me because I'm too dumb to know when to quit" (106). Although Beverly Danzinger, the client who hired her to find Elaine Boldt in *"B" Is for Burglar,* wants to give up the search, Kinsey is too caught up in the case to stop. She just switches clients in order to stay on the investigation (45–46). And in *"M" Is for Malice,* when she is paid off by the Malek family for finding Guy Malek, she then works for Lonnie Kingman to track down the identity of Guy's murderer. In *"J" Is for Judgment,* Kinsey continues past the final payment from CF without any paying client because she thinks it would be morally right to find out if Wendell Jaffe has been murdered.

Perhaps because we ourselves are so caught up in the stories, we rarely question why Kinsey, a paid professional, sometimes works on a case without being paid. Her reasons are varied but understandable and admirable. Kinsey sees herself as an individual struggling in her small way to redress wrongs. Her pursuit of justice (*Judgment* and *Killer*), combined with her curiosity (*Lawless*), her affection for others, including at times the victims (*Corpse, Killer,* and *Malice*), and the need to clear her own name (*Evidence*) are all reasons that keep her going even though she may not be paid. It is fortunate that Kinsey's frugality permits her to save enough money to sustain her through the nonpaying cases, because her passions for balancing the scales of justice and assisting the powerless are strong.

Her tenacious persistence carries her beyond any initial problems. For example, in *"E" Is for Evidence,* Kinsey wants to interview Lyda Case but has no address or phone number for her. First, she finds Lyda Case in an old telephone directory, then gets the old address from the crisscross, and locates a former neighbor who tells her Lyda moved to Dallas. Information in Dallas has a phone number for Lyda, but when Kinsey calls her, she hangs up on her. Undeterred, Kinsey checks Lyda's voter registration in order to obtain her birth date and

Social Security number. Knowing that Lyda used to be a bartender, Kinsey next calls the local bartender's union, pretending to be someone with the Chamber of Commerce addressing invitations to the annual Board of Supervisors dinner and needing the name of the receptionist answering the phone so that she could receive an invitation. She next calls the local bartender's union in Dallas, claiming this time to be the assistant in the Santa Teresa local—whose name she has just gotten—doing a status check on a Lyda Case. With this neat series of interlocking moves, she succeeds in getting Lyda's current employment, address, and work phone number. Kinsey calls Lyda at work, but is temporarily stymied in her quest because Lyda uses the normally effective device of simply hanging up a second time on her caller. Terrier pup that she is, Kinsey doesn't turn her loose. She flies to the Dallas airport, catches the woman leaving her airport bartending job, and persuades her to talk. After the interview, Kinsey takes the next flight home, having gotten exactly what she worked so hard for (*E* 83–85).

Kinsey can get so focused on following her leads and solving the case that she works right through the pain of serious injuries. In *"C" Is for Corpse*, she suddenly realizes with surprise that with the distraction of being on the job again, she hasn't noticed any pain at all in her injured arm (174). She is similarly surprised when, searching her face in a mirror in *"E" Is for Evidence* and in *"G" Is for Gumshoe*, she sees how bruised and battered she looks because she had forgotten about her injuries in the excitement of the searches.

Kinsey's occasional frustrations are always couched in humor. How can we forget her hiding in the bathroom when she is interrupted in her search by Lila Sams' unexpected return? Crouched down in the tub, hiding behind a shower curtain, and listening to Lila use the commode, Kinsey jokes, "This is not a dignified way to make a living" (*C* 153). In *"E" Is for Evidence* she is similarly struck with humor by the indignities of her profession as she crawls around the floor of Andy Motycka's apartment collecting bits of paper that in fact turn out to be of no use whatsoever (202). And when she decides to use a maid's uniform as a disguise in *"L" Is for Lawless* and ends up on her hands and knees dusting baseboards, she quips, "even in Texas I don't think impersonating a maid would classify as a crime" (113).

Step Four: Solving the Murder

Keeping track of all the information she has collected from all of her sources and working past her frustrations, Kinsey, like all fictional detectives, reaches that moment when all the various threads come together and she knows who the murderer is. The moment is not reached in an identical fashion in all the novels. In *"J" Is for Judgment,* one could argue that it is not reached during the action of the novel at all. Not until the Epilogue does Kinsey realize that Renata Huff may have duped her. Yes, she did murder Wendell Jaffe, but she may have staged a fake suicide and may be enjoying her illegally gotten money on some beach somewhere.

In most of the novels, though, we find that Kinsey reaches the moment of insight into the murderer's identity through one of several ways: straight deduction, a twist of luck, or a deduction that leads her *almost* to the identity of the murderer. (In *"D" Is for Deadbeat,* she's right about everything except *which* family member committed the murder.) As she says, "I don't always succeed in ways that I anticipate, but I haven't yet failed to bring a case to resolution" (*J* 119). And sometimes she flushes out the killer into self-revelation just by stirring things up. In every case, Kinsey solves the crime through her own hard work, but there are various triggers for the final discovery of the killer.

Sometimes, for example in *"F" Is for Fugitive,* Kinsey follows the logic of the clues straight to the murderer. To find the killer of teen-aged Jean Timberlake, murdered seventeen years earlier, Kinsey studies all the usual print sources of court records, newspapers, and high school records; she interviews everyone she can find with any potential for information, and she scrutinizes all the sites of the lives of the people potentially involved and the murder site as well. Thanks to her ability to read others, she recognizes that the erratic behavior of one of the witnesses could be explained only if that is the guilty person, and she immediately heads for the murderer's room to search for proof. Straight deduction and accurate reading of the clues lead her directly to the murderer.

Kinsey herself is the first to admit that luck often plays a role in figuring out a murderer's identity. A striking example occurs in *"K" Is for Killer* when Kinsey examines the shattered photographs from Danielle Rivers' apartment, wanting to see if the frames can be repaired. In a photo of Lorna and Danielle, she finds that the mat had been hiding the figures of two men. This is the first time there has been any proven connection between Lorna and these men, one of whom is already Kinsey's primary suspect. Suddenly Kinsey remembers that the man claimed to have had a phone conversation with Lorna on a day when Kinsey now knows *for certain* she was dead. Thanks to a bit of luck in looking behind a picture frame, Kinsey has her killer.

And sometimes Kinsey reaches the critical moment only by beating the bushes until she flushes the murderer out into the open. In *"E" Is for Evidence*, for instance, Kinsey follows trail after trail but can't seem to put together a case against any one person. Deduction is getting her nowhere. Nonetheless, she keeps on poking around, asking questions of anyone she can find, even provoking arguments—just to see what she gets. "I didn't have a clue to what was going on. I was driving randomly from one side of the city to the other, hoping that I could shake something loose" (201). What she finally gets, of course, is the shock of her life as she opens her own front door to find the murderer hiding in her bathroom with a gun in his hand, having just left a bomb on her kitchen counter. Only through his arrogant willingness to talk during this moment when he thinks he has won is Kinsey finally able to put all the pieces together and understand how and why the killer framed her for arson fraud and murdered his own wife in an earlier bomb blast.

Step Five: Confrontation with the Murderer

"E" Is for Evidence is typical of only a few of the novels in the series in having the revelation of the murderer occur in the same scene in which Kinsey confronts the murderer. *Corpse, Deadbeat,* and, arguably, *Malice* fit this pattern of surprising the reader and Kinsey together in the final big scene. And, of course, *Lawless* is totally anomalous: there is no killer for Kinsey to pursue until the final scene when Ray Rawson shoots Gilbert Hays and escapes with the loot.

More typical is the pattern followed in *Alibi, Burglar, Fugitive, Gumshoe, Judgment,* and *Killer* in which Kinsey concludes who the murderer must be and either names the killer or, more often, gives enough hints that we also can deduce for ourselves who she thinks is guilty, and then she goes to confront the killer. The impetus for setting up the final scene naturally differs from novel to novel. In *Alibi*, Kinsey figures out who the murderer of Laurence Fife is, confronts her, and she readily confesses. The *real* confrontation scene comes later as Kinsey realizes there must be a second murderer, goes to find evidence to prove it, and is caught by the killer who chases her across the beach with a butcher knife. In *Burglar*, Kinsey has figured out what the murder weapon was and simply wants to secure it before the killers can remove it, but the killers catch her in the act and they have a violent fight with fists, an axe handle, and finally a gun. In *Fugitive*, Kinsey goes to search the killer's room and is horrified to find the killer waiting with a shotgun in her hands, while *Killer* turns the pattern upside down by having Kinsey seek the killer not to challenge him but to warn him that she has just called the Mafia to kill him. *Gumshoe* offers another interesting twist with its dual confrontations: Kinsey goes to search the house of one killer, Patrick Bronfen, only to be doubly horrified when he returns early to find her, *and* when another killer, Mark Messinger, also shows up. He has tailed her to the house. He kills Bronfen and kidnaps her, taking her to a final showdown at a private airport. The confrontation in *Judgment* seems too easy—and Kinsey later realizes why it was too easy. Kinsey deduces that Renata Huff must have killed Wendell Jaffe, and when she confronts her, Renata promptly confesses without any struggle. She then jumps into the ocean and the only real sense of confrontation is Kinsey's futile efforts to save Renata from apparently committing suicide.

Most of the novels' violence occurs in these scenes. Many confrontations with the killers seem to be typical of hard-boiled detective fiction: Kinsey and the killers fight it out at the end of *"B" Is for Burglar;* they shoot it out at the end of *"I" Is for Innocent.* But we notice a sophisticated toying with the basic technique. Grafton deliberately plays off Kinsey's particular phobias. The author is especially tough on Kinsey by making her confront not only the killer but also some of her own worst fears at the same time, making the confrontation both external and internal in nature. Is Kinsey scared of needles? Okay, have the killer in *Corpse* stalk her through a morgue carrying a large syringe full of tranquillizer. She hates garbage bins after her first homicide case involved children stuffed into a garbage can? And she didn't like the tension of playing hide-and-seek as a child, fearing she would wet her pants? Fine, make the only refuge she can find to hide in on the beach in *Alibi* be a garbage bin. And then let's make her hide in the dark beside the Xerox machine from David Barney who's stalking her in *Innocent*. She doesn't like heights? Let's perch her on the edge of an eight-story building, trying to prevent a suicide at the end of *Deadbeat*. She doesn't like swimming in the ocean? Oh good, let her have to swim after Renata in the conclusion of *Judgment*. She loves her apartment and feels secure for the first time in her life? Make her come home to find a killer ready to bomb it out of existence in *Evidence*. She fears loss of autonomy and personal control above all? Great, let's have the killer use a taser gun to stun her into immobility in the final scene of *Killer*.

Lord, that woman is strong—physically and psychologically.

"Can I ask about the autopsy?": Kinsey's Relationship with the Police

Private investigators are frequently portrayed at odds with the police. Simply put, the police are paid from public funds to solve crimes. When citizens use their own private funds to hire investigators, a normal assumption might be that the police haven't done their job properly. This is a likely reading when private investigators work on crimes that the police are simultaneously investigating, and the police may be understandably resentful of what they see as both interference and insult. Fictional detectives who cross paths with police detectives are, therefore, often antagonized, cross-examined, and threatened with loss of their licenses and livelihood. Kinsey's relationship with the police occasionally reflects this stereotypical assumption, for example, when she tangles with Lt. Santos from the LAPD in *"H" Is for Homicide*, but it is typically much richer, more complex, and more collegial. "Just for the record, I like cops . . . anyone who stands between me and anarchy" (*J* 2).

First, Kinsey has a number of friends and acquaintances in the Santa Teresa Police Department from her stint there as a police officer. Although she left, she did so without trailing bitterness or ill will behind her. We are not completely surprised to find her defending the police to critical, cynical, disappointed citizens. She refutes accusations that the police can be bought off (*C* 90). When her client in *"D" Is for Deadbeat* thinks the police officers don't have enough emotional concern about the case, Kinsey defends them. "Cops don't have to *care*. . . . If it's homicide, they have a job to do and they'll do it well" (41). She strongly defends them as "serious professionals" to a skeptical Janice Kepler in *"K" Is for Killer* (15).

Kinsey often calls the police to arrange backup or cooperative action. On a case, she falls smoothly into the procedures she learned on the force, relaxing into them rather than struggling against them. In *"E" Is for Evidence,* she says: "The next two hours were filled with police routine, comforting procedures, as formalized as a dance. All of the responsibility belonged to someone else" (186). Even when provoked by police action, Kinsey can show amazing restraint. Again in *Evidence,* she has little critical to say about the police when she is threatened with possible arrest, even though she knows that she is innocent. The only time she strikes a police officer occurs in *"H" Is for Homicide,* and that punch is prompted more by her desire to stay in disguise for Bibianna's benefit than by inability to control her temper.

There are a few police officers or staff to whom Kinsey frequently turns for information or assistance:

Detective Lt. Con Dolan appears in almost every book prior to *"M" Is for Malice.* In *"A" Is for Alibi* he is responsible for referring Nikki Fife to Kinsey, thus starting the ball rolling in the first case in the series. This referral sets the tone for the relationship between Kinsey and the lieutenant. Nikki was properly, if unjustly, convicted of the murder of her ex-husband, Lawrence, and served eight years in prison. Yet when she wants to clear her name, maintaining her innocence, Dolan not only refers her to Kinsey, but also encourages Kinsey to take the case. It turns out Dolan thinks Nikki killed a second person and hopes Kinsey will turn up evidence to support his supposition. He shows her all the paperwork—autopsy reports, whatever she wants—the police have collected. Their interaction is tense and far from trustful, but she tells him she respects his skills, and he allows that he believes that she is honest and not a bad detective (15).

In *"B" Is for Burglar,* Kinsey comes up against the resistant side of Dolan when she wants to question him about her missing persons case. They sound more like the typical policeman and private eye than they did in the previous novel. " 'I won't discuss it with you. . . . department policy,' he said. His favorite phrase. 'Jesus, Lieutenant Dolan. Big deal. Who asked you?' I knew he was protecting the integrity of his case, but I get tired of his being such a tight-ass. He thinks he is entitled to any information I have, while he never gives me a thing. I was hot and he knew it. 'I just thought I'd head off that tendency of yours to stick your nose in where it doesn't belong' " (50). After she leaves the office, Kinsey admits to herself that she lets Dolan get to her. And the further we get in the series, the more we realize how unfair Kinsey is being to Dolan here; in fact, he does give her a lot—more than she might reasonably expect from a disinterested police official.

In *"E" Is for Evidence,* Dolan interviews Kinsey in her hospital room, showing concern for her injuries, but also digging for information to help him solve his case. He acknowledges that her observations and impressive memory for details are especially helpful. But their relationship is still dominated by his dislike of P.I.s and her anger at having to defend her livelihood. She describes his professional demeanor as "that mask of studied neutrality all cops tend to wear—taking in everything, giving nothing back" (136).

When Kinsey's life is in danger in *"G" Is for Gumshoe,* Dolan openly assists her, providing her bodyguard with information about the hired killer, Mark Messinger, sending her a bulletproof vest, and helping her to find Messinger's former wife, who ultimately saves Kinsey's life. He will even stoop to helping her with a license tag check if it is related to a case he is working on ("Full Circle," *K & M* 170).

Kinsey and Dolan are in a position to help each other in *"H" Is for Homicide.* She's been arrested, and Dolan and a Los Angeles police detective, Santos, try to get Kinsey to do undercover work for them upon her release. Like every stereotypical policeman, Santos tries to bully her into it by threatening to take away her license. Kinsey blows up at the very idea, and it is Dolan who signals Santos to back off this strategy. He knows Kinsey well enough to realize this is precisely the way to make her refuse the request. He also knows her well enough to come up with the one appeal that will get her to cooperate—that the man they want her to investigate was probably responsible for the death of her colleague, Parnell. When she agrees, he thanks her and holds out his hand. In short, Dolan gains her cooperation by appealing to her humanity and by treating her as a fellow professional (108–12).

Unfortunately, Dolan is down with the flu in *"I" Is for Innocent* and Kinsey must rely on other allies. He is only a voice on the phone in *"L" Is for Lawless,* although his is an important voice because he vouches for Kinsey to the Kentucky police and secures her release. Since we learn in *"M" Is for Malice* that Dolan has retired, it is reasonable to assume we will not see him often in the future. (Unless he goes to work for her. Now *that* would be fun.)

Officer Jonah Robb presents a special case for Kinsey's police network, because they become lovers. But they have a professional relationship as well. She meets him during *"B" Is for Burglar* when she files a missing persons report for her client. Sgt. Robb handles missing persons cases. Later he tracks her down at Rosie's and gives her the information he's found about her case. She can hardly believe it when he offers to let her look at department files—she tells him that Dolan would never show them to her and Jonah simply says, "Ask me. . . . What do you want to see? Autopsy? Incident Report? Follow-up interviews? Lab Reports?" (97). And it's Kinsey who feels anxious about this, not Jonah. He implies that homicide detectives are too uptight about information. He's fine with sharing.

Jonah agrees to help again in *"D" Is for Deadbeat,* violating department rules and federal regulations to get Kinsey information from the National Crime Information Computer. Such help is invaluable to her because the police can obtain in minutes what would take her days to find, if she can find it at all (29–30). In the course of *Deadbeat,* Jonah and Kinsey become lovers, which complicates things for them personally but doesn't significantly alter her professional relationship with this important source of information. Even while recollecting "cavorting stark naked" (*D* 211) with Jonah, she discusses handmade silencers with him. They freely exchange information throughout the book.

Kinsey relies on Jonah for more than information. In *"I" Is for Innocent,* for example, she calls him at his home late at night asking for backup for a meeting that may prove dangerous. In spite of the late hour or any inconvenience, he instantly agrees to help.

Jonah is promoted to lieutenant by *"J" Is for Judgment* and he moves to the Homicide Division. By *"M" Is for Malice,* he replaces Dolan as chief of Homicide and he seems less willing to give information to Kinsey than when he worked in Missing Persons and sneered at the secretiveness of homicide detectives, but his manner remains cordial.

Emerald is another link in Kinsey's regular police resource network. She is an African-American woman who is a clerk in Identification and Records and appears in many of the books and short stories. Starting with *Alibi,* Emerald is frequently the one who actually gets specific police files for Kinsey (13). In this first instance, she is told to do so by Dolan, but on other occasions, such as in *"E" Is for Evidence,* Kinsey bypasses the officer in charge, if he is unlikely to help, and goes straight to Emerald. "Technically she's not supposed to give out the kind of information I needed, but she's usually willing to help if no one's around to catch her" (85). Because she's "a sucker for gossip" ("Full Circle," *K & M* 161), Emerald offers more than official information from their files.

Lt. Cheney Phillips appears in a significant way only in *"K" Is for Killer,* but he is extremely important in that one novel. Kinsey is investigating the death of Lorna Kepler some months earlier. Told that Lt. Phillips in Homicide handled the case, she tracks him down at a local bar frequented by the police and arranges to meet him there. He tells her everything he can remember about the case, including his informal impressions. At the time he suspected murder, but the body was so decomposed they could not even determine the cause of death. Seeming to welcome her fresh look at the case, Cheney even offers to arrange for her to see all the police files (32). Later Lieutenant Dolan agrees to let her see the autopsy photographs, though he warns her that they will be upsetting (75). Cheney also puts Kinsey in contact with Danielle Rivers, the prostitute who provides her with the most useful information about Lorna. And he responds immediately when Kinsey calls 911 after Danielle is assaulted (209 and 215).

Although Kinsey normally has a good relationship with the individual police personnel she encounters, she is not without a healthy distrust of the community of law enforcement officers, aware that they, like any other group, will have some incompetents and rotten apples. For example, in *"H" Is for Homicide* the police bureaucracy makes a mistake and Kinsey is released into her undercover role without appropriate preparation, including the wire. She's angered by the negligence, but she still does her job. And in *"F" Is for Fugitive,* Kinsey learns that the police knew their chief witness had lied, but they remained silent while an innocent man was sent to jail for murder (190).

Homicide and *Killer* are the most critical of the police and contain vivid incidents of police corruption. In *Homicide,* Jimmy Tate—who went through the police academy with Kinsey and later joined the L.A. County Sheriff's Department—explains that he and six other deputies were indicted "in a money-skimming scandal that was rocking the department" (60). In spite of being guilty, he was acquitted on a technicality. He was nonetheless fired and lost his benefits. He then turned around and sued the department, winning a hefty settlement. Especially chilling in his account is the easy assumption of universal corruption. "Come on, Kinsey. You know how it is. I palmed cash sometimes. Hell, everybody does. I saw guys palming cash the first day I ever went to work" (69).

Kinsey must believe something of Tate's perspective. In *"K" Is for Killer,* when she is unable to find the $20,000 Lorna Kepler took out of the bank the day before she died, she wonders aloud to Cheney if the first officer on the scene stole it (173). But her major disillusionment comes when she tells Cheney who the murderer is. He knows she is right, but says they can do nothing. There is not enough evidence to convict. Kinsey, "propelled by the hot urge to act, by the blind need to strike back at the man who had dealt me this blow," calls her Mafia contact and, in effect, signs the murderer's unofficial death warrant (278). Kinsey, then, has come full circle, from her defense of the police to Lorna's grieving mother, through cooperation with the police, telling Cheney and Dolan everything she discovers, to a complete rejection of the police as a vehicle of justice.

In Kinsey's usual complex way, though, this is not her final word on the subject. We learn in the Epilogue that she told Lt. Dolan everything she had done, but absent a dead body, he takes no action against her.

Killer offers an extreme instance of Kinsey trusting no one more than herself to be able to effect a bit of justice in an unjust world.

KINSEY'S CASE LOG

NOVEL	KINSEY'S CLIENT	OBJECT OF INVESTIGATION	ULTIMATE CONFRONTATION	KINSEY'S ROLE IN OUTCOME
A	Nikki Fife	1. Find murderer of Laurence Fife	1. Confronts murderer who confesses	1. Questions killer
		2. Solve related murders of Libby Glass and Sharon Napier	2. Is chased along beach by killer with a butcher knife	2. Shoots and kills murderer
B	1. Beverly Danzinger	1. Locate Elaine Boldt	Collecting murder weapon, Kinsey is caught and attacked by killers	Subdues killers; she's injured in the fight
	2. Mrs. Ochsner	2. Find Boldt's murderer		
C	Bobby Callahan	Find person trying to kill him (who later succeeds)	Finds key evidence at morgue but is caught and attacked by killer	Subdues killer with a 2' × 4'
D	1. John Daggett	1. Deliver check to Tony Gahan	Tries to talk Daggett's young killer out of jumping from building	1. Delivers check
	2. Barbara Daggett	2. Solve her father's murder		2. Fails to prevent suicide

continued

NOVEL	KINSEY'S CLIENT	OBJECT OF INVESTIGATION	ULTIMATE CONFRONTATION	KINSEY'S ROLE IN OUTCOME
E	1. California Fidelity Insurance	1. Investigate arson at Wood/ Warren	Killer/person who framed her traps her with a bomb in her own apartment	Shoots killer. She is wounded and murderer is killed in explosion
	2. Herself	2. Refute conspiracy charge in arson and solve related murder		
F	Royce Fowler	Clear his son of old charge of murdering Jean Timberlake	Killer lies in wait with shotgun for Kinsey coming to search her room	Trapped by killer, who wounds herself when her father tries to subdue her
G	1. Irene Gersh	1. Check on her mother, Agnes Grey	1 & 2. Killer catches Kinsey searching his kitchen	1 & 2. Killer is shot by the contract killer
	2. No client	2. Find Agnes's killer		
	3. Herself	3. Protect herself from contract killer	3. Killer holds his ex-wife, Kinsey, and Dietz at gunpoint at airport	3. Contract killer is shot by ex-wife
H	1. California Fidelity	1. Check insurance claim of Bibianna Diaz	1 & 2. Kinsey chases killer/ insurance fraud leader through hospital	1. Helps Bibianna escape leader of fraud ring
	2. LAPD and Santa Teresa Police Department	2. Uncover insurance scam and find link to murder of Parnell Perkins		2. Catches killer and, enraged, almost shoots him

continued

NOVEL	KINSEY'S CLIENT	OBJECT OF INVESTIGATION	ULTIMATE CONFRONTATION	KINSEY'S ROLE IN OUTCOME
I	Lonnie Kingman	1. Gather information for wrongful death suit against David Barney 2. Solve related murder of Morley Shine and a hit-and-run	Kinsey is ambushed and shot by killer in her office	Kinsey shoots and kills the murderer
J	1. Mac Voorhies at CF 2. Herself	1. Find out if Wendell Jaffe is alive 2. Find out if Jaffe has been killed	1 & 2. Kinsey confronts killer on breakwater; she confesses and dives into the water	Dives in but fails to prevent killer from suicide; on reflection, decides killer escaped
K	Janice Kepler	Prove her daughter Lorna was murdered and find the killer	Kinsey tries to warn killer in water treatment plant but is attacked by him	Killer presumed killed by Mafia on Kinsey's tip
L	1. Favor to Henry Pitts 2. Chester Lee	1. Establish deceased neighbor's veteran status 2. Track down theft from his father's apartment	1 & 2. Kinsey locates stolen money at cemetery. One robber kills another and Kinsey is knocked out	While Kinsey is unconscious, thief/killer escapes with money
M	1. Cousin Tasha on behalf of Malek family	1. Locate missing heir, Guy Malek	1 & 2. Kinsey tracks killer to busy highway and killer confesses	After Kinsey's questioning, killer runs into traffic and is killed

continued

NOVEL	KINSEY'S CLIENT	OBJECT OF INVESTIGATION	ULTIMATE CONFRONTATION	KINSEY'S ROLE IN OUTCOME
	2. Lonnie Kingman	2. Find Guy's murderer		

KINSEY LAUGHS AT:

Importance of a paper trail:

"Small comfort to an attorney who could end up in court with nothing in his hand but his dick." (*I* 98).

Her job:

"Thinking is hard work, which is why you don't see a lot of people doing it." (*I* 265–66)

Social and Political Issues

*"Other days, I concede
the dark forces are
gaining ground."*

Grafton spares us lengthy diatribes on the ills of our society and her versions of how to remedy societal problems. Most often, through the use of short witty insights, the novels reveal deep concerns about a variety of social issues, concerns that are thought-provoking but never didactic.

Class

Each of the novels contains real sensitivity to class differences in the American social structure. Kinsey is working class and proud of it. She tells us in *"G" Is for Gumshoe,* "I was strictly blue-collar lineage" (252).* Unlike many of her fellow Americans, upward mobility never

---

* Kinsey's insistence on her working-class background and lack of higher education is clearly a statement about her chosen persona more than a factual description of parentage and upbringing. Her father and her aunt held clerical positions, not blue-collar jobs. Kinsey occasionally goes against expectations for this persona: she alludes to Marcel Proust (*J* 154) or paraphrases William Wordsworth (*F* 145). She easily refers to "echolalia" (*C* 138) and "paresis" (*C* 203) and she knows the *Oxford English Dictionary* (*C* 76). She casually observes the "helix" of someone's ear (*F* 40). She reads French (*M* 254). Granted, Kinsey is curious about everything and reads a lot; even so,

seems to be on her mind. Perhaps one of the attractions of this independent and highly competent woman is that she is refreshingly comfortable with a small rented apartment, a car praiseworthy only for its efficiency, and a minimalist wardrobe totally incapable of uttering a fashion statement. Although Kinsey sometimes expresses a fleeting desire for some element of the lives of the well-to-do—the silence of their large estates or the magically prepared elegant meals, for example—her attitude toward the wealthy is usually one of bewilderment or distaste.

We most frequently encounter her class views during visits to the wealthy neighborhoods of Montebello and Horton Ravine and those upper middle-class sections with aspirations to grandeur, where she goes to interview witnesses or deal with clients. Typical is her description of one such pretentious middle-class neighborhood: "The Copse at Hurstbourne is one of those fancy-sounding titles for a brand-new tract of condominiums on the outskirts of town. . . . It was hard to understand why it couldn't have just been called Shady Acres, which is what it was. Apparently people aren't willing to pay a hundred and fifty thousand dollars for a home that doesn't sound like it's part of an Anglo-Saxon land grant. These often quite utilitarian dwellings are never named after Jews or Mexicans. Try marketing Rancho Feinstein if you want to lose money in a hurry. Or Paco Sanchez Park. Middle-class Americans aspire to tone, which is equated, absurdly, with the British gentry. . . . The Copse at Hurstbourne was surrounded by a high wall of fieldstone, with an electronic gate meant to keep the riffraff out" (*E* 57). Since she assumes that means her, she sneaks through the barrier by tailgating an incoming car. Her portrayal of the snobbery and bigotry of these neighborhoods helps us to understand why she has no desire for a mortgage there.

The upper class suffers defects similar to the middle class. They may actually dwell on land-grant property, but she usually spots their superficial approach to living. She has a hard time finding the person behind the facade, and hypocrisy is something Kinsey despises. Visiting one such home, Kinsey looks at the furnishings and concludes, "Aside from the conventional good taste, there was no indication that

---

there are startling aspects of her language, vocabulary, and habits that challenge stereotypes of the working-class.

they listened to music or read books. No evidence of shared interests. There was a current copy of *Architectural Digest* on the coffee table, but it looked like a prop." As far as Kinsey is concerned, the upper class might all be done with smoke and mirrors, or they might be a completely different species from the creatures Kinsey knows as people. "I've never known rich people to read *Popular Mechanics, Family Circle,* or *Road & Track.* Come to think of it, I have no idea what they do at night" (*E* 113).

Fascinated in spite of herself, Kinsey frequently tries to figure out what lies behind the snobbery of the wealthy. Even when they have all the material goods they may want, they continue to try to distinguish themselves as wealthier than other members of their class. She sarcastically expresses what she understands as their credo, "What's the point of achieving status if you can't still be compared favorably with someone else in your peer group?" (*I* 63). She presents us with an amusing scorecard of real property indicators that rich people use to establish their superiority to the less wealthy members of their class: "The size and location of the property should be given first consideration. Additionally, the longer the driveway, the more points will be accorded. The presence of a private security guard or a pack of attack-trained dogs would naturally be counted more discerning than mere electronic equipment. . . . Beyond that, one must factor in such matters as guesthouses, spiked gates, reflecting pools, topiary, and excessive outdoor lighting. Obviously the fine points will vary from community to community, but none of these categories should be overlooked in assessing individual worth" (*I* 63–64).

Kinsey lets us know how much in error it is to ascribe superior values to the wealthy. The rich she meets may have leather tomes instead of paperbacks, and sophisticated sound systems instead of boom boxes, but they rarely read or listen to music. Or they may be so involved in making money that other values seem to fade into a distant second. Many—especially the men who marry for money— seem to use their wealth only to control others or purely for self-indulgence. We assume from Bobby Callahan's description of his absent father that he falls into the category of those who give new meaning to the term "idle rich." Bobby replies to Kinsey's question about where his father is: "Tibet. He's taken to mountain climbing of late. Last year, he lived in an ashram in India." Bobby adds dryly,

"His soul is evolving at a pace with his VISA bill" (*C* 23). Police detective Cheney Phillips confirms Kinsey's impression that his background is monied. That's something that would ordinarily put a barrier between them, but Cheney confides that his father, a prominent banker in the area, had little time for his family, and his mother, who sold "high-end" real estate, had little more time for him. "I was raised in an atmosphere of benign neglect" (*K* 81). Cop shows on television made more of an impression on him than did his parents, hence his job choice.

Food is often a class marker for Kinsey. She's comfortable with her fast food when dining out or jars on the table if she's eating at home. She enjoys the greasy fingers brought on by a gooey ham and grilled cheese sandwich and a pile of fries, which, she tells us, are "heaven to a person of my low appetites" (*J* 112). Yet, when offered a treat, she enjoys the extravagant hors d'oeuvres or snacks of the rich even as she exhibits flashes of guilt for the pleasure, as if she has betrayed her own class by liking the tomato aspic. Thoroughly impressed by the maid's almost instantaneous delivery of a lovely meal to Bobby's room, Kinsey wonders, "Did these people eat like this every day? Bobby never batted an eye. I don't know what I expected him to do. He couldn't squeal with excitement every time a supper tray showed up, but I was impressed and I guess I wanted him to marvel, as I did, so I wouldn't feel like such a rube" (*C* 38). She both likes and laughs at the elegant food. And she normally finds a way to contrast their fine wine with her jug wine or their fancy canapés with her cheeseburgers.

People may aspire to join the economic elite, but Kinsey would warn them to be careful what they wish for. Francesca Voigt tells Kinsey that she has the same "sense of amazement" at her own expensive home as Kinsey does. "My father was a grade-school custodian and my mother worked in a pharmacy, stocking shelves with dental floss and Preparation H." Francesca describes how easy it was to fit herself into her husband's social group. "It's just a series of tricks. I could teach you in an afternoon." But after falling in love and snagging her wealthy husband, she now finds him difficult to be around. The superficiality has not proven satisfying for the long haul. "He turns out to be rather shallow. . . . He doesn't read. He doesn't think about things. He has opinions, but no ideas" (*I* 157–58).

Francesca and Kinsey are not alone in the series in making their way successfully in life in spite of humble beginnings. Julia Ochsner in *"B" Is for Burglar,* for example, believes that she and her ten siblings did well. "I came from a family of shriekers and face slappers. They all threw things. . . . Now that I look back on it, I see we were all common as mud, but effective. We all got what we wanted in life and no one ever accused us of being helpless or fainthearted" (*B* 166). Another set of characters who came from the working class are Henry Pitts and his siblings. Although their father died young, the five siblings all made out quite well. Strength of character and personal determination appear to be associated in Kinsey's mind with the working class more than with the middle or upper classes.

The members of the upper class whom Kinsey encounters usually vindicate her class bias. Many of them are arrogant, demanding, self-satisfied, and treat the people around them as objects. Partly due to her instinctive distaste, and partly from a lack of social self-confidence, Kinsey is uncomfortable in the extreme with wealthy people. Meeting the family and friends of Bobby Callahan in *"C" Is for Corpse,* Kinsey reveals her uneasiness and expects their negative judgment even before entering the house. Once there, nothing seriously alters her expectations, although she is surprised to hear one of the women describe buying fabric remnants to make her own dress (25–26). At a gathering of the same people later in the novel, one group is talking about "long-term paper," and she keeps herself going by imagining a possible contribution to the discussion: "Such a nuisance, that shit, isn't it?" She watches the maid consolidating hors d'oeuvres so that the plates would continue to look impressive, and she sarcastically thinks to herself, "God, there was a lot to this business of being rich." And she places herself so she won't have to talk to anyone. "I'd rather have chatted with some hooker down on lower State Street than try to exchange pleasantries with this crew" (114).

Kinsey contrasts these wealthy stuffed shirts with Alicia, the Chicana maid of the household, who brings the tray of food to Bobby's room. Kinsey clearly identifies with Alicia, and she wonders what this world looks like from the maid's perspective. "If she knew what was happening, she gave no indication of it. . . . She murmured something and departed." Kinsey observes how the wealthy tend to ignore

their domestic employees, as if they were invisible or part of the furniture. "I felt uncomfortable that it was all so impersonal. I wanted to
ask her if her feet hurt like mine, or if she had a family we could talk
about. I wanted her to voice curiosity or dismay about the people she
worked for" (38).

In the series, wealthy characters range from the merely irritating
to the downright evil. Irene Gersh is a hothouse flower who would
not survive outside a monied environment (*G* 6–7). Even when we
discover the cause of her nervous disorders, we can't completely forget her pampered dependency on her husband. The bickering selfish
Malek sons in *"M" Is for Malice* are also tributes to the harmful effects
of financial indulgence.

Most damning of all is the fact that the wealthy seem able to get
away with murder. In *"C" Is for Corpse*, two of these same arrogant,
distant, controlling people are responsible for two murders. At the
conclusion of *Corpse*, both are out of jail. One, Nola Fraker, pleads
guilty to manslaughter but serves no time. Her husband, who killed
two people and tried to kill Kinsey, is out on bail, and it is not at all
clear that he will serve time either. David Barney, the wealthy murderer in *"I" Is for Innocent*, escaped a guilty verdict in a criminal trial
and is busy spending his dead wife's wealth until Kinsey is brought in.
Renata Huff *apparently* escapes punishment of any kind in *"J" Is for
Judgment* and has millions of dollars to play with.

Despite this bias, over and over in the Grafton novels individuals
defy any generalizations she might seem to be making about any
group or community to which they belong. This iconoclasm is obvious in Grafton's portrayal of the wealthy. Against the background of
a group of unprincipled, amoral, superficial rich, a few individuals
emerge who markedly elude the worst effects of their class. Bobby
Callahan, whose mother is so wealthy she has a street named for her,
is one such. Likewise Guy Malek, after a period of irresponsibility, has
become an engaging man who earns Kinsey's good opinion. Cheney
Phillips comes from a monied background, but he, too, wins Kinsey's
approval. All of them have strength and moral fiber, qualities that
always attract Kinsey.

It's not only rich men who can occasionally rise above their class.
Occasionally, a wealthy woman has the strength of character and independence so valued by Kinsey. For example, Bobby's mother, Glen

Callahan, is one of the wealthiest people Kinsey meets, but Kinsey comes to hold a genuine respect for her. She is impressed by Glen's use of her money to help the community (she "launched the Santa Teresa Girls' Club just about singlehandedly. The Rape Crisis Center too," *C* 36) and by her overwhelming love for her son. Glen, who lavished money on physicians and hospitals to help her son survive the first car crash, had stayed constantly by his hospital bed willing him back to life. When he is killed in the second car crash, her grief is boundless.

Given her distaste for the wealthy, we can't help but wonder if much of Kinsey's reluctance to embrace her recently discovered family is because they represent a fundamental challenge to her working-class assumptions. Her aunt Virginia taught her that money only encourages people to abuse those without money. With this childhood lesson drummed into her head, how can she now embrace a wealthy family whose daughters made social debuts?

Family

If there is one social institution that is consistently portrayed throughout the series as both unhelpful and damaging, it is the American family. In *every* book in the series, we encounter families who could be described, at best, as dysfunctional. These families are so unpleasant to be around that they inspire in Kinsey a genuine gratitude for orphanhood.

The people in Kinsey's world, like most of her readers, appear to have been duped into assuming that other people must be luxuriating in the love and nurturance of a happy family, à la *Leave it to Beaver* and *The Cosby Show*. So deeply rooted is this misconception that even those who have found other satisfactions remain haunted by the desire for the family experience. But those who have lived with an intact family of parents and siblings know its defects well. Julia Ochsner tells Kinsey that her large family has all died. Kinsey responds that her only family, her aunt, has also died. Instead of lamenting their losses, Julia surprises Kinsey and us with her crisp analysis: "We're in the same boat. Restful, isn't it?" (*B* 166).

In *"M" Is for Malice*, the four Malek sons had a financially privileged childhood. But Guy recalls their childhood as lacking any moral compass. He was always testing his limits and never found them because his weak-willed father blustered a lot and then backed down every time (66–67). His mother was only nominally present (134). As adults, his brothers are greedy, bickering men with the social skills and moral responsibility of a three year old. Guy's only problem as an adult apparently is that he still longs for his family to *be* a family.

Similarly, Barbara Daggett, in *"D" Is for Deadbeat,* grew up in a family in which her father was a drunk, irresponsible and often absent. Rather than feeling good about the success she has made of her life, she continues to want to win approval from her despicable absent father. She gives voice to what could be called the major underlying social theme of the Grafton series: "There are laws for everything except the harm families do" (*D* 48).

Starting with *"A" Is for Alibi,* we find seriously flawed families everywhere throughout the series. Charlie Scorsoni paints a grim picture of his family, headed by a drunken abusive father who beat him and his mother. His father's painful death from cancer elicited from the son only a sense of "just desserts." His mother died four months after his father, surprising Scorsoni that her reaction to her husband's death was not relief, but loss, having become dependent on the abuse. And what of Charlie himself? His house tells one story. "Charlie's house was a two-story structure with a painted-yellow-shingle exterior and a dark shingled roof, a bay window in front, a long narrow driveway to the left. It was the sort of house that might appear in an establishing shot for a television family show, something that might come on at 8:00 p.m., everything looking regular and wholesome and suitable for kids" (264). But a few pages later, we learn another story—that this safe and wholesome media-perfect dwelling is, in fact, the home of a multiple murderer. As Stephanie Coontz points out in her study of the American family, *The Way We Never Were,* " 'Leave It to Beaver' was not a documentary" (29).

For the most part, the families in the rest of the series appear to have fundamental problems. The latest, *"M" Is for Malice,* offers the Maleks, whose sibling rivalry makes fratricide not only understandable, but likely. We are amazed only that Guy, who has escaped these jackals, wants to return. The Rawsons in *"L" Is for Lawless* have a wonderful Granny, but the father has been in jail most of his adult life, maintaining no contact with his daughter, and acknowledges her only as part of a caper to recover money he has stolen. Wendell Jaffe in *"J" Is for Judgment* has also abandoned his wife and children in order to get away with millions in embezzled funds and a new lover. His sons are scarred by the abandonment, with the younger one having taken to a criminal life. The Keplers, the Gershs and the Greys, the Fowlers, the Daggetts, the Callahans, the Boldt sisters, the Barneys, the Weidmans, the Snyders, and the Voigts are hardly families we are likely to see in a television sitcom, and we would never want to see them across our own breakfast tables.

The media's model family reappears as a frequent point of reference in Kinsey's mind, a reflection of the source of so many people's notions of what a family should be. The unpleasant Fowlers prompt Kinsey to observe, "As a child, I didn't experience much in the way of family and I usually find myself somewhat taken aback to see one at close range. 'The Donna Reed Show' this was not. People talk about 'dysfunctional' families; I've never seen any other kind" (*F* 114–15). The popular-media family portrayed in *Family Circle* magazine has little connection to what she sees in real life. The magazine has "articles about children, health and fitness, nutrition, home decorating, and inexpensive home-building projects meant for Dad in his spare time—a wooden bench, a tree house, a rustic shelf to support Mom's picturesque garden of container herbs. To me, it was like reading about life on an alien planet" (*K* 95–96).

Throughout the series, from *"B" Is for Burglar* through *"M" Is for Malice,* we learn bits and pieces about the highly problematic family life of Jonah Robb. He and his childhood sweetheart, Camilla, have an on-again–off-again marriage, which features separation or an "open marriage" on a periodic basis, but not divorce. Their relationship has its bizarre side—when Camilla leaves Jonah in *Burglar,* she leaves him a year's worth of frozen dinners, all with identical directions for their heating in case he forgets somewhere between dinner #1 and dinner #365. There are two children in this family about whom we know very little, except that they are tossed about on their parents' emotional tides. Their father has a brief affair with Kinsey and then, with no warning, takes off for a Christmas holiday with the family. We learn in *Malice* that the two are separated again and that Camilla is pregnant and Jonah is not the father.

The combination of Kinsey's own experience with and without family, her two divorces, and her keen observations of families encountered during her cases has led her to a sophisticated understanding of family dynamics. Sometimes her insights resemble those of a family therapist because of her clear understanding of what sociologists and psychologists call the family as a "system," in which each member has a designated psychological role to play. Her musings on the dysfunctional Wood family in *"E" Is for Evidence* are a case in point. Of Ebony Wood, she says: "In the family mythology, she was the thrill-seeker, addicted to the sorts of treacherous hobbies that can spell early death: sky-diving, helicopter skiing, climbing the sheer faces of impossible cliffs. In the family dynamic, maybe she'd been designated to live recklessly, just as Bass [Wood] lived with vanity, idleness, and self-indulgence" (206).

Sibling rivalry is another part of the family system, and although she has seen how bad sibling rivalry can be (for example, in *Fugitive* and *Killer),* Kinsey herself misses even this negative experience. Her comic delight in fighting with Laura in *Lawless* is, fortunately, too funny to make us sad. "I felt a laugh bubble up. 'Be a sport. This is fun. I'm the adopted daughter. This is "family dynamic." Isn't that what it's called? I read about this stuff, but I never got to experience it. Sibling rivalry's a hoot' " (208).

We occasionally hear a more poignant yearning from Kinsey for the comfort she hopes a "real" family would provide. Images evoke strong emotions in her, even when the people she is watching are singularly unadmirable. For example, in *"B" Is for Burglar,* the greedy Grices are willing to kill a friend and murder their neighbor in order to boost up their lifestyle several notches. Yet immediately after she has engaged in a fight with the crazed wife, Kinsey looks on, gun in hand, as Leonard Grice puts his arm protectively around his wounded wife and she says, "In that moment, I wished there was someone to comfort me" (228).

She experiences similar stirrings watching Wendell Jaffe parting from his son, Michael. "They rocked back and forth in an ancient dance. Michael made a small sound at the back of his throat, his eyes squeezed shut. For that one unguarded moment, he and Wendell were connected. I had to look away. I couldn't imagine what it must feel like to find yourself in the presence of a parent you thought was dead" (*J* 203). She experiences a similar envy at the reuniting of Ray Rawson and Laura, the daughter he'd never seen. Thoughts of her own possible reunion with Grand and Cousin Tasha come unbidden and unwelcome to her mind (*L* 150).

The desire is so deep that, in *"L" Is for Lawless*, she is willing to make the effort to build family connections with people whom she knows to be completely dishonest and who are strangers to her. Little surprise to us that they do her physical harm and leave her with no reason to believe they even looked over their shoulders as they took off with the money. Yet this behavior comes as something of a surprise to Kinsey. "I stood there thinking about Ray and Laura and Helen, wondering where they'd gone. I know it's absurd, but I found it painful they hadn't cared enough to stick around and see that I was okay. In some curious way, they'd become my family. I'd seen us as a unit, facing adversity together, even if it was only for a matter of days. It's not that I thought we'd go on that way forever, but I would have liked a sense of closure—thanks, fare-thee-well, drop us a line someday" (290). Later she may see these moments as hollow shells, precious moments off a mass-produced Hallmark card. But in the instant, she feels a desire for the love that our culture associates with the generic family.

Kinsey retains important and affecting memories of her mother. These seem highly singular and particular to Kinsey. However, her thoughts about fathers are often more generalized. One moving reflection comes at the conclusion of *"F" Is for Fugitive*, as Kinsey comes to an understanding of what Ann Fowler has done and why. She flashes back to the almost unbearably sad memory of herself at age five in a wrecked car, holding her father's hand for reassurance. Pondering the pathos of taking comfort from a father who was already dead, she senses a kinship with Ann and others, like Barbara Daggett, who have felt injuries, intended and unintended, inflicted by their fathers. "None of us had survived the wounds our fathers inflicted all those years ago. Did he love us? How would we ever know? He was gone and he'd never again be what he was to us in all his haunting perfection. If love is what injures us, how can we heal?" (260). Her immediate response to this question is her resolution to allow Henry to be more like a father with her and to accept the concern he exhibits, which she had rejected at the opening of the novel.

One flaw in the essential family structure is linked to a basic societal problem, that of stereotypical roles into which men and women are cast. Both women and men seem to reproduce the behavior of their parents (and other important adults in their lives), behavior designated as appropriate according to their genders. These designated roles cause problems for those who accept them as well as for those who break them. Kinsey especially notices the societal demands most women feel to marry and become the wife everyone seems to want her to be. She is firmly resistant to this expectation for herself: "Where is it written that being part of a couple is a measure of anything?" (*D* 34). Kinsey admits she gets "faintly misty-eyed when she sees "old couples toddle down the street together holding hands," but everything she sees in her work and life leads her to suspect "it is all the same clash of wills behind closed doors" (*B* 64).

Kinsey encounters a woman who was totally committed to the entire wifely role when she meets Gwen Fife in the first book of the series. Her situation is shared by many women in the later novels—among them, Olive Kohler, Christie Malek, Francesca Voigt, Dana Jaffe—all women who live their lives by someone else's script. Gwen is especially eloquent in describing her former identity as a wife. She speaks with a detachment born of hard work to recreate herself and her life:

"Anyway, in those days [married to Laurence] I was the dutiful wife, and I mean I played the part with a dedication few could match. I cooked elegant meals. . . . I cleaned the house. I raised the kids. I'm not saying I'm anything unique for that, except that I took it awfully to heart. I wore my hair up in this French roll, not a pin out of place, and I had these outfits to put on and take off, kind of like a Barbie doll. . . . When it was over, I was pretty angry—not so much at him as at myself for buying into the whole gig. I mean, don't get me wrong. I liked it at the time and it suited me fine, but there was also a form of sensory deprivation going on so that when the marriage blew up, I was totally unequipped to deal with the real world" (*A* 39–40).

After two divorces and many cases involving wretched marriages,

Kinsey has a healthy disrespect for the entire institution of marriage. She concludes that the pretty wedding gift wrap only covers a Pandora's box of horrors. We see a fascinating picture of the wedding game when Kinsey visits Dana Jaffe, a bridal consultant, and overhears her conversation with an upset client. "I wondered idly if Dana ever told these young brides the problems they were going to run into once the wedding was over with: boredom, weight gain, irresponsibility, friction over sex, spending, family holidays, and who picks up the socks. Maybe it was just my basic cynicism rising to the surface, but cost-per-person food and drink breakdowns seemed trivial compared to the conflicts marriage generated" (*J* 106). It's enough to make fiancées all over America cancel their subscriptions to *Bride* magazine.

Ironically, the woman who is giving all the wedding advice is herself a part of a very disturbed family. Dana's husband faked his own death and disappeared, leaving his wife with two sons: Michael, still angry over his father's abandonment, and Brian, indicted for murder, a cap to a long history of juvenile offenses that began with his father's disappearance. Kinsey gives us her opinion of the father, Wendell Jaffe, while interviewing the man's partner, who's trying to convince her that Jaffe was concerned about his sons. "He was a very good father," he tells Kinsey. She snaps, "The kind of parent every kid needs. . . . I'll pass that on to them. It'll help them with their therapy" (255).

In *"K" Is for Killer,* the Kepler family was ostensibly normal until the murder of the youngest daughter. Remaining are the mother, father, and two daughters. Yet, Mrs. Kepler cannot talk to her husband about her despair over their daughter's death and her need to have the cause of death determined. It turns out that one of the "loving" sisters, Berlyn, actually discovered her sister's body, but, instead of calling the police, she stole jewelry off the body and walked out, leaving the body to decompose for days. Also, jealous of her mother's affection for her dead sister, she anonymously sends her a tape of a pornographic movie the sister had made. Ann Fowler is also a member of an apparently normal intact family, but she is content to let her brother go to jail for a murder she herself committed. Plus, she ends up killing her own mother and considers shooting her own father to keep her crimes from being uncovered and to be free of looking after them. Lest we are sympathetic with the rest of the family, we might recall how manipulative the invalid mother, Ori, is in using her illness to bully everyone else, and how utterly blind the father, Royce, has been about his blazingly obvious preference for his son over his daughter. This is a genuinely repulsive set of blood-related humanoids.

And what of Kinsey's own family? We know that she is far from thrilled to have discovered a family connection in Lompoc, and as readers we've been anxiously awaiting her foray into the details of the people who make up this family. But as late as *Malice,* when she finally agrees to meet her cousin Tasha face to face and even takes on a job for her, she still refuses to get involved with the family in any personal or intimate way. She explains her feelings to Cheney Phillips in *Killer.* "As it turns out, I do have family up in Lompoc, but I haven't decided what to do about them yet. . . . They've ignored my existence now for twenty-nine years, and suddenly they want to make nice. It doesn't sit well with me. That kind of family I can do without" (81). Cheney's response makes Kinsey laugh. "Look at it this way. I feel the same way about mine, and I've been in touch with them since birth" (82).

The *only* family in the series that seems genuinely happy and nurturing is the Pitts family. Henry and his brothers and sister may be quirky and at times irritating, but fundamentally there is love and mutual support. In *Lawless,* Henry's family appears throughout the novel in contrast to the Rawsons, Hays, and Lees, and it appears throughout the series as the lone and striking exception to the "families do harm" rule.

Domestic Violence

Kinsey encounters several families so dysfunctional that they shelter wife and child abuse. Physical violence and sexual abuse are certainly not an inevitable part of the family structure, but the structure seems to make it difficult for some families to take the necessary steps to stop the abuse. For years the very wealthy and socially prestigious Wood family hid the fact that an older son sexually abused his young sister. When the abuse was discovered, the father beat the son within an inch of his life and sent the daughter away to school (*E* 187). This ultrapolite family never discussed it, thus creating serious strains within the family and serious problems for the young girl, problems that stayed with her throughout her life. The abuse is also one of the root causes of the series of murders that form the plot of *"E" Is for Evidence*. "Olive died because Helen was too bloody polite to deal with the truth" (215).

The entire plot of *"G" Is for Gumshoe* is a study in domestic violence. Patrick Bronfen killed two of his sisters and his wife, Sheila. Because he has terrified his other sister, Anne (alias Agnes Grey), she is afraid to tell anyone the stories of the murders. Years later, Agnes stumbles across him and he winds up killing her, too. It is not clear that he would have been caught or suffered any punishment had he been able to kill Kinsey, as he tries to do in one of the novel's final scenes. Even the novel's subplot involves a dysfunctional family. Here, the contract killer, Mark Messinger, is a father who, in some wild perversion of parental concern, kidnaps his own son and takes him along on his "work." In the novel's finale, Messinger kills Bronfen and takes Kinsey hostage. But the gods of marital vengeance are watching, and Messinger's ex-wife shows up in time to shoot him right between the eyes, thus rescuing herself, her son, Kinsey, and Dietz.

"H" Is for Homicide also explores an abusive relationship, this one between Raymond Maldonado and Bibianna Diaz. He holds Bibianna and Kinsey virtual prisoners in his apartment and he threatens, very believably, to kill Bibianna if she refuses to marry him. When Bibianna escapes, Maldonado sends one of his sidekicks to kill her. As is often the case, his violent behavior is part of a family pattern; we learn that Raymond was himself abused as a child by his father.

Kinsey meets a stalker who kills his wife and almost gets away with it in *"I" Is for Innocent*. Her investigation reveals that after their separation, David Barney continued to stalk and otherwise harass his wife, Isabelle. He left a flower every day on her car, jewelry on her doorstep, cards in the mail. The more she rejected these efforts, the harder he tried. He called her day and night. When she got an unlisted number, he found it and continued to call at all hours. When she got an answering machine, he talked until the tape ran out. Isabelle described her situation to friends as being "under siege." He followed her everywhere, letting up only when she got a restraining order. The effects on Isabelle were severe: "She was a nervous wreck, eating little, sleeping poorly, subject to anxiety, panic, and tremors. She was pale. She was haggard. She was drinking too much. She was agitated by company and frightened to be alone" (18).

Kinsey also encounters battered wives. The bigamist John Daggett makes a practice of beating up his wife, Lovella, in *"D" Is for Deadbeat.* Kinsey meets her shortly after one of these episodes. "Her upper lip was puffy, like the kind of scrape children get falling off bicycles when they first learn to ride. Her left eye had been blackened not long ago and it was streaked now with midnight blue, the surrounding tissue a rainbow of green and yellow and gray" (11–12). In a similar fashion, in *Lawless,* Gilbert Hays leaves his marks. "Laura's tears had streaked through the many layers of makeup, bringing ancient bruises to the surface. It was clear she'd recently suffered a black eye. Her jaw was tinged a drab green, washing out to yellow around the edges" (151). Her body is also covered with older bruises. She tells Kinsey and Ray she has tried to get away, twice going to shelters for battered women, but "he always finds me and brings me back" (163). Yet, as so often the case with abuse, Laura sentimentalizes Gilbert, saying: "He can really be so sweet. Sometimes when he drinks, he busts out crying like a baby. Breaks my heart." To which an unimpressed Kinsey replies, "Along with your nose" (200).

Both these men are stalkers, like David Barney, and equally capable of violence. They beat their partners, threaten them with worse if they leave, and go after them to bring them back. When Kinsey asks Lovella why she doesn't leave Daggett, she explains angrily, "Because he'd come after me is why. . . . You don't know him. He'd kill me without giving it a second thought. Same thing if I called the cops. Talk back to that man and he'll punch your teeth down your throat. . . . Of course, when he sobers up, he can charm your socks off" (*D* 15).

Much of what we know about the pattern of wife and child abuse from reading our local newspapers is painfully replicated in Grafton's novels. The cyclical familial repetition, the reluctance to tell, the alternation of mental humiliation and physical violence with gestures of charm and apology, the lifetime impact on the victims—all the details are chillingly familiar to Grafton's readers. As with all the troubling issues she faces, Kinsey doesn't sermonize at length about abuse within the family. She doesn't work at a women's shelter and she doesn't tell women to report their husbands. She merely understands what she sees and she tells us all about it. She asks only the occasional question and offers the occasional snide remark. We are left to be appalled by the pervasiveness of the problem as a contemporary social issue. We are not given guidance by Kinsey about ways to solve the problem, but we have no doubt it's a serious problem.

Child Abuse Outside the Family

Child abuse is not limited to the family. Even an institution that would appear completely safe can harbor an individual who will take advantage of a young child. In *"F" Is for Fugitive*, for example, the institution is a Christian church and the abuser is a minister. Reverend Haws is a highly respected member of his community, yet he abuses the trust his parishioners have placed in him by sexually abusing a teenaged girl working at the church. Plus, he succeeds in escaping any penalty for his behavior. Kinsey learns of his actions during an interview with the local pharmacist, who was a witness to the acts. "She [Jean, the sixteen-year-old] worked at the church, cleaning Sunday-school rooms. Wednesdays at four o'clock before choir practice started, he would pull his pants down around his knees and lie back across his desk while she worked on him. I used to watch from the vestry" (157).

The school as well can become a site for child abuse, rather than the nurturing place it is expected to be. In *"F" Is for Fugitive*, Kinsey learns that that same teenager was also abused by her school principal. His sexual abuse of his student is still hidden at the close of the novel; thus he has escaped any penalty for his actions. After Kinsey figures out his actions, he excuses his secrecy both then and now as necessary to keeping his job. Kinsey expresses our own lack of sympathy for this man when she sarcastically replies: "Yeah, unlawful sexual intercourse being what it is" (245).

As with the wealthy, the church and the schools do have moral, responsible individuals who are the exception to any blanket condemnation implied. Kinsey's search through Jean's school records impresses her with the effort *most* of the school staff made to assist the troubled girl: "To the credit of the faculty, a general alarm seemed to sound. From the paper trail left behind, it looked as if every effort had been made to bring her back from the brink" (*F* 146).

Inadequacies in the Judicial System

Although Kinsey normally defends the local police force as generally honest, hard-working, and competent, she rarely has reason to afford similar praise to the judicial system. We learn about one of her first recorded encounters with the system during an interview in *"A" Is for Alibi*. Her first homicide investigation, she says, was for the public defender's office. A woman killed her three children by tying them up, taping their mouths, and leaving them to suffocate in garbage cans. "She got off, of course. Pleaded temporary insanity" (143). We might remember that the main plot of *Alibi* is built on Kinsey's efforts on behalf of Nikki Fife, who spent eight years in jail for a crime she didn't commit. We also hear the unjust story of Gwen and Laurence Fife—the husband Nikki Fife was convicted of killing. Although Laurence had numerous barely hidden affairs with other women, when Gwen became interested in another man, Laurence, a prominent divorce attorney, was able to divorce her easily. And, as the expression goes, he took her to the cleaners. Although Gwen had been the perfect, submissive wife, entertaining Laurence's business clients and friends and devoting her entire life to him, she lost her home, her source of income, and custody of their children. *Alibi* leaves us with nothing but contempt for a judicial system that sells justice to the wealthy and powerful through expensive lawyers while denying it to innocent murdered children through legal chicanery.

After Kinsey gets an office with the law firm of Kingman and Ives, we hear a bit more about lawyers and the process of the courtroom, all of which confirms Jack Clemson's assessment: "Going to trial is a crapshoot" (*F* 35). Truth seems repeatedly to be lost in the showmanship and game-playing of a trial. Lonnie Kingman explains why the state's prosecutor lost his case against David Barney, who was guilty of his wife's murder. The state's attorney was not untalented or without a case. Rather, he committed the crime of having no lawyerly style, no flair for theatrics in the courtroom. Lonnie tells Kinsey, "He thought he could win on the merits of the case," and then "Lonnie snorted at the absurdity of the assumption" (*I* 10).

Not being convicted of crimes or getting off with light sentences seems to be the norm in Kinsey's world. John Daggett gets only a few months in jail for vehicular manslaughter when he kills five people while driving drunk. Prior to that fatal "accident" he had been picked up *fifteen* times for drunk driving, but he had only paid a few fines and once served thirty days (*D* 96). In *"E" Is for Evidence,* it turns out that the murderer had gotten away with killing his foster mother by pleading temporary insanity years earlier. Kinsey's frustrated response on hearing about the old crime and outcome makes it clear that such injustices are familiar to her: "Oh geez, I get it. No prison for him" (215).

Lawyers are an integral part of the judicial system. Perhaps surprisingly, in light of all the lawyer jokes rampant in our litigious age, they are not generally on the receiving end of Kinsey's biting humor. They are not, however, totally safe from attack. Usually it is their manner, more than their function, that provokes a venomous jab from Kinsey. "Attorneys," according to Kinsey, "are the people who can say things in the mildest of tones that make you want to shriek and rend your clothes" (*E* 36). On one of the few occasions when Kinsey needs a lawyer for herself, she turns to Lonnie Kingman, who performs his lawyerly role to perfection, scaring Kinsey half to death with his assessment of her situation. She has been accused of conspiring in an arson case. Lonnie laid out his view of the problem and "sighed like he was going to hate to see me in a shapeless prison dress" (*E* 36). A nastier lawyer is Laurence Fife, who was "vindictive" and "absolutely merciless" (*A* 52). He not only made sure that his clients got every penny possible, regardless of what might seem a fair distribution of property, but, more disturbingly, he violated basic professional ethics by seducing his female clients, already made vulnerable by being in the middle of a divorce process.

Kinsey doesn't speak directly about her opinion of the final stage in the judicial process, the prison system. Clearly she believes that people who commit violent illegal acts ought, generally, to be put away. But where and under what conditions? We get some hint that she may think prison is not the rehabilitative experience it claims to be. When she learns that Bailey Fowler has created a whole new and rather successful life for himself after his escape from prison, she is fascinated and impressed. She also gives some thought to how he might have turned out after a long prison term. "I wondered if serving out his sentence in prison would have had as laudatory an effect as being out in the world, getting on with his life" (*F* 17).

Kinsey herself is jailed once in the series. In *"H" Is for Homicide,* she and Bibianna Diaz are jailed overnight because they were witnesses to a shoot-out and then resisted cooperating with the police. The account Kinsey gives stresses the impersonality of the procedures and her own distaste for being locked up behind chain-link fencing, in a cinder-block facility with no windows, a communal lidless commode, and other inmates who might be dangerous (91–99). But there is no real condemnation of her treatment.

Health Care

The medical profession and medical facilities arouse Kinsey's suspicions, but not her condemnation because she's had too many experiences in which she or people she cared about depended on them. She follows her aunt's advice not to waste time and money on general medical care. We see her under medical care only in times of emergency, and even then she's argumentative and resistant just as soon as she reaches an energy level that makes these behaviors possible. Her opinion is quite clear: "Hospitals are dangerous. People make mistakes. Wrong blood, wrong medication, wrong surgeries, wrong tests. I was checking out of this place 'toot sweet'" (*E* 140).

Doctors, as a group, are a subject for Kinsey's skepticism, although a few physicians who take care of her own injuries win the status of exceptions to the rule. What Kinsey dislikes is that the medical system appears to place physicians above and beyond their patients. Such a class division always offends Kinsey. A typical pompous physician appears in *"F" Is for Fugitive.* Kinsey manages to break through the outer defenses and get into his office, where she asks him some very pointed questions. He is amazed at her assertiveness and her refusal to leave. "He stared at me blankly, accustomed to his pronouncements being taken as law. He probably never had to deal with pushy people like me. He was protected from the public by his receptionist, his lab tech, his nurse, his billing clerk, his answering service, his office manager, his wife—an army of women keeping Doctor safe and untouched" (164).

One physician we get to know well is the monstrous Dr. James Fraker in *"C" Is for Corpse*. Not only is he arrogant and condescending, but, more important, he is a ruthless killer. He enjoys tormenting his wife by reminding her of the evidence he holds proving that she murdered her first husband. He engineers Bobby Callahan's first disastrous car "accident," which kills one of Bobby's friends and almost kills Bobby, leaving him with debilitating and painful injuries. He follows this by setting up a second "accident" that results in the young man's death. When he traps Kinsey at the morgue, he sadistically enjoys pursuing her through the halls, all the while armed with a deadly syringe and singing a romantic Gershwin song.

With families, physicians, and hospitals not very nurturing, we might hope for better from the final place for many of us—nursing homes. But the nursing homes in the novels are pretty sad places. We can hardly fail to be moved by Kinsey's description of the patients at the Rio Vista Convalescent Hospital, where Agnes Grey is a temporary resident. "They seemed as motionless as plants, resigned to infrequent watering. Anyone would wither under such a regimen: no exercise, no air, no sunlight. They had outlived not only friends and family, but most illnesses, so that at eighty and ninety, they seemed untouchable, singled out to endure, without relief, a life that stretched into yawning eternity" (*G* 46–47). The nursing home staff are often supportive, however, as exemplified by the nurses and managers in both *"G" Is for Gumshoe* and *"I" Is for Innocent*. At least there's one bright spot in the bleak picture.

Corporate America

Kinsey has a similarly low opinion of many corporations she encounters, the primary one being the insurance company with which she had the longest employment history. California Fidelity, a name belying its total lack of reliability, is interested only in its profits and pays little attention to basic morality. As early as *"A" Is for Alibi,* we learn not to trust California Fidelity Insurance (CF). The company is fully prepared to pay off a small claim they know to be fraudulent, rather than take on the expense of a potential lawsuit. The claim is smaller than the cost of going to court. Weighing only dollars makes sense to the company, but Kinsey has a moral streak that is offended by letting Marcia Threadgill get away with a fraudulent claim. CF will, however, fight claims that are large even if they know they are valid, just because they are large (*Judgment*). Kinsey sees that big companies seldom put the concept of money and morality into the same sentence. Trying to get something done at CF, Kinsey says, "I even had to stoop so low as to mention principles, which never sits that well with the claims manager" (*A* 82).

Kinsey does not lay all the blame for corporate corruption at the feet of the company or its officials, although they deserve their fair share. There are private citizens who take advantage of the company whenever they can, almost as if robbing a company is not the same thing as robbing a person. "It's been my observation, after years in the business, that a certain percent of the population simply can't resist the urge to cheat. This inclination seems to cut across all class and economic lines, uniting racial and ethnic groups who otherwise might have little to say to one another. Insurance is regarded as equivalent to the state lottery" (*H* 11).

California Fidelity Insurance also fosters toadyism, encouraging low-level management to bootlick those above while abusing their staff. Darcy Pascoe finds common ground with Kinsey over their resentments of the claims manager, Andy Motycka, who bullies, belittles, and scapegoats them to avoid criticism from his bosses. Even Kinsey's friend at the company, Mac Voorhies, refuses to stand up to the efficiency expert sent from the home office, who fires Kinsey, in spite of the fact her work brought a multi-million-dollar auto insurance scam to an end. The fraud, described in detail in *"H" Is for Homicide,* went on for years with little concern from the company. In fact, it is the police, not California Fidelity, who uncover it. What kind of message do they intend to send to law abiding citizens by firing the individual most responsible for ending the crime ring?

The telephone company is another corporation unworthy of trust.

In *"E" Is for Evidence,* Kinsey is advising Lance Wood, who has been accused of arson. His office may have been bugged. When he confides to Kinsey that he feels foolish calling the phone company about this problem, she is amused. "That's like asking the fox to secure the henhouse" (176).

And what does Kinsey think of the corporate news media? That it is so "riddled with commercials" it leaves the viewer knowing "more about dog food than . . . about world events" (*M* 55–56).

Kinsey, then, does not expect much from her dealings with corporate America except irritation and at times a good laugh. There may not be overt corruption, but there's frequently less than humane or efficient service. "In my experience, banks are the least helpful institutions on earth" (*E* 1). In a "bad, bad, bad" mood one morning because of an error in her bank statement, she calls the bank—"almost with an eye toward comic relief"—to try to correct the mistake that gave her $5,000 extra. Of course, no one can make the correction without umpteen more phone calls. And what starts as a simple bank inquiry in *"D" Is for Deadbeat* ends in a full-blown urge to bite the teller. "How can you call it customer service when you don't do shit?" (18–19).

Her skepticism is fueled by her professional work with corporations. For example, investigating a high-level executive just before the opening of *"H" Is for Homicide,* she learned he had falsified his credentials (1). We might also recall that Derrick Wenner was a trust executor who met wealthy Glen Callahan in the course of his job and, after their marriage, immediately quit the bank to live a life of spoiled leisure. It's not corruption, but he is a greedy unsavory person who has secretly taken out an insurance policy on his stepson after the first accident (and who fails to understand why the boy's mother would be upset). He's not the kind of person any bank customer hopes would be managing a family trust.

Sex Roles

Kinsey's aunt taught her the most fundamental defense against sexual discrimination: a belief that women were the equals of men and capable of leading an independent life. Somewhere along the way, Kinsey decided to lead the examined life, and she is neither ignorant of, nor indifferent to, the manner in which stereotypical sex roles work to the disadvantage of women. She often notices instances in which male bosses fail to treat women employees the same way they treat men. In her first case report, in "A" Is for Alibi, she hears about the partner in the accounting firm where one of the murder victims, Libby Glass, worked. "Old man Haycraft was a petty tyrant, the original male chauvinist pig. Libby thought if she worked hard, she'd get a promotion and a raise, but no such thing" (159). When Kinsey goes to the Crow's Nest, she notices the skimpy and uncomfortable waitress uniforms: "I wonder how long uniforms like that would last if the night manager was required to squeeze his hairy fanny into one" (D 173).

Kinsey lets us know the depth of her antagonism to confining roles for women by quick expressions of genuine surprise and candid rejection. Perusing a magazine, Kinsey is led to consider the insidious ways that women are given messages about how to be a woman and the products necessary to the proper female role. "All the ads showed such perfect women. Most were thirty years old, white, and had flawless complexions. Their teeth were snowy and even. None of them had wide bottoms or kangaroo pouches that pulled their slacks out of shape. There was no sign of cellulite, spider veins, or breasts drooping down to their waists. These perfect women lived in well-ordered houses with gleaming floors, an inconceivable array of home appliances, oversize fluffy mutts, and no visible men. . . . Intellectually I understood that these were all highly paid models simply *posing* as housewives for the purpose of selling Kotex, floor covering, and dog food. Their lives were probably as far removed from housewifery as mine was. But what did you do if you actually were a *housewife*, confronted with all these images of perfection on the hoof?" (K 96).

Having at first assumed a wealthy woman's stay-at-home lifestyle was easy, she reassesses the situation upon seeing Olive's response to the "Honey, I'm home" appearance of her husband. "She didn't exactly perk up and pant, but that's the impression she gave. Maybe her job was harder than I thought. I wouldn't do that for anyone" (E 112).

Of course, playing the stereotypical role as wife requires finding a man with whom to play the part. Ann Fowler in *Fugitive* seems a stereotypical daughter trapped into caring for her parents, when she'd like to find a man and start her own family. She ends up committing a series of murders all in order to catch and keep a man—a bizarre example of female socialization gone awry.

Since she is in a profession heavily populated by men, Kinsey encounters the effects of sex-role discrimination firsthand. She is sometimes irritated, sometimes bemused, when people are surprised at the phenomenon of a female private investigator. In *"B" Is for Burglar*, Aubrey Danzinger explains his trip from Los Angeles to Santa Teresa by confessing that "it amuses me to think about a girl detective" (142). Once she's on the job, she is more than occasionally asked to take on "feminine" tasks. When Irene Gersh asks her to calm her mother, Agnes Grey, Kinsey thinks, "What really bugged me was the suspicion that nobody would have even *suggested* that a boy detective do likewise" (*G* 61). Even though she's a trained professional, Kinsey initially gets paid less than her male counterparts. She mentions in a dinner conversation that she feels people often hire her because they believe they can pay a woman less. Much to her dismay, she discovers the precise dollar amount of that truth and promptly boosts her rates in *"I" Is for Innocent* (23).

Prostitution

The only two jobs where women typically earn more than men are modeling and prostitution. Kinsey's most extensive involvement with prostitutes and society's complex attitudes toward them occurs in *"K" Is for Killer*. Lorna Kepler was a prostitute who knew how to earn top dollar and invest it wisely. She appears to have succeeded in operating without a pimp. Yet, as smart and savvy as she was, she ultimately became a victim. She had connections with the Mafia and was about to be married to a Mafia leader, but this derivative power from a man was not sufficient to keep her from being murdered. And her killer was one of her johns who murdered her because *he* talked too freely about his criminal activities in front of her, not because of anything she had done.

Throughout *Killer,* we get a close view of the world of the prostitute. Even at its higher end where Lorna worked independently, making her own choice of clients, the women are victimized. Serena Bonney, an emergency-room nurse, tells Kinsey about what she has seen of women who work on the streets for pimps and even of the higher paid, independent prostitutes like Lorna. They all come into the emergency room battered, and sometimes dying, from the assaults of their clients, men who take out their rage at their own impotence on the women they hire for sex. The women seldom go to the police for protection because their profession is unlikely to get them much in the way of assistance. Lt. Dolan wishes they would come to him for help, but he understands why they think the police are only out to hassle them. Kinsey sees that the police have varying degrees of compassion for the homicide victim if she was a prostitute.

Closely allied to physical sex for hire is video sex for purchase. Having seen the pornographic movie in which Lorna played a role, Kinsey makes fun of the acting and plot. "I've seen elementary school pageants with more talent in evidence. . . . I suspect [the female lead] was actually hired because she was the only one who owned a real garter belt in this age of panty hose" (*K* 22). Kinsey's opinion of such videos is condemnatory and sincere. "I tried to watch with the same detachment I affect at homicide sites, but the mechanism failed and I found myself squirming. I do not take lightly the degradation of human beings, especially when it's done solely for the financial gain of others" (22).

Ageism

In a society that worships youth, especially in the female sex, Kinsey enthusiastically enjoys seniors who live their lives with gusto. "I'd always been fond of the elderly" (*F* 174). Kinsey's closest friend is in his eighties. The novels are full of feisty older folk who refuse to disappear into the woodwork of nursing homes. Who can forget the wonderful havoc that Agnes Grey gloriously creates in her convalescent home? "I heard Agnes Grey before I ever laid eyes on her. . . . I'd picked up the blast of a television set turned up loud enough for failing ears. . . . It wasn't a television set at all. Without even asking,

I knew this was Agnes. She was stark naked, dancing a dirty boogie on the bed while she accompanied herself by banging on a bedpan with a spoon. . . . She seemed to be having the time of her life" (*G* 46–47).

Kinsey tells us, "I like older women as a rule" (*C* 15). Typical is her enjoyment of Ruth, the secretary in Charlie Scorsoni's office, who is sixty-nine, "a chatty little thing, full of pep, and I wondered if she wasn't about perfect for Henry Pitts," an ultimate in compliments from Kinsey (*A* 28). Ruth describes the difficulty she had finding a job when she was divorced at the age of sixty-two, something Kinsey understands immediately. "She was quick, capable, and of course was being aced out at every turn by women one-third her age who were cute instead of competent" (28–29).

Another elderly joy is Mrs. Julia Ochsner in *"B" Is for Burglar,* who becomes so enchanted by Kinsey's profession as a detective that she asks, only half-jokingly, to become Kinsey's partner. To get ready, she starts reading Mickey Spillane, because she's afraid she won't know enough four-letter words to do her share of the work.

Nell Pitts, older sister of Henry, energetically continues to enjoy her life, convinced that at ninety-five, thanks to her mother's good genes, she has at least another eight years to go. She makes a quilt for Kinsey, in spite of her fading eyesight. When Nell comes for William and Rosie's wedding, Kinsey finds her energetically cleaning Henry's stove and refrigerator. Kinsey lets her know that Henry cleaned the refrigerator two days earlier, but Nell is determined to do the job thoroughly. She tells Kinsey that she taught Henry his cleaning skills in 1912, but knows that he never gets it quite right (*L* 70–71). And Henry himself retains all of his appeal and attraction as he moves energetically through his eighties, baking cinnamon rolls and brownies, gardening, and designing incredibly challenging crossword puzzles.

We'd all love to have met Mother Pitts, who had ten children (five survived childhood) and lived to be a hundred and three. Nell tells Kinsey, "Right about the time she turned ninety, she got so crabby we threatened to withhold her sour mash whiskey if she didn't straighten up. She only required six tablespoons a day, but she believed it was absolutely essential to life. We put the bottle right up on the shelf where she could see it but couldn't reach. That settled her right down, and she went on for another thirteen years just as gentle as a lamb" (*L* 72).

Kinsey humorously sums up the boundless energy of the Pitts siblings, all of whom plan to live as long as their mother: "At ten, when they hauled out the Monopoly board and the popcorn paraphernalia, I excused myself and went home. I knew the game would continue until midnight or one, and I wasn't up to it. Not old enough, I guess" (*L* 49).

Even when others appear to be making fun of the old, Kinsey doesn't dismiss them. In *"B" Is for Burglar,* Mr. Snyder patronizes his elderly wife, May, calling her mentally confused and hard of hearing. But what May Snyder insists she heard on the night of the murder (64) turns out to be crucial to Kinsey's solving the crime, and her hearing once again comes to the rescue when she is the only one who hears Kinsey's calls for help and phones the police at the end of the novel.

Gilbert Hays, the nasty thief and abuser in *"L" Is for Lawless,* learns much to his dismay that it doesn't pay to make fun of little old ladies. He laughs heartily at elderly Helen Rawson when she pulls out a twelve-gauge shotgun and shakily tries to aim it at him in spite of her hazy eyesight. He should have known that her late husband used to call her "Hell on Wheels" instead of "Helen" (223). His laughter turns to screams moments later when she drops her pretense of feebleness, corrects her aim, and blasts him with shotgun pellets right in the face.

Afterward, Helen answers questions from an impressed Kinsey and Ray. "Just because you get old doesn't mean you lose your nerve. . . . Frieda's got me into lifting weights now, and I can bench-press twenty-five pounds. Did you hear what he said? He thought I couldn't even hold up a seven-pound shotgun. I was insulted. Stereotyping the old. That's your typical macho horseshit" (242–43).

Kinsey doesn't plan to cover up her own aging. She will exercise regularly to ward off the softening process that comes with age, but when a woman who's had several face-lifts tells her she'll need to have her eyes done in a couple of years, Kinsey laughingly replies, "I like lines. . . . I earn mine" (*A* 79).

But growing old is not simple or easy. After her fearless handling of the shotgun, Helen throws up. (Still, she remains determined to come out swinging and she carries a baseball bat for protection throughout the rest of the novel.) And Henry tells Kinsey, "You can keep your spunk, but you have to give up your vanity early on" (*M* 84). With acceptance and a humor that reminds us of Kinsey, he describes the physical effects of growing old as he and his sibs are experiencing them—shrinking in size, losing hearing and sight, and incontinency. "We've talked about this and it's our contention that the shrinkage is nature's way of assuring you don't take up so much space in your coffin. . . . Makes it easy on the pallbearers." He concludes, "We're all in diapers. Well, I'm not, but then I'm the baby in the family" (84).

Scenes in nursing homes highlight what many people say is the hardest part about growing old—the loneliness of having outlived family and friends and, finally, one's own body. Kinsey is keenly attuned to this. As she walks through Rio Vista and hears the hiss of machines in the rooms, she thinks, "Hearts would go on beating, lungs would pump, kidneys filtering all the poisons from the blood. But who would diagnose their feelings of dread, and how would anyone provide relief from the underlying malady, which was despair?" (*G* 62).

Sexual Orientation

Kinsey's open-minded attitude is never clearer than in her easy acceptance of people's sexual orientation. One highly memorable character in the series is the deliciously ironic Cherie Stanislaus, roommate of Russell Turpin, in *"K" Is for Killer*. Kinsey goes to interview Russell, who had made a pornographic video with the murder victim, Lorna Kepler. Encountering Cherie rather than Russell, Kinsey is happy to wait for him in their apartment. After a drink and some patter, Cherie confides to Kinsey that Russell is "very screwed up" (135). Moments later, when Cherie changes her persona along with her clothes and reveals herself to *be* Russell, Kinsey is fascinated by the illusion. She is transfixed by the cleverness of it all, rather than judgmental. When asked by Russell, she frankly admits to preferring Cherie, and he is in complete agreement. "I can't tell you how obnoxious it is waking up every morning to a

beard. And a penis? My gawd. Picture *that* in your lacy little underpants" (137).

Kinsey also has a completely accepting attitude toward homosexu-
ality, as revealed by her lack of comment or judgmental tone when
encountering gay men and lesbians. Her opinion of Wim Hoover in
"B" Is for Burglar is seemingly unaffected by his sexual orientation.
When she catches sight of his partner as she's leaving the apartment,
her reaction is simply admiration for his good looks (102). Even
when she discovers, eight years after the fact, that her second husband, Daniel Wade, left her for another man, her angry response is
for his recent betrayal of her trust and hospitality, not for his sexual
orientation, and she seems to have no problem understanding his
physical attraction to Bass Wood. In fact, later in the series, she makes
a comment about catching her ex-husband with his lover, without
feeling the necessity of mentioning that the lover was male.

We find Kinsey feeling nothing but admiration for the (presumably) lesbian couple in *"L" Is for Lawless,* Freida Green and Minnie
Paxton. Their willingness to watch out for Helen Rawson and to teach
her to hide and use a shotgun, as well as lift weights, probably saves
her life and the lives of her guests (239–43).

Does Kinsey ever tell us what to do about all the corporate and judicial messes? About inadequate family structures? About prejudice
against individuals whose age, sex, sexual orientation, or career
makes other people want to ignore or abuse them? No, of course not.
Kinsey is an investigator, not a preacher or a social worker. She tells
us what she discovers, not what to do with it. Plus, let us point out, she
does not highlight social issues as heavily as having a chapter in this
book devoted to the topic may imply. This chapter has isolated a
thread that is only one of many making up the pattern of the novels.

At the same time, the issues constituting that thread are the social
context of twentieth-century America. Significantly, Grafton has said
that she sees "the detective novel as a serious examination of contemporary issues" ("Breaking and Entering" 18–28). We recognize our
own concerns captured in Kinsey's words and actions. Kinsey does
have opinions about many of the issues. She is a strong and competent woman, acting in a world that has been shaped by men. Her own
experiences and feelings are often at odds with this world. She does

what she can to keep her individual corner of the world a place where she can be herself, a woman much of her own creating. She confronts the injustices around her with a range of tactics—subtle repartee, outraged condemnation, ingenuity, intelligence, and physical force when necessary, and always hard work and her wonderful sense of humor.

KINSEY LAUGHS AT:

The rich:

"It's been my observation that the rich like to subdivide into the haves and the have-mores." (*I* 63)

"We were in the section of Montebello known as the slums, where the houses only cost $280,000 each." (*I* 93)

"Pay enough for anything and it passes for taste." (*I* 61)

Growing old:

Ruth, who's in her sixties, says, "The only cleavage I got left, I sit on." (*A* 29)

Homophobia:

She describes a stained-glass window in a Floral Beach church as "depicting Jesus in an ankle-length nightgown that would get him stoned to death in this town." (*F* 213)

Paying taxes:

She can't be mugged: "Any money I had, I was being forced to give to the feds at pen point." (*K* 4)

Sex roles:

"He'd probably spent most of his married life being waited on hand and foot, and my guess was he took household chores for granted, as if the elves and fairies crept in at night and cleaned pee off the rim of the toilet bowl whenever he missed." (*E* 61)

Cosmetic surgery:

"She looked like she'd had softballs surgically implanted on her chest. Hug a woman like that and she was bound to leave dents." (*E* 108)

Is Justice Possible?

"I'm still a good person, aren't I?": Kinsey's Personal Moral Code

K insey doesn't believe that an angry, or kindly, old man micromanages our world, and she doesn't look to some other magical or superstitious force running things either. "I don't believe in palmistry, any more than I believe in numerology, astrology, the Easter Bunny, or the tooth fairy" (*H* 201). She knows well enough that people often do bad things and get away with them. ("Cheaters win all the time. It wasn't big news but it was worth remembering," *A* 228.) She still continues to wish that they would not, and her choice of careers is in no small measure reflective of her desire to get things right and into balance. She encounters bad guys in her own life who, in fact, get away with their bad behavior. Their injustices, like that of Marsha Threadgill with her insurance scam in *"A" Is for Alibi,* bother her. She does what she can to stop the injustice, but if she can't, she moves on to the next problem. A good example is the dastardly Mr. Gordon "Tight Ass" Titus, who arrogantly imposes his own efficiency scheme on the company and fires her. "In a world presided over by Agatha Christie, Gordon Titus might have ended up on the conference room floor with a paper spindle through his heart. In the real world, such matters seldom have such a satisfactory ending" (*H* 10).

Kinsey, then, does not base her own moral code on an established religion or sense of a presiding deity of any kind. She does, however, have a firm, if somewhat generic, set of moral behaviors by which she chooses to live.

Need for Answers and Order

In the classic detective story, an ordered world, large or small, is disrupted by a murder, and the detective's role is to identify the guilty party and remove the individual, thus restoring the original social order. The acknowledged queen of this form of detective fiction is Agatha Christie, and we are not surprised that Kinsey is a fan. Kinsey loves order of every sort: in her apartment, her office, her relationships, and most of all her cases.

Her preference for an ordered space is coupled with a tendency to follow, rather than break, rules. "I pay my bills on time, obey most laws, and I feel that other people should do likewise . . . out of courtesy, if nothing else" (*D* 1). Or, as she puts it: "I'm a model citizen, give or take a civil code or two" (*E* 126). Just to keep her life interesting, we know that Kinsey loves a good breaking and entering escapade, and, of course, a juicy lie. Fortunately for her, she can say with a smile, "Inconsistency has never troubled me" (*D* 1).

She is impatient for solutions and she longs for resolution. She says of one frustrating case, "I wanted closure, surcease. I wanted peace of mind again" (*E* 216). Even if she is paid off or fired, she continues to work, without pay, simply because otherwise she would sit up nights wondering about the answer to the puzzle. "I wasn't ready to let go" (*B* 37).

Desire for Justice

In addition to wanting answers for the sake of achieving a sense of order and closure, Kinsey wants the answers in order to restore a moral balance to the scheme of things. Especially when murder or abuse of others is involved, the answers are an essential step toward achieving justice. While Kinsey, like most fictional detectives, does not spend much time pondering metaphysical questions about the creation of the universe and the source of human evil, she does believe that solving the puzzle of "whodunit" and then taking some equalizing steps can restore a kind of balance to the universe. Throughout the series she says something similar to her gritty assertion in *"A" Is for Alibi* that there's a need for "the payment of old debts. That's what the notion of 'justice' was all about anyway: settling up" (245). The spirits of the murdered wander about, seeking a resetting of the scales. Kinsey is content to be their handmaiden, carrying on until the murderers are identified and punished. She answers an inquiry about why she will continue to investigate even though her client is dead by saying, "To settle accounts. I believe in clearing the ledger" (*C* 118).

Sometimes Kinsey's desire for order and her desire for justice appear to conflict; in these instances, we find her giving a higher priority to justice. In the opening of *"A" Is for Alibi,* order is already present, but not justice. Eight years earlier, Nikki Fife was convicted of murder and she has now served her time. Social order has been nominally established by the criminal justice system. No one seems to be worried that this reestablished order is rotten, no one except Nikki, that is, who knows she did not commit murder. She hires Kinsey, who becomes the disrupter of order by taking on the case and seeking the real murderer. In the process, she discovers that the murder was committed by Laurence Fife's first wife, Gwen. She also uncovers a second, tangentially related murder. Fife's law partner, Charlie Scorsoni, had murdered Libby Glass, their accountant, because she had discovered he was embezzling money. The Glass murder had not been resolved at the time because, although Nikki had been suspected of that murder also, the police did not have enough evidence to indict her. Even Lt. Dolan, who is convinced of Nikki's guilt, still isn't willing to do anything about it officially. Instead, he, the representative of the official justice system, encourages an outsider, Kinsey, to investigate what his system will not. Kinsey's investigation triggers Scorsoni's fear of disclosure, and he murders twice more in his efforts to protect himself.

Kinsey, then, disrupts the superficial order created by the incarceration of Nikki, but she is able to bring about a more just settlement by determining the real murderer. In the process, as readers, we are led to question who the true victims were and to wonder how *just* the *justice* system really is. Nikki, Gwen, and Kinsey were all seduced and mistreated (and Gwen murdered) by Laurence and Charlie. True, at the end of the case, both Fife and Scorsoni are dead, but what are we supposed to conclude about the law enforcement system? Identifying the guilt of these men did not come through the official justice system, but through the action of a private detective. And even more unsettling is our awareness that the next step, punishment, also happened through the actions of two women, Gwen and Kinsey, each acting on her own, and not as part of the official justice system.

Perhaps the most troubling problem of conflicting order and justice appears in *"D" Is for Deadbeat*. Kinsey addresses the confusion directly as she thinks about the death of the alcoholic John Daggett. Normally, she would feel a need to find and punish his murderer. "Usually the morality of homicide seems clear to me. Whatever the shortcomings of the victim, murder is wrong and the penalties levied against the perpetrator had better be substantial to balance out the gravity of the crime" (97). This case elicits a more complex response, however, because Daggett had killed five people in a car accident several years earlier. He was drunk at the time, clearly guilty of vehicular homicide. Now his body has been discovered. He either drowned accidentally, according to the police, or was murdered, according to his daughter.

Kinsey ponders her usual response to murder and realizes it may not apply to this situation. "In this case, that seemed like a simplistic point of view. It was *Daggett* who had caused the world to tilt on its axis. Because of him, five people had died, so that his death, whatever the instrument, was swinging the planet upright again, restoring a moral order of sorts" (97). She does agree to investigate his death, though, primarily because she is so moved by his daughter's pain and determination.

Later she is shocked to discover that the murderer is Tony Gahan, the teenaged son of one of the families killed in Daggett's DUI, a discovery that makes her wonder if Daggett may have gone willingly to his death as a kind of expiation of his guilt. She is further dismayed by her failure to prevent Tony from committing suicide in the novel's final scene. Yet, since Tony has murdered two people (a witness, in addition to Daggett), balancing the scales in detective fiction would appear to require his own death regardless of how much we may understand his motivation. But the resolution is an especially grim one—*all* killers must pay for what they've done—and Kinsey's sense of justice is only partially satisfied. "Some debts of the human soul are so enormous only life itself is sufficient forfeit. Perhaps in this case, all of the accounts are now paid in full . . . except mine" (229).

Throughout the novels, in fact, we continue to find Kinsey troubled by the lack of clear and immediate punishment for murderers, those people whose actions form the worst violation of moral and legal codes. We may be tempted to conclude that the answer to the question heading this chapter is "No, there is no justice" if we expect the judicial system to exact appropriate punishment for murder. "The problem is that so often the law seems pale in its remedies, leaving us restless and unfulfilled in our cravings for satisfaction" (*K* 285). Even where there is an arrest, it is often unclear that a prosecution will ever take place. There is, however, an essential kind of justice in the large number of cases in which the murderer is killed by the novel's conclusion, thus balancing the scales. But there is also a disturbing number who simply get away with murder. The overall pattern in the novels is troubling.

MURDERERS WHO ARE KILLED BY KINSEY IN SELF-DEFENSE

MURDERER	VICTIMS	MOTIVE	REASON FOR KINSEY'S ACTION	NOVEL
Charlie Scorsoni	Libby Glass Sharon Napier Gwen Fife	Prevent exposure of crimes	Self-defense	*"A" Is for Alibi*
Terry Kohler (Chris Emms)	Hugh Case Lyda Case Olive Kohler (foster mother years earlier)	Prevent exposure Jealousy Unknown	Self-defense	*"E" Is for Evidence*

continued

MURDERER	VICTIMS	MOTIVE	REASON FOR KINSEY'S ACTION	NOVEL
David Barney	Isabelle Barney Morley Shine	Money and jealousy Prevent exposure	Self-defense	"I" Is for Innocent

NOT IN SELF-DEFENSE				
MURDERER	VICTIMS	MOTIVE	REASON FOR KINSEY'S ACTION	NOVEL
Roger Bonney	Lorna Kepler	Protect real estate scheme	Retaliation on behalf of a friend	"K" Is for Killer
	Danielle Rivers Clark Esselmann	Prevent exposure		

KILLED BY SOMEONE OTHER THAN KINSEY				
MURDERER	VICTIMS	MOTIVE	REASON KILLED	NOVEL
Gwen Fife	Laurence Fife	Revenge	Charlie wants to prevent exposure of his own murders	"A" Is for Alibi
John Daggett	Five passengers in car he hit	Driving while drunk	Revenge	"D" Is for Deadbeat
Patrick Bronfen	Lottie Bronfen Emily Bronfen	Money	Got in the way of a contract killer	"G" Is for Gumshoe
	Anne Bronfen (alias Agnes Grey)	Prevent exposure		

continued

MURDERER	VICTIMS	MOTIVE	REASON KILLED	NOVEL
	Sheila Bronfen	Money		
	One of his nursing home residents	Money		
	Two unknown bodies	Unknown		
Mark Messinger	Patrick Bronfen	Expediency (trying to get to Kinsey, whom he's been hired to kill)	Self-defense and protect child	*"G" Is for Gumshoe*
	Rochelle's brother Roy	Expediency		

MURDERERS WHO KILL THEMSELVES				
MURDERER	VICTIMS	MOTIVE	REASON & METHOD OF SUICIDE	NOVEL
Tony Gahan	John Daggett	Revenge	Revenge unsatisfying; life is pointless; jumps from 8-story building	*"D" Is for Deadbeat*
	Billy Polo	Prevent exposure		
Claire Maddison (alias Myrna Sweetzer)	Guy Malek	Revenge	Revenge unsatisfying; runs into traffic	*"M" Is for Malice*

MURDERERS WHO ARE ARRESTED

MURDERER	VICTIMS	MOTIVE	HOW CAUGHT	NOVEL
Ann Fowler	Jean Timberlake	Jealousy and desire to protect a man	Subdued by her own father; turned over to police	*"F" Is for Fugitive*
	Shana Timberlake Ori Fowler	Prevent exposure Get away from home		
Brian Jaffe	Unidentified woman and man	Expediency in course of escape from juvenile detention	Tracked down and turned over to police by Kinsey	*"J" Is for Judgment*

ARRESTED, OUTCOME UNCLEAR

MURDERER	VICTIMS	MOTIVE	LEGAL STATUS	NOVEL
Marty Grice (alias Pat Usher) and Leonard Grice	Elaine Boldt	Money	Both are arrested, but Kinsey is "cautious" about what the courts will do	*"B" Is for Burglar*
	Wim Hoover	Prevent exposure		
James Fraker	Rick Bergen Bobby Callahan	Jealousy and control over wife	Charged, but out on bail	*"C" Is for Corpse*
Raymond Maldonado	Parnell Perkins Chopper (died carrying out Raymond's orders)	Prevent exposure	Charged, but will probably "work out a deal"	*"H" Is for Homicide*

KILLERS WHO GET AWAY WITH IT

MURDERER	VICTIMS	MOTIVE	METHOD OF "ESCAPE"	NOVEL
Nola Fraker	Dwight Costigan	Shoots husband when he catches her with a lover	Pleads guilty to voluntary manslaughter but serves no time	*"C" Is for Corpse*
Tippy Parsons	Mr. McKell	Hit-and-run	Statute of limitations expired	*"I" Is for Innocent*
Renata Huff	Wendell Jaffe	Revenge, jealousy, and money	*Implied* escape with millions after faked suicide	*"J" Is for Judgment*
Ray Rawson	Gilbert Hays	Money and revenge	Escapes with money	*"L" Is for Lawless*

We can see that of the novels' twenty murderers, half of them—ten—are dead by the novels' conclusions. This may be seen as a settling of accounts at its most basic level; however, this settling has not happened through the actions of any of society's systems for justice, but through the actions of individuals. Eight murderers either get away with their crimes or Kinsey seriously doubts they will be punished. Only *two* out of the twenty are headed for certain prosecution for their crimes.

If we consider the failures or limitations of the judicial system suggested by the novels' endings, we are not at all surprised that Kinsey's world is full of conflict and confusion about what constitutes justice. If the official legal and judicial systems cannot be relied upon, what part should individuals assume in seeing that justice prevails? In all her case reports, Kinsey continues to wonder about how she can and should act in her own little part of the world in order to realize some small measure of fairness. Sometimes she thinks the answer is clear. When someone questions why she would continue to work for Bobby Callahan after he's been killed, Kinsey replies heatedly, "He's dead now and he's got no way to rectify the situation, but *I* do and if you think I'll back off this sucker, you don't know me" (*C* 195). In other instances, such as the Daggett murder case, she is far less sure of what constitutes the right action. Until Billy Polo is killed, she seriously wishes she could drop the case: justice may have already been achieved with the death of Daggett. We respond to Kinsey's dilemma because she is grappling with one of life's largest issues: individual human life and its meaning in an infinite universe.

If the legal system cannot be trusted to exact appropriate punishment, Kinsey does seem prepared to take action herself. In "F" Is for Fugitive, she has a revealing discussion with Shana Timberlake about her daughter's murder having never been solved. Kinsey tells Shana, "If I had a kid and somebody'd killed her, I wouldn't be drunk in the middle of the day. I'd be out pulling this town apart until I found out who did it. And then I'd manufacture some justice of my own if that's what it took" (107). This willingness to execute punishment herself occurs most dramatically in "K" Is for Killer, where the lack of response by the official system leads Kinsey to arrange with the Mafia for the death of the man who had murdered both Lorna Kepler and Danielle Rivers. She shouts at Cheney, "I'm tired of the bad guys winning. I'm sick of watching people get away with murder. How come the law protects them and not us?" (277).

But vigilante action is not something Kinsey feels comfortable with. She fully understands that personal action of this kind lies outside her moral code of acceptable behavior. Thinking, "Oh, Jesus. What had I done?" she immediately tries to undo the hit she has arranged, and when she cannot do that, she goes personally to warn the murderer (278). Failing in her efforts, she tries to learn to live with the consequences of her decision. She remains haunted by the discovery of the unsavory depths of her own nature and she monitors herself carefully so that she will be better able to resist the impulse for personal vengeance the next time she senses its pull.

She also sees that the efforts of other people to take vengeance, to restore justice through private action, are fraught with serious repercussions. Tony Gahan takes Daggett's life, almost as an obsession, to restore order in his own emotionally disturbed world. This action initially seems fair to him, because Daggett was responsible for the death of his entire family. Won't this balance the scales? But he finds that the murder doesn't end his trauma. He is more troubled, not less, and he ultimately commits suicide. In "M" Is for Malice, Claire Maddison kills the wrong person in her effort to avenge the deaths in her family. She, too, finds that the completion of her plan for vengeance brings no consolation, and she, too, seeks the release of suicide. Kinsey herself is learning to live with the implications of her own private search for justice, and by the time of *Malice*, her nights are full of ghosts and dreams.

Like most of us, Kinsey wants to think that events in life have an order and that she can decipher patterns and come to an understanding of them. Her understanding is a key to revealing the identity and motives of the murderers she pursues and restoring some sort of order to her piece of the world. But defining a *patterned* universe is not the same as describing a *meaningful* universe. Kinsey says, chillingly, "Everything happens for a reason, but that doesn't mean there's a point" (*C* 102). Even more emphatically, Kinsey tells Tony Gahan, who's planning suicide because he doesn't see the point of life, "There isn't a point. That's the part you invent" (*D* 225).

Distaste for Hypocrisy

Kinsey hates hypocrisy and posing and is comfortable making cutting comments to deflate windbags. She uses her wit and sarcasm freely in the presence of fools, although her jokes at their expense often seem to fly over their heads, just as her cousin Liza misses her irony in feigning relief that her father was not "just" a waiter (*J* 171), and Dwight Shales misses the depth of her outrage over his hypocrisy in *"F" Is for Fugitive* (243–45).

One of Kinsey's many virtues is that she accepts herself as part of the human network. She knows that she, too, can fall into complacency or larcenous thinking or prejudice. In *"H" Is for Homicide*, for example, she begins to feel superior when she is being taught Raymond's con scheme. Almost before she realizes what has happened, she absorbs and then replicates his attitude of blaming the "mark" for being gullible enough to fall for the trap. "Mentally, I had to shake myself off, though I suppose it never hurts to be reminded that none of us is that far away from larceny" (*H* 233).

Horror at Killing

Because Kinsey is so appalled by the act of one human being killing another, she is deeply disturbed by her first experience of taking someone's life. *"A" Is for Alibi* opens with Kinsey's statement, "The day before yesterday I killed someone and the fact weighs heavily on my mind" (1). What follows is the story leading up to that act, the shooting of Charlie Scorsoni in self-defense. Kinsey worries about what the action of killing will do to her sense of herself. Whether it was self-defense or not, the brutal fact is that she has now joined the ranks of killers. "The shooting disturbs me still. It has moved me into the same camp with soldiers and maniacs" (275). In the next novel, Kinsey is still troubled: "What took me by surprise was realizing that I'd killed someone and didn't much care. No, that wasn't true. I did care, but if my life was threatened, I knew I'd do it again. I'd always believed I was a good person. Now I didn't know what 'good' meant. Surely good people didn't kill other human beings, so where did that put me?" (*B* 49).

Kinsey has a serious discussion with Henry about the event. She is struggling to establish some kind of high moral ground from which it is all right that she has killed someone. But Henry speaks bluntly to her, telling her that she is wasting her time looking for moral justifications for killing: "You can drop the rhetoric. It's bullshit. . . . You did what you did. Just don't try to turn it into a philosophical statement, because it doesn't ring true" (*B* 83).

Kinsey's response to Henry is a tentative question, "I'm still a good person, aren't I?" Henry replies, "What happened to you doesn't change that, Kinsey, but you have to keep it straight. Blow somebody's brains out and you don't brush that off. And you don't try to turn it into an intellectual stance" (84).

Kinsey appears to take Henry's advice seriously. In many ways, he simply reinforces her own tendencies. She is a thoughtful person. She considers her actions both in the context of the world around her and in the context of her own scheme of values. She thinks about how the world, her beliefs, and her actions fit together or clash. She looks hard to discern any pattern that might be visible behind the fit or the collision. But her efforts to understand must not prevent her from taking decisive action. Leaving Henry's house, she says, "I had to put it out of my mind again. Back the subject went, into its own little box" (84). She goes for her three-mile jog and gets back to the case at hand. But the box is never sealed.

We know that Kinsey seems to enjoy the excitement and even exhaustion of a physical scuffle, but she tries to avoid using her gun if she can do so sensibly and without endangering her own life. When she does use it to threaten or take life, she tries to reconcile the action with her rational, as well as subjective, sense of what is "good." Her inability to achieve this reconciliation in an easy fashion convinces us of the sincerity of her values and her commitment to maintaining her moral code. In other words, she doesn't easily make exceptions from the code, even to ease her own conscience.

Importance of Honesty

Kinsey is basically honest. She reveals her honesty in large and small ways. In her work, she is scrupulous in telling clients the truth about her progress on a case and she normally tells the truth to the police. Honesty is an automatic part of her daily life. When she finds $5,000 in her bank account and knows she didn't deposit it, she immediately calls the bank. She never considers keeping it. In fact, she worries about the person to whom she assumes it properly belongs, fearing he or she is writing checks against it that will bounce (*E* 3).

Her whole approach to her business is one of honesty and fairness. We see her trying to discourage people from hiring her if she believes their money may be wasted. She offers to teach Beverly Danzinger the basic steps for tracing a missing person, explaining that, rather than hiring Kinsey, she could do it more cheaply herself (*B* 6). She is always scrupulous about her expense account, staying at modest places, buying the least expensive airline tickets. We never see her fudge or pad her expenses to make more money, just the reverse: she appears to carry her own thrifty lifestyle over into her business dealings.

Willingness to Lie

Kinsey is quite explicit on this topic: "I'm a purist when it comes to justice, but I'll lie at the drop of a hat" (*D* 1). In spite of her overall honesty, Kinsey is proud of her ability to lie convincingly, an apparent aberration in Kinsey's moral code, but we notice that the lies are either part of her disguise during an investigation or harmless.

In either case, Kinsey likes the fun of creating a persona or a story with which she can fool other people. It's her most extreme method of creating herself her way. She considers herself an accomplished liar and she is seldom caught out. "I'm a born liar myself and I know how it's done. You stick as close to the truth as you can. You pretend to volunteer a few bits of information, but the facts are all carefully selected for effect" (*B* 30). Kinsey derives a great deal of pleasure from spontaneous lies, as well as from planned ones needed for a disguise in her investigation. "Lying is fun. I can do it all day myself" (*D* 5).

Yet, with all of her lying, we never expect her to lie to her readers. She is amazingly open and honest with us. If she thinks or feels something, she tells us, censoring nothing. Also, we have never seen her tell a serious lie to a friend, a client, or the police. Her moral code allows deception in the performance of her work, or the polite white lie, or the harmless lie that is a self-indulgent game for Kinsey, but she makes an effort to keep her personal relationships honest. A telling and painful example of her personal honesty occurs when she is unable to lie convincingly to Tony Gahan to prevent his suicide jump from a ledge. She asks him for help getting inside the building, and he in turn asks if it's a trick. " 'No,' I said, but I could hear my voice shake and the lie cut my tongue like a razor blade. I've always lied with ease and grace, with ingenuity and conviction and I couldn't get this one out" (*D* 227).

Daniel Wade may toss into a conversation with Kinsey that they share the tendency to lie, but we are able to distinguish between his use of lies as a way of life and Kinsey's use of them. We would find it exceedingly difficult, for example, to imagine Kinsey bugging Daniel's apartment while pretending to be his friend, as Daniel does to her.

Acceptance of the Duality of Human Nature

Kinsey believes that her work shows her the worst of human behavior. "So often, humankind just seems tacky to me, and I don't know what the rest of us are supposed to do in response" (*E* 216). Like many of us, she changes her attitude toward her fellow humans with changes in her mood and in the people she meets. Sometimes we hear from her the idea that some people are just bad, if not by nature, at least by very early in their lives. Kinsey appears to agree when Bass Wood's own mother says of him, "He knew about wickedness even at that age [13 years] and he enjoyed it all so very much" (*E* 211).

Kinsey may not see the world and its inhabitants through rose-colored glasses, but she usually takes a positive, if unsentimentalized, view. She defines herself as a person who expects the positive: "Kinsey Millhone, perpetual optimist" (*E* 175). Strength, humor, and honor can appear in the most amazing situations or people. Danielle Rivers may be a prostitute and uneducated, but she has guts, loyalty, and a sense of playfulness. Raymond Maldonado may be a gangster, but he proves to be a good teacher, he has endured much sadness and a debilitating illness, and he responds admiringly to Kinsey's strengths— and so the list goes. Kinsey can see both the good and the bad.

She also understands that there are emotional lows, but she expects a high time will eventually come along. Arguing with Tony Gahan on the ledge of a building, she tries to keep him from jumping. Her desperate words ring true as she tells him, "Life is hard. Life hurts. So what? You tough it out. You get through and then you'll feel good again, I swear to God. . . . There are days when none of us can bear it, but the good comes around again. Happiness is seasonal, like anything else. Wait it out" (*D* 226).

Kinsey occasionally suffers mild depression. In *Evidence,* she is lonesome when all of her friends are away for the Christmas holidays. In *Innocent,* she struggles to regain her sense of self-confidence after being fired. By *Malice,* she is going through a serious self-evaluation as a new year begins. "Who was I, really, in the scheme of things, and what did it all add up to? . . . Some days I see myself (nobly, I'll admit) battling against evil in the struggle for law and order. Other days, I concede the dark forces are gaining ground" (2). Again, though, the depression and self-questioning never prevent her from moving forward with the case at hand.

There's a power hierarchy operating everywhere, and as much as anyone, Kinsey knows that to save your sanity and stay an individual you need to stand up to it sometimes. But, in order to save your work, your life, and occasionally your other values, you sometimes have to sidestep the confrontation. Take the route around, rather than through. Not every battle can or should be fought. "All of us are subjected to somebody else's power at some point. So once in a while you kiss ass. So what? Either you make your peace with that early, or you end up living your life as a crank and a misfit" (*H* 22). Billy Polo properly sizes up Kinsey as a strong woman and speculates, "I bet you don't take crap from anyone, am I right?" But Kinsey is quite realistic about accepting the world as it is. She replies, "We all take crap from someone" (*D* 76).

Kinsey sees herself as part of the human network and always subject to the same vulnerabilities and temptations as other people. One of the aspects of her job that gives her some concern is that she finds her work increasingly leading her to bend the rules. She is self-conscious about such decisions. For example, on one occasion she is trying to get information from a seventeen-year-old who is cute, a punk, and a drug dealer. She knows he will trade the information she wants, which turns out to be the key to solving the murder mystery, in exchange for not reporting him to the police. "I had to make quick peace with my own corruption and it wasn't that hard to do. Times like this, I know I've been in the business too long" (*B* 126).

"Opening the door so all the ghosts could move on": Kinsey Considers Death

Many of Kinsey's values are played out around her encounters with death. Quite simply, death has an all too salient place in the life of Kinsey Millhone.

Readers expect one or more deaths in a detective novel, but the deaths are usually simply plot devices. A murder normally triggers the entire story and the case for the detective. But, significantly, while the death is the catalyst for the whole novel, the concept of death itself, or the value of the life of the murder victim, is rarely a subject of much contemplation. The central question of the detective formula is "Who Done It?" not "To Whom Was It Done?"

Death in a mystery novel is paradoxically both present and absent, typically offering the presence of death without the concomitant need to think about or analyze the meaning of death in any metaphysical way. Many readers enjoy detective fiction for the very reason that they can be entertained by that which in real life would frighten and disturb them.

Kinsey is unusual, then, in her occasional confrontations with death as a cosmic event, one we will all encounter, and in her grappling not only with the death of a specific person, but with death as a phenomenon. "Death is insulting, and I resented its sudden appearance, like an unannounced visit from a boorish relative" (*E* 140). "Sometimes I picture death as a wide stone staircase, filled with a silent procession of those being led away. I see death too often to worry about it much, but I miss the departed and I wonder if I'll be docile when my turn comes" (*D* 130).

Ultimately death teaches Kinsey and us about life, a lesson we might learn less often than she, except that we keep choosing to read her adventures. "Sometimes the hardest part of my job is the incessant reminder of the fact we're all trying so assiduously to ignore: we are here temporarily . . . life is only ours on loan" (*K* 156). Her language ranges from gritty to sublime, inviting the reader to struggle with her, simply because we want to understand Kinsey, or perhaps because we like the appealing opportunity to mull over life's largest question within the safe confines of an entertaining novel. One of the reasons readers continue to follow Kinsey on these potentially depressing and disturbing journeys is her ability to lead us to valuable insights and yet leave us with a smile, or even a laugh.

At the most concrete level, Kinsey straightforwardly confronts the physical reality of death. She recognizes death as inevitable and, in her no-nonsense attitude toward life, she does not shy away from this fact, or dress it up as the will of a caring deity. She can't go along with the Christians she meets who tell her that a particular death is God's will. And she often finds herself angered or saddened by a death that, to her, can have no comforting explanation—Danielle, Bobby, and Guy are victims whom she mourns and misses. She doesn't try to delude herself that their deaths are anything other than wasteful loss.

A frequent way that we encounter death with Kinsey is as she views police photographs of homicide victims, in varying stages of deterioration and with different signs of the traumas suffered by the victim. One of her first such experience made a deep impression on her: three young children had been bound, gagged, and left in a garbage can to suffocate. "I had to look at the glossy eight-by-ten police photographs. I got cured of any homicidal urges" (*A* 143). As readers, we share her first reaction to these horrible images, and we are grateful for her lack of specificity about the condition of the bodies. "Violent death is repellent. My first impulse, always, is to turn abruptly away, to shield my soul from the sight" (*B* 122). Her revulsion is still as deep in her eleventh reported case as in her second, in spite of the fact that she has learned to manufacture some detachment (*K* 77). As readers, we are carried along in her vivid disturbing encounters, and regardless of our own beliefs, we learn to see death through her eyes. She generally describes these encounters in straightforward and sometimes witty terms, without resorting to sentimentality or euphemisms, leaving us unable to join the general societal game of pretending that we will never die. "I'm well aware that immortality is simply an illusion we carry with us to keep ourselves functional from day to day" (*G* 28).

At times Kinsey comes close to her own death because, of course, her work is dangerous, but also because, as she is quick to remind us, death is often a random visitor anywhere. Part of the shock of death is its sudden and arbitrary appearance. For example, while unloading groceries with Olive Kohler, Kinsey offers to carry a package that Olive takes instead. The package contains a bomb that explodes, damaging the house and killing Olive. "Her casual refusal had saved me. Death sometimes passes us by that way, with a wink, a nod, and an impish promise to return for us at another time" (*E* 204–05). Kinsey's personification of impish death is haunting and not easily dismissed.

Kinsey also encounters the more frightening persona of death as a malevolent force. The murderer in *"E" Is for Evidence* kills someone and deliberately uses the body as a warning to Kinsey. He murders a young woman and leaves her body in a car parked outside Kinsey's apartment. He covers the car, maximizing the heat inside, so that by the time the body is discovered, it is bloated, gaseous, ugly, and vile smelling. Kinsey has such a visceral reaction to this discovery that we sense with her a palpable form of malignant death, almost as an infectious disease. We readily understand her physical cleansing as an effort to wash death away, shampooing her hair, and tossing all of her clothing, including her running shoes, into the trash (*E* 187–88).

Common in Western thought is a belief in the separation of body and soul. Most simply put, the body can be viewed as only a shell for the more important mind or spirit. At times, Kinsey appears to share this belief. Watching people viewing the body at a wake, she observes, "I don't know why people stand and study the dead that way. It makes about as much sense as paying homage to the cardboard box your favorite shoes once came in" (*D* 89).

More often, however, this detached strategy does not appear to work for her. For example, she's more contemplative upon seeing the body of her California Fidelity colleague, Parnell Perkins, at the opening of *"H" Is for Homicide.* "What is life that it can vanish so absolutely in such a short period of time? Looking at Parnell, I was struck by the loss of animation, warmth, energy, all of it gone in an instant, never to return. His job was done" (7). Here Kinsey is less distant from the body, and at these times she observes a confluence of body and spirit. The absence of life in the body is simply the outward sign, the way that we know that a death has occurred.

A major drawback of accepting individuals, especially the deceased, as both body and spirit is the greater difficulty in detaching oneself in the face of death. Kinsey is well aware of her own desire for detachment but also of its dangers. When she begins the investigation in *"I" Is for Innocent,* she considers it necessary to look at the photographs of Isabelle Barney's body, but she steels herself for the experience because Isabelle was killed in an especially ugly way, shot in the eye through the peephole of her front door. Kinsey prepares herself: "I disconnected my emotional machinery while I studied the autopsy x-rays and photographs. I work best when I'm armed with an unflinching view of reality, but the detachment is not without its dangers. . . . Unplug yourself often and you risk losing touch with your feelings altogether" (16). Kinsey's ability to detach temporarily when necessary is almost always balanced by her very genuine engagement with the good and evil she encounters in her work.

In *Killer,* she is engaged with a dead Lorna Kepler re-created through the memories of those who cared about her. In *Corpse* and *Malice,* she becomes emotionally attached to the victims, Bobby Callahan and Guy Malek. When she finally identifies Bobby's murderer, she writes up her report for her client, even though he has died. She includes in the report a personal letter to Bobby telling him how much she misses him, and she concludes her report to us, "I hope, wherever he may be, that he sails among the angels, untethered and at peace" (*C* 243).

Even as wicked a man as David Barney seems to be more than his body. Kinsey shoots him in self-defense and watches him die. "His eyes had gone empty and his fingers opened slowly as he released his own life. Something like a moth fluttered off into the dark" (*I* 283). Although Kinsey does not believe in an afterlife according to the tenets of any organized religion, she clearly has her own personal sense of the human soul, of there being something more to the human being than a collection of cells that decay and return to the earth.

Kinsey also bravely engages the meaning of specific deaths in her personal life. We know that the deep feelings evoked by the death of her parents and later of her aunt led Kinsey to change in fundamental ways. She also allows herself to respond emotionally to the deaths she encounters in her work. At first, like most of us confronting the death of someone we care for, she tries to detach her emotions in order to stay in control. We see her attempt detachment at Bobby Callahan's funeral, where she says, "[I tried] surviving the eulogy by neatly disconnecting myself from what was said. I wasn't going to deal with Bobby's death today. I wasn't going to lose control in a public setting like this." But Kinsey awakens within herself and within us our shared human experience of loss that each death is capable of evoking. "It was more than this loss. It was all death, every loss—my parents, my aunt" (*C* 103). She feels her face flush and her eyes fill with tears. Yet, she still cannot come to terms with her loss.

Pure anguish rushes through her when Tony Gahan leaps to his death. "I thought I heard a siren wailing, but the sound was mine" (*D* 228). Her deep feeling is not muted by Tony's having been responsible for the deaths of two people. Likewise, her regret and sadness are obvious at the death of Billy Polo, one of Tony's victims, in fact. She hears the shot that fatally wounds him, reaching him in time to hold his hand as he dies. "Polo sighed, his gaze still pinned on my face. His hand relaxed in mine, but I held on" (*D* 200). She won't sully his final moments with questions about the case, and she is deeply moved by his death, never minimizing it with reference to his less than stellar life.

Rather than remain immobilized by her sadness, Kinsey is able to link her grief to anger and then to action. "I was spoiling for a fight, which I suspected would feel better than grief" (*C* 111). Often it is this ability to transform her emotions into actions that helps Kinsey to keep going and to track down those responsible for the deaths.

Although she has no children and never wishes to become a mother, Kinsey is especially understanding about the death of a child. She observes the varied strategies parents adopt to cope with their losses. Several novels focus on parents trying to cope with the loss of a child, all suffering psychic pain with no end in sight. Bobby Callahan's mother, Glen, was able to bring him through the first attempt on his life, but the depth of her caring is not enough to save him from the second and she is defenseless against the pain of his death. John Daggett's victims include the parents of children killed during the car crash he caused while driving drunk. The families of the victims are explicit about the absolute endlessness of their grief (*Deadbeat*). Shana Timberlake continues to mourn the death of her daughter, Jean, seventeen years later. She tells Kinsey that she keeps the pain of the loss alive as a continuing tribute to her love of her only child (*Fugitive*). Janice Kepler tells Kinsey that her entire life is overshadowed by the death of her daughter. She has joined a support group to help her cope, but nothing really seems to have dimmed the pain of her loss (*Killer*).

Kinsey also considers the ways in which death may have an impact on a group of people, again holding our interest by expressing feelings we often experience, but less often try to analyze. When Parnell Perkins is murdered, everyone at California Fidelity is perturbed. "He seemed a perfectly ordinary human being just like the rest of us. . . . Since there were never any suspects, we were made uncomfortably aware of our own vulnerability, haunted by the notion that perhaps we knew more than we realized. We discussed the subject endlessly, trying to dispel the cloud of anxiety that billowed up in the wake of his death" (*H* 8).

The group of friends surrounding Glen Callahan after Bobby's death are subdued and quiet throughout the funeral service and burial, but Kinsey notices a "much lighter" mood when the people arrive at the family home afterward. "People seemed to shrug death aside, comforted by good wine and lavish hors d'oeuvres. I don't know why death still generates these little têtes-à-têtes. . . . It was filler, just something to smooth the awkward transition from the funeral to the bone-crushing sleep that was bound to come afterward" (*C* 106).

Throughout the series, Kinsey breaks tension with humor and she makes no exception for the pain of death. When she begins to wonder if Marty Grice had been killed by one of her neighbors, several of whom regularly played bridge together, she speculates, "I didn't think Marty Grice had been killed for messing up a small slam, but with bridge partners one can never tell" (*B* 122). Although initially she is reluctant to disturb the bodies at the morgue (in *"C" Is for Corpse)*, out of respect, she gradually subdues her reluctance by assuming a lighthearted attitude more attuned to a cocktail party than a morgue. She engages the corpse she wants to move into another room in a necessarily one-sided conversation, which has the reader laughing out loud. All the wit and ease, which often elude her in gatherings of the living, flow freely in this gathering of the dead (232).

Kinsey often deals humorously with all the group rituals surrounding death. Miss Manners she is not. *Corpse, Deadbeat, Evidence,* and *Innocent* have funerals, all very different, but having in common a strong sense of the absurd. The funeral for John Daggett in *Deadbeat* is probably the most hilarious. We begin by sharing Kinsey's uneasiness with her surroundings and the feeling we might have had as a child that misbehaving here would be the baddest thing we could do, so, of course, the baddest possibilities invade our brains. "Being with devout Christians is like being with the very rich. One senses that there are rules at work, some strange etiquette that one might inadvertently breech. I tried to hold bland and harmless thoughts, hoping I wouldn't blurt out any four-letter words" (24).

Kinsey also deals with a range of emotions about her own death. Unlike most readers, Kinsey must constantly confront this possibility. She fully accepts, rather than evades, this reality. At the conclusion of *Burglar,* she has barely escaped death, but she has not escaped a vicious and painful beating and shooting, leaving her with a broken arm and broken nose. Standing in her apartment, she contemplates her own mortality with a calm resignation: "I stare out the window at the palms and wonder how many times I'll dance with death before the orchestra packs it in for the night" (229).

She has no wish for death, however. She may relish the thrill of playing with it, but she fully intends to be the victor in that match for as long as possible. She stays in shape; she calls for backup; she thinks through her strategies; she keeps her gun clean and ready and gets in her target practice. She swears, "Honestly, my sole object in life is to protect my own ass" (*C* 224).

As we would expect, Kinsey considers her possible death in much the way she considers her life—with quick snatches of philosophical contemplation sandwiched between distracted attention to details and completely irresistible one-liners. Kinsey opens her account of the Barney case in *"I" Is for Innocent,* for example, by poking fun at spiritual accounts of dying. "I feel compelled to report that at the moment of death, my entire life did not pass before my eyes in a flash. There was no beckoning white light at the end of the tunnel, no warm fuzzy feeling that my long-departed loved ones were waiting on The Other Side. What I experienced was a little voice piping up in an outraged tone, 'Oh, come on. You're not serious. This is really *it*?' " What she minds most is that she didn't tidy up her bureau as she had planned to the previous night. "It's painful to realize that those who mourn your untimely demise will also carry with them the indelible image of all your tatty underpants" (1).

When she actually comes to experience the near-death scene that she refers to in the opening pages, she is bleeding on the carpet and trying to think of ways to outwit her assailant. Even here we see the same combination of the serious and the comic. "The notion of dying is at the same time, trivial and terrifying, absurd and full of anguish. Ego clings to life. Self lets it go, willing to free-fall, willing to soar. If I regretted anything, it was simply not knowing how all the stories would turn out. Would William and Rosie fall in love sure enough? Would Henry reach the age of ninety? With all the blood oozing out, would Lonnie ever get his carpet clean?" (281–82).

Kinsey is convinced that somehow the dead remain with us. Essentially, this means that people live on in the influence they have on the lives of others, whether for good or ill. She never disagrees with Barbara Daggett's assessment of her alcoholic father's continuing impact on her life. "I've hated him with every cell in my body for as long as I can remember. And now I'm stuck with it. He won, didn't he? He never changed . . . never gave us an inch. . . . I don't even know why I care how he died. I should be relieved, but I'm pissed. The irony is that he's probably still going to dominate my life" (*D* 47–48). Many people had been affected by John Daggett. After he is killed by Tony Gahan, the pain will continue because, as Kinsey points out, the consequent suicide of Tony will haunt the life of the aunt who had adopted him when his family was killed by Daggett. And as Daggett's daughter made clear, she will never have resolution to the dysfunctional relationship she had with her father.

Homicide victims, in particular, have a special effect on the living, including Kinsey. In the opening pages of *"K" Is for Killer,* her darkest report, she conjures up for us an unearthly vision of those whose murders have not been solved. "The victims of unsolved homicides I think of as the unruly dead: persons who reside in a limbo of their own, some state between life and death, restless, dissatisfied, longing for release. It's a fanciful notion for someone not generally given to flights of imagination, but I think of these souls locked in an uneasy relationship with those who have killed them" (1–2).

Kinsey goes on to explain the powerful bond she feels with these ghosts. "In the hazy zone where wakefulness fades into sleep, in that leaden moment just before the mind sinks below consciousness, I can sometimes hear them murmuring. They mourn themselves. They sing a lullaby of the murdered. They whisper the names of their attackers, those men and women who still walk the earth, unidentified, unaccused, unpunished, unrepentant. On such nights, I do not sleep well. I lie awake listening, hoping to catch a syllable, a phrase, straining to discern in that roll call of conspirators the name of one killer" (2). Kinsey goes into the night, exhausts herself, endangers her own life, and, as the title indicates, becomes a killer herself, behavior we can better understand if she is being haunted by Lorna's mournful spirit seeking rest.

Kinsey encounters more than dreams or fancy in *"M" Is for Malice.* She experiences a ghost. She first meets the death presence—a sense of cold and the smell of earth—on the steps of the house in which Guy Malek was murdered. Although she tries to deny any ghostly presence to Enid, the Maleks' cook, her denial is in vain. Enid explains, "Ghosts don't haunt us. That's not how it works. They're present among us because we won't let go of *them.*" Kinsey attempts to reject the idea: " 'I don't believe in ghosts,' I said faintly." But Enid has the last word. "Some people can't see the color red. That doesn't mean it isn't there" (*M* 280). From Enid's questioning, we know that she has had the same experience on the stairway that Kinsey did.

After the case is solved, Guy comes to Kinsey in a dream. "Somehow in the dream, I knew he'd come to say good-bye." Kinsey tries to hold onto Guy, but he lets her know that his time on earth is done and that he has other places to go. "In the end, I set him free, not in sorrow, but in love. It wasn't for me. It was something I did for him" (*M* 300).

Her thoughts of the connection to other deaths and her abiding sense of loss is evoked once again by Guy. "The tears I wept for him then were the same tears I'd wept for everyone I'd ever loved. My parents, my aunt. I had never said good-bye to them, either, but it was time to take care of it. I said a prayer for the dead, opening the door so all the ghosts could move on. I gathered them up like the petals of a flower and released them to the wind. What's done is done. What is written is written. Their work is finished. Ours is yet to do" (300).

KINSEY LAUGHS AT:

Social responses to death:

"Violent death is a spectator sport and I could hear them comment about the way the final quarter had been played." (*D* 201)

Food brought to the house:

"It had only been an hour and a half since Bailey fled the courthouse in a blaze of gunfire. I didn't think gelatin set up that fast, but these Christian ladies probably knew tricks with ice cubes that would render salads and desserts in record time for just such occasions. I pictured a section in the ladies' auxiliary church cookbook for Sudden Death Quick Snacks." (*F* 85)

Grafton on Kinsey

"Often I feel she's peering over my shoulder, whispering, nudging me, and making bawdy remarks."

"Kinsey is my alter ego—the person I might have been had I not married young and had children. . . . While our biographies are different, our sensibilities are the same. . . . I think of us as one soul in two bodies and she got the good one."

Sue Grafton, *Kinsey and Me*

Unlike many writers, Sue Grafton is happy to acknowledge that her fictional character is her own alter ego. As she told us, "Kinsey is the undomesticated and adventurous side of me." She enjoys Kinsey's company and watches enthusiastically as Kinsey does many things she would like to do herself. In fact, the character and the plot of *"A" Is for Alibi* in part grew out of Grafton's frustrations over a difficult divorce and a series of custody battles with her second husband. Like so many of us in the midst of the divorce process, she lay awake at night thinking up ways to kill her ex. But she didn't think actually doing this would be a good idea; murder is the last taboo. And besides, she has suggested, serving prison time would be a nuisance. So she used her imagination to do away with him. Kinsey closes the novel with what must have been a satisfying line for Sue—"I blew him away"—as she shoots her lover, who is a murderer.

Grafton says she drew Kinsey's first name from a birth announcement column in *The Hollywood Reporter* in 1977. She liked the name because it was not exclusively male or female and it sounded vaguely Southern. At the time Grafton was writing movies for television and living in Columbus, Ohio, while her husband was completing a doctorate at Ohio State. She considered using the name in a screenplay, but she chose instead to save it for some special project of her own. When she decided to try writing a detective novel, she knew this was the right name. Looking for a strong surname with the double or triple cadence to go with "Kinsey," she searched the telephone directory until she found "Millhone." She had the name. Kinsey tells us in *"M" Is for Malice* to pronounce it with the accent "on the first syllable. The last rhymes with bone" (38).

One of Grafton's readers told her she admired the last name because "to mill" means "to grind" and "hone" means "to sharpen," both apt descriptions for Kinsey's work. "I like that idea," Sue has said, "but I swear I did not consciously think of those associations when I picked the name." She also liked our suggestion that the name "Millhone" has echoes of all the working-class neighborhoods surrounding Southern textile mills called "millhills," but denied she had ever consciously thought of that either. Laughing, she said, "I guess the Right Brain strikes again." Sue's reference to the intuitive right brain—which she calls by the acronym of "RB"—influencing things the more logical left brain is unaware of, calls to mind Kinsey's own awareness of those sudden leaps of intuition that move her forward in a case. For example, in *"L" Is for Lawless,* Kinsey, trying to figure out where the money could be, suddenly says, "I heard the sound an idea makes when your brain ignites, a tiny implosion, like spontaneous combustion at the base of your skull" (147). We learn that Kinsey's flash of insight was triggered by her recall of seeing tampons in supposedly pregnant Laura's purse: she's *not* pregnant, but she has a large belly so the money must be inside her padding. Kinsey refers often to something along the lines of the mind making "magic little leaps" (*C* 5).

Just as Kinsey will work at rational solutions to a problem and finally just set it aside while she jogs or cleans or sleeps, so Sue will turn things over to her subconscious when she gets stuck in her writing. Her husband, Steve, teases her that in writing every one of her novels she hits a point where she claims *this* is the hardest book she's ever written and she'll never figure how to get out of this one. Sue keeps a journal about the writing of every novel and when she gets stalled, she notes it. Here, for example, is one of the journal entries for *"J" Is for Judgment.*

> March 25, 1992:
> Dear RB,
> Please use your massive intelligence, wit, and ingenuity to come up with some sparkling twist or device to give "J" a lift.
> It wouldn't hurt my spirits either while you're at it . . .
> Thanks.
> Your pal,
> Sue

The *Judgment* journal is filled with references to the Right Brain's intuitive messages to her during her periods of escape from the logical thought processes of the Left Brain. "Coming up on the interchange between Kinsey & the drunk and RB quizzed me in the dead of night on the subject of how to make this scene play" (1-14-92). "Had my teeth cleaned this morning under nitrous and RB suggested the following. . . . RB also reminded me that I described the hotel as three stories high and then mention rooms 414 & 416 which implies a fourth floor" (1-9-92). "What RB suggested in the dead of night is that thematically I might play Wendell Jaffe and the guy who cut out on his child support as a comment on the abandonment of responsibility. Not condemning, but letting these guys have a voice . . ." (2-26-92).

Both Sue and Kinsey can compartmentalize their intellectual and creative lives and they are tidy, organized people about everything they do. Grafton says she really likes Kinsey's ability to organize her work and her home, and she considers herself to be an orderly person, too. Certainly Grafton's offices, where she writes every morning, reflect extreme tidiness. Looking out over green lawns and part of the vegetable garden, her California office is filled with resource books, her awards, and all the computer-related paraphernalia needed to write, as well as a good-luck witch (The Mysterious Stranger Award from the Cloak and Clue Society) perched on the monitor. Her files are as neat and up-to-date as Kinsey's, for which only partial credit goes to her capable assistant, Barbara Toohey, because Sue likes to do much of her own letter-writing and filing. "What pleases me most are letters from readers that prove somebody really is out there" (Goodman 82).

As do many writers, Sue Grafton talks about her fictional character as if she were a living, breathing person who might walk through the door at any moment—and one who clearly has a mind of her own. Sue describes the relationship between the two of them during her writing as "almost a form of channeling. . . . I just be with her and things come through" (Nance F1). "Often I feel she's peering over my shoulder, whispering, nudging me, and making bawdy remarks" (*K & M* 5). The experience is so intense that Grafton claims, "Later, because I've been so very focused and concentrated, I haven't the faintest idea what I've written until I read it again on the page" (Nance F1). In fact, Kinsey does seem to make her own decisions. When we commented that we were surprised to see Kinsey wearing a skirt in *"M" Is for Malice,* a substantial deviation from her normal jeans and T-shirts, Sue initially denied making this wardrobe modification. Rereading the passage (152), she immediately laughed and exclaimed, "Oh, that was *my* new denim skirt. I guess Kinsey was jealous and had to have one too."

Grafton gave Kinsey much of herself in nature and in details, starting with the basic similarity: gender. "I elected to write about a female protagonist at the outset because I'm female (hot news, huh?) and I figured it was my one area of expertise" (*K & M* 3). In addition to sharing a sense of order and a fondness for jeans and turtlenecks (and denim skirts), both have been married and divorced twice; both are independent and strong-willed, tough with an essential core of compassion. Kinsey may be physically tougher, but Grafton considers herself "tough in a psychic sense. I'm certainly tough in my persona" (Herbert 33). They dislike pretension and they both feel rage at abuse of the powerless. They distrust many things about the system, but they both believe in following the rules themselves. Kinsey's all-purpose dress, two of her guns, and both of her cars are really hand-me-downs from Sue, who owned them first. And Sue started jogging three miles every morning well before Kinsey did. Sue began taking Spanish classes the same time Kinsey did. Neither of them likes getting injections and they both have a bit of dental phobia. Their mutual distrust of the excesses of the Christian church comes from Sue's background as the granddaughter of missionaries: her grandparents on both sides were Presbyterian missionaries in China, and Sue grew up hearing stories of the church and its foibles. She says she would *never* make fun of other religions, but she feels she can laugh at the Christian church because it is her own and she knows it so well from the inside.

Even when Kinsey behaves badly by Grafton's more genteel standards, Sue embraces her completely. Sue is very interested in the work of Jung and his notion of the shadow self, and she calls Kinsey her "evil twin" (Nance F1) who can cuss, act out, strike an attitude, punch somebody in the nose, and express opinions that may be far from tactful or popular, but are oh so satisfying.

Grafton even made their birth dates similar, and they share the same astrological sign. They are both Tauruses, "organism[s] of the earth . . . never born of air, of water, or of fire" (*D* 220). Sue's birthday is April 24, 1940, or 4/24/40 and she went for a similar repetition for Kinsey, whose birth date is May 5, 1950, or 5/5/50. Only *after* she chose this date did she learn that "5" is the number associated with investigation and action. That Right Brain strikes again.

Grafton plays with the birth date for Kinsey in *"H" Is for Homicide*. While they are in jail, Bibianna Diaz gives Kinsey (using the alias "Hannah Moore," chosen by Grafton for the powerful pair of double letters) a quick read of the numbers for her birthday. "Five is the number of change and movement. You got three of them. That's hot. You know, travel and like that. Growth. You're the kind of person has to be out there doing things, moving. The zero out here means you don't have any limits. You can do anything. Like whatever you tried, you'd be good at, you know? . . . You'd need to have the kind of job that would never be the same. Know what I mean? You have to be in the middle of the action." It's all enough to make one believe in numerology, although Kinsey herself appears unimpressed. " 'Weird,' I said for lack of anything better" (98).

If Grafton gives Kinsey so much of herself, what does Kinsey give back to Grafton? Kinsey "is a marvel for which I take only partial credit, though she probably claims *all* the credit for me. It amuses me that I invented someone who has gone on to support me" (*K & M* 5). Obviously, Kinsey has given Grafton and her family a gracious lifestyle well beyond Kinsey's own means, something Sue acknowledges with a car tag reading "THNX KNZY." Creating Kinsey has also been a kind of education for Grafton, who said that when she began *"A" Is for Alibi,* "I wasn't even sure what a private investigator did. In the course of writing that first book, I began the long (and continuing) task of educating myself. I read books on forensics, toxicology, burglary and theft, homicide, arson, anatomy, and poisonous plants, among many others. My personal library has grown since I began writing about Kinsey and I now have quite a storehouse of information at my fingertips" (*K & M* 3–4). We can certainly attest to the variety of her library, which includes such intriguing and varied volumes as Conna's *How to Hide Anything,* Arnog's *History of the Crossword Puzzle,* Jung's *Modern Man in Search of a Soul,* Richmond's *How to Disappear Completely and Never Be Found,* McCauley's *The Way Things Work,* plus a slew of reference works on police procedures, the California civil and criminal penal codes, weather, history, medicine, literature, pornography, numerology, geology, and travel. Sue always keeps handy up-to-date road atlases, Spanish dictionaries, and Susan Derecskey's *The Hungarian Cookbook* for Kinsey's dinners at Rosie's. She also does her own version of fieldwork, interviewing real detectives and police officers, visiting three morgues while writing *"C" Is for Corpse,* taking a self-defense class, and taking classes in criminal law. She drives to all the locales for the novels, making notes and taking photos to help her describe the settings accurately. "Kinsey Millhone's growth is a parallel to my own and my job in life is to make sure I keep progressing and growing and changing and exploring myself so that she can grow, because if I shut down she shuts down" (Herbert 37).

In addition to learning a great deal from her association with Kinsey, Grafton also increasingly uses her as a kind of barometer for her own personal behavior. "Kinsey has given me a little backbone. She's a little bullshit meter. I find myself asking if Kinsey would put up with this. If she wouldn't, then I don't see why I should either." The identification between the two women is very strong, and those shared "sensibilities" are moving them closer and closer together, according to Grafton. She has said she feels herself increasingly absorbed into Kinsey so that "by the time of *"Z" Is for Zero,* there will be no Sue Grafton. There will only be Kinsey Millhone" (Nance F1).

Although Kinsey has a job that is more physically dangerous than Grafton, dealing with guns, axe handles, and fists in a way that Sue does not, both women have had their share of profoundly difficult problems. And Grafton has faced hers with a bravery and self-reliance that appear quite Kinseyesque even though weapons were not involved. Perhaps the most striking, because of its connection to Kinsey, is Grafton's childhood.

Grafton's parents were alcoholics. This fact appears to have dominated everything about Sue's growing up in Louisville, Kentucky, where her father, C. W. Grafton, was a municipal bond attorney. Sue's earliest memories are of living at home with her mother, Vivian Harnsberger, and her sister, Ann, who is three years older, while her father served in the army during World War II. Those memories seem to be happy ones because her mother was able to maintain control over the alcohol and to function responsibly and lovingly. But her father's return—when Sue was five years old (the connection to Kinsey is obvious)—shattered that family structure. It is clear that Sue loved her father and still loves and respects his memory, taking great pleasure in the number of municipal projects throughout the state of Kentucky for which he was responsible and in his influence on her becoming a mystery writer, but his return led to serious family disruptions. The minute her father returned, her mother no longer had to maintain control and she sank ever more deeply into a nonfunctioning state of alcohol dependency. She periodically recovered, only to lapse again, until her death from cancer on Sue's twentieth birthday (we might note that Kinsey's parents died very close to her birthday as well). Her father was "the family's functioning alcoholic." He "downed two jiggers of whiskey and went to the office" every day, leaving Sue and Ann home with a mother who, "similarly fortified, went to sleep on the couch" (*K & M* 207).

As Sue puts it, rather dryly, "From the age of five onward, I was left to raise myself, which I did as well as I could, having had no formal training in parenthood" (207). Without adult supervision, she did whatever she wanted—playing with neighborhood children, creating and performing plays, exploring the city of Louisville on foot and bus, attending movies on all three days of the weekend, and reading mystery novels. The latter activity was encouraged by her father, who kept the house filled with them and wrote three well-received mysteries himself. Both of her parents read a great deal (her mother had a degree in chemistry) and books were always available. "We read all the time, and we were allowed to read *anything*" (Herbert 42). She was a keen observer and analyst of her surroundings—both inside the family and without—and was always on the alert to figuring out the rules by which she was supposed to operate. "Children of alcoholics are always very rules-governed," she says. In addition, Sue had a very good memory for details and pictures. She remembered what she observed and even as a youngster wrote stories about much of it. Writing was both an escape from her daily life and a way of imposing some kind of order and meaning on that life: "The writing was my journey into the self" (*K & M* 208). By the age of eighteen, she knew she wanted two things: to be a writer and "to get out of that house." Her marriage at eighteen, primarily a means of escape, was "a detour" on her way to becoming a writer, a detour into a world for which she was ill-prepared because of the few usable skills she brought from her own family (208).

Such an independent childhood may have lacked much in guidance and nurturance for a growing child, but Grafton is convinced that it was excellent preparation for making her into the writer she has become. "Not surprisingly, I grew up confused, rebellious, fearful, independent, imaginative, curious, free-spirited . . . anxious . . . [and] obsessed with writing" (208). "It was the perfect training for a writer. It was the great gift of my life that I was raised not only with intellectuals and with people who valued the language and the written word, but with people who were somehow incapable of parenting me very well, so that I was left to my own devices, and I think in that respect Kinsey and I are very connected at the core" (Herbert 39).

The subject for her writing is equally a consequence of her childhood and her complicated relationship with her parents. From her mother, Sue has said, "I learned all the lessons of the human heart" (*K & M* 207), and most of those lessons were painful. The highly personal, limited edition *Kinsey and Me* contains eight *non*-Kinsey stories Sue wrote in the decade after her mother's death as "my way of coming to terms with my grief for her . . . that rage, that pain, all the scalding tears I wept, both during her life and afterwards. All of it is part of the riddle I think of now as love" (209).

The connection to the Kinsey novels lies not just in her frequent portrayals of the impact of alcoholism on a family, as in the powerful account given by Barbara Daggett of life with her father in *"D" Is for Deadbeat,* but, more importantly, to the overall series theme of "the harm families do" (*D* 48) and to the core of Kinsey's character as a self-created survivor who is extremely cautious about establishing relationships.

During her childhood, Sue and her sister assumed responsibility for the care of their mother, becoming mothers to their mother. Her father was apparently a strong figure who expected certain behavior from the two girls, and he especially expected them to look after their mother because she needed it. "When life seemed unbearable, my father, to comfort me, would sit on the edge of my bed and recount in patient detail the occasion when the family doctor had told him he'd have to choose between her and us and he'd chosen her because she was weak and needed him and we were strong and could survive" (*K & M* 208). He praised the girls for being the strong and capable ones. Sue says that at the time she valued the trust her father was placing in her and her sister. Only later as an adult, when he was making a similar case for leaving Sue's stepmother virtually everything in his will, did she see that action for what it really was. "Only then," she says, "did I realize he had coopted me to agree to my own abandonment." Her father died in 1982 just before *"A" Is for Alibi,* dedicated to him, was published.

We are not surprised that Kinsey's major personal issues all relate to her parents' deaths when she was five and to her consequent sense of abandonment. The biographical facts for Grafton and Kinsey may differ, but the psychological history for the five-year-old girls is identical: "death" of family, "abandonment" by parents, forced assumption of adult responsibilities, and teaching oneself to grow up. No wonder Sue can say of Kinsey: "She is a stripped-down version of my 'self'—my shadow—my projection—a celebration of my own freedom, independence and courage. . . . Through Kinsey, I tell the truth, sometimes bitter, sometimes amusing. Through her, I look at the world with a 'mean' eye, exploring the dark side of human nature—my own in particular" (*K & M* 209).

Grafton found elementary school just as terrifying as Kinsey did, but she insists that *she* never misbehaved there. She was not a truant and she was never sent to the principal's office; she "was Miss Goody Two Shoes." She was "Little Mary Sunshine, tap dancing my way through life just to the left of stage center where the big battles took place" (*K & M* 208). There are, in fact, several ways in which Kinsey is different from her creator, aside from the obvious differences in age, financial status, career, and education (Sue is a 1961 graduate of the University of Louisville, where her major was English). Sue is happily married to Steven Humphrey, a professor of philosophy, whom she met when they lived in the same apartment building in L.A. and with whom she has written a number of screenplays and teleplays. (Their cats introduced them.) She is a much more domestic and social creature than Kinsey. The homes she and Steve share in Santa Barbara and Louisville are spacious and beautiful, with both plants and pets: two cats sleep in baskets on the granite-topped island in the kitchen in California. A neighbor's cat wanders freely into the Kentucky house for extra food and affection. Asked how she could live in such Edenic settings and write about the gritty world in which Kinsey operates, Sue replied, "Kinsey spends a lot of time in the houses of the wealthy, going around gaping at them. So do I."

She and Steve are very sociable people, enjoying the company of family and friends on a frequent basis; this includes three adult children and two grandchildren, one of whom is named Kinsey. She and Steve are both excellent cooks. They also make an effort to eat healthily. Sue is, in fact, appalled by Kinsey's eating habits. "Kinsey's in danger from fast food. Nutritionally she walks a razor's edge" (Goodman 82).

Sue is more admiring of other differences between the two of them. "She'll always be thinner and younger and braver, the lucky so-and-so" (Goodman 81). She seems especially to like Kinsey's gutsiness in physically threatening situations. Although Grafton is not fond of the excessive violence that is almost savored in some detective novels, she says, "Still, I like to bring conflict to a physical contest. Perhaps it's because, in my life, I never associate with violence and avoid ugly or out-of-control people. So these books allow me to vicariously experience something I have so carefully removed from my life" (Goodman 80–81). She also envies Kinsey's freedom to do what she wants. Kinsey may have to work on her cases, but she chooses most of them and can pace herself however she wants, while Grafton feels she is in some way at work on her books all the time. As Sue sees it, "She can play while I have to work."

While Grafton is herself happily married, she wants Kinsey to "celebrate singlehood." She is certain that Kinsey will never marry or have children. Although Kinsey will continue to meet men and develop professional and personal relationships with them, Grafton says she will never have a mate or a partner. "I don't want to write Nick and Nora Charles. I don't want to do the Kinsey and George Detective Agency. Otherwise you're stuck with all the little domestic scenes where they cook up these gourmet treats and have witty repartee. Not cool" (Goodman 76).

The only man so far who might make readers question whether Kinsey would ever in fact marry again is Robert Dietz, who appears in *"G" Is for Gumshoe* and *"M" Is for Malice*. Grafton decided to introduce him after listening to one of her readers, a carpenter in Mendocino, who said, and we quote, "It's high time Kinsey got laid." Grafton says she spent a lot of time planning this male character because she wanted someone "as richly textured and complex as Kinsey herself." She wanted him to be Kinsey's equal in every way. Kinsey herself calls Dietz "my twin" (*G* 178). Since she was created as a play on the male hard-boiled detective, the risk here was that the male equal to her might turn back into the stereotypical private eye. Grafton says she worked hard to make him strong but to avoid the cliches that gave the male private detective fists of steel and "a dick the size of Utah."

Where can we expect Grafton to take Kinsey in *N* through *Z*? How will she change? What will happen to her friends in Santa Teresa? Grafton says, "The particulars of her history usually come to me in the moment of writing" (*K & M* 5), but we already have hints that we may hear the story of her leaving the police force (*M* 2). And Sue has told us that she will reveal the story of that first marriage sometime.

There are a few constraints on future action that Grafton has set for Kinsey's world, constraints established by her character, her past, and her sensibilities. For example, Kinsey's landlord, Henry Pitts, is destined for eternal life in the series. Grafton once considered the possibility of Henry's having a heart attack. To begin her research, she visited the Coronary Care Unit in Santa Barbara Cottage Hospital, where the nurses recognized the author and ferreted out her intentions. They refused point-blank to admit her into the unit if she was going to make Henry have a heart attack. Facing their resolve, Sue realized that she and her readers were too attached to Henry to let anything happen to him. She assures us Henry will make it to Z, at which point he will be a presumably still healthy eighty-nine.

In addition to the unlikelihood of Kinsey marrying or having a child, Grafton also says she can't imagine ever sending Kinsey to Europe. "She's too American, too rooted in her culture" to be transportable to the world of European history and customs. And we know that Kinsey would never put up with all the immunization shots required for more exotic destinations.

Asked if she feels any other regrets or limitations as a result of the character she has created, Grafton said, "I wish I'd never started all that family business in *Judgment.*" It set off a firestorm of reader demand for the full story on the Burton Kinseys in Lompoc, something Grafton is not ready to invent. She says she really has no idea where to go with that family story. "Maybe it will never be any more than just an occasional lunch with Tasha" as in *"M" Is for Malice.* Grafton says, "After all that's what families are—one lunch and then you've got all these friggin' relationships."

Another frustration Grafton has expressed is the result of the time in which the novels are set. The first novel, published in 1982, also takes place in 1982. Subsequent novels are separated by only a few months in Kinsey's life, while the publication dates are now approximately a year and a half apart. Thus, with each novel Kinsey's life gets further and further away from the year of the novel's publication. Grafton would love to be able to play with some of the technology available to us now in the late 1990s—DNA, computers, and genetic engineering, for example—but she can't impose current technology onto the decade of the '80s. Grafton worries that what seemed so current about Kinsey in *"A" Is for Alibi* will seem out-of-date and old-fashioned by the time of *"Z" Is for Zero.*

One thing we can expect from Kinsey in the future is that she will *not* be what readers may expect. Grafton doesn't want Kinsey to "line up neatly" with any genre or camp or even with earlier descriptions. She is complex, inconsistent, and unpredictable. If she were capable of being categorized, she would become boring, a concept that is anathema to her creator. Grafton is equally adamant about "not wanting Kinsey ever to be idealized or larger than life." Her vulnerabilities will continue to be apparent. Grafton likes this display of vulnerability as one of the ways she "makes fun of the self-aggrandizing of the male detectives."

At the same time, Grafton also considers herself now somewhat free of her original intent of playing off the male private investigator stereotype. She is fully prepared to experiment more with the genre. Kinsey began the series with a "jaded eye," Grafton says, but she does not feel compelled to maintain that perspective. If Kinsey changes and grows, becomes "softer and more mellow," then Grafton will be perfectly happy to channel that right onto the page.

Asked if her unwillingness to make Kinsey idealized negated her statement in a CBS interview that she considered Kinsey "Everywoman," Grafton explained that her remark did not mean she thought of Kinsey in generalized terms at all. If a character is made generic, that is, a *type,* then no one believes in or can identify with the character. The most credible fictional characters are so richly detailed as creatures of their time and place that we fully accept them as real. In one of the basic ironies of literature, the more uniquely specific characters are, the more we accept and understand them. Grafton wants to be "so specific—to give so many specific details about Kinsey—that you can always recognize something of yourself in her."

Grafton's Writing Style

"A quick visual survey"

Most readers of Grafton's novels are happy to talk about what they like about tough, funny, vulnerable Kinsey, or what they like about the action or the other characters. They are usually less likely to account for their interest in the novels in terms of Grafton's writing style, yet, writing style—the way in which an author uses, maneuvers, and manipulates words—determines our emotional and intellectual response to a work. Readers may not be consciously aware of the impact of the specific arrangement of the words, but it is quite real, making a reader anxious or thoughtful or satisfied, or whatever the author intends. Style is a kind of subliminal technique for an author to achieve a desired response in a reader, similar to the musical score accompanying a movie.

Tone and Descriptions

The laconic, breezy, wise-cracking style associated with hard-boiled detective fiction from its beginnings is characteristic of Grafton's writing. Kinsey deals with tough situations and tough people and she often does so with a joke, a put-down, or a blunt assessment that brooks no sentimentality. She says "fuck" and "shit" when she damn well feels like it, and, in spite of her self-proclaimed ability to lie persuasively, she is unflinchingly honest about what she sees in others and herself.

Because all the novels in the series are first-person narratives, we see everything through Kinsey's eyes alone. The novels are written as if they are reports (to whom is not always clear) and usually have an Epilogue, once a Prologue. This report format invites Kinsey to be factual, precise, and unemotional. Add to this objective format the fact that Kinsey is by nature a close observer and, as she often tells us, terribly nosy, and the consequence is that we're treated to a wealth of descriptions of people and places.

The initial emphasis in these descriptions is on the external surface Kinsey sees as she looks at a particular scene. We know how things look, smell, and feel.

Grafton is perhaps at her best in making us see eccentric buildings and people. Long after readers have forgotten the details of who killed whom, memory recalls the way the Grices' burned-out blackened skeleton of a house looked: "like the frail bones of an overcooked fish" (*B* 16); the office building with its parapet eight dizzying stories above street level in the final scene of *Deadbeat;* the raunchy, thumping "lowlife bar called the Meat Locker" (*H* 52) where the waitress's buns are "hanging out like water-filled balloons" (53); the pipe- and noise-filled water-treatment plant in *Killer;* the inside workings of the Desert Castle Hotel in *Lawless,* or Agnes Grey's filthy, vandalized trailer in the Slabs (*Gumshoe*).

Even more vivid may be our mental pictures of a whole gallery of distinctive characters: elderly Agnes Grey herself, naked, wrinkled, toothless, dancing wildly on her nursing-home bed and beating her own accompaniment on a bedpan; fat, domineering Ori Fowler on her sick bed (*Fugitive*); short, bespectacled, astonished Harris Brown when he finds Kinsey in his hotel room (*Judgment*); young drug-dealing Mike with his bizarre Mohawk haircut in *Burglar;* the amazing Cherie, who lets her hair down while Kinsey watches—and turns out to be Russell Turpin (*Killer*).

Not all the people we remember are outlandish or ugly, of course. Amid the hard-boiled squalor and dirt are moments of respite and beauty, plus, a whole cadre of engaging friends, such as Henry Pitts, whose appealing looks and nature are warmly described in every novel.

Grafton's style of allowing Kinsey to give many descriptions about the externals of things can lull us into thinking that that's all there is. Kinsey, however, is sometimes proven wrong in her initial assumptions about people. As readers, we can get lazy and let Kinsey do all the work for us. But if we do that, if we ignore what *Grafton* is telling us, we may be led astray. Readers, therefore, had better stay on their figurative toes and draw their own conclusions about characters. For example, let's consider Luis in *"H" Is for Homicide*. Kinsey is virtually kidnapped by Raymond Maldonado, and en route to L.A., she describes his chauffeur and second-in-command, Luis: "a Latino with a dark knit watch cap pulled down to his ears. His eyes were black, as flat and dull as spots of old paint. He had acne scars on his cheeks and a mustache made up of about fourteen hairs, some of which looked like they were drawn on by hand. He was my size. He wore sharply pressed khaki pants with numerous pleats across the front and an immaculate white undershirt. Tufts of underarm hair were visible, straight and dark. His bare arms were muscular, tattoos extending from his shoulders to his wrists—a graphic rendition of Donald Duck on his right and Daffy Duck on his left" (120).

Here's a good example of Kinsey looking at someone and giving us a detailed, factual description. What she sees, and what we accept, is Luis as a hoodlum, almost the stereotyptical portrait of the Latino hood. We may unthinkingly accept Kinsey's account of this tough guy with his dull, flat eyes and a fourteen-hair mustache at face value (pun intended). When Luis fulfills our expectations by immediately drawing a gun on Kinsey, we are ready to believe, with Kinsey, that he is a thoroughly menacing, sullen criminal and up to no good whatsoever.

Kinsey is, therefore, astonished in the novel's final scene when Luis stops her from killing Raymond, flashes an LAPD badge at her, and then arrests Raymond. As soon as he can pry Kinsey's hands from around Raymond's neck, that is.

But if we had been paying careful attention to what *Grafton* has told us by manipulating the action and the language, and not just what Kinsey said at the beginning, we would not be completely surprised by the revelation that Luis is a cop—one of the good guys. The careful reader will notice two key points that undercut the portrait of Luis as a hood. First, there's the humor of his two tattoos of harmless little cartoon characters. Kinsey's first words to Luis are about Donald and Daffy: " 'That's a copyright violation,' I remarked, nearly giddy with anxiety" (120). We seldom fear that which elicits our laughter. And we glimpse a human being behind the stereotype.

Second, and more important, are the scenes in Maldonado's kitchen in which Luis cooks. In one scene, Kinsey watches him prepare enchilada sauce and she is struck by the precision and care with which he operates. "Every act was small, precise" as he peeled an onion, flattened cloves of garlic, charred, seeded, and chopped peppers, added tomatoes and, finally, concentrated on tending the sauce as it simmered. There is admiration in Kinsey's voice: "I always find myself fascinated by expertise. . . . There was a certain style to the work, a fastidious ordering of events" (155).

In this scene, we can reach our own conclusions about Luis. We can observe that Luis is not only a human being, rather than a stereotype, but he is also a human being much like Kinsey herself. His cooking demonstrates many of the best traits of Kinsey at work. A fondness for precision, detail, organization, and accuracy; a concern for one's work; a following of routine; an ability to concentrate—all these are skills that Kinsey values and embodies. We, then, are less surprised than Kinsey when Luis turns out to be on the good-guy team. We've already been challenged to rethink our quick acceptance of the first description of Luis. In this way, *Grafton* has prepared us to accept a plot twist that *Kinsey* does not know about.

In addition to buildings and people, Grafton also gives attention to the beach, the weather, and the natural scene in every novel. Kinsey can claim she doesn't like nature, but she still creates potent word-pictures that evoke it. The most frequent opportunity for this comes with Kinsey's early morning three-mile jog along the beach. She typically tells us how the morning world looks, sounds, and smells.

"To the right of me, the ocean was pounding at the beach, a muted thunder as restful as the sound of rain. Sea gulls were screeching as they wheeled above the surf. The Pacific was the color of liquid steel, the waves a foamy mass of aluminum and chrome. The sand became a mirror where the water receded, reflecting the softness of the morning sky. The horizon turned a salmon pink as the sun crept into view. Long arms of coral light stretched out along the horizon, where clouds were beginning to mass from the promised storm front. The air was cold and richly scented with salt spray and seaweed" (*H* 19–20).

Kinsey always seems sensitive to the color of things. In the description above, there's a wonderful sense of the grayness of the dawn implicit in the linked images of the "liquid steel" ocean and the "aluminum and chrome" waves. Against this monochromatic backdrop are the dramatic flashes of the dawn colors of "salmon pink" and "coral." And she seems equally responsive to smells. Here the smell is of salt and seaweed. We might recall that one of her first attractions to Henry's apartment was the smell of his cinnamon rolls and his flowers—she liked the smell of the place before she liked the sight of it. Kinsey's highly tactile and sensory descriptions are also typically full of motion and sound. Here, the ocean pounds, the gulls screech and wheel, the sun creeps, the dawn stretches, and the clouds mass together. We can see and hear and smell and almost taste dawn's arrival on the beach.

Another colorful dawn is described as "laid out on the eastern skyline like water-colors on a matte board: cobalt blue, violet, and rose bleeding together in horizontal stripes. Clouds were visible out on the ocean, plump and dark, pushing the scent of distant seas toward the tumbling surf" (*D* 28). Not only are the vivid colors of the sky and the shape of the clouds visually impressive, but the scene's movement and sound are again powerful. Consonance unites the pl*u*m*b* clouds with the t*u*m*b*ling surf, the s*cent* with di*stant* seas. Connections are further underscored by the repetition of the "u" sound in pl*u*mp, p*u*shing, and t*u*mbling. And finally, the combined repetition of the sibilant sounds and the vocative "t," "k," and "p" sounds in "*p*lum*p* and dar*k*, pushing the s*cen*t of di*stan*t seas *t*oward the *t*umbling surf" is highly onomatopoeic, i.e., it reproduces the actual sound of the ocean waves splashing against the sand. This is skillful, evocative writing of a caliber that takes Grafton well beyond being categorized as "merely" a writer of detective fiction and into the so-called mainstream of "serious" American fiction.

Even the constructed world of the city has vivid colors, although often with a gritty, hard-boiled tarnish. There are frequent descriptions of Santa Teresa and the places Kinsey goes. The houses on Daggett's street in Los Angeles in *"D" Is for Deadbeat* "had been painted in pastel hues, odd shades of turquoise and mauve, suggestive of discount paints that hadn't quite covered the color underneath" (8). Daggett's building "was painted the color of Pepto-Bismol and sported a sagging banner of Day-Glo orange that said NOW RENTING. . . . Spiky weeds had sprung up along the base of the wall and trash had accumulated like hanging ornaments in the few hearty bushes that managed to survive the gas fumes. . . . There was something meanspirited about its backside, and the entrance turned out to be worse" (8).

Figures of Speech

A key part of Grafton's descriptive style is a heavy use of figurative language. Generally less jarring than her primary progenitor, Raymond Chandler, in her imagery, Grafton often uses metaphors and similes to compare people, objects, and actions to something usually considered dissimilar. This can help the reader see the primary subject; for example, elderly nursing-home patients are "as motionless as plants, resigned to infrequent watering" (*G* 46–47). The comparison of elderly people to stationary plants elicits our understanding of their stillness, their sense of abandonment, and their desperate need for nurturance more powerfully than stating the same idea in a literal way. For example, a literally description might be: "They lay extremely still on their beds, with resigned looks on their faces." The sentence contains the same facts, but there's no emotional punch to it. Again, calling police cars a "stutter of blue lights" (*K* 208), or palm trees "Spanish exclamation points" (*A* 45) succinctly captures the scenes far better than several literally descriptive sentences could. There is a power, an immediacy, an engagement that comes only with figures of speech. The best writers make readers participate in the fictional action or emotion. This happens most powerfully with figurative, rather than literal, speech.

Several types of figurative language appear in Grafton's novels, but the most frequent devices are similes and, somewhat less often, metaphors. A metaphor is an implicit comparison of two unlike things, such as "the long slender arm of the breakwater curved around the marina, cradling sailboats in its embrace" (*I* 148), which compares the breakwater to a person. A simile makes the comparison directly through using "like" or "as." An example might be, "The chill felt like liquid pouring over my skin" (*K* 84–85), which compares the feeling of cold air to liquid.

Short, perfect images are everywhere in Grafton's writing. A tiny street is "the size of an ingrown hair" (*C* 89), or an ash falls from a cigarette, "leaving an empty socket like a pulled tooth" (*C* 51). The pictures evoked are vivid and clear, and we feel that we see precisely what Kinsey sees. Much of the figurative language does this, and only this—it makes the reader see the scene more clearly. But some of the passages go beyond this simple function to reach a highly sophisticated level of writing that places Grafton among the better contemporary writers.

Images from Nature

With all of Kinsey's general disdain for nature and fear of attack by myriad creatures in the wild, it is surprising to find so much use of the natural world in the figurative language used by Kinsey. Like Raymond Chandler, Sue Grafton places her detective in a highly urban setting and then puts scores of natural comparisons in the detective's mouth or uses the mechanical world to describe the bits of nature that do surround her (calling the waves "a foamy mass of aluminum and chrome"). She simultaneously startles readers by the unexpected comparisons and seduces us into thinking we are looking at a whole world where the mechanical and the natural exist side by side. Examples of her use of images from nature include the description of Mrs. Snyder's small head, "like a little pumpkin off the vine too long, looking shrunken from some interior softening" (*B* 61). (After this image, it's not surprising to learn that she is presumed to be a little soft in the head by her husband.) The Ayers' red brick house has "aged to the color of ripe watermelon" (*K* 127), and the tops of Henry's brownies are "light brown, as fragile-looking as dried tobacco leaves" (*J* 163). Greg Fife lives in "an aluminum trailer that looked like a roly-poly bug" (*A* 135). The voices of Lonnie Kingmen and some other lawyers sound like the "droning on the warm air [of]

big fat bumblebees" (*I* 97). In his postcoital stupor, Wim Hoover
regards Kinsey on his doorstep "with all the boredom of a boa con-
strictor after a heavy meal of groundhog" (*B* 99). Rosie is "as aggressive as a Canada goose" (*G* 19). And, although Kinsey never expresses
an opinion about cats, a number of her metaphorical passages refer
to them, usually in a positive way. (Grafton herself is fond of cats and
works with a local group that rescues feral cats.) Typical is her observation that elderly and ill Agnes Grey "reminded me of certain old
cats I've seen whose bones seem hollow and small, who seem capable
of levitating, so close are they to fairylike" (*G* 63). And Colin Fife's
eyes are peaceful and intelligent: "I have seen the same look in cats,
their eyes wide, aloof, grave" (*A* 178).

　　Like other good writers, however, Grafton uses these images for
an organic effect beyond that of creating a vivid picture of the scene.
When Kinsey searches for Bibianna Diaz and is frustrated to find that
the address she's been given is a vacant lot, she describes the ugly,
weedy, bottle-strewn spot: "A condom dangled limply from a fallen
palm frond, looking like a skin shed by some anemic snake" (*H* 26).
The used and limp condom, the fallen frond, and the shed snake
skin—from an anemic snake, no less—add up to a point that Kinsey
might have made in other, more explicit, hard-boiled detective language: "You've been fucked." What has seemed a casual detail included to magnify the grittiness of the scene has a much richer, more
subtle function than at first we thought. The image is making a point
and the point is not being given to the reader in the literal words at
all.

　　Similarly, when Kinsey is fed, nursed, and wrapped in a quilt by
the LaRues after Messinger forced her car into a ditch, she describes
herself, shuffling to the car that will take her to the hospital, as "still
wrapped in the puffy quilt like a bipedal worm" (*G* 77). The comparison of Kinsey, encircled by a quilt, to a segmented worm on legs is
both funny and startling because the two objects, Kinsey and a worm,
seem so unlike each other. Further consideration, however, shows us
two ways in which the comparison is perfect. On a superficial level,
the segments of a quilt and the segments of a worm *are* alike. On the
psychological level, the new vulnerability felt by Kinsey as she is pursued by a hit man is emphasized by her assessment of herself as a
lowly worm, long perceived as one of the most helpless and smallest

creatures in the animal kingdom. She feels like a worm and now she looks like a worm.

At the same time that we feel sympathy for Kinsey's revelation of personal vulnerability, we have to laugh at the image. Why? Primarily because of that little word "puffy." A "puffy" quilt is a light high quilt and a "puffy" worm has to be a Disneyesque caterpillar of the *Alice in Wonderland* variety. We are not seriously worried about any character who can portray her vulnerabilities in so ludicrous and lighthearted a fashion. The word choice by Grafton is exquisite.

Grafton's sophisticated ability to create images that elicit complex responses in the reader is demonstrated time and time again. Beauty and blood are juxtaposed in Kinsey's characterization of Patrick Bronfen's shooting: "Blood and torn flesh bloomed in his chest like a chrysanthemum, shreds of cotton shirting like the calyx of a flower" (*G* 248). A bullet wound and the center of a flower—not a ready duo for comparison for most of us. But Grafton sees it and Kinsey makes us see it. The image is stunning in its portrayal of ugly violence as beautiful. As with the worm simile, the comparison is startling because it seems so wrong, but, of course, unlike the worm simile, this comparison is not at all funny. In fact, this picture is so extremely wrong that it can offend us, making us want to object. Kinsey's clinical detachment and precision of detail at that terrifying moment seem totally inappropriate. The image is repugnant.

Yet, at the same time, we can't help recognizing the accuracy of the picture. A circle of blood spreading outward from a single bullet wound *does* look like the opening of a flower as it blooms. Tattered shreds of a destroyed shirt *do* look like the fringes of a flower's calyx. The comparison is physically right, regardless of whether our higher sensibilities approve of it as morally right. What we are forced to do, then, by Grafton's powerful image, is to see both blood and beauty as a normal part of the world. They both exist at the same time, and, yes, we can see some ways in which they are alike, whether we want to or not. Grafton has given Kinsey an image that has forced us to rethink our view of the world. This is imagery at work at a level far above merely evoking a word picture of a scene.

Domestic Images

Perhaps the most frequently used vehicles for Kinsey's figurative language are domestic objects and activities. Again, this is a surprising choice—and certainly not the vehicle of choice for Chandler and the other male writers of detective fiction—because Kinsey makes such a point of explaining throughout the novels that she does not cook. Her aunt deliberately did not teach her to cook, and she is never shown preparing anything beyond the ubiquitous peanut-butter-and-pickle, sliced egg, or cheese-and-pickle sandwiches.

Grafton's own interest in cooking is revealed by the frequency with which literal descriptions and figurative passages draw on culinary knowledge and experience. Some passages are simply quick vivid comparisons that let us see or sense the scene with perfect clarity. The stucco exterior of the wealthy Woods' house is compared to the "frosting on a wedding cake, roofline and windows edged with plaster garlands, rosettes, and shell motifs that might have been piped out of a pastry tube" (*E* 65). Kinsey covers herself with sunscreen that makes her "smell like a freshly baked coconut macaroon" (*J* 5). The disc jockey, Hector, has a voice as "smooth and satiny as fudge" (*K* 40). Rain on a car roof sounds "like uncooked rice grains falling on a cookie sheet" (*H* 85). The list of examples could go on and on.

For some readers, cooking images in a novel about a woman detective may seem traditional and appropriate, almost cozy. But those readers shouldn't get too comfortable with that notion, not only because Kinsey is such an outspoken noncook herself, but also because so many of the cooking images are just as grotesque as anything we saw in the blood-flower comparison.

For example, we can understand that Kinsey's unwillingness to go to a hair salon is caused by more than her notorious cheapness if we listen to the way she describes one in *"I" Is for Innocent*. The beautician sets a customer's hair, "inserting small white plastic rollers as dainty as chicken bones" and a perm fills "the air with the scent of spoiled eggs" (34). Just as grotesque as the idea of setting one's hair with chicken bones is the ugly picture of sloppy construction in *"B" Is for Burglar*. When Kinsey reaches the area where the Howes live, she observes that the houses "were shabby and the evidence of poor construction floated on the surface like chicken fat on homemade soup" (73). We may question how the noncooking Kinsey would even know about fat rising to the top on homemade soup, but we don't question her observation that the Thrifty Motel was "painted the strange green that yolks turn when they've been hard-boiled too long" (*I* 117), because she does hard-boil eggs for her egg sandwiches.

Unexpected comparisons may underscore the brutal impact of a scene. Early in *"H" Is for Homicide,* Kinsey gets caught in the middle of a shoot-out in the street, during which a man is killed and a woman wounded. She describes the peak of the action: "The ensuing shots sounded like kernels of popcorn in a lidded saucepan" (77). Something so innocent as the sound of corn popping surely wouldn't cause death and mayhem, would it? But it does, and it is the more frightening precisely because the sound carries so little malice.

Some of the most repulsive images refer to uncooked meats. Ori Fowler, for whom Kinsey can muster little sympathy in spite of her ill health, is said to have legs "like haunches of meat not yet trimmed of fat" (*F* 24). In *"A" Is for Alibi,* when Sharon Napier's body bleeds a great deal, Kinsey observes, "Blood had soaked into the carpet under her head and it had darkened now to the color of uncooked chicken liver" (127). Equally unpleasant is Kinsey's description of Franklin's corpse as she moves him onto the morgue's gurney: "He was surprisingly light, and cold to the touch, about the consistency of a package of raw chicken breasts just out of the fridge" (*C* 232). None of these images is as startling, perhaps, as the blood-flower association for Patrick Bronfen—blood, meat, and bodies do have a natural affinity—but they are more repellant in their linking of dead bodies with things we humans routinely eat. Kinsey seems to be trying to be as tough as she can in these intense moments in order to give herself some distance from the victims. Elsewhere she tells us that she has to deaden her feelings in order to be able to look closely at a homicide victim, and these cooking images would certainly distance her from feeling any human compassion for the bodies. They are just dead meat.

At the same time, such images would certainly dampen anyone's enthusiasm for doing any cooking with raw chickens any time soon. After watching Dr. Fraker casually dumping out "a glistening blob of organs" and poking through "this small pile of human flesh" with his tweezers (*C* 218), Kinsey is forced to admit, "I didn't think I'd ever look at stew meat in quite the same way" (219). And later she asks, "Why do I plague myself with these domestic images? I'd never be motivated to learn to cook at this rate" (232). We sympathize completely.

The novels have happier images drawn from other domestic activities. Sheets and fabrics appear to come frequently, easily—and rather pleasantly—to mind. For example, Barbara Daggett has "skin as finely textured as a percale bedsheet" (*D* 32), while elderly Mrs. Wood has skin hanging down "like tissue-thin kid leather, lined and seamed" (*E* 68). A lake in the moonlight is "as glossy as a remnant of gray silk" (*C* 173). The blades of a ceiling fan are "sueded with dust" (*J* 234). The hills near San Luis Obispo "look like soft humps of foam rubber, upholstered in variegated green velvet" (*F* 44). The beach, during a morning jog, "looked as fine and as supple as gray leather, wrinkled by the night winds, smoothed by the surf" (*J* 131).

Since Kinsey prides herself on keeping her apartment neat and tidy, we are not surprised by the number of instances in which she uses images related to cleaning. Too much coffee makes Kinsey's "brain vibrate like an out-of-balance washing machine" (*K* 35). Age has given Dr. Fraker's face "a softly crumpled look, like a freshly laundered cotton sheet that needs to be starched and ironed" (*C* 76). And clouds overhead look "like dark gray vacuum cleaner fluff" (*D* 36).

Problems with Writing a Series

For an author writing a series of novels involving one central character and a number of reappearing ancillary figures, there are special problems with descriptive passages. How many different ways can such an author give necessary information for new readers, who may pick up a book out of sequence, while simultaneously creating a consistent atmosphere for earlier readers—and do all this without boring the socks off those previous readers?

A basic challenge is the description of Kinsey herself. Grafton circumvents much of the difficulty by having Kinsey begin the early novels up until *"E" Is for Evidence*, with some version of the statement that she is writing a report of a case and that "I start by asserting who

I am and what I do, as though by stating the same few basic facts I can make sense out of everything that comes afterward" (*B* 1). This will be followed by a terse summary that sounds like an entry in a police log: "I'm female, age thirty-two, single, self-employed. . . ." (*B* 1). From *Fugitive* on, this brief self-description may appear anywhere in the opening chapters. The more interesting personal details about family, personal quirks, likes and dislikes, will gradually unfold in tiny bits as Kinsey works on her case. One method is for Kinsey to give information to someone else when that seems expedient. For example, the first time we hear about the deaths of her parents in a car accident occurs in *"A" Is for Alibi*, as Kinsey responds to a question about her father from an interview subject, Greg Fife, whose own father was murdered. Kinsey's account is offered in order to encourage Greg's willingness to talk about his family situation. The information is interesting to the readers who want to know more about Kinsey and her background, but in terms of the literary success of the novel, we should note that the account is offered in a psychologically credible way. There is a valid reason for Kinsey to tell this to Greg.

We learn more about Kinsey's background in each novel as something about the current case will trigger a memory or will prompt action from Kinsey. We learn about her long-estranged family in *"J" Is for Judgment* when a minor interview subject, Lena Irwin, thinks Kinsey looks a lot like the Kinseys up in Lompoc, causing Kinsey to look up her parents' marriage certificate; Simone's tiny, perfect house in *Innocent* reminds her of the cardboard box she lived in for months after her parents were killed. *Evidence* actually gives us the brief reappearance of her second husband, Daniel Wade. Worth noting is the extent to which all the details are spread richly throughout all the novels, rather than being concentrated in only the early books or only the beginnings of the books.

Devising ways to give Kinsey's physical appearance offers more problems to Grafton, who solves this difficulty by a variety of means. Her age is frequently given in the police-log-style description of herself opening the novels. Sometimes this includes height and weight, but more often these, along with hair color, are given in comparison to a suspect or witness (Mace "was probably six feet four to my five feet six," *K* 47). Interestingly, the comparisons with men tend to be about height and weight, as if Kinsey is sizing them up as potential opponents, while the comparisons with women tend to refer to coloring, hair, or faces, as if Kinsey is comparing her looks to those of the women she sees.

Sometimes the physical information is triggered by the action; for example, in the opening of *"C" Is for Corpse,* Kinsey is working out at a gym in order to regain strength in the arm that was injured at the conclusion of *"B" Is for Burglar,* and she says that since she only weighs 118 pounds, there isn't a lot of upper body to rehabilitate (3). Revelations about Kinsey's appearance are often funny. We learn just what an unruly mess her trimmed-every-six-weeks-with-nail-scissors hair must look like when a hair stylist says her hair looks like it's "been whacked off with a ceiling fan" (*I* 35).

An easy way for an author to describe her main character is to have the character get dressed, as Kinsey does often and with commentary in every novel, or look in a mirror, as Kinsey does in *"J" Is for Judgment* when she learns that Mac Voorhies, whom she hasn't seen for several months, is about to walk into her office (4). Kinsey also sees something of herself in another kind of mirror, her newly discovered cousin Tasha, whose "very white and square" teeth remind her of her own (*J* 169). Or Kinsey may talk with another character who comments on the way she looks. Lyda Case tells her, "That hair of yours looks like a dog's back end" (*E* 96). Mrs. Ochsner asks her what color her eyes are, prompting Kinsey to answer, "Hazel" (*B* 31).

As clever as Grafton is in developing new and credible ways for us to see what Kinsey looks like, the strain of doing the same thing for Henry and Rosie—inside whose head we never see—shows in some of the novels. In how many ways, for example, can Grafton say that Henry has intensely blue eyes? In *Alibi* and *Burglar,* his eyes are "periwinkle blue" (191 and 81), as they implicitly must be in *Evidence,* because the "periwinkle-blue mohair muffler" Kinsey knits him for Christmas matches his eyes (6); in *Corpse,* they are a more fanciful "violet-blue, the color of ground morning glories" (13) and "the color of gas jets" in *Fugitive* (10); *Deadbeat* and *Homicide* have no reference to the color of his eyes, while they're just plain "blue" in *Gumshoe* (3) and *Judgment* (162–63) and "bright blue" in *Killer* (20); in *Innocent,* they are "blue eyes that seemed to burn in his tanned face" (78); and, similarly, in *Lawless,* "His blue eyes seem ablaze in his lean, tanned face" (4). The first cluster of images compares the color of

Henry's eyes to various blue flowers, while the second cluster associates the intensity of his eyes with blue flames. In between these two clusters is the nonemotive label of "blue," as if all of us had one crayon labeled blue and therefore knew precisely the hue, intensity, and effect Grafton had in mind when she says Henry's eyes are "blue." Most readers will be far more engaged by the figurative descriptions, although some may point out that blazing eyes in a tanned face may sound more like a hero in a romance novel than a sidekick in a detective novel. Those readers may respond more positively to the freshness and appropriateness of Henry's eyes being compared to "gas jets"—the heat and the intensity are there, but in a fresh and noncliché image.

Description of Action

Grafton can be at her best in creating action in which Kinsey is at great physical risk. The novels' final scenes are especially powerful with their portrayal of Kinsey confronting the murderer in settings that play on basic human fears and especially on Kinsey's particular phobias. In the final scene of *"A" Is for Alibi,* for example, Kinsey runs along the beach at night, trying to escape Charlie Scorsoni. The scene is vividly real: the dark night, the running pursuit by a former lover who's now revealed as a murderer, the alternation of pain, fright, and determination to live, the emptiness of the beach, the inability to outrun her pursuer or to find a safe place to hide—all of the details play on basic human fears. The short choppy sentences perfectly capture Kinsey's thought processes as she tries to catch her breath and find a way to escape ("I watched the beach, seeing little, searching for Charlie. Car lights still on. Nothing. No one." 272). The rhythm of the scene builds nicely as Kinsey is startled by Charlie's arrival, then goes through several small vignettes of near escape before finally hiding in the foul-smelling garbage bin, an especially macabre refuge if we recall Kinsey's earlier memory of her revulsion over her first homicide case—the bodies of three children had been stuffed into a garbage can by their demented mother. Even inside the bin, Kinsey's reactions vacillate as she hears Charlie call to her and thinks he sounds just like he always did. What if she is just crazy and Charlie really means her no harm? Then he lifts the lid of the can,

and the "beams from his headlights shone against his golden cheek.
He glanced over at me. In his right hand was a butcher knife with a
ten-inch blade." This boyish, innocent-looking, golden-cheeked man
is a killer. The novel's famous last line is, "I blew him away" (274).

Contradictory World

Arguably the most dominant characteristic of Grafton's writing style is
her use of contradictions. As suggested above, grotesque comparisons
of unlike objects are frequent in moments of intense fear. Ambiguity
and paradox go beyond this, however. Even the most literal descriptions and the most mundane occasions can be the opportunity for
Grafton to show us how two contrary perspectives, or two contradictory facts, can both be true at the same time. Looking down at Kinsey
in the garbage bin, Charlie is "golden-cheeked," but he's also a killer
who systematically wooed her in order to follow her investigation of
the case. While waiting to learn whether Danielle, a prostitute with
whom she's become friends, will live after being brutally beaten, Kinsey browses through women's magazines with their unreal, prettified
picture of a woman's world in a perfect house with perfect kids and
perfect kitchen appliances (*Killer*). Deputy Tiller spouts outrage
against the depth of corruption now exhibited by teenage hoodlums
and considers young Brian Jaffe a good example of those soulless
psychopaths, but *he* is the one who permits Brian to make a jail-break
(*Judgment*).

   An extended set of contradictions that may serve to illustrate the
technique throughout all the novels occurs in Kinsey's trip to the
shooting range in *"B" Is for Burglar*. Depressed by her two-martini
lunch with wealthy Aubrey Danziger, Kinsey says, "I needed air and
sunshine and activity" (148). The next line is not what we might
expect—there are no picnics or swims at a nearby pool in a hard-
boiled detective novel. Instead, Kinsey gets on the phone to Jonah:
"You want to go up to the firing range and shoot?" On the way up to
the mountains on their excursion for target practice and fresh air,
Kinsey describes the vegetation she sees. The picture is pretty: there
are fluffy white clouds, sage and mountain lilac, and the underbrush
"scented the still air with camphor." But note the description that
immediately follows the idyllic sight of "bright little faces of monkey

flowers" and hot pink phlox: "The poison oak was thriving, its lush growth almost overwhelming the silvery leaves of the mugwort which grew alongside it" (148). Next to beauty is the potential for pain. And not only that, the poisonous plant is "thriving" and "lush"—it too looks beautiful. Just as we know that Charlie's golden cheek hides a killer, so too this appearance of innocent exterior and poisonous interior should not be a surprise. It's part of the contradictory and complex world we've come to expect from Grafton.

We see a Zen-like acceptance of the duality of the world demonstrated perfectly when Kinsey and Jonah spend the next few hours practicing their shooting skills. Ironically, they are both rejuvenated as individuals and they interact as a couple by working with instruments of destruction, and, in a further irony, this firing range, with its collection of noisy man-made gadgets for death, is set in a quiet location of great natural beauty. Destruction and creation are intertwined.

In a further play on this idea, the lush setting contains its own contradictions. The area around the shooting range bears the scars of a fire that swept through a few years ago, destroying everything in its path. But many of the shrubs and flowers now blooming owe their existence to that fire because their seed pods will burst only in the intense heat of a brush fire. Death in life, life in death—the circle is endless. Even those instruments of destruction, Kinsey's guns, can also be used to help—to keep Charlie from killing her, to keep Mark Messinger from killing her, to keep David Barney from killing her, to save Jimmy Tate, and so on.

Kinsey doesn't comment on the applicability of this natural cycle to her view of human life, but we see it. After all, we remember the end of Kinsey's sentence about the poison oak—the mugwort that grew beside the poison oak *"is its antidote"* (emphasis added). The solution to a problem does not come from a different world—it comes from the same world in which the problem originates, a valuable lesson Kinsey learned as a child in that cardboard box and continues to relearn again and again as she solves her cases and leads her adult life.

Themes

Grafton returns time and again to certain social issues, in particular, troubled families, class divisions, and corrupt social structures. Not surprisingly, then, some themes recur time and again throughout the series. These are made especially powerful by appearing in both the main plotline of Kinsey's current case and a supporting subplot, usually from her personal life, occasionally from a secondary case.

Abandonment and Betrayal

As Kinsey says in *"M" Is for Malice,* about an old love affair, "I was always too caught up in my own abandonment issues" (201). No kidding. Her childhood was dominated by the loss of her parents in an automobile accident when she was five years old. Granted, the act was not deliberate on their part, but the effect was that her parents left her to deal with the world on her own. Her aunt died when she was twenty-two, and her second husband left her without explanation, further exacerbating her sense of always being abandoned by the people she loves. This heightened sensitivity to what it means to be abandoned, left, betrayed, colors the way Kinsey reacts to the many acts of betrayal and abandonment she sees in her investigative work. Throughout the series, we see a variety of ways in which family members, and to a lesser extent friends, can abandon the people to whom they are supposedly tied. Betrayal of familial bonds lies at the heart of every single novel, beginning with Gwen's murder of her unfaithful husband in *"A" Is for Alibi* and concluding (for now) with Jack Malek's framing his own brother for forgery and allowing him to be disinherited for it in *"M" Is for Malice.*

The Search for Resolution/Answers

This may seem an obvious theme for detective novels. Naturally, the detective searches for answers. Who killed Laurence Fife? Isabelle Barney? Name the murder victim(s) in any novel and the major plot question is "Who killed so and so?" The genre is even referred to as "Whodunit." But Grafton takes the probing well beyond the immediate questions about who committed a murder and how and why it was committed. Curious about everything, Kinsey always wants to know what could drive a person to choose to commit murder and she wants to understand the pyschology behind the action for virtually everyone she meets. For example, in *"I" Is for Innocent*, when she learns about Tippy's involvement in a hit-and-run several years earlier, it is not enough that she knows about the action; she genuinely wants to understand what could motivate Tippy to drive away from the scene, she wants to understand her reactions now, and she wants her to take responsibility now for her earlier action.

Kinsey's investigations trigger her thinking about her own motives and character, as well as how her own behavior fits within a larger system of justice or order. She keeps wanting to see a point to it all. Her attempts to understand human behavior clearly include her own behavior, and she responds strongly to what she sees of herself in the people and problems in her cases. What she concludes about human nature is not always cheery. In *"I" is for Innocent*, thinking of David Barney as a suspect for his wife's murder, she says, "Murder is an aberrant deed, often born of passions distorted by obsessiveness and torment. Emotion doesn't travel in a straight line. Like water, our feelings trickle down through cracks and crevices, seeking out the little pockets of neediness and neglect, the hairline fractures in our character usually hidden from public view. Beware the dark pool at the bottom of our hearts. In its icy, black depths dwell strange and twisted creatures it is best not to disturb. With this investigation, I was once again uncomfortably aware that in probing into murky waters I was exposing myself to the predators lurking therein" (177).

The Value of Individual Bravery

In spite of Kinsey's recognition that her investigations take her into murky waters—literally and figuratively—she continues to do so. She is personally brave and she always responds positively to the exercise of courage by others. If the systems we depend on—the church, law, business, or the family—cannot be trusted, then the only resource we have left is personal bravery in our individual niche of the world. In general, the good guys in the novels demonstrate notable courage of some kind, whether it is Bobby Callahan's personal courage in fighting the physical and emotional effects of his car "accident" in *Corpse*, or Danielle Rivers' courage in the face of abuse from customers in *Killer,* or Guy Malek's courage in changing himself after his youthful mistakes in *Malice,* or Rochelle Messinger's walking toward her ex-husband across the airport tarmac in spite of the gun in his hand in *Gumshoe.* Even little things, such as Dietz's instantaneous decision to give up smoking, can demonstrate a character's determination to retain personal autonomy in a dark and chaotic world, another way to think of courage.

Plot Structure

Grafton creates a self-contained world in each of her novels. Granted, the same central figure and assorted friends and colleagues appear throughout the books, and most are set primarily in the single locale of Santa Teresa, but each novel is nonetheless given its own distinctive ambience. For example, *"K" Is for Killer,* the novel in which Kinsey becomes a killer, takes place primarily at night, unlike all the other novels and against Kinsey's natural instincts as a day person. In this book, which Grafton says she intended as Kinsey's "descent into the Stygian underworld," Kinsey drinks pots of coffee, can't sleep, stays up until the wee hours, gets involved with the people of the night, from emergency-room nurses and all-night disc jockeys to prostitutes and pimps, and questions a number of basic assumptions she has about the way the world operates.

Because Grafton was also reading Joseph Campbell at the time, the novel reflects its author's growing interest in Jungian psychology and Greek myths. Jung's association of water with the workings of the id lies behind all the attention to water—the water-treatment plant that is the backdrop for the confrontation between Kinsey and the killer, or even Danielle's last name "Rivers" and the minor character Delbert "Squalls"—in the one novel in which Kinsey succumbs to the primitive human drive for revenge and becomes a killer herself. The identification of the water-treatment plant with the river Styx in Hades is underscored by the use of such names as Hector, Mace, and Leda, all from mythology, for characters in the novel. While Kinsey is grappling with the moral implications of having arranged for a Mafia hit—she has descended into her own moral hell—she concludes the Epilogue by asking, "Having strayed into the shadows, can I find my way back?" (285). Her metaphorical question is emphasized by our memory of all the literal and symbolic shadows darkening the novel.

One of the key ways in which Grafton creates this self-contained world for each novel is her skillful use of subplots. The novels typically contain two story lines, one from the current primary case and a second one from a minor case being investigated at the same time or from Kinsey's personal life or the personal life of one of her friends. The ways in which the main plot and the subplot tie together either factually or thematically becomes clear by the novel's conclusion.

This richness of texture may be as small as the occasional reference in *"A" Is for Alibi* to the insurance fraud being attempted by Marcia Threadgill, who's falsely claiming she was injured. CF chooses to let her get away with it because the amount of the claim is too small to be worth a legal fight. This minor case, pursued by Kinsey at the same time she is pursuing her major investigation of Laurence Fife's murder, underscores the main plot's themes that appearances can be extremely deceiving and that systems intended to assist us, such as insurance companies or the legal structure, often fail us.

As the series develops, so does the use of the subplot. By the writing of *"C" Is for Corpse,* Grafton goes well beyond a minor case offering a small echo to the main plot. In this third novel, the story of Lila Sams, a con artist who betrays Henry Pitts, is a fully developed underscoring of the main plotline about Kinsey seeking the murderer of Bobby Callahan. In the main plot, Nola Fraker killed her first husband when he caught her in bed with her lover, Jim Fraker, who became her second husband and blackmailed her into absolute submission to his will. She was conned by him, just as Henry was conned by Lila. The difference was in the goals of the two sexual cons. Lila wants only money, while Dr. Fraker is a psychotic who wants total control of Nola and is willing to kill to keep her with him. This play on the varieties of love-sex-control-power-betrayal-and-death is implied by the many aliases Lila uses: they are all some version of the name "Delilah Samson." The Biblical account of Delilah's sexual seduction and subsequent betrayal of Samson forms a perfect paradigm for all the sexual betrayals of this novel.

Perhaps the fullest example of the mutuality of the main plot and the subplot—and the way in which the two plots elucidate a single theme—occurs in *"J" Is for Judgment.* Kinsey's attempts to locate Wendell Jaffe, who abandoned his family, are paralleled by her discovery of a family that has, in a sense, abandoned her. The main plot is, of course, Kinsey's search for Wendell, but along the way, one of her interviewees triggers Kinsey's search for her own family in Lompoc, and the pattern of her personal investigation being interwoven with the Jaffe investigation continues throughout the novel. Kinsey begins her report with this observation: "It was my investigation into the dead man's past that triggered the inquiry into my own, and in the end the two stories became difficult to separate" (1).

The novel's opening initiates the motif of familial abandonment. Kinsey is doing a routine skip-trace on a "client's ex-husband, who was six thousand dollars in arrears on his child support" (3). The search for this deadbeat dad is not pursued any further in the novel. It serves its fictional purpose by framing the action with a little reminder that irresponsible parents are a fact of life these days. Other reminders of the frequency of betrayal, or abandonment of expected codes of behavior, include the name Wendell Jaffe chose for his boat: the *Captain Stanley Lord*. Wendell's partner, Carl, explains the name to Kinsey: "Stanley Lord was captain of the *Californian*, allegedly the only boat close enough to the *Titanic* to have helped with the rescue. Lord claimed he never picked up the distress signal, but a later investigation suggested he ignored the SOS" (80). Interestingly, Carl's account not only gives us an infamous example of abandoning one's responsibilities, but the explanation for the action comes in two different versions, neither of which can now be proven to be correct. Lord may have been incompetent, or he may have been deliberately wicked. In either case, though, the effect was to abandon the passengers on the *Titanic* to their deaths in the dark icy waters of the North Atlantic. And we will never know exactly why Captain Lord failed to respond to the other ship's distress signals.

Carl's account of Captain Lord is historically accurate. In another technique, Grafton creates an entire history for the two fictitious towns, Perdido (loosely based on Ventura) and Olvidado (loosely based on Oxnard). The ponderous weight of the past is underscored by Kinsey's lengthy—and completely fictional—description of eighteenth-century political machinations in the California missions when Father Olivarez's dream of twin churches was squelched, either because of his own increasing secularism or because of the jealousy of a rival priest, Father Perdido. As with Captain Lord, we don't know the motive behind the (fictional) action. There are conflicting accounts. "Whatever the truth, cynical observers renamed the dual sites Perdido/Olvidado, a mongrelization of Prospero Olivarez's name. Translated from Spanish, the names mean Lost and Forgotten" (123).

The truth about the past in this novel may often be *lost* in the welter of ambiguous, confusing stories from Wendell, or Brian, or cousin Tasha, and especially Renata, but the past will certainly not be *forgotten*. In any detective story, the past is crucial—after all, the detective is searching for the killer in a murder that occurred in the past, whether recent or distant—but in *Judgment* the need to understand human behavior in the past and how it shapes the present becomes an obsession for Kinsey.

As the novel progresses, Kinsey sees much of herself in Wendell, as well as in those he abandoned. The parallels between Kinsey and the Jaffe family are obvious: Wendell abandoned his wife and two sons five years ago through staging a fake suicide, while Kinsey's Lompoc family failed to come forward when Kinsey's parents were killed when she was five years old. The parallels between Kinsey and Wendell himself are less obvious, but Kinsey feels the connection. Not only is she intrigued by the idea of reinventing oneself as Wendell did, but also she sees that "In some curious way we were in the same position, Wendell Jaffe and me: trying to understand what our lives might have been if we could have enjoyed the benefits of family life, looking at the mislaid years and wondering how much we'd missed" (255). For both Kinsey the detective and Kinsey the person, understanding the past is the key to understanding the present. "The past has a way of catching up with all of us" (12).

The past is a burden carried by each of the novel's characters. Immediately after Brian Jaffe tells Kinsey about his broken family and his years without a father, she heads for the Hall of Records to try to trace her own broken family and her years without either parent. The weight of the past for both Brian and Kinsey is portrayed literally in Grafton's description of the Hall of Records, the place where the past is neatly written down and filed away, waiting for someone to need it. The Hall is a large, dark wing of the Santa Teresa Courthouse with "heavy" oak tables, "leather" chairs, "thick" ceiling beams, and a "dark red" stone floor. Colors are either "faded" or "muted." Even the windows carry the sense of weight: "leaded-glass panes" are "pierced with rows of linked circles" (140).

Significantly, Kinsey also points out that the Courthouse was re-built in the late 1920s after an earthquake in 1925. The motif of reconstruction applies not only to this particular building, but also to all the characters in the novel who have to rebuild their lives after emotional earthquakes of various kinds—the Jaffe sons and Dana Jaffe, Carl Eckert, Harris Brown, Rosie and William, Kinsey herself, and, of course, Wendell Jaffe, who tried first to reinvent himself after a pseudosuicide and tries now to recreate the family he lost. Perhaps one can reinvent oneself for the future, but a revision of the past is ultimately impossible. As Kinsey tells Jaffe, "You can't just step back into the life you left and make all the stories come out differently" (205). For herself, Kinsey staunchly resists the reconstruction of her past that is imposed by discovery of the Kinseys in Lompoc. Knowl-edge of their existence forces her to rewrite her own history, and, unlike Jaffe, this is not something she wants to do. From this novel through *"M" Is for Malice,* her cousins keep wanting to get together and behave like a family, whatever that means, but Kinsey continues to refuse. In *"L" Is for Lawless,* Kinsey echoes her earlier words to Jaffe when she tells her cousin Tasha, "What's done is done. It came down the way it came down, and I can live with that. It's folly to think we can go back and make it come out any different" (28).

The difficulty of understanding the past—and the high cost of making the attempt—are obvious in the conclusion to the main plot: Wendell disappears on his boat again, presumed by some to have killed himself for real this time and presumed by others to have faked suicide once again. Yet, there is a third way to view the action, and it is probably the correct way. Kinsey is proven right in her conclusion that Jaffe was murdered when his bullet-riddled body washes up a few days later. And she thinks she knows who killed him—his lover, Renata. When Kinsey confronts Renata, she promptly confesses to the murder and gives a plausible account of being furious that she had given up so much for Jaffe, who then wanted to go back to his wife and sons. Kinsey accepts this version of the immediate past and deeply regrets her inability to prevent Renata from swimming out to her death. But later she begins to question this entire scene. Surely by now she knows, as well as the reader does, that there will always be conflicting explanations about the events of the past. Perhaps Renata staged the entire confession scene and faked a suicide. After all, her body never turned up. And what caused the death of her first, wealthy husband? "I'd been viewing this as Wendell Jaffe's story," says Kinsey, "but suppose it was hers?" (288).

Grafton's skills in description and her thematic sophistication take her well beyond the level of many authors of detective fiction. Not all examples of formula fiction continue to reward the reader in a second reading. Knowing who the murderer is and whether the detective escapes alive is enough, and you get those plot details the first time through the novel. A second reading can be pretty pointless for such works. But good literature—and that includes Grafton—rewards the reader again and again. Grafton's complex and thoughtful awareness of how people behave as individuals and as social beings is rich enough to provoke us into rethinking our own views of the world and to offer new insights on every reading.

Grafton's Place in the Development of the Detective Novel

"The story's not over yet."

When some of us heard P. D. James at the Pump Room a few years ago, she said she must have had the mind of a crime writer even as a child, because when she first heard the nursery rhyme about Humpty Dumpty, her thought was 'Did he fall, or was he pushed?' " (Lovesey 23).

This delightful story about P. D. James is told by one of the characters in Peter Lovesey's recent Peter Diamond novel *Bloodhounds*. We don't know if it is true, but we hope so, because it is a perfect description of the most basic appeal of a detective novel, or mystery novel, or crime fiction, or whatever we want to call the broad category of novels about catching murderers. Since the time of the Bible, Anglo-Saxon riddles, and Aesop's fables, we human beings have been fascinated by puzzles and riddles and by our own propensity for violence.

Sue Grafton would probably have shared P. D. James' early curiosity about Humpty Dumpty since she "was raised on a steady diet of mystery and detective fiction" ("An Eye for an I").* In their house filled with enthusiastic readers, Sue was allowed to read anything she found on the packed bookshelves, and she turned most often to detective fiction. "In my early teens, on the occasions when my par-

---

* In press; see Bibliography

ents went out for the evening, I'd be left alone in the house with its tall, narrow windows and gloomy high ceilings. . . . Usually, I sat downstairs in the living room in my mother's small upholstered rocking chair, reading countless mystery novels with a bone-handled butcher knife within easy reach. I worked my way from Nancy Drew through Agatha Christie and on to Mickey Spillane," a wildly diverse set of twentieth-century detective writers. "From Mickey Spillane, I turned to James M. Cain, then to Raymond Chandler, Dashiell Hammett, Ross Macdonald, Richard Prather, and John D. MacDonald, a baptism by immersion in the dark poetry of murder" ("An Eye").

The detective novel is an invention of the nineteenth century, springing up nearly simultaneously in England and America. Couple the basic human sense of curiosity, fondness for puzzles, and interest in violence with the growing need for public police forces to maintain order and prevent violence during the dislocations of the nineteenth century and the result was an ideal cradle for the beginnings of the detective novel. Prior to that, tales of outlaws appeared in literature, of course, but they were usually romanticized stories of attractive rogues, such as Thomas Nashe's *The Unfortunate Traveller* in 1594, or allegedly true accounts of villains who met bad ends and whose punishments served as warnings to readers. The appeal of the first group was escapism and the second was, nominally, education. Daniel Defoe's *General History of Pyrates,* in 1724 and 1728, and Henry Fielding's *Jonathan Wild,* in 1743, were intended to warn readers about how *not* to live their lives, but the fact that such major eighteenth-century novelists were attracted to writing these criminal biographies tells us that the popular appeal of the genre actually lay more in its entertainment than its educational value.

The emphasis in these stories of outlaws prior to the nineteenth century was the villain. Whether romanticized or demonized, it was always the robber or murderer who was the centerpiece of the story, not the person who caught the villain.

So how did the shift to a focus on the figure of the detective come about?

Interestingly, the word "detective" did not appear in the English language until 1842, according to the *Oxford English Dictionary,* when its first recorded use was in the name of a new department of the

Metropolitan Police Force in London: the Detective Division. (We should remember that the concept of a *publicly* funded police force was itself less than two decades old in England at that time and was just beginning in America. The enormous growth in population and attendant problems with crime in both countries had necessitated the establishment of the first public police forces.) The word "detected" had been in existence as far back as the fourteenth century, when it meant "disclosed," "open," or "exposed" (*Oxford English Dictionary*). Put simply, during the Medieval and Renaissance periods, crime tended to be solved by confession, usually obtained by torture, or by the testimony of a witness or an informant, also frequently obtained by torture. For centuries, self-revelation of guilt by the criminal was the basic method of solving a crime.

Transformation of the adjective "detected" into the noun "detective" indicates the nineteenth century's recognition that there was a new method of solving crime. This new method centered around the abilities of someone to think through the details of the crime and rationally conclude the identity of the criminal. Exposure of the criminal was done by the detective, not by the criminal. This new method, which seems blindingly obvious to contemporary readers, was a radical consequence of a great modern shift in popular thinking about the way in which the world originated, operated, and could be understood.

The shift had begun in the eighteenth century with the Enlightenment and its reliance on rational thought instead of divine revelation as a way to understand the universe. People came to believe that an individual was not merely a passive receptacle of divine knowledge but was instead capable of *generating* knowledge (hence the development of the concepts of plagiarism and copyright during the eighteenth century). This increased awareness that a single human being could observe the natural world, postulate a theory to explain a phenomenon, and prove that theory through experimentation and analysis reached a logical apotheosis in the publication of Charles Darwin's *On the Origin of Species* in 1859.

Darwin's techniques aboard the *Beagle* would remind any devotee of the detective novel of Sherlock Holmes, or Auguste Dupin, or Hercule Poirot at work. The scientist/detective observes the scene in minute detail, notices the unexpected, speculates about the possible causes of the anomaly, and then tests out each theory until only one is left. The process is highly rational, orderly, and thorough. Success occurs because one brilliant and tenacious individual finds the solution to a puzzle.

The theological implications of Darwin's work were profoundly disturbing to many people. At the same time, the notion that the world was a knowable entity and that the human mind was capable of knowing it was both appealing and reassuring, to judge by the rapidity with which the scientist/detective seized the popular imagination, especially in the figure of Arthur Conan Doyle's Sherlock Holmes. Readers were the Dr. Watsons of the world—awed by Holmes' amazing skills of ratiocination, astonished by his revelation of the murderer's identity, and satisfied by the murderer's arrest. The world had an order after all; its temporary disruption had been righted by Holmes. Once everything was explained, readers could see the essential pattern and order underlying the superficial confusion created by the murderer.

The Holmesian model of the brilliant, eccentric, rational amateur detective dominated the mystery genre throughout the nineteenth and early twentieth centuries in both England and America. Peaking in England in the twenties and thirties with the novels of Dorothy Sayers, Agatha Christie, and Margery Allingham, and continuing through the forties with the novels of Ngaio Marsh, the period is often called the Golden Age of detective fiction, a term coined by Howard Haycraft in *Murder for Pleasure*. The age deserves its title in more ways than one. Many fans of the detective novel consider this period the highest accomplishment of the style. It established the basic formula of the genre and, additionally, married the English comedy of manners with a strong sense of nostalgia for a "golden" past that the post–World War I English reader feared would never come again. If, in fact, it had ever existed at all.

The result is a slew of murders in nice quiet English villages or lovely aristocratic country homes where such aberrant acts might never be expected to occur. They do, however, and, in a further demonstration of their abnormality, they occur in the most bizarre ways possible—through touching a poisoned walking cane, or being caught in a wool baler, for example. The witty and arch aristocrats are suitably shocked—and they do so hope "the butler did it" and not one of their own people. (The number of times a fictional murder was done by the butler was virtually nil—the cliché represents a class-based hope of considerable intensity.) What follows is formulaic: A brilliant man, or occasionally a shrewd spinster, takes a logical look at a string of clues that bewilder the local policemen and deduces the identity of the murderer, who turns out to be the one bad apple in an otherwise pristine aristocratic barrel. The clever detective traps the murderer, who is promptly arrested by the (finally useful) police, and the ripples in the village pond can smooth out again. Class, order, and tranquility are restored.

What a lovely concept. What complete balderdash.

The latter reaction was the response of Raymond Chandler and Dashiell Hammett, the leading writers of detective stories for the popular American pulp magazine *Black Mask*.

Hammett and Chandler looked with amusement at the effete and elegant novels of the English Golden Age and at its American practitioners, among them, Arthur Reeves, S. S. Van Dine, and Ellery Queen. These Americans offered enormously popular versions of the Holmesian detective, and they were just "as aristocratic in attitude and as eccentric in habit as the stuffiest of [their] British counterparts" (Geherin 3)* Van Dine's Philo Vance, an extreme example of the type, spoke with a pseudo-English accent, wore a monocle, lived in a penthouse in New York, and used a gold cigarette holder as he cogitated about amusing little problems of murder. He could—and often did—lecture his friends on anything from botany to Egyptian hieroglyphics. One can sympathize with Ogden Nash's exasperation when he observed, "Philo Vance needs a kick in the pance" (quoted in Geherin 15).

Hammett and Chandler delivered exactly the kick needed.

Chandler summarized his irritation with Americanized versions of the British Golden Age mystery in "The Simple Art of Murder," a landmark article in *The Atlantic Monthly* (1944) in which he described Hammett's transformation of the genre and his own aims in writing detective fiction. Chandler intensely disliked what he saw as the artificiality of the "pseudo-English versions" offered by his American co-

* David Geherin's *The American Private Eye: The Image in Fiction* is an excellent survey of the genre (see Bibliography).

horts. He thought Van Dine and company always presented "the same careful grouping of suspects, the same utterly incomprehensible trick of how somebody stabbed Mrs. Pottington Postlethwaite III with the solid platinum poignard just as she flatted on the top note of the 'Bell Song' from *Lakmé* in the presence of fifteen ill-assorted guests; the same ingenue in fur-trimmed pajamas screaming in the night to make the company pop in and out of doors and ball up the timetable; the same moody silence next day as they sit around sipping Singapore slings and sneering at each other, while the flatfeet crawl to and fro under the Persian rugs with their derby hats on" (56).

Chandler praised Hammett because he took "murder out of the Venetian vase and dropped it into the alley," where it belonged (58). He especially liked *The Maltese Falcon* (1929), the novel in which Sam Spade appeared as a loner private eye caught up in an incredibly confusing case of theft, betrayal, and corruption. Dashiell Hammett had himself been a detective for the Pinkerton Detective Agency and he well understood the seamy side of the real life of a detective. (The Pinkerton logo of an open eye and the words "We Never Sleep" was the origin of the term "private eye.") He also understood firsthand how confusing criminal cases actually were; he once compared the private eye's investigation of a crime to the actions of a "blind man in a dark room hunting for the black hat that wasn't there" ("The Black Hat" 140). *Real* investigations were neither neat, rational, nor orderly. Whole chunks of key information—such as the name of Hammett's early detective, known only as the "Continental Op," short for "operative"—were missing in the dirty world of real-life crooks.

Recalling her own reading of detective fiction as a teenager, Grafton says, "I can still remember the astonishment I felt the night I leapt from the familiarity of Miss Marple into the pagan sensibilities of *I, The Jury*" ("An Eye") by Mickey Spillane, one of the hardest of the hard-boiled writers. It must have been a shock. The two worlds—Golden Age and hard-boiled—had been created from very different sensibilities and to this day have widely differing appeal to readers.

Most people respond to trauma in one of two ways: they deny it or they fight it. The Golden Age detective novels tended to reflect the English capacity for denial. Agatha Christie's *The Body in the Library* was written in 1939 and '40, with Europe just entering another war, something Christie certainly knew plenty about since she had worked in a hospital dispensary during the First World War and her first husband was a decorated pilot in the Royal Air Force. But the novel contains only three or four references to current political or military crises, and they are so fleeting and so vague that they lack any relevance or impact. In stark contrast, Hammett, Chandler, and their colleagues chose to fight back. They too had seen firsthand the traumas caused by World War I. Hammett had contracted TB while serving in the ambulance corps and Chandler had served first with the Canadian Air Force, then with the Royal Air Force. The men also saw the traumas caused by the American prohibition of alcohol in 1920, the 1929 stock market crash, and the consequent worldwide depression in the thirties, and they were angered by what they saw. They squarely faced the implications that the universe was neither rational nor benevolent. Even the legal system seemed capricious. After all, the act of Prohibition had transformed almost everyone's next door neighbor and half of one's family into criminals overnight. And crime appeared to be everywhere, as bootleggers and gangsters dominated newspaper headlines in the major American cities (see Geherin 4).

In the same year that Christie began writing *The Body in the Library*—1939—Chandler's *The Big Sleep* was published. About the only things the two novels appear to share is that murders do occur in both and some of the action takes place in the homes of wealthy men. But these two homes—Colonel Bantry's aristocratic home, where the major noise in the morning is the maid opening the curtains before she serves tea, and General Sternwood's *nouveau riche* L.A. house, where the major noise is the screaming of one of his daughters high on drugs—might as well be on separate planets.

Chandler's shabby, sunbaked Los Angeles is filled with the mean streets of contemporary American life—ugly, corrupt, unstable, replete with violence and confusion. In this setting, wealthy men may be as wicked as the gang boss and one must not make assumptions about who the good guys are. This is a world, Chandler says, "where the mayor of your town may have condoned murder as an instrument of money-making, where no man can walk down a dark street in safety because law and order are things we talk about but refrain from practicing" ("Simple Art" 59). Murder is no longer the result of one rotten apple; in this world one suspects that almost the whole damn barrelful of apples is rotten, and termites are probably destroying the barrel itself.

In *The Big Sleep,* Chandler introduced Philip Marlowe as his proto-typical hard-boiled detective. There is as yet no accepted source for the term "hard-boiled," although there are two possibilities: in an after-dinner speech to the Army and Navy Club of Connecticut in 1887, Mark Twain used the term to indicate a tough style of speech* and, according to mystery novelist Donald E. Westlake, it was later routinely applied to tough drill sergeants during World War I (DeAndrea 153†).

Whatever the origin, "hard-boiled" as applied to a detective—such as Sam Spade, Philip Marlowe, and later Lew Archer and a legion of others—meant a tough male professional private eye who tells the story of the investigation himself. No admiring Dr. Watsons here. This detective works alone to fight crime because he is good at it, and someone needs to do it. The investigation is a job, not an intellectual game. The hard-boiled detective makes no claim to being the great rational puzzle-solver—indeed, one has the impression in this world that a Hercule Poirot would promptly be tossed into the river wearing concrete booties. Instead, in order to survive in a world without controls, this detective must use his fists, guns, wits, luck, physical bravery—anything he can—in order to remove whatever evil force he can. As Grafton sees him, "He smoked too much, drank too much, screwed and punched his way through molls and mobsters with devastating effect. In short, he kicked ass" ("An Eye").

The hard-boiled detective speaks in a wisecracking colloquial style in keeping with the disillusioned world around him. Cynicism colors his speech, but not his essential heroic core, for his progenitors were the American cowboy and the Medieval knight, those lone heroes who cleaned up a local mess and then moved on to the next adventure.

The murder he tackles is not the refined and complex affair of poisoned walking sticks, but the direct and raw brutality of shotguns

---

* We are indebted to Matthew J. Bruccoli, University of South Carolina, for calling this early usage to our attention. For the Twain passage, see Louis J. Budd (ed.), *Mark Twain: Collected Tales, Sketches, Speeches, and Essays.*
† See Bibliography.

flashing in the dark, or tire irons crashing over heads. Further, the murder may not even be the most important plot device in the novel. A murder may occur early in the novel, but sometimes the murder does not occur until late in the story, or the detective may have a whole string of casual deaths to deal with, or death may be subordinate to embezzlement, or blackmail, or some other form of corruption. One never knows what to expect in this world of random violence.

Understandably, then, hard-boiled novels don't end with a general sense of order restored because the basic systems are themselves flawed. Instead, the novels conclude with a highly limited sense of satisfaction that one specific source of human evil has been contained. Until Thursday, at least. And assuming the novel concludes on a Wednesday.

The emphasis is not on the detective solving an intellectual puzzle, then, but on the detective surviving a physical challenge. In the Golden Age novel, the amateur detective typically concludes the case by springing a psychological trap during which the murderer confesses. But in the hard-boiled novel, the professional investigator typically faces the villain in a final violent confrontation scene in which the protagonist may suffer considerable physical pain and is at constant risk to life and limb. In the end, the detective subdues or kills the villain because of his brawn, his stamina, his skill with a pistol, or his ability to outbluff the other guy—seldom because of the exercise of Poirot's famous "little gray cells" beyond the rudimentary level of trickery. Reason will take the detective only so far in this arbitrary and capricious world.

This cursory look at the originating shape of the detective novel—which blithely ignores the subgenres of police procedurals, the inverted whodunit in which the murderer's identity is known from the beginning, the spy story, the thriller, and so on—focuses on what we consider two key points about the dual basic lines of development, the Golden Age and the hard-boiled. First, the impact of the Golden Age is quite conservative—it gives pleasure through the extent to which the status quo is maintained, while the impact of the hard-boiled is emphatically not conservative—it gives pleasure through the extent to which the social status quo is questioned. Second, the appeal of both strands is closely tied to the character of the detective and the unique kind of world embodied by that character.

Grafton's sensibilities, both as a teenaged reader and now, respond most strongly to the hard-boiled tradition. "There was something seductive about the primal power of the hard-boiled narrative, something invigorating about its crude literary style. For all its tone of disdain, the flat monotone of the narrator allowed us to 'throw' our own voices with all the skill of ventriloquists. I was Mike Hammer. I was Sam Spade, Shell Scott, Philip Marlowe, and Lew Archer, strengthened and empowered by the writers' raw-boned prose. Little wonder, years later, in a desire to liberate myself from the debilitating process of writing for television, I turned to the hard-boiled private eye novel for deliverance" ("An Eye").

Having written a number of screenplays and teleplays, Grafton tired of that in the late seventies and wanted to switch exclusively to writing her own novels. She turned to her first love—private-eye fiction. Grafton began planning her detective series with the intention of playing against the character of hard-boiled Philip Marlowe. Her first step was to try out the role in the hands and voice of a woman. Her original introduction of Kinsey for *"A" Is for Alibi* began:

"My name is Kinsey Millhone. I'm what they call a 'dick,' though the term is somewhat of a misnomer in my case. I'm a woman . . . a female adult. Maybe you know the kind. I'm also a private investigator. I'm thirty-six, married twice, no kids. I'm not very tough, but I'm thorough. . . ."

Grafton describes "this piece of silliness" with its "mocking Mae West accent" sitting on her desk for two years while she continued to work in developing what she calls a "plot map" outlining a sequence of events and profiles of characters (18). "I knew that I could never sustain an entire book in this manner. Furthermore, I had no desire to do so. I wanted a 'real' detective novel, not a *spoof* of one" ("Breaking and Entering," 17).

The real detective who emerged as Kinsey Millhone in *"A" Is for Alibi* retains much of the flip tone of the original Kinsey, but thanks to Grafton's growing sense of the detective novel as a serious exploration of contemporary social issues, the flipness is only one aspect of a highly complex character who would be recognized by Philip Marlowe and Sam Spade as a kindred soul. Kinsey is a loner, a financially struggling private investigator who takes her cases in order to put Quarter Pounders on the table, and she's a breezy talker, who shoots her lover in a terrifying final scene reminiscent of Sam Spade's turning Brigid O'Shaughnessy over to the police (Spade: "I won't play the sap for anyone" vs. Millhone: "He'd played me for a sucker"), yet she maintains an inviolable moral core.

In "The Simple Art of Murder," Chandler says that he does not "care much about [the] private life" of his detective (59). We never learn exactly why Marlowe is such a loner or much about his family and personal history. Similarly, Hammett gives us virtually nothing about the interior trappings of his detectives. The Continental Op often says, "I went home to bed." Period. The end. There is not even a single emotion *named,* much less explored, in Hammett's *The Glass Key.* In *The Maltese Falcon,* we can register the existence of emotion only by whether a character's eyes widen, squint, narrow, glint, or darken.

In contrast, Grafton takes a keen interest in the private life of her private eye.

If Chandler gives us a loner hero, so does Grafton, but she takes it one step farther by explaining *why* Kinsey is a loner. If Chandler gives us a hero who does investigative work because he's good at it and he needs to earn money on which to live, so does Grafton, but she explains *why and how* Kinsey turns to investigation for a career. If Chandler gives us a hero who lives simply, so does Grafton, but, again, she explains *the history behind* Kinsey's fondness for small living quarters and sandwiches. The list could go on. All the major characteristics of the hard-boiled detective appear in Kinsey. What Grafton does that is different is emphasize the psychology behind those characteristics. We know the whys and hows that lie behind Kinsey's actions because as Grafton points out, "Kinsey keeps nothing back—she is irrepressible."

Grafton also says she wanted to try her hand at writing detective fiction because she likes "the rules of the genre." Her toying with the nature of the central character did not come from any disdain for the form. On the contrary, Grafton believes a detective novel offers "the perfect blend of ingenuity and intellect, action and artifice" ("An Eye"). She describes herself as "a very rules-governed person who loves details," much as her readers do if we can judge by the content of the mail Grafton receives about her novels. (One woman counted the number of times Kinsey said "shit" in a novel.) The formulaic quality of the genre dismissed by some literary critics is precisely what she finds appealing, reassuring, and admirable. Because, says Grafton, *all* fiction writing is the unfolding of a story with some key elements withheld until the conclusion, mysteries are actually superior to the so-called mainstream novels because they force an author to allow the plot to blossom in a way that must be simultaneously codified *and* natural. It is both real and a game. "Mystery at its best is the most divine form of manipulation," as Grafton sees it.

Her father, C. W. Grafton, wrote three much-admired mystery novels during her youth in the forties and early fifties, something that clearly elicited both pride and curiosity from Sue. She says, "I wanted to see if I could pull off what my father did." She decided she wanted the fun of trying to play the divine game of manipulation herself and to do it by the boys' rules, plus she wanted to create a female character who *succeeded* in playing by the boys' rules within the game of detection. Having a woman as the central figure was easier because she knows this world from her own experience—writing a cross-gender narrative can be laden with problems—plus it gave her a way to have fun by playing with the characteristics of the genre. She wanted to turn some things upside down or inside out and see if they would still work. For instance, Charlie Scorsoni was Grafton's version of the blond bombshell with whom the male private eye became dangerously involved or against whose sexual machinations he was resistant. Grafton says she enjoyed making fun of this device from so many previous hard-boiled novels and was surprised by the lack of outrage from readers to this and other variations on the genre. Things she thought might offend readers just seemed to amuse them.

At the time Grafton decided she wanted into the game, female private eyes were scarce creatures in novels and only occasionally found in short stories. Fictional women detectives had existed as far back as the 1860s in both England and America, but the most popular ones were usually amateurs of the Miss Amelia Butterworth or Miss Jane Marple variety of genteel spinster, or professionals of the equally genteel Miss Maud Silver variety, and almost never of the hard-hitting, fast-action professional mold of the American male private eyes. Marcia Muller is credited with being first to create a popular female private eye in a novel: Sharon McCone, who first appeared in *Edwin of the Iron Shoes* in 1977. Significantly, Muller had a difficult time getting the book accepted for publication because publishers assumed that a tough-talking and tough-acting female private eye would not be accepted by the reading public. And, indeed, Muller's earliest books, though popular, were not runaway best-sellers, and she continued for several years to have trouble finding a willing publisher. Not until Sue Grafton and Sara Paretsky published their initial ventures in 1982 was the new wave of women private eyes firmly established. With the appearance of *"A" Is for Alibi* and *Indemnity Only,* the genre of detective fiction was significantly reshaped, and bookstore shelves are now packed with novels featuring women private eyes.

In addition to wanting to give new dimensions to the established figure of the hard-boiled detective, Grafton responded to the sense of game-playing pervading the entire genre of mystery fiction from its inception in the mid–nineteenth century. The mystery plot, according to Grafton, is a game she plays with the reader, one in which she has to play fair and give just enough misleading hints to trick the reader, while simultaneously giving just enough accurate information for the reader to feel satisfied when the conclusion arrives. "The reader and the writer are pitted against each other, and my job is to stay one step ahead of the reader, but in a way that both of us agree is fair." Make the identity of the murderer too obvious and the reader feels cheated; likewise, make the identity too implausible and again, the reader feels cheated. The reader needs to feel that the competition is rigorous, not rigged. When Jane Marple or Kinsey Millhone says something akin to, "I thought I knew now who it was" (*A* 252) without naming names, we want to have been given enough accurate clues that we think we know who she means.

The game board on which the author and reader play was established from the beginning by such playful devices as Grafton's use of the alphabet in every title and by the supporting use of the alphabet for the locales and families involved in most cases. If *"B" Is for Burglar,* then part of the story takes place in *B*oca Raton and the family involved is named *B*oldt; if *"F" Is for Fugitive,* then the story takes place in *F*loral Beach and involves the *F*owler family, and so on. Even the center of the novels' game board—Santa Teresa—is a part of the fun shared by author and reader. "Santa Teresa" is the fictitious name Ross Macdonald gave to Santa Barbara for his detective series. Grafton says she chose the name as an appreciative "way of tipping my hat" to Macdonald, whose work she greatly admires, and to "let the town live on." Grafton's nod to Dashiell Hammett is more amusing: in *"A" Is for Alibi,* when Kinsey goes to interview Gwen Fife at the dog-clipping parlor, she finds Gwen clipping a poodle named "Dashiell"— and in good hard-boiled fashion, he steps right in a pile of dog shit.

The basic device of titling the novels with the letters of the alphabet is an obvious call to game playing. What prompted Grafton to use this playful device? She was aware, she says, that publishers were very interested in series novels and she was deliberately looking for a device to signal that she was beginning a series. Two of her father's mysteries had used lines from a children's nursery rhyme, *The Rat Began to Gnaw the Rope,* and *The Rope Began to Hang the Butcher.* She was actively looking for something similar. One night she was reading one of her favorite books, Edward Gorey's *The Gashlycrumb Tinies,* a lovely little book of poetry about Victorian children being maimed and killed (!), when she had a "Eureka" moment. In typical Gorey fashion, *The Gashlycrumb Tinies* is funny, irreverent, and bloody, and importantly for our story, it is organized alphabetically: "A is for Amy who fell down the stairs. B is for Basil assaulted by bears." Thinking this device might work for mystery novels, Grafton sat right down and began to make a list of all the words associated with murder that she could use if she based a series on the alphabet.

Grafton's notes at the time reveal a number of names that made it into print, as well as some interesting rejected options. The list may be long, but it's too much fun for us not to give the entire set of options for those already published:

A was always for "alibi."

B was for either "bum" or "burglar."

C was always for "corpse."

D was for either "Dietz," "danger," "dagger," "dynamite," or "deadbeat." (Yes, Grafton considered the name Dietz very early; she has very rough ideas about some major figures who come in and out of Kinsey's life several books ahead.)

E was for "ever." Grafton really liked this play on words,
    but decided to give it up when she "just couldn't make it
    work," and she turned to "evidence" instead.
F was for either "fugitive," "Fahrenheit," "felony," or
    "forgery."
G was for either "gumshoe," "gun," "gambler," "gambit,"
    "gallows," or "gone." Again Grafton says she liked the
    play on "for gone," but she settled very quickly on
    "gumshoe" as the obvious choice.
H was always for "homicide."
I was always for "innocent."
J was a large number of possibilities before "judgment" was
    finally chosen during the writing of the novel. Options
    included "justice," "jury," "jealousy," and "jeopardy."
K was always for "killer."
L was either for "lunatic," "line-up," or "lock-up." "Law-
    less" came later during the writing.
M was either for "marathon," "mission," "murder," or
    "motive." "Malice" came later during the writing.
N is the one Grafton is currently writing. As of this writing,
    she has not settled on a title. Her original notes offer
    options of "notary," "negative," "narcotics," and she
    has said since only half-jokingly, "none of the above."

The sense of fun created by playing with titles and names, the feeling
that the plot itself is a game played between the author and the
reader—plus Kinsey's irreverent sense of humor—all embody the artificial side of the genre.

Playing with how much to hide and how much to reveal in this
divine game is a challenge Grafton obviously enjoys, but her ultimate
interest lies in a more realistic aspect—the psychology of her characters. Her dominant interest, she says, is learning what motivates her
characters, not just Kinsey, but all of them. "I want the story line to
come out of character" (*Judgment* journal for 1-31-92). From childhood on, Grafton has used her writing as a way to understand the
complex and often ugly realities of human behavior. So the author's
games of "hide the murderer under the shell" must be handled

carefully in order that every action be true to the psychological makeup of the character whose action is moving the plot forward.

The careful attention Grafton pays to relating an action to the psychology of the actor is demonstrated throughout the journals she maintains as she is writing each novel. One illustration about a detail in *"J" Is for Judgment* is typical of the care Grafton takes. When she was writing *Judgment,* she wanted to have someone object to William and Rosie moving in together. Her journal reveals her efforts to find the right person to register this objection directly to Rosie. It wouldn't be in Kinsey's nature to object, so who could? For a long time, Grafton tried to put the objections in the mouth of Moza Lowenstein, one of Rosie and Kinsey's neighbors and a rather naive sweetie who could be a logical spokesperson for conventional behavior. But in her journal entry on 2-16-92, Grafton had reservations, "It gives me a scene to play, but I'm not sure it rings true." She reread the portions of *"C" Is for Corpse* that feature Moza and realized that Moza is "way too unsure of herself" to open her mouth to Rosie (*Judgment* journal 3-13-92). Grafton tried inventing a new neighbor, Mrs. Snavely, who would express moral outrage and persuade Henry to object, but this too was later rejected as artificial. As we know, Grafton ended up by giving minor objections to Henry himself and they are expressed to Kinsey, not Rosie. It would not be in his nature to espouse mere conventionality, thus his objections are grounded in what he sees as the mismatch between these two very different people. And his objections are deliciously undercut by his own relief at having his cranky hypochondriac brother out of his hair now. The remarks ring true from Henry; they are amusingly complex, and they are countered by Kinsey's amusement.

Grafton's concern for the psychology of her characters and the human richness of her central detective obviously strike a responsive chord in contemporary readers. Of course, fully realized fictional characters have always found a receptive readership, but the popularity of Grafton and many other writers of detective fiction, especially the women authors who as a group spend more time developing richly textured characters than devising shocking methods of murder, seems to us to require a little more comment than relegating it simply to "strong characterization."

It is in the last thirty years or so that we have witnessed an absolute onslaught of *series* of detective novels. Why would this be the case?

This is the same period in American social history that has seen a growing sense of isolation and loneliness in all our lives, a trend brought to our attention in the past five years by an increasing number of articles in professional journals and popular newsprint about the subject. For example, *Time* ran a feature article about the topic, which included a set of photos of people in urban settings, each one looking away from the others, alone in the middle of a crowd. This loss of a sense of community is attributed to many forces, including a number of initiatives that had seemed innately good at first: for example, the widespread introduction of air-conditioning was certainly a welcome relief, but it moved entire families from the front porch or the fire escape, where they talked with neighbors, into the privacy of their own homes. Here they talked only to each other, or with the arrival of television, not even each other. Later they turned to that great magic box in the study—the computer—which was normally used by only one person at a time.

Now, we doubt if any of us would willingly forgo any of our gadgetry—the more we get, the more we want. Certainly neither of us is willing to give up the dishwasher in order to regain the family unit gathering to wash dishes together, or the clothes drier in order to return to conversations with neighbors as we hang out the clothes on the line. But that loss of opportunity for human interaction is very real and quite serious. Psychologists tell us that we all need human contact in order to be emotionally healthy. And most of us figure out some way to have that contact.

Sherry Turkle, author of *The Second Self: Computers and the Human Spirit*, popularized the term "High Tech–High Touch" to describe contemporary American life and our efforts to have both advanced technology and human contact. Just at the point we have developed some of the most amazing technological advances in history, we are also awash in television shows and films about angels, unsolved mysteries, aliens, psychics, and other rationally inexplicable phenomena. There is clearly a part of us that refuses to succumb to the purely rational and strictly technical, a part that insists on maintaining human relationships and an awareness of the irrational aspect of human life. New Age music, Scientology, and titles on just about every other magazine on the newsstand remind us of the importance of feelings and emotion and the value of a single individual. Bookstores are packed with books with titles such as *How to Be Your Own Best Friend* or *Making Your Spouse Your Friend*. Interestingly, what is one of the first uses we human beings have made of the computer's Internet? We've created "Chat Rooms," so that while we sit in isolation in our studies, we can still have the illusion of maintaining personal relationships. Just as we can delight in driving our gadget-laden cars on the highway—alone, moving fast, but with an ear glued to the cell phone.

Talk with any group of detective-fiction readers and they will tell you that they can hardly wait for the next one so that they can see what *their friend* Kinsey Millhone (or V. I. Warshawski, or Sharon McCone, or Neil Hamel, or Carlotta Carlyle, or Anna Pigeon, or whoever) is up to now. This warmth with which readers talk about their favorite detectives reveals the importance of these characters in the readers' lives. They fill a genuine void in contemporary American life. We're tempted to draw a parallel to the current popularity of soap operas, now prevalent on the evening as well as the afternoon television schedules, but we would not want this misunderstood to suggest a parallel in the quality of writing. We want the similarity to be understood only in the sense that both soaps and series detective novels are extremely popular because they meet a contemporary need for ongoing friendships and relationships in our lives.

This sense that readers feel they know the characters personally is reflected by the letters Grafton receives daily. Readers talk about the characters as if they live just down the street. They worry about Kinsey's eating habits and her sex life; they want to see more of Cheney Phillips or Mike with the Mohawk. Some want her to settle down with Dietz; others want her to throw Dietz out. The great variety of characters in Grafton's novels—wealthy, derelict, middle-class, young, old, conservative, unconventional, police, lawyers, criminals, friends, lovers, killers, and so on—elicits passionate responses. One of the characters about whom Grafton receives frequent questions and comments is Henry Pitts, who is clearly adored.

Readers feel equally free to act as if they know Sue Grafton. Many feel free to give her personal advice about herself. One woman wrote to express great concern over Sue's mental or physical health because she thought the dust-jacket photo for *"M" Is for Malice* revealed that

Grafton was seriously worried about a current crisis in her life. Grafton was able to reassure her that the photo had been taken three years earlier and revealed nothing except dramatic lighting by the photographer. Another objected to the violence and bad language from Kinsey, a surprising comment in light of the many current detective novels by other authors with far more blood and profanity.

Detective fiction has always been intensely responsive to, and reflective of, the needs of its own time. Detective fiction is almost obsessively *au courant*. When Anna Katherine Green wrote the first American detective novel in 1878, *The Leavenworth Case,* she presented inquest testimony about new techniques in ballistics that was right out of contemporary newspaper headlines. The entire novel, in fact, was based on current events—it was a fictionalized account of a celebrated unsolved murder case in New York on which her attorney father had worked. Raymond Chandler's scene was the dark crime-laden world of gangsters that dominated L.A. newspaper headlines—and those of most cities in the U.S. at the time. It is unsurprising, then, that contemporary detective fiction—again, especially that written by women—touches time and again on current American fears. Patricia Cornwell makes us face our fears of that modern phenomenon, the serial killer, and of loss of personal privacy through someone else's manipulation of the computer sitting on our desk. Judith Van Geison, Karen McQuillen, Dana Stabenow, and Nevada Barr play on our fears that the environment will be vandalized beyond repair. Grafton, Muller, Paretsky, as well as Linda Barnes, Barbara Neely, Barbara D'Amato, Sandra Scoppotone, and a host of others touch our deep-seated fears that the social and legal systems, which should enable our society to function, are themselves so essentially corrupt that we may never be able to put Humpty Dumpty together again.

Grafton's novels explore a variety of troubling contemporary social issues—class distinctions, prostitution, real-estate scams, corrupt lawyers and politicians, sexism, the stranglehold of bureaucracy and flaws in the basic structures of government, the church, and, even closer to home, the family. Grafton says she reads several newspapers each day, looking for ideas for her novels. She does not want to use an actual case for her novels—she won't name real names—but she likes to borrow the motive or the murder or the method of discovery that she sees in current news. Contemporaneousness is a deliberate emphasis on the part of the author of detective fiction, then, and an important reason for enthusiastic reader response.

Part of being contemporary is being realistic, making the characters and the action seem natural. Chandler praised Hammett—and he himself was praised—for creating a fictional world that was much more natural than the artificial world of the Golden Age British "cozies." Yet, when a reader in the 1990s reads a Chandler or a Hammett novel, much of it seems enormously dated, even artificial, as precious in its own way as anything by Arthur Conan Doyle or Dorothy Sayers. The contemporary nature of the genre leads, or course, to a wealth of superficial detail about dress, or slang, or drinks that can make a novel appear out-of-date very quickly.

But, it seems to us that there is a more profound outdating process going on, one that is indigenous to the genre itself. By this we mean that much of what we fear, as a society, changes as social conditions change. The sheer numbers of the rapid population growth frightened nineteenth-century readers, who feared loss of public order and control. The horrors of trench warfare in World War I made the English afraid that there was not a benign deity in charge after all. The economic chaos of the thirties, coupled with the threat of another war, made Americans despair that anyone could ever put the world right again. The complacency of the fifties made many people apprehensive that there were no more adventures to be had. For each shift in popular consciousness, there is a corresponding shift in the character of the detective and the world in which the detective operates. The one action humanity has *always* feared is murder; it is the one fear that requires no social construct. Thus, this is the action that becomes the generic metaphor for all the specific fears for our individual time. It is freighted with all of society's current worries and apprehensions. Chandler seems dated to us, then, not only because gangster talk has changed, but also because what frightens us is not what frightened his readers in the thirties. The terrors offered by crooks and dirty postcard dealers that were natural then seem odd, artificial, and even laughable to us now. We have our own fears ("our" drug lords are *much* worse than "their" bootleggers), which doubtless will appear equally odd to the readers of 2010.

One of the key reasons for the popularity of Sue Grafton, then—and for many of her colleagues—is her ability to give voice to our contemporary fears, while, at the same time, giving us the reassurance of a central figure, credible by current standards, who can hold back the darkness for one more day. In Grafton's own words, "The hard-boiled private eye in current fiction represents a clarity and vigor, the immediacy of a justice no longer evident in the courts, an antidote to our confusion and our fearfulness. In a country where violence is out of control, the hard-boiled private eye exemplifies containment, order, and hope, with the continuing, unspoken assertion that the individual can still make a difference. . . . The hard-boiled private eye novel is still the classic struggle between good and evil played out against the backdrop of our social interactions" ("An Eye").

Grafton is not alone, nor was she the first, in her use of a woman as the professional investigator, her interest in the psychology of her characters, her subordination of gratuitous violence to social issues, and her variety of characters beyond gangland thugs and P.I.s. As Grafton considers the current literary scene for detective fiction, she believes that "The P.I. has been transformed from a projection of our vices to the mirror of our virtues. The hard-boiled private eye has come to represent and reinforce not our excess, but our moderation. In the current hard-boiled private eye fiction, there is less alcohol, fewer cigarettes, fewer weapons, greater emphasis on fitness, humor, subtlety, maturity, and emotional restraint. It is no accident that women writers have tumbled onto the playing field, infusing the genre with a pervasive social conscience" ("An Eye" 5).

Grafton is a leader, arguably *the* leader, of the team reshaping the genre into a more psychologically interesting and socially aware form.

While Grafton's Kinsey is similar to several other women detectives in some of her strengths, her kick-ass manner, and her effective detective abilities, she is unique and especially admirable for the way in which she has learned an important lesson about life: the solution to a problem lies within the problem itself—*if* one has the ability to see it and act on it. This concept colors everything about Kinsey's life and work. The concept was vividly illustrated in the quick snapshot in *"B" Is for Burglar* of the poison oak and its antidote, mugwort, growing side by side. We see it developed more fully every time we learn more about Kinsey's childhood or personal life. The tragic loss of her parents could have been an excuse for collapsing into victimhood, but given her innate courage (and her aunt's nudges), Kinsey turned the problem into the core of her strength. She is tough, strong, and self-reliant because of what she created out of a tragedy.

Grafton speaks of growing up with her alcoholic parents in terms that sound like Kinsey: "I wouldn't change my childhood for anything. And the truth is, the minute you understand what your life is about, you're *responsible*. And what I don't have any patience for is people who want to blame, and want to find fault. The minute you understand what's going on, the mantle of responsibility passes to you! From that moment on, your life is your own and you may make of it whatever you choose" (Herbert 40).

Grafton says, "One always rescues oneself in this world!" (Herbert 41), a dictum demonstrated by Kinsey in every novel.

This powerful sense of responsibility and self-creation is greatly appealing to a reading public awash in newspaper headlines that suggest rampant apathy and random violence throughout the country. Although Kinsey is the purest embodiment of the lesson of personal responsibility developed in the cauldron of personal catastrophe, it is echoed throughout the novels through such major characters as Bobby Callahan (*Corpse*) and Guy Malek (*Malice*), and a whole host of lesser figures such as Dana Jaffe (*Judgment*) or Francesa Voigt (*Innocent*). Francesa is an especially clear instance. She has a thriving business making turbans for cancer patients who lose their hair during chemotherapy, a business that exists only because she went through cancer and chemo herself. "One morning in the shower, all my hair fell out in clumps. I had a lunch date in an hour and there I was, bald as a egg. I improvised one of these from a scarf I had on hand. . . . The idea for the business got me through the rest of the chemo and out the other side. Funny how that works. Tragedy can turn your life around if you're open to it" (*I* 155).

The lesson of personal responsibility is never offered by Grafton in a sentimentalized or saccharine fashion. And suffering doesn't automatically lead to strength of character—witness Ori Fowler. On the contrary, you have to have strength of character to make something out of the suffering ("*if* you're open to it"). There is nothing of the Pollyanna about these figures who prevail in situations that often crush others. And there is no brushing aside of the depth of pain suffered by a Bobby Callahan or by Kinsey herself.

Stylistically, the novels are appealing for their clarity of expression, satisfying plot twists, vivid figures of speech, and striking characters. They are easy to read, but this does not mean they are simple. Far from it. Grafton creates a fictional world for Kinsey in which contradiction, complexity, and balance are the keynotes, and readers are constantly teased into rethinking something in the novels or their own lives they had taken for granted. The grace note hovering above everything—the line that keeps the serious moments from becoming preachy or depressing and keeps readers coming back for more—is Grafton's keen sense of humor.

Grafton is a leader for changing the genre, then, because she creates an entire world that is credible, thought provoking, and amusing. We believe her creation of complex Kinsey Millhone and we accept the validity of the world in which Kinsey operates. We can see ourselves reflected in Kinsey and our fears embodied in her world. In Grafton's detective novels of humanity and complexity, we like being puzzled and frightened and then escaping unscathed; we like being teased—not pushed—into thinking; we like being challenged to find our own strengths; and we just love being verbally tickled into laughing out loud.

Sue Grafton's Awards

Christopher Award, 1979, for teleplay, *Walking Through Fire*.

Mysterious Stranger Award, 1982–83, for *"A" Is for Alibi* from Cloak and Clue Society, Mystery Book Store, Milwaukee, Wisconsin.

Shamus Award, 1986, for *"B" Is for Burglar* as Best Hardcover Private Eye Novel of 1985 from Private Eye Writers of America.

Anthony Award, 1986, for *"B" Is for Burglar* as Best Hardcover Mystery of 1985 from Bouchercon.

Macavity Award, 1986, for "The Parker Shotgun" as Best Short Story from Mystery Readers International.

Anthony Award, 1987, for *"C" Is for Corpse* as Best Hardcover Mystery of 1986 from Bouchercon.

Anthony Award, 1987, for "The Parker Shotgun" as Best Short Story from Bouchercon.

Doubleday Mystery Guild Award, 1989, for *"E" Is for Evidence* as Best Hardcover Novel.

American Mystery Award, 1990, for "A Poison That Leaves No Trace" as Best Short Story.

The Falcon Award, 1990, for *"F" Is for Fugitive* as Best Mystery Novel from the Maltese Falcon Society of Japan.

Doubleday Mystery Guild Award, 1990, for *"F" Is for Fugitive* as Best Hardcover Novel.

Doubleday Mystery Guild Award, 1991, for *"G" Is for Gumshoe* as Best Hardcover Novel.

Anthony Award, 1991, for *"G" Is for Gumshoe* as Best Hardcover Mystery of 1990 from Bouchercon.

Shamus Award, 1991, for *"G" Is for Gumshoe* as Best Hardcover Private Eye Novel of 1990 from Private Eye Writers of America.

Doubleday Mystery Guild Award, 1992, for *"H" Is for Homicide* as Best Hardcover Novel.

American Mystery Award, 1992, for *"H" Is for Homicide* as Best Private Eye Novel.

Doubleday Mystery Guild Award, 1993, for *"I" Is for Innocent* as Best Hardcover Novel.

Doubleday Mystery Guild Award, 1994, for *"J" Is for Judgment* as Best Hardcover Novel.

Doubleday Mystery Guild Award, 1995, for *"K" Is for Killer* as Best Hardcover Novel.

President, Private Eye Writers of America, 1989–90.

President, Mystery Writers of America, 1994–95.

Works by Sue Grafton

Novels

Keziah Dane. New York: Macmillan, 1967, and London: Peter Owen Ltd., 1968.

The Lolly-Madonna War. London: Peter Owen Ltd., 1969.

"A" Is for Alibi. New York: Holt, Rinehart & Winston, 1982.

"B" Is for Burglar. New York: Holt, Rinehart & Winston, 1985.

"C" Is for Corpse. New York: Henry Holt, 1986.

"D" Is for Deadbeat. New York: Henry Holt, 1987.

"E" Is for Evidence. New York: Henry Holt, 1988.

"F" Is for Fugitive. New York: Henry Holt, 1989.

"G" Is for Gumshoe. New York: Henry Holt, 1990.

"H" Is for Homicide. New York: Henry Holt, 1991.

"I" Is for Innocent. New York: Henry Holt, 1992.

"J" Is for Judgment. New York: Henry Holt, 1993.

"K" Is for Killer. New York: Henry Holt, 1994.

"L" Is for Lawless. New York: Henry Holt, 1995.

"M" Is for Malice. New York: Henry Holt, 1996.

All except *Malice* are currently available in paperback through Bantam or Fawcett. Foreign publication in over twenty languages include those in Iceland, Finland, Denmark, Sweden, Norway, England, Holland, France, Italy, Germany, Poland, Spain, Portugal, Israel, Russia, Japan, China, and Australia.

Short Stories

Kinsey and Me. Santa Barbara: Bench Press, Limited Edition, 1992. Contains non-Kinsey short stories about her mother and the following Kinsey short stories:
"Long Gone," which first appeared as "She Didn't Come Home" in *Redbook*, April 1986.
"Between the Sheets," which first appeared as "Murder Between the Sheets" in *Redbook*, October 1986.
"The Parker Shotgun," which first appeared in *Mean Streets: The Second Private Eye Writers of America Anthology*, ed. Robert J. Randisi, Mysterious Press, 1986.
"Non Sung Smoke," which first appeared in *An Eye for Justice: The Third Private Eye Writers of America Anthology*, ed. Robert J. Randisi, Mysterious Press, 1988.
"Falling Off the Roof," which first appeared in *Sisters in Crime*, ed. Marilyn Wallace, 1989.
"A Poison That Leaves No Trace," which first appeared in *Sisters in Crime II*, ed. Marilyn Wallace, 1990.
"Full Circle," which first appeared in *A Woman's Eye*, ed. Sara Paretsky and Martin H. Greenberg, 1991.
"A Little Missionary Work," which first appeared in *Deadly Allies: Sisters in Crime and Private Eye Writers of America*, ed. Marilyn Wallace and Robert Randisi, 1992.

Articles

"Breaking and Entering." *The Writer*, January 1983: 16–18, 28.
"How to Find Time to Write When You Don't Have Time to Write." *The Writer*, December 1986: 7–10.
"What I'm Reading: Sue Grafton." *Entertainment Weekly*, 16 September 1994: 105.
"The Use of the Journal in the Writing of a Private Eye Novel." In *Writing the Private Eye Novel: A Handbook by the Private Eye Writers of America*. Ed. Robert J. Randisi. Cincinnati: Writer's Digest Books. In press.
"An Eye for an I: Justice, Morality, the Nature of the Hard-boiled Private Detective, and All That Existential Stuff." In *Crown Crime Compendium*. New York: Random House. In press.

Editions

Writing Mysteries: A Handbook by the Mystery Writers of America. Cincinnati: Writer's Digest Books, 1992.

Film

Screenplay for *Lolly-Madonna XXX*, adapted from her novel *The Lolly-Madonna War*, MGM 1973.

Television

Episode, "With Friends Like These," *Rhoda*, CBS, April 1975.

Teleplay, *Walking Through the Fire*, adapted from the book by Laurel Lee, CBS, April 1979.

Teleplay, *Sex and the Single Parent*, adapted from the book by Jane Adams, CBS, September 1979.

Teleplay, *Nurse*, adapted from the book by Peggy Anderson, CBS, April 1980. (Became the basis for the series, *Nurse*, CBS, 1981–82.)

Teleplay, *Mark, I Love You*, adapted from the book by Hal Painter, CBS, December 1980.

Pilot, *Seven Brides for Seven Brothers*, adapted with Steven Humphrey from the MGM movie, CBS, October 1982. Served as story editor with Steven Humphrey for the series *Seven Brides for Seven Brothers*, CBS, 1982–83. They jointly wrote two episodes: "I Love You, Molly McGraw" and "A House Divided."

Story Credit, *Svengali*, teleplay by Frank Cucci, CBS, March 1983.

Teleplay, *A Caribbean Mystery*, adapted with Steven Humphrey from the novel by Agatha Christie, CBS, October 1983.

Teleplay, *A Killer in the Family*, with Steven Humphrey and Robert Aller, ABC, October 1983.

Teleplay, *Sparkling Cyanide*, adapted with Steven Humphrey and Robert Malcom Young from the novel by Agatha Christie, CBS, November 1983.

Teleplay, *Love on the Run*, with Steven Humphrey, NBC, October 1985. (Nominated for a Mystery Writers of America Edgar Award, 1986.)

Teleplay, *Tonight's the Night*, with Steven Humphrey, ABC, February 1987.

Bibliography

Works cited in addition to those of Sue Grafton

Anthony Mason Interview with Sue Grafton in Santa Barbara, *CBS Sunday Morning*, 3 February 1997.

Baker, Robert A., and Michael T. Nietzel. "Kinsey Millhone—Sue Grafton." In *Private Eyes: 101 Knights*. Bowling Green, Ohio: Bowling Green State University Popular Press, 1985.

Budd, Louis J., ed. *Mark Twain: Collected Tales, Sketches, Speeches, and Essays, 1852–1890*. Vol. I. New York: Library of America, 1992.

Chandler, Raymond. "The Simple Art of Murder." *The Atlantic Monthly*, December 1944: 53–59.

Coontz, Stephanie. *The Way We Never Were*. New York: BasicBooks, 1992.

DeAndrea, William L. "Sue Grafton," "C. W. Grafton," "Kinsey Millhone," and "The Hard-Boiled Detective." In *Encyclopedia Mysteriosa: A Comprehensive Guide to the Art of Detection in Print, Film, Radio, and Television*. New York: Prentice Hall, 1994.

Fuller, Daniel. "Is That Cordite I Smell, or Just a Red Herring: Firearm Facts and Follies in Detection." Annual Meeting of the Popular Culture Association, San Antonio, March 28, 1997.

Geherin, David. *The American Private Eye: The Image in Fiction*. New York: Frederick Ungar, 1985.

Goodman, Susan. "Sue Grafton and Tony Hillerman." *Modern Maturity*, July–August 1995: 74–82.

Gorey, Edward. *The Gashlycrumb Tinies*. In *Amphigorey*. New York: G. P. Putnam's Sons, 1972.

Hammett, Dashiell. "The Black Hat That Wasn't There." *Ellery Queen Mystery Magazine*, June 1951: 131–42.

Herbert, Rosemary. "Sue Grafton." In *The Fatal Art of Entertainment: Interviews with Mystery Writers*. New York: G. K. Hall, 1994.

Lovesy, Peter. *Bloodhounds*. New York: Warner, 1996.

Murray, J. A. H., ed. *A New English Dictionary on Historical Principles* (commonly known as *Oxford English Dictionary*, or *OED*). Oxford: Clarendon Press, 1897.

Nance, Kevin. "Fear Drives Author." *The State*, 12 June 1994: F 1–2 (rpt. from *Lexington Herald-Leader*).

Schaffer, Rachel. "Grafton's Black Humor." *The Armchair Detective*. Summer 1997: (In press).

Selected Related Works of Interest

Ames, Katrine. " 'A' Is for Alibi." *Newsweek*, 7 June 1982: 72.

———. " 'G' Is for Gumshoe." *Newsweek*, 14 May 1990: 66.

———. "The Alphabet Sleuth." *Savvy Woman*, June 1989: 21.

———. "Sue Grafton's Alphabetic Mystery Tour." *Newsweek*, 18 July 1988: 55.

Ames, Katrine, and Ray Sawhill. "Murder Most Foul and Fair." *Newsweek*, 14 May 1990: 66–67.

Binyon, T. J. *"Murder Will Out:" The Detective in Fiction*. Oxford: Oxford University Press, 1989.

Bernikow, Louise. " 'G' Is for Gumshoe." *Cosmopolitan*, May 1990: 56.

Brooks, Terry. " 'G' Is for Gumshoe." *People*, 23 April 1990: 30–31.

Cawelti, John G. "The Gunfighter and the Hard-Boiled Dick: Some Ruminations on American Fantasies of Heroism." *American Studies*, Fall 1975, 49–63.

Chambers, Andrea, and David Hutchings. "Make No Bones About It, Sue Grafton's Detective Heroine Is a Real Pistol." *People*, 10 July 1989: 81–82.

Christianson, Scott. "Talkin' Trash and Kickin' Butt: Sue Grafton's Hard-Boiled Feminism." *Feminism in Women's Detective Fiction*. Ed. Glenwood Irons. Toronto: University of Toronto Press, 1995.

Cimons, Marlene. " 'R' Is for Running." *Runner's World*, June 1992: 36–38.

Dye, Nancy S. "Who Is Kinsey Millhone? She Isn't Sure." *New York Times Book Review*, 28 July 1991: 8.

" 'E' Is for Evidence." *Publisher's Weekly*, 3 November 1989: 60.

Eaglen, Audrey. "Murder, They Write." *School Library Journal*, January 1989: 39.

Geherin, David. "Grafton, Sue." In *Twentieth Century Crime and Mystery Writers*. Ed. Lesley Henderson. Third edition. Chicago and London: St. James Press, 1991, 459–60.

Gorman, Ed, Martin H. Greenberg, Larry Segriff, with Jon L. Breen, eds. *The Fine Art of Murder*. New York: Carroll & Graf Publishers, 1993.

Haycroft, Howard. *Murder for Pleasure: The Life and Times of the Detective Story*. New York: Appleton, 1941.

Herbert, Rosemary. "Aiming Higher." *Publisher's Weekly*, 13 April 1990: 30–32.

Hoyser, Catherine Elizabeth. "Sue Grafton." In *Great Women Mystery Writers: Classic to Contemporary*. Ed. Kathleen Gregory Klein. Westport, Conn.: Greenwood Press, 1994.

Irons, Glenwood. "New Women Detectives: 'G' Is for Gender-Bending." In *Gen-

der, Language, and Myth: Essays on Popular Narrative. Ed. Glenwood Irons. Toronto: University of Toronto Press, 1992.

Kerr, Nora. "Stockpiling the Alphabet." *New York Times Book Review,* 28 July 1991: 8.

Klein, Kathleen Gregory. *The Woman Detective: Gender and Genre.* Urbana: University of Illinois Press, 1988.

Knight, Stephen. *Form and Ideology in Crime Fiction.* Bloomington: Indiana University Press, 1980.

Keating, H. R. F., ed. *Whodunit? A Guide to Crime, Suspense and Spy Fiction.* New York: Van Nostrand Reinhold Co., 1982.

Kozinski, Alex. "Trouble in Santa Teresa." *New York Times Book Review,* 27 May 1990: 13.

Lange, Pam. " 'H' Is for Homicide." *Mostly Murder,* June 1991: 1–2.

Lehman, David. *The Perfect Murder: A Study in Detection: A Guide to the Best Mysteries Ever Written.* New York: The Free Press, 1989.

Monaghan, Pat. "Writers Dreaming." *Booklist,* 1 June 1993: 1773.

Morgan, Susan. "Books: Female Dick." *Interview,* May 1990: 152–53.

Nemy, Enid. " 'A' Is for Alter Ego." *New York Times Book Review,* 4 August 1994: C1+.

Nicholls, Jane, and Bonnie Bell. "Banishing Old Ghosts." *People,* 30 October 1995: 115–16.

Nolan, Tom. "It Was a Dark and Stormy Night. . . ." *Los Angeles Magazine,* November 1988: 168–77.

Patrick, Vincent. "Lifestyles of the Rich and Quirky." *New York Times Book Review,* 1 May 1988: 11–12.

Prescott, Peter S. "Beachy Keen Summer Reads." *Newsweek,* 9 June 1986: 77.

Rabinowitz, Peter J. " 'Reader, I Blew Him Away': Convention and Transgression in Sue Grafton." *Famous Last Words: Changes in Gender and Narrative Closure.* Ed. Alison Booth. Charlottesville: University of Virginia Press, 1990.

Reddy, Maureen T. "The Feminist Counter Tradition in Crime: Cross, Grafton, Paretsky, and Wilson." *The Cunning Craft: Original Essays on Detective Fiction and Contemporary Literary Theory.* Ed. Ronald G. Walker. Western Illinois University Press, 1990.

———. *Sisters in Crime: Feminism and the Crime Novel.* New York: Continuum, 1988.

Rich, B. Ruby. "The Lady Dicks: Gender Benders Take the Case." *Village Voice Literary Supplement,* June 1989: 24–26.

Richler, Daniel. "Interview with Sue Grafton." *Imprint.* Toronto: TVOntario, 1992.

Rubins, Josh. "Miss Marple They Ain't." *New York Times Book Review,* 8 October 1995: 24.

Stasio, Marilyn. " 'I' Is for Innocent." *New York Times Book Review,* 24 May 1992: 25.

———. " 'J' Is for Judgment." *New York Times Book Review,* 2 May 1993: 22.

———. " 'K' Is for Killer." *New York Times Book Review,* 1 May 1994: 24.

———. "What's Happened to Heroes Is a Crime." *New York Times Book Review,* 14 October 1990: 1, 57–58.

Steinberg, Sybil. " 'D' Is for Deadbeat." *Publisher's Weekly,* 27 March 1987: 38.

————. " 'E' Is for Evidence." *Publisher's Weekly,* 11 March 1988: 89.

————. " 'F' Is for Fugitive." *Publisher's Weekly,* 17 March 1989: 80–81.

————. " 'G' Is for Gumshoe." *Publisher's Weekly,* 30 March 1990: 54.

Symons, Julian. *Bloody Murder: From the Detective Story to the Crime Novel.* Third Revised Edition. New York: The Mysterious Press, 1992.

Taylor, Bruce. " 'G' Is for (Sue) Grafton: An Interview with the Creator of the Kinsey Millhone Private Eye Series Who Delights Mystery Fans as She Writes Her Way Through the Alphabet." *The Armchair Detective,* 1989: 4–13.

Walton, Priscilla L. " 'E' Is for En/Gendering Readings: Sue Grafton's Kinsey Millhone." In *Women Times Three: Writers, Detectives, Readers.* Ed. Kathleen Gregory Klein. Bowling Green, Ohio: Bowling Green State University Popular Press, 1995.

Weiner, Ed. "Who Killed the Town Lolita?" *New York Times Book Review,* 21 May 1989: 17.

White, Jean M. "Alphabetical Murder." *The Washington Post,* 18 May 1986: Book World Section, 8,13.

————. "Sensitive Shamus." *The Washington Post,* 21 June 1987: Book World Section, 8.

Wilson, Ann. "The Female Dick and the Crisis of Heterosexuality." *Feminism in Women's Detective Fiction.* Ed. Glenwood Irons. Toronto: University of Toronto Press, 1995.

Zaslow, Jeffrey. "Sue Grafton." *USA Weekend,* 7–9 February 1997: 18.

Sue Grafton's Website

www.suegrafton.com

Index